S0-BRI-493

Ultimate Recipes

Chinese

Ultimate Recipes

Chinese

DP

DEMPSEY
PARR

This is a Dempsey Parr Book
This edition published in 2000

Dempsey Parr is an imprint of Parragon

Parragon
Queen Street House
4 Queen Street
Bath BA1 1HE, UK

Copyright © Parragon 1999

All rights reserved. No part of this publication may be reproduced,
stored in a retrieval system or transmitted, in any form or by any means,
electronic, mechanical, photocopying, recording or otherwise, without the
prior permission of the copyright holder.

ISBN 1-84084-967-3

Printed in Indonesia

Produced by Haldane Mason, London

Notes
Use all metric or all imperial quantities, as the two are not interchangeable.
Cup measurements in this book are for American cups. Tablespoons are assumed to be 15 ml.
Unless otherwise stated, milk is assumed to be full fat, eggs are medium and pepper is freshly
ground black pepper.

The nutritional information provided for each recipe is per serving or per portion.
Optional ingredients, variations or serving suggestions have not been included in the
calculations. The times given for each recipe are an approximate guide only as the
preparation times may differ as a result of the type of oven used.

Contents

Introduction   10

Soups

Appetizers

Appetizers (continued)

Salads & Pickles

Poultry

Meat

Fish & Seafood

Vegetables

Tofu

Rice

Rice
(continued)

Noodles

Desserts

Introduction

The abundance of Chinese restaurants testify to the fact that Chinese cuisine is hugely popular in the West. This book will show you how to recreate authentic Chinese dishes in your own home. Along with the more famous Cantonese and Szechuan specialities, there are also less familiar but equally delicious recipes from other regions for you to try.

There can be few places in the world these days that are unfamiliar with Chinese cuisine. It first became known in the West with the arrival of Chinese workers in North America during the Gold Rush years and today there are Chinese restaurants from San Francisco to Helsinki and from Sydney to Edinburgh. Home-cooked Chinese food is a more recent phenomenon—at least, in the Western kitchen—but, once the ingredients and the wok became easily available and people realized how quick and easy it is to prepare, it soon became popular.

Besides being quite delicious, which is undoubtedly its most attractive characteristic, Chinese food is both healthy and economic. Carbohydrates, such as rice, which release energy slowly and are recommended by nutritionists as an important part of a healthy diet, are served at every meal. Vegetables, too, play a starring role and they are cooked in ways, such as stir-frying and steaming, which preserve most

Introduction

of their vitamins and minerals. With a few exceptions, high-cholesterol, high-fat ingredients, such as dairy products and red meat, are either absent altogether or are served sparingly.

To a considerable extent, the distinctive flavors of Chinese food resulted from the need to be economical. Bulky but bland foods, such as noodles, were served in relatively large amounts to satisfy the appetite. Expensive ingredients, such as meat and fish, could be used in only small quantities, so they had to be prepared in ways that made the most of them—combined with herbs, spices, and other flavorings. As a result, Chinese cuisine probably has the largest repertoire of any in the world. Fuel was scarce, so "fast food" was a necessity, resulting in the art of stir-frying in which ingredients are tossed in a round-based, cast-iron wok over a high heat to cook in a short time. This preserves their flavor, color, texture and nutrients. Steaming, also a favorite Chinese cooking technique, similarly results in flavorsome, attractive, and nutritious dishes. Bamboo baskets are stacked one above another over a single heat source, thus saving fuel.

A desire for balance and harmony has permeated all aspects of Chinese life since the days of Confucius and this applies to food as well as everything else. Spicy dishes are complemented by sweet-and-sour ones, dry-cooked dishes are balanced with those bathed in sauce, meat is matched with seafood. Dishes are chosen to complement each other in texture, flavor, and color, and it is not considered correct to serve more than one dish with the same main ingredient or to cook them using the same technique. Consciously or unconsciously, Chinese cooks, from the homemaker to the professional chef, all work to this ancient Taoist principle of Yin and Yang in which balance and contrast are the key. Mealtimes, too, are a time of harmony, when the family—often three generations—gather and share a selection of different dishes, as well as their daily news.

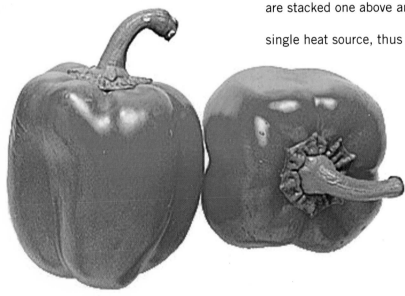

Regional Cooking

China is a huge country and the terrain and climate vary dramatically from one region to another. The crops grown and the livestock raised are equally diverse, giving rise to distinctive regional culinary traditions.

The North

Beijing has been the capital of China for about 1,000 years and, as befits such an important city, its culinary tradition is venerable. The Emperor's chief chef was a highly respected figure whose responsibilities included maintaining the health of the Imperial family through a careful balance of herbs, spices, and other ingredients, not simply creating appetizing dishes. Each newly appointed chef considered it a matter of honor to outdo his predecessors and there was also much rivalry with visiting chefs who accompanied dignitaries from other provinces when they came to Beijing. As a result, Beijing cuisine, which still tends to be called Peking in culinary circles, is varied and elegant. It has also been influenced by the Moslem culinary traditions of Central Asia through a number of Tartar invasions. Sesame seeds and the oil and paste made from them, which now feature in the cooking of all regions of China, were originally introduced by the Tartars. The popularity of lamb, rather than pork, unique to the Northern provinces, is probably also a result of Moslem influences. Outside the city, the cooking is simpler and lacks the light-handed touch that is characteristic of Beijing. Sauces and dips tend to be strongly flavored and leeks, onions, and garlic are popular vegetables. Mongolian or chrysanthemum fire pot dishes—a kind of stock-based fondue—are a speciality.

Wheat, rather than rice, is the staple ingredient in Northern Chinese cuisine and it is used to make noodles, dumplings, crêpes, and steamed buns. The climate can be quite harsh, but produce in this region includes bok choy, onions, grapes, and peaches. Freshwater fish, especially carp, are popular in the area around the Huang Ho River and shrimp and other seafood are abundant in the coastal regions. Drying, smoking, and pickling are typical preserving techniques.

The South

The first Chinese emigrants came from Kwangtung in the nineteenth century, so this is probably the best-known style of Chinese cuisine in the West. The capital of the province, Canton, was the first major trading port in the country and so was open to many foreign influences. However,

Regional Cooking

probably the most important influence, from the culinary point of view, was internal. In 1644 the Ming dynasty was overthrown and the Imperial Household, together with its retinue of chefs, fled to Canton from Beijing. This has resulted in a style of cooking that is renowned for its variety, sophistication, and excellence.

Steaming is a characteristic technique in Southern China and small fish, little parcels of meat or patties, and, above all, dumplings are often cooked this way. Dim sum, which literally means "to please the heart" are a Cantonese speciality. These small, steamed, filled dumplings are as popular in the West as they are in China, but there, they are never served as an appetizer. Rather, they are eaten as snacks at teahouses in the morning or afternoon. In fact, an alternative way of saying going to a

dim sum restaurant is going out for morning tea.

Char siu roasting is another Cantonese technique. No kind of roasting is common in Chinese homes, which often do not have ovens, but this method is popular in restaurants. Meat is seasoned and marinated well and then roasted at a very high temperature for a short time. This results in the marinade becoming encrusted on the meat in a crisp outer layer, while the inside remains succulent and juicy. Only very tender cuts of meat, particularly pork, can be prepared in this way.

Agricultural produce in this semi-tropical region is abundant and varied. Vegetables are often simply stir-fried and served plain or just with oyster sauce. They may also be combined with meat or fish. Spinach, bok choy, and dried mushrooms feature widely. Fresh fruit, frequently served on its own as

a dessert, may also be combined with meat or fish in sweet-and-sour dishes. Fish and seafood, particularly abalone, crab, lobster, shrimp, and scallops, are plentiful. They are usually stir-fried or steamed, often flavored with ginger, and cooking meat with fish is typically Cantonese. Generally, food is not highly spiced, as the Cantonese prefer to enjoy the natural flavors of the ingredients. Light soy sauce is a popular flavoring and other typical sauces include hoisin, oyster, black bean, and plum.

The East

The delta of the Yangtse River makes this one of the most fertile regions in China. The abundant produce includes broccoli, green onions, sweet potatoes, bok choy, soya beans, tea, wheat, rice, corn, and nuts, and the region is well known for its superb vegetarian dishes, noodles, and dumplings. Freshwater

Regional Cooking

fish are found in the many streams and lakes, especially in Kiangsu, which also has a long tradition of deep-sea fishing.

The provinces that comprise this region each have a particular style of cooking, but all are characterized by their richness. The vast cosmopolitan city of Shanghai has assimilated many influences from both other parts of China and abroad. Its cuisine is unusual in that it features dairy products and uses lavish quantities of shortening. Shanghai dishes are typically rich, sweet, and beautifully presented. The school of cooking in the surrounding area is known as Kiangche, the name being an amalgamation of the two provinces of Kiangsu and Chekiang. Duck, ham, and fish dishes are specialities, often prepared with piquant spices.

This region produces the best rice wine in the country. It is one of the most prosperous parts of China and has a long gourmet tradition. In Fukien to the South, the cuisine is less sophisticated, relying mainly on fish and a wealth of fresh produce. It is strongly influenced by neighboring Kwangtung.

The West

Surrounded by mountains, Szechuan has a mild, humid climate and rich fertile soil. Its cuisine is most noted for its robust, richly colored dishes flavored with hot spices, such as chilies and Szechuan peppercorns. Strongly flavored ingredients, such as garlic, ginger, onions, leeks, and sesame seed paste are typical and hot pickles are a speciality.

Food preservation techniques, for which Western China is famous, include smoking, drying, salting, and pickling. Yunnan, to the South of Szechuan, produces superb cured, smoked raw ham.

Szechuan cooking is traditionally described as having seven kinds of flavors - sweet, salty, sour, bitter, fragrant, sesame, and hot - based respectively on honey or sugar, soy sauce, vinegar, onions or leeks, garlic or ginger, sesame seeds and, finally, chilies. Methods of cooking are varied, ranging from dry-frying with very little oil and no additional liquid to cooking in a clear, well-flavored stock, which is then reduced to make a thick rich sauce. Deep-fried, paper-wrapped parcels of marinated meat or fish are a Szechuan speciality.

Equipment

It is not essential to buy a vast array of special equipment for Chinese cooking, but some items, especially a good-quality wok, are easier to use than their Western equivalents and will result in more authentic-tasting dishes. Most utensils are inexpensive and easily available from Chinese supermarkets and good kitchenware stores.

Wok

This bowl-shaped "skillet" with sloping sides is designed to ensure that heat spreads quickly and evenly over the surface so that food can be cooked rapidly, which is crucial for stir-frying. Once the ingredients have been added to the wok, they are tossed and stirred constantly for a short time over a very high heat. It is possible to stir-fry in a Western-style skillet, but it is more difficult and the texture of the dish is likely to be less crisp. Woks can also be used for a variety of other cooking techniques, including braising, deep-frying, and steaming.

Traditionally made from cast-iron, they are now available in a variety of metals and in a wide range of prices. Carbon steel is a good choice, but stainless steel tends to scorch. Non-stick woks are also manufactured, but the lining cannot really withstand the high temperature required for stir-frying. Handles may be single or double, semi-circular or long, or a combination of the two. Wooden handles are safer than metal ones. It is important that a wok is large enough for the ingredients to be stirred and tossed all the time they are cooking and a range of sizes is available. One with a diameter of about 14 inches is adequate for most Western families without being so heavy, whatever it is made of, that it is an effort to use. Flat-based woks are now manufactured for use on electric stovetops.

New woks, apart from those with a non-stick lining, must be seasoned before they are used. First wash well with hot water and a cream cleanser to remove the protective coating of oil. Rinse and dry the wok and then place it over a low heat and add about 2 tablespoons of vegetable oil. Rub the oil all over the inner surface of the wok with a thick pad of paper towel, being careful not to burn your fingers. Heat the oil for about 10 minutes, then wipe it off with a fresh pad of paper towel, which will become black. Repeat this heating and wiping process until the kitchen paper remains clean; it will take quite a long time.

Once the wok has been seasoned, it should not be washed with cream cleanser or detergent. Simply wipe it out with paper towels, wash in hot water, and dry thoroughly. If the wok is used only occasionally, it may become rusty. In this case, scour the rust off and season again.

Wok Accessories

Some woks are supplied with lids, but if not, these can be bought separately. They are dome-shaped, usually made of aluminium and are tight-fitting. A lid is necessary when the wok is used for steaming, but a dome-shaped saucepan lid will work as satisfactorily.

A metal stand is an essential safety feature when the wok is used for steaming, braising or deep-frying. It may be an open-sided frame or a perforated metal ring.

A wok scoop is a bowl-shaped spatula with a long handle. Some resemble a perforated spoon and others are made from reinforced wire mesh. The handle may be wood or metal. The scoop makes it easier to toss the ingredients during stir-frying, but a long-handled spoon is an adequate substitute. Chinese cooks also use the scoop for adding ingredients to the wok.

A trivet is used for steaming. It is placed in the base of the wok and supports the dish or plate containing the food above the water level. It may be made of wood or metal. A wok brush of split bamboo is used for cleaning the wok.

Bamboo Steamer

Bamboo baskets with lids are available in a range of sizes and can be stacked one on top of another. They are designed to rest on the sloping sides of the wok above the water level.

Cleaver

This finely balanced tool is seen in every Chinese kitchen and is used for virtually all cutting tasks, from chopping spare ribs and halving duck to slashing fish and deveining prawns. Cleavers are available in a variety of weights and sizes and although they look unwieldy, they are precision instruments. The blade should be kept razor sharp.

Chopsticks

Long wooden chopsticks may be used for adding ingredients to the wok, fluffing rice, separating noodles and general stirring. They are not essential, but are useful and add a feeling of authenticity. Because they have a lighter touch than a spoon or fork, they are less likely to break up or squash delicate ingredients. Chopsticks are easy to handle once you have acquired the knack. Place one chopstick in the angle between your thumb and index finger, with the lower part resting on your middle finger. Hold the other chopstick between the thumb and index finger as you would hold a pencil; this is the one you manipulate.

Ingredients

Many ingredients used in Chinese cooking are also typically found in the Western kitchen – eggs, meat, poultry, fish, bell peppers, spring onions, carrots, cucumbers, and so on. Some, such as bean sprouts and soy sauce, have become familiar. A few, such as won ton skins and chili sauce, may not be so well known. A comprehensive range of specialist ingredients can be obtained from Chinese foodstores and many can be purchased from good supermarkets.

Bamboo Shoots

Used for their texture rather than their flavor, which is very bland, bamboo shoots are readily available in cans. Fresh young bamboo shoots can sometimes be obtained. To prepare them, remove the tough outer skin and boil them in water for 40–50 minutes. Adding two red bell peppers to the water helps to remove the bitter taste.

Bean Sauce

Also known as bean paste, this savory paste may be black or yellow. It is made from crushed, salted soya beans, flour, and spices and is often used instead of soy sauce when a thicker consistency is required. It is available in cans and jars. Sweet bean sauce is red and is used as a basis for sweet sauces and as an accompaniment to char siu dishes.

Bean Sprouts

This term usually refers to the shoots of the mung bean, although the shoots of many other legumes and grains can also be eaten. They are widely available, fresh and in cans from supermarkets. It is easy to sprout beans at home to provide a fresh supply when needed. They are used to give texture to dishes and can be stored in the refrigerator for two or three days.

Black Beans

Salted fermented soy beans are available in cans and packets. They should be soaked in cold water for 5–10 minutes before use to remove some of their saltiness. They have a distinctive flavor and are always combined with other ingredients, such as meat or fish.

Cellophane Noodles

Also known as transparent noodles or bean threads, these opaque white noodles are sold in bundles that resemble candy floss in appearance. They should be soaked in hot water for 5 minutes before using, when they will become translucent. They

Ingredients

their own and are good combined with soups and soupy dishes because they absorb a lot of liquid, making them very tasty.

Chili Bean Sauce

This fermented soya bean sauce flavored with chilies and other spices is available in cans and jars. Some varieties are fiery hot, so use with caution.

Chili Oil

This is a very hot, red-colored oil used for flavoring spicy dishes. It should always be used with caution. Some varieties contain chili flakes. You can make your own by adding a few dried chilies to a small bottle of bland vegetable oil.

Chilies

Many varieties of both red and green fresh chilies are widely available and they range from relatively mild to scorchingly hot. It is often not possible to tell which variety you are buying and some look very similar to each other, but taste quite different. As a general rule, large, round chilies are usually milder than small, pointed ones. The seeds are the hottest part, so if you prefer a milder flavor, remove and discard them before use. Take care when handling chilies because the juice can burn. Wear protective gloves if you have sensitive skin and avoid touching your face, especially the eyes. Always wash you hands well afterwards. Dried red chilies are also used in Chinese cooking. They are often hotter than fresh chilies and can also burn.

Chinese Five-Spice Powder

This flavoring contains star anise, fennel seeds, cinnamon, cloves, and Szechuan pepper. It has a distinctive taste and a pungent aroma, so it should be used sparingly. It is a popular flavoring for soy-braised dishes and roast meat. It will keep more or less indefinitely in an airtight container. When buying, make sure you look for Chinese five-spice powder because the Indian flavoring is a different mixture.

Chinese Cabbage

Also known as Chinese leaves, the commonest variety of this leafy vegetable resembles a tightly packed, pale green romaine lettuce. Another variety is rounder with curly leaves. A large proportion of the vegetable consists of the crunchy stems, which add texture to stir-fries and other dishes.

Chinese Pancakes

These are made from flour and water and are available fresh and frozen. Frozen pancakes should be thawed before steaming.

Chinese Pickles

A variety of pickles is available from Chinese foodstores in jars and cans. They include salted cabbage, salted mustard greens, Szechuan hot pickle, made from kohlrabi, and Szechuan preserved vegetable, made from the root of mustard greens. They should be rinsed well before using.

Chinese Rice Vinegar

White rice vinegar, which is distilled from Chinese rice wine, has a stronger flavor than the red variety, which is made from fermented rice. Cider vinegar or white wine vinegar may used as a substitute.

Chinese Rice Wine

Made from glutinous rice, this has a rich, sherry-like flavor and is golden in color. In fact, its alternative name is yellow wine. The best type, called Shaoxing, comes from Chekiang in Western China and is made from glutinous rice, millet, ordinary rice, and mineral water. Another famous wine, Chen Gang, comes from nearby Fukien. These are both well-matured and quite expensive. Ordinary quality rice wine, made from glutinous rice alone, is adequate for cooking, and dry or medium sherry may be used as a substitute. Be careful not to buy Mao Tai, which is also sometimes marketed as a "wine", as it is a spirit distilled from sorghum and is even stronger than pure vodka.

Cilantro

Also known as Chinese parsley, the fresh leaves are widely used in Chinese cooking. Tearing the leaves, rather than chopping them, produces a more subtle flavor. Although it resembles flat leaf parsley in appearance, cilantro tastes quite different.

Dried Mushrooms

Dried Chinese or shiitake mushrooms are used many dishes. They are expensive, but as their flavor is very strong, only a few are required. Soak them in hot water for 20–30 minutes before using. The soaking water can be used as stock. Dried mushrooms keep more or less indefinitely in a cool, dry place.

Ingredients

Egg Noodles

These yellow noodles range in size and shape from long, narrow strands, like spaghetti, to broad, flat ribbons, like tagliatelle. They are available both fresh and dried.

Ginger

The fresh root is an essential ingredient in many Chinese dishes. Ground ginger is no substitute, as it will burn during stir-frying and does not impart the same delicate flavor to other dishes. Choose plump sections of fresh ginger with shiny, unblemished skins. To use, peel with a swivel vegetable peeler or a small sharp knife and thinly slice, finely chop, or grate, according to the recipe. Fresh ginger will keep for several weeks in a cool, dry place.

Hoisin Sauce

Sweet and spicy, this dark brownish red sauce is made from soy beans, sugar, flour, vinegar, garlic, chilies, sesame oil, and salt. It is often combined with soy sauce for flavoring stir-fried dishes and may also be used on its own when cooking seafood, spare ribs, and duck. It is sometimes provided in a small bowl at the table as a dipping sauce.

Lemon Grass

This aromatic herb has a mild citrus flavor. It is available fresh, in jars or powdered. Use only the lower part of the stem, which should either be removed from the dish before serving or very finely chopped, as it is quite woody.

Lily Buds

Tiger lily buds, also called golden needles, are dried flower buds with a rather musty flavor that is something of an acquired taste. They should be soaked in water for 20 minutes before use.

Lotus Leaves

The leaves of the lotus plant are very large and are used to enclose food to be steamed and although they are not eaten, they impart a subtle flavor to the contents of the parcels. They are sold dried and should be soaked in warm water for 20 minutes before use.

Lotus Root

Available dried or canned, lotus root is cooked as part of a mixed vegetable dish. Soak the dried root in cold water overnight before use. Fresh lotus root is not usually available in the West.

Ingredients

Lotus Seeds

These oval seeds, about $\frac{1}{2}$ inch long, are available dried or canned. They are used in vegetable dishes and soups.

Oyster Sauce

Made from boiled oysters and soy sauce, this salty, brown sauce should be used moderately. It is widely used in Cantonese cooking. Vegetarians can use soy sauce as a substitute. Oyster sauce will keep in the refrigerator for several months.

Pak Choi

Also known as bok choy, this is an attractive vegetable with white stems and dark green leaves.

Plum Sauce

Especially popular in Cantonese cooking, this thick, rich, spicy fruit sauce is available in jars and cans.

Rice Stick Noodles

About 10 inches long, these white thread noodles are more popular in Southern than Northern cuisine and go well with fish. They do not require soaking before cooking.

Sesame Oil

Made from toasted sesame seeds, this oil is strongly flavored and aromatic. It is rarely used for frying, but a little is often added to a dish at the end of the cooking time for extra flavor. Be sure to buy a Chinese variety, as Middle Eastern sesame oil is less aromatic and flavorsome.

Sesame Seeds

Widely used in all Chinese cooking, sesame seeds add a nutty flavor, pleasant aroma, and crunchy texture to many dishes.

Soy Sauce

This is the sauce most widely used in Chinese cooking and is made from fermented soy beans, salt, yeast, and sugar. Light soy sauce has a stronger flavor than dark and is mainly used in cooking. Dark soy sauce is sweeter and richer and is frequently used as a condiment. When used in cooking, it imparts a rich color to the food and is integral to the technique known as red-cooking. Japanese soy sauce has a much lighter flavor and is not an adequate substitute.

Spring Roll Skins

These are made from wheat flour or rice flour and water and are wafer-thin. They are available in a variety of sizes. Wheat-flour skins are sold frozen and should be thoroughly thawed before separating and using them. Rice-flour skins must be soaked before use.

Straw Mushrooms

Named because they grow on beds of rice straw, these mushrooms are used for their unusual slippery texture rather than their flavor, which is quite bland. They are widely available in cans, but fresh straw mushrooms cannot be obtained in the West.

Szechuan Peppercorns

These reddish brown or pink peppercorns, also known as farchiew, grow wild in Western China. They are very aromatic, but not so hot as either black or white peppercorns. They are often roasted and ground before use.

Tofu

Also known as bean curd, this soya bean product is used extensively in Chinese cooking. It has a fairly bland flavor, but readily absorbs the flavors of other ingredients. Firm tofu, ideal for stir-frying, is usually sold in cakes. It should be handled carefully, as it breaks up fairly easily. It can be sliced, diced, or shredded. Silken tofu has a more jelly-like consistency. Tofu is high in protein, making it a very popular vegetarian food. It can be stored, submerged in water and covered, in the refrigerator for several days. Dried tofu is sold in cakes and can be cut into strips or slices before being cooked with other ingredients. Smoked and marinated tofu is also available, but these are less suitable for Chinese cooking.

Water Chestnuts

These roots of an aquatic plant resemble chestnuts in appearance only and peeling them reveals crisp, white, sweet-tasting flesh. They are available fresh and in cans, but the latter have less flavor and texture. Store fresh water chestnuts, submerged in water and covered, in the refrigerator for up to a month, changing the water every two or three days.

Won Ton Skins

These are made from flour, egg, and water. You can make your own or buy them ready-made.

Wood Ears

Dried fungi that grow on trees, wood ears and the similar cloud ears are like mushrooms. They are used more for their texture than flavor and provide contrasting color in some dishes. They are available dried and should be soaked in hot water for 20-30 minutes and thoroughly rinsed before use. Discard the soaking water.

Basic Recipes

Chinese Stock

This basic stock is used in Chinese cooking not only as the basis for soup-making, but also whenever liquid is required instead of plain water.

MAKES 10 CUPS

1 lb 10 oz chicken pieces

1 lb 10 oz pork spare ribs

15 cups cold water

3-4 pieces fresh ginger, crushed

3-4 green onions, each tied into a knot

3-4 tbsp Chinese rice wine or dry sherry

1 Trim off any excess fat from the chicken and spare ribs; chop them into large pieces.

2 Place the chicken and pork in a large pan with the water; add the ginger and green onion knots.

3 Bring to a boil, and skim off the froth. Reduce the heat and simmer uncovered for at least 2-3 hours.

4 Strain the stock, discarding the chicken, pork, ginger, and green onions; add the wine and return to a boil, simmer for 2-3 minutes.

5 Refrigerate the stock when cool; it will keep for up to 4-5 days. Alternatively, it can be frozen in small containers and be defrosted as required.

Fresh Chicken Stock

MAKES 7½ CUPS

2 lb 4 oz chicken, skinned

2 celery stalks

1 onion

2 carrots

1 garlic clove

few sprigs of fresh parsley

9 cups water

salt and pepper

1 Put all the ingredients into a large saucepan.

2 Bring to a boil. Skim away surface froth using a large flat spoon. Reduce the heat to a gentle simmer, partially cover, and cook for 2 hours. Allow to cool.

3 Line a strainer with clean cheesecloth and place over a large jug or bowl. Pour the stock through the strainer. The cooked chicken can be used in another recipe. Discard the other solids. Cover the stock and chill.

4 Skim away any fat that forms before using. Store in the refrigerator for 3-4 days, until required, or freeze in small batches.

Fresh Vegetable Stock

This can be kept chilled for up to three days or frozen for up to three months. Salt is not added when cooking the stock: it is better to season it according to the dish in which it its to be used.

MAKES 6¼ CUPS

9 oz shallots

1 large carrot, diced

1 celery stalk, chopped

½ fennel bulb

1 garlic clove

1 bay leaf

a few fresh parsley and tarragon sprigs

8¾ cups water

pepper

1 Put all the ingredients in a large saucepan and bring to a boil.

2 Skim off the surface froth with a flat spoon and reduce to a gentle simmer. Partially cover and cook for 45 minutes. Leave to cool.

3 Line a strainer with clean cheesecloth and put over a large jug or bowl. Pour the stock through the strainer. Discard the herbs and vegetables.

4 Cover and store in small quantities in the refrigerator for up to three days.

Fresh Lamb Stock

MAKES 7½ CUPS

about 2 lb 4 oz bones from a cooked joint or raw chopped lamb bones

2 onions, studded with 6 cloves, or sliced or chopped coarsely

2 carrots, sliced

1 leek, sliced

1-2 celery stalks, sliced

1 bouquet garni

about 2 quarts water

1 Chop or break up the bones and place in a large saucepan with the other ingredients.

2 Bring to a boil and remove any froth from the surface with a perforated spoon. Cover and simmer gently for 3-4 hours. Strain the stock and leave to cool.

3 Remove any fat from the surface and chill. If stored for more than 24 hours the stock must be boiled every day, cooled quickly, and chilled again. The stock may be frozen for up to 2 months; place in a large plastic bag and seal, leaving at least 1 inch of headspace to allow for expansion.

Fresh Fish Stock

MAKES 7½ CUPS

1 head of a cod or salmon, etc., plus the trimmings, skin and bones or just the trimmings, skin and bones

1-2 onions, sliced

1 carrot, sliced

1-2 celery stalks, sliced

squeeze of lemon juice

1 bouquet garni or 2 fresh or dried bay leaves

1 Wash the fish head and trimmings and place in a saucepan. Cover with water and bring to a boil.

2 Remove any froth with a perforated spoon, then add the remaining ingredients. Cover and simmer for about 30 minutes.

3 Strain and cool. Store in the refrigerator and use within 2 days.

Cornstarch Paste

Cornstarch paste is made by mixing 1 part cornstarch with about 1½ parts of cold water. Stir until smooth. The paste is used to thicken sauces.

Plain Rice

Use long-grain rice or patna rice, or better still, try fragrant Thai rice.

SERVES 4

9 oz long-grain rice

1 cup cold water

pinch of salt

½ tsp oil (optional)

1 Wash and rinse the rice just once. Place the rice in a saucepan and add enough water so that there is no more than $3/4$ inch of water above the surface of the rice.

2 Bring to a boil, add salt and oil (if using), and stir to prevent the rice sticking to the bottom of the pan.

3 Reduce the heat to very, very low, cover, and cook for 15-20 minutes.

4 Remove from the heat and let stand, covered, for 10 minutes or so. Fluff up the rice with a fork or spoon before serving.

Fresh Coconut Milk

To make it from fresh grated coconut, place about 9 oz grated coconut in a bowl, pour over about 1 pint of boiling water to just cover and leave to stand for 1 hour. Strain through cheesecloth, squeezing hard to extract as much "thick" milk as possible. If you require coconut cream, leave to stand, then skim the "cream" from the surface for use. Unsweetened shredded coconut can also be used in the same quantities.

How to Use This Book

Each recipe contains a wealth of useful information, including a breakdown of nutritional quantities, preparation and cooking times, and level of difficulty. All of this information is explained in detail below.

The nutritional information provided for each recipe is per serving or per portion. Optional ingredients, variations or serving suggestions have not been included in the calculations.

The number of chef's hats represents the difficulty of each recipe, ranging from easy (1 chef's hat) to difficult (5 chef's hats).

This amount of time represents the preparation of ingredients, including cooling, chilling, and soaking times.

This represents the cooking time.

The ingredients for each recipe are listed in the order that they are used.

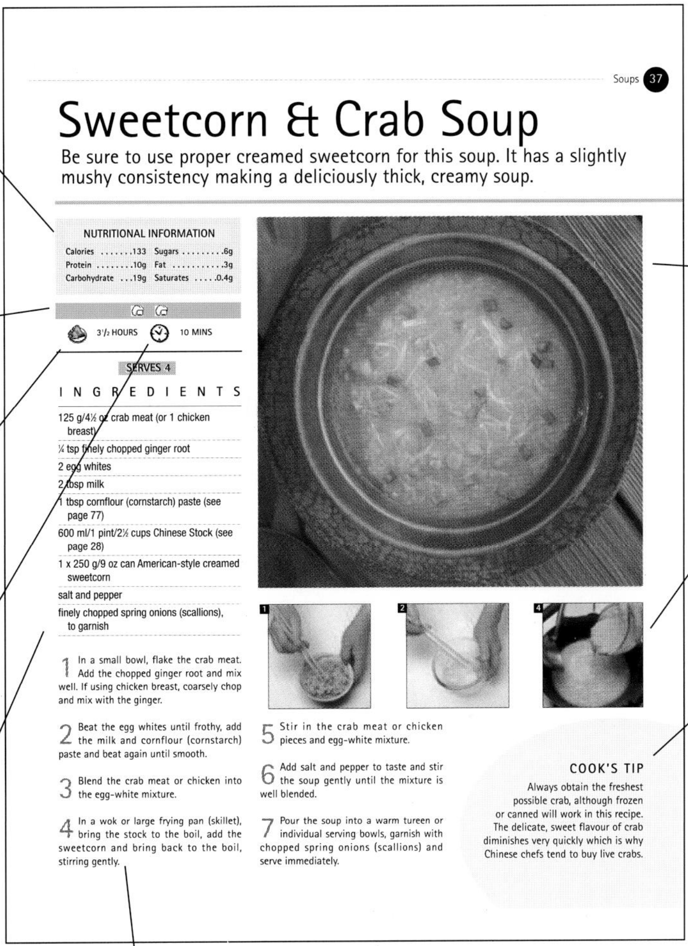

Soups 37

Sweetcorn & Crab Soup

Be sure to use proper creamed sweetcorn for this soup. It has a slightly mushy consistency making a deliciously thick, creamy soup.

NUTRITIONAL INFORMATION

Calories	133	Sugars	6g
Protein	10g	Fat	3g
Carbohydrate	19g	Saturates	0.4g

3½ HOURS 10 MINS

SERVES 4

INGREDIENTS

- 125 g/4½ oz crab meat (or 1 chicken breast)
- ¼ tsp finely chopped ginger root
- 2 egg whites
- 2 tbsp milk
- 1 tbsp cornflour (cornstarch) paste (see page 77)
- 600 ml/1 pint/2½ cups Chinese Stock (see page 28)
- 1 x 250 g/9 oz can American-style creamed sweetcorn
- salt and pepper
- finely chopped spring onions (scallions), to garnish

1 In a small bowl, flake the crab meat. Add the chopped ginger root and mix well. If using chicken breast, coarsely chop and mix with the ginger.

2 Beat the egg whites until frothy, add the milk and cornflour (cornstarch) paste and beat again until smooth.

3 Blend the crab meat or chicken into the egg-white mixture.

4 In a wok or large frying pan (skillet), bring the stock to the boil, add the sweetcorn and bring back to the boil, stirring gently.

5 Stir in the crab meat or chicken pieces and egg-white mixture.

6 Add salt and pepper to taste and stir the soup gently until the mixture is well blended.

7 Pour the soup into a warm tureen or individual serving bowls, garnish with chopped spring onions (scallions) and serve immediately.

COOK'S TIP

Always obtain the freshest possible crab, although frozen or canned will work in this recipe. The delicate, sweet flavour of crab diminishes very quickly which is why Chinese chefs tend to buy live crabs.

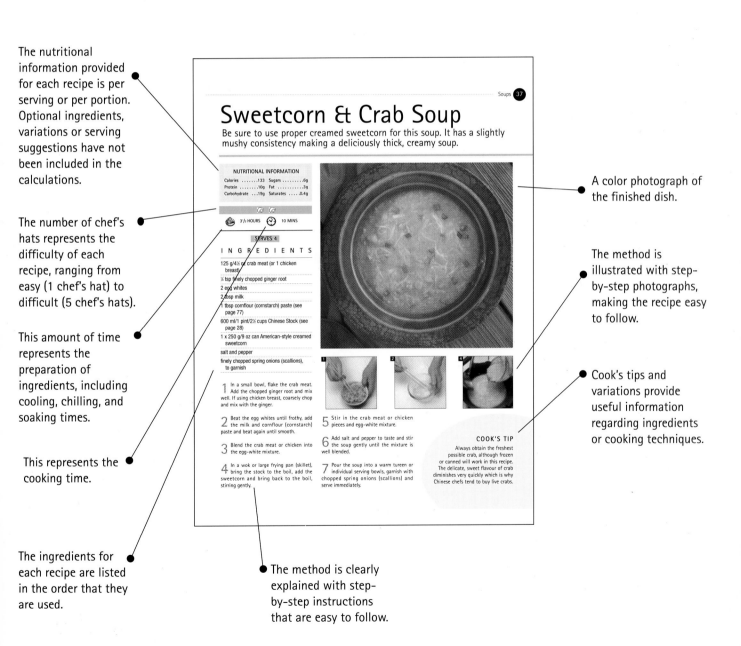

A color photograph of the finished dish.

The method is illustrated with step-by-step photographs, making the recipe easy to follow.

Cook's tips and variations provide useful information regarding ingredients or cooking techniques.

The method is clearly explained with step-by-step instructions that are easy to follow.

Soups

Soup is an integral part of the Chinese meal but is rarely served as a first course as it is in the Western world. Instead, soup is usually served between courses to clear the palate and act as a beverage throughout the meal. The soup is usually presented in a large tureen in the center of the table for people to help themselves as the meal

progresses. The soups in this chapter combine a range of flavors and textures. There are thicker soups, thin clear consommés, and those which are served with wontons, dumplings,

noodles, or even rice in them. Ideally the soup should be made with fresh stock, but if this is unavailable, use a stock cube and reduce the amount of seasonings, otherwise the soup will be too salty. It is always worth making your own Chinese Stock (see page 30) if you have time.

Chicken & Corn Soup

A hint of chili and sherry flavor this soup while red bell pepper and tomato add color.

NUTRITIONAL INFORMATION

Calories	199	Sugars	.........8g
Protein	........12g	Fat	..........8g
Carbohydrate	...19g	Saturates	.......1g

5 MINS   20 MINS

SERVES 4

I N G R E D I E N T S

1 skinless, boneless chicken breast,
    about 6 oz

2 tbsp sunflower oil

2–3 green onions,
    thinly sliced diagonally

1 small or ½ large red
    bell pepper, thinly sliced

1 garlic clove, crushed

4½ oz baby corn-on-the-cob, thinly sliced

4 cups chicken stock

7 oz can of corn
    kernels, well drained

2 tbsp sherry

2–3 tsp bottled sweet chili sauce

2–3 tsp cornstarch

2 tomatoes, quartered
    and seeded, then sliced

salt and pepper

chopped fresh cilantro or parsley, to garnish

1 Cut the chicken breast into 4 strips lengthwise, then cut each strip into narrow slices across the grain.

2 Heat the oil in a wok or skillet, swirling it around until it is really hot.

3 Add the chicken and stir-fry for 3–4 minutes, moving it around the wok until it is well sealed all over and almost cooked through.

4 Add the green onions, bell pepper, and garlic, and stir-fry for 2–3 minutes. Add the baby corn-on-the-cob and stock and bring to a boil.

5 Add the corn kernels, sherry, sweet chili sauce, and salt to taste, and simmer for 5 minutes, stirring from time to time.

6 Blend the cornstarch with a little cold water. Add to the soup and bring to a boil, stirring until the sauce is thickened. Add the tomato slices, season to taste, and simmer for 1–2 minutes.

7 Serve the chicken and corn soup hot, sprinkled with chopped cilantro or parsley.

Corn & Crab Soup

Be sure to use proper creamed corn for this soup. It has a slightly mushy consistency making a deliciously thick, creamy soup.

NUTRITIONAL INFORMATION

Calories	133	Sugars	.........6g
Protein	........10g	Fat	...........3g
Carbohydrate	...19g	Saturates	.....0.4g

 3¹/₂ HOURS   10 MINS

SERVES 4

I N G R E D I E N T S

4½ oz crab meat (or 1 chicken breast)

¼ tsp finely chopped fresh ginger

2 egg whites

2 tbsp milk

1 tbsp cornstarch paste (see page 297)

2½ cups Chinese Stock (see page 30)

1 x 9 oz can creamed corn

salt and pepper

finely chopped green onions, to garnish

1 In a small bowl, flake the crab meat. Add the chopped fresh ginger and mix well. If using chicken breast, coarsely chop and mix with the ginger.

2 Beat the egg whites until frothy, add the milk and cornstarch paste, and beat again until smooth.

3 Blend the crab meat or chicken into the egg-white mixture.

4 In a wok or large skillet, bring the stock to a boil, add the corn, and bring back to a boil, stirring gently.

5 Stir in the crab meat or chicken pieces and egg-white mixture.

6 Add salt and pepper to taste and stir the soup gently until the mixture is well blended.

7 Pour the soup into a warm tureen or individual serving bowls, garnish with chopped green onions, and serve immediately.

COOK'S TIP

Always obtain the freshest possible crab, although frozen or canned will work in this recipe. The delicate, sweet flavor of crab diminishes very quickly, which is why Chinese chefs tend to buy live crabs.

Seafood & Tofu Soup

Use shrimp, squid, or scallops, or a combination of all three in this healthy soup.

NUTRITIONAL INFORMATION

Calories	97	Sugars	.........0g
Protein	........17g	Fat	...........2g
Carbohydrate	....3g	Saturates	.....0.4g

 3¹/₂ HOURS   10 MINS

SERVES 4

INGREDIENTS

9 oz seafood: peeled shrimp, squid, scallops, etc., defrosted if frozen

½ egg white, lightly beaten

1 tbsp cornstarch paste (see page 31)

1 cake tofu

3 cups Chinese Stock (see page 30)

1 tbsp light soy sauce

salt and pepper

fresh cilantro leaves, to garnish (optional)

1 Small shrimp can be left whole; larger ones should be cut into smaller pieces; cut the squid and scallops into small pieces.

2 If raw, mix the shrimp and scallops with the egg white and cornstarch paste to prevent them from becoming tough when they are cooked. Cut the cake of tofu into about 24 small cubes.

3 Bring the stock to a rolling boil. Add the tofu and soy sauce, bring back to a boil, and simmer for 1 minute.

4 Stir in the seafood, raw pieces first, pre-cooked ones last. Bring back to a boil and simmer for just 1 minute.

5 Adjust the seasoning to taste and serve, garnished with cilantro leaves, if liked.

COOK'S TIP

Tofu, also known as bean curd, is made from puréed yellow soya beans, which are very high in protein. Although almost tasteless, tofu absorbs the flavors of other ingredients. It is widely available in supermarkets, and Oriental and health-food stores.

Hot & Sour Soup

This well-known soup from Peking is unusual in that it is thickened. The "hot" flavor is achieved by the addition of plenty of black pepper.

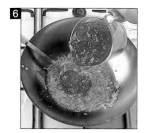

NUTRITIONAL INFORMATION

Calories 124	Sugars 1g	
Protein 5g	Fat 8g	
Carbohydrate 8g	Saturates 1g	

3¹/₂ HOURS   25 MINS

SERVES 4

I N G R E D I E N T S

2 tbsp cornstarch

4 tbsp water

2 tbsp light soy sauce

3 tbsp rice wine vinegar

½ tsp ground black pepper

1 small fresh red chili, finely chopped

1 egg

2 tbsp vegetable oil

1 onion, chopped

3¾ cups chicken or beef consommé

1 open-cap mushroom, sliced

1¾ oz skinless chicken breast, cut into very thin strips

1 tsp sesame oil

1 In a mixing bowl, blend the cornstarch with the water to form a smooth paste.

2 Add the soy sauce, rice wine vinegar, and black pepper.

3 Finely chop the red chili and add to the ingredients in the bowl. Mix well.

4 Break the egg into a separate bowl and beat well. Set aside while you cook the other ingredients.

5 Heat the oil in a preheated wok and fry the onion for 1–2 minutes until softened.

6 Stir in the consommé, mushroom, and chicken and bring to a boil. Cook for about 15 minutes or until the chicken is tender.

7 Gradually pour the cornstarch mixture into the soup and cook, stirring constantly, until it thickens.

8 As you are stirring, gradually drizzle the egg into the soup, to create threads of egg.

9 Pour the hot and sour soup into a warm tureen or individual serving bowls, sprinkle with the sesame oil, and serve immediately.

Lamb & Rice Soup

This is a very filling soup because it contains rice and tender pieces of lamb. Serve before a light main course.

NUTRITIONAL INFORMATION

Calories 116   Sugars 0.2g
Protein . . . . .9g   Fat 4g
Carbohydrate . . .12g   Saturates 2g

5 MINS   35 MINS

SERVES 4

INGREDIENTS

5½ oz lean lamb

¼ cup rice

3¾ cups lamb stock

1 leek, sliced

1 garlic clove, thinly sliced

2 tsp light soy sauce

1 tsp rice wine vinegar

1 medium open-cap mushroom,
    thinly sliced

salt

1 Using a sharp knife, trim any fat from the lamb and cut the meat into thin strips. Set aside until required.

2 Bring a large pan of lightly salted water to a boil and add the rice. Bring back to a boil, stir once, reduce the heat, and cook for 10–15 minutes, until tender.

3 Drain the rice, rinse under cold running water, drain again and set aside until required.

4 Meanwhile, put the lamb stock in a large saucepan and bring to a boil.

5 Add the lamb strips, leek, garlic, soy sauce, and rice wine vinegar to the stock in the pan. Reduce the heat, cover, and leave to simmer for 10 minutes, or until the lamb is tender and cooked through.

6 Add the mushroom slices and the rice to the pan and cook for 2–3 minutes more, or until the mushroom is completely cooked through.

7 Ladle the soup into 4 individual warmed soup bowls and serve immediately.

VARIATION

Use a few dried Chinese mushrooms, rehydrated according to the pack instructions and chopped, as an alternative to the open-cap mushroom. Add the Chinese mushrooms with the lamb in step 4.

Noodle & Mushroom Soup

This soup is very quickly and easily put together, and is cooked so that each ingredient can still be tasted in the finished dish.

NUTRITIONAL INFORMATION

Calories	74	Sugars	.........1g
Protein	........13g	Fat	...........3g
Carbohydrate	....9g	Saturates	.....0.4g

4 HOURS   10 MINS

SERVES 4

I N G R E D I E N T S

¼ cup dried Chinese mushrooms or 1⅓ cups field mushrooms

4 cups hot Fresh Vegetable Stock (page 28)

4½ oz thread egg noodles

2 tsp sunflower oil

3 garlic cloves, crushed

1 inch piece fresh ginger, shredded finely

½ tsp oyster mushroom sauce

1 tsp light soy sauce

2 cups bean sprouts

cilantro leaves, to garnish

1 Soak the dried Chinese mushrooms, if using, for at least 30 minutes in 1¼ cups of the hot vegetable stock. Remove the stalks and discard, then slice the mushrooms. Reserve the stock.

2 Cook the noodles for 2–3 minutes in boiling water. Drain, rinse, and set aside until required.

3 Heat the oil over a high heat in a wok or large, heavy skillet. Add the garlic and ginger, stir, and add the mushrooms.

Stir over a high heat for 2 minutes.

4 Add the remaining vegetable stock with the reserved stock and bring to a boil. Add the mushroom sauce and soy sauce and mix well.

5 Stir in the bean sprouts and cook until tender. Serve over the noodles, garnished with cilantro leaves.

COOK'S TIP

Dried mushrooms are highly fragrant and add a special flavor to Chinese dishes. There are many different varieties, but Shiitake are the best. Although not cheap, a small amount will go a long way and they will keep indefinitely in an airtight jar.

Wonton Soup

The recipe for the wonton skins makes 24 but the soup requires only half this quantity. The other half can be frozen for another time.

NUTRITIONAL INFORMATION

Calories 278   Sugars 2g
Protein ....10g   Fat 5g
Carbohydrate ...50g   Saturates 1g

 45 MINS   5 MINS

SERVES 4

INGREDIENTS

WONTON SKINS

1 egg

6 tbsp water

2 cups all-purpose flour, plus extra for dusting

FILLING

½ cup frozen chopped spinach, defrosted

1 tbsp pine nuts, toasted and chopped

¼ cup minced Tofu

salt

SOUP

2½ cups vegetable stock

1 tbsp dry sherry

1 tbsp light soy sauce

2 green onions, chopped

1 To make the wonton skins, beat the egg lightly in a bowl and mix with the water. Stir in the flour to form a stiff dough. Knead lightly, then cover with a damp cloth and leave to rest for 30 minutes.

2 Roll the dough out into a large sheet about ¼ inch thick. Cut out 3 inch squares. Dust each one lightly with flour. Only 12 squares are required for the

soup so freeze the rest to use on another occasion.

3 To make the filling, squeeze out the excess water from the spinach. Mix the spinach with the pine nuts and Tofu until thoroughly combined. Season with salt to taste.

4 Divide the mixture into 12 equal portions. Using a teaspoon, place one

portion in the center of each square. Seal the wontons by bringing the opposite corners of each square together and squeezing well.

5 To make the soup, bring the vegetable stock, sherry, and soy sauce to a boil, add the wontons, and boil rapidly for 2–3 minutes. Add the green onions and serve in warmed bowls immediately.

Spicy Chicken Noodle Soup

This filling soup is filled with spicy flavors and bright colors for a really attractive and hearty dish.

NUTRITIONAL INFORMATION

Calories 286   Sugars 21g
Protein . . . . .22g   Fat 6g
Carbohydrate . . .37g   Saturates 1g

 15 MINS   20 MINS

SERVES 4

I N G R E D I E N T S

2 tbsp tamarind paste

4 red chilies, finely chopped

2 cloves garlic, crushed

1 inch piece Thai ginger, peeled
   and very finely chopped

4 tbsp fish sauce

2 tbsp sugar

8 lime leaves, roughly torn

5 cups chicken stock

12 oz boneless chicken breast

3½ oz carrots, very thinly sliced

12 oz sweet potato, diced

3½ oz baby corn-on-the-cob, halved

3 tbsp fresh cilantro, roughly chopped

3½ oz cherry tomatoes, halved

5½ oz flat rice noodles

fresh cilantro, chopped,
   to garnish

1 Preheat a large wok or skillet. Place the tamarind paste, chilies, garlic, ginger, fish sauce, sugar, lime leaves, and chicken stock in the wok and bring to a boil, stirring constantly. Reduce the heat and cook for about 5 minutes.

2 Using a sharp knife, thinly slice the chicken. Add the chicken to the wok and cook for 5 minutes more, stirring the mixture well.

3 Reduce the heat and add the carrots, sweet potato, and baby corn-on-the-cob to the wok. Leave to simmer, uncovered, for 5 minutes, or until the vegetables are tender and the chicken is completely cooked through.

4 Stir in the chopped fresh cilantro, cherry tomatoes, and flat rice noodles.

5 Leave the soup to simmer for about 5 minutes, or until the noodles are tender.

6 Garnish the spicy chicken noodle soup with chopped fresh cilantro and serve hot.

Spicy Shrimp Soup

Lime leaves are used as a flavoring in this soup to add tartness.

NUTRITIONAL INFORMATION

Calories . . . . .217 Sugars 16g
Protein . . . . .16g Fat 4g
Carbohydrate . . .31g Saturates 1g

10 MINS   20 MINS

SERVES 4

I N G R E D I E N T S

2 tbsp tamarind paste

4 red chilies, very finely chopped

2 cloves garlic, crushed

1 inch piece Thai ginger, peeled and very finely chopped

4 tbsp fish sauce

2 tbsp sugar

5 cups fish stock

8 lime leaves

3½ oz carrots, very thinly sliced

12 oz sweet potato, diced

1 cup baby corn-on-the-cob, halved

3 tbsp fresh cilantro, roughly chopped

3½ oz cherry tomatoes, halved

8 oz butterfly shrimp

1 Place the tamarind paste, red chilies, garlic, ginger, fish sauce, sugar, and fish stock in a preheated wok or large, heavy skillet. Roughly tear the lime leaves and add to the wok. Bring to a boil, stirring constantly to blend the flavors.

2 Reduce the heat and add the carrot, sweet potato, and baby corn-on-the-cob to the mixture in the wok.

3 Leave the soup to simmer, uncovered, for about 10 minutes, or until the vegetables are tender.

4 Stir the cilantro, cherry tomatoes, and shrimp into the soup and heat through for 5 minutes.

5 Transfer the soup to a warm soup tureen or individual serving bowls and serve hot.

COOK'S TIP

Thai ginger or galangal is a member of the ginger family, but it is yellow in color with pink sprouts. The flavor is aromatic and less pungent than ginger.

Chicken Wonton Soup

This Chinese-style soup is delicious as a first course to an oriental meal or as a light meal.

NUTRITIONAL INFORMATION

Calories . . . . 101 Sugars 0.3g
Protein . . . . .14g Fat 4g
Carbohydrate . . . .3g Saturates 1g

15 MINS   10 MINS

SERVES 4-6

INGREDIENTS

FILLING

12 oz ground chicken

1 tbsp soy sauce

1 tsp grated, fresh ginger

1 garlic clove, crushed

2 tsp sherry

2 green onions, chopped

1 tsp sesame oil

1 egg white

½ tsp cornstarch

½ tsp sugar

about 35 wonton skins

SOUP

6 cups chicken stock

1 tbsp light soy sauce

1 green onion, shredded

1 small carrot, cut into very thin slices

1 Place all the ingredients for the filling in a large bowl and mix until thoroughly combined.

2 Place a small spoonful of the filling in the center of each wonton skin.

3 Dampen the edges and gather up the wonton skin to form a small pouch enclosing the filling.

4 Cook the filled wontons in boiling water for 1 minute or until they float to the top. Remove with a slotted spoon and set aside.

5 Bring the chicken stock to a boil. Add the soy sauce, green onion, and carrot.

6 Add the wontons to the soup and simmer gently for 2 minutes. Serve.

COOK'S TIP

Make double quantities of wonton skins and freeze the rest. Place small squares of baking parchment in between each skin, then place in a freezer bag and freeze. Defrost thoroughly before using.

Vegetarian Hot & Sour Soup

This popular soup is easy to make and very filling. It can be eaten as a meal on its own or served as an appetizer before a light meal.

NUTRITIONAL INFORMATION

Calories.........61	Sugars.........1g
Protein.........5g	Fat.........2g
Carbohydrate....8g	Saturates.....0.2g

30 MINS   10 MINS

SERVES 4

INGREDIENTS

4 Chinese dried mushrooms (if unavailable, use open-cap mushrooms)

4½ oz firm tofu

1 cup canned bamboo shoots

2½ cups vegetable stock or water

⅓ cup peas

1 tbsp dark soy sauce

2 tbsp white wine vinegar

2 tbsp cornstarch

salt and pepper

sesame oil, to serve

1 Place the Chinese dried mushrooms in a small bowl and cover with warm water. Leave to soak for about 20–25 minutes.

2 Drain the mushrooms and squeeze out the excess water, reserving this. Remove the tough centers and cut the mushrooms into thin shreds. Shred the tofu and bamboo shoots.

3 Bring the stock or water to a boil in a large saucepan. Add the mushrooms, tofu, bamboo shoots, and peas. Simmer for 2 minutes.

4 Mix together the soy sauce, vinegar, and cornstarch with 2 tablespoons of the reserved mushroom liquid.

5 Stir the soy sauce and cornstarch mixture into the soup with the remaining mushroom liquid. Bring to a boil and season with salt and plenty of pepper. Simmer for 2 minutes.

6 Serve in warmed bowls with a few drops of sesame oil sprinkled over the top of each.

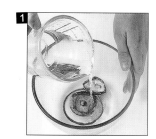

COOK'S TIP

If you use open-cap mushrooms instead of dried mushrooms, add an extra ²/₃ cup vegetable stock or water to the soup, as these mushrooms do not need soaking.

Corn & Lentil Soup

This pale-colored soup is made with corn and green lentils, and is similar in style to the traditional crab and corn soup.

NUTRITIONAL INFORMATION

Calories	171	Sugars	9g
Protein	5g	Fat	2g
Carbohydrate	30g	Saturates	0.3g

5 MINS   30 MINS

SERVES 4

I N G R E D I E N T S

2 tbsp green lentils

4 cups vegetable stock

½ inch piece fresh ginger, chopped finely

2 tsp soy sauce

1 tsp sugar

1 tbsp cornstarch

3 tbsp dry sherry

11½ oz can corn kernels

1 egg white

1 tsp sesame oil

salt and pepper

TO GARNISH

green onion, cut into strips

red chili, cut into strips

 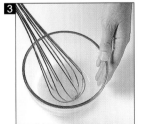 

1 Wash the lentils in a strainer. Place in a saucepan with the stock, fresh ginger, soy sauce, and sugar. Bring to a boil and boil rapidly, uncovered, for 10 minutes. Skim off any froth on the surface. Reduce the heat, cover, and simmer for 15 minutes.

2 Mix the cornstarch with the sherry in a small bowl. Add the corn with the liquid from the can and cornstarch mixture to the saucepan. Simmer for 2 minutes.

3 Whisk the egg white lightly with the sesame oil. Pour the egg mixture into the soup in a thin stream, remove from the heat, and stir. The egg white will form white strands. Season with salt and pepper to taste.

4 Pour into 4 warmed soup bowls and garnish with strips of green onion and red chili. Serve the soup immediately.

COOK'S TIP

To save time use a 15 oz can of green lentils instead of dried ones. Place the lentils and corn in a large saucepan with the stock and flavorings, bring to a boil, and simmer for 2 minutes, then continue the recipe from step 2, as above.

Chinese Potato & Pork Broth

In this recipe the pork is seasoned with traditional Chinese flavorings – soy sauce, rice wine vinegar, and a dash of sesame oil.

NUTRITIONAL INFORMATION

Calories 166   Sugars 2g
Protein ....10g   Fat 5g
Carbohydrate ...26g   Saturates 1g

 5 MINS   20 MINS

SERVES 4

I N G R E D I E N T S

4½ cups chicken stock

2 large potatoes, diced

2 tbsp rice wine vinegar

2 tbsp cornstarch

4 tbsp water

4½ oz pork tenderloin, sliced

1 tbsp light soy sauce

1 tsp sesame oil

1 carrot, cut into very thin strips

1 tsp fresh ginger, chopped

3 green onions, sliced thinly

1 red bell pepper, sliced

8 oz can bamboo shoots, drained

VARIATION

For extra heat, add 1 chopped red chili or 1 tsp of chili powder to the soup in step 5.

1 Add the chicken stock, diced potatoes, and 1 tbsp of the rice wine vinegar to a saucepan and bring to a boil. Reduce the heat until the stock is just simmering.

2 Mix the cornstarch with the water then stir into the hot stock.

3 Bring the stock back to a boil, stirring until thickened, then reduce the heat until it is just simmering again.

4 Place the pork slices in a dish and season with the remaining rice wine vinegar, the soy sauce, and sesame oil.

5 Add the pork slices, carrot strips, and ginger to the stock and cook for 10 minutes. Stir in the green onions, red bell pepper, and bamboo shoots. Cook for 5 minutes more. Pour the soup into warmed bowls and serve immediately.

Lettuce & Tofu Soup

This is a delicate, clear soup of shredded lettuce and small chunks of tofu with sliced carrot and green onion.

NUTRITIONAL INFORMATION

Calories	113	Sugars	.........2g
Protein	.........5g	Fat	..........8g
Carbohydrate	....3g	Saturates	.......1g

  5 MINS   15 MINS

SERVES 4

INGREDIENTS

7 oz tofu

2 tbsp vegetable oil

1 carrot, sliced thinly

½ inch piece fresh ginger,
  cut into thin shreds

3 green onions, sliced diagonally

5 cups vegetable stock

2 tbsp soy sauce

2 tbsp dry sherry

1 tsp sugar

1½ cups romaine lettuce, shredded

salt and pepper

1 Using a sharp knife, cut the tofu into small cubes.

2 Heat the vegetable oil in a preheated wok or large saucepan, add the tofu, and stir-fry until browned. Remove with a perforated spoon and drain on paper towels.

3 Add the carrot, fresh ginger, and green onions to the wok or saucepan and stir-fry for 2 minutes.

4 Add the vegetable stock, soy sauce, sherry, and sugar. Stir well to mix all the ingredients. Bring to a boil and simmer for 1 minute.

5 Add the romaine lettuce to the wok or saucepan and stir until it has just wilted.

6 Return the tofu to the pan to reheat. Season with salt and pepper to taste and serve the soup immediately in warmed bowls.

COOK'S TIP

For a prettier effect, score grooves along the length of the carrot with a sharp knife before slicing. This will create a flower effect when the carrot is cut into circles. You could also try slicing the carrot on the diagonal to make longer slices.

Chili Fish Soup

Chinese mushrooms add an intense flavor to this soup which is unique. If they are unavailable, use open-cap mushrooms, sliced.

NUTRITIONAL INFORMATION

Calories	166	Sugars	.........1g
Protein	........23g	Fat	...........7g
Carbohydrate	....4g	Saturates	.......1g

 15 MINS   15 MINS

SERVES 4

INGREDIENTS

½ oz Chinese dried mushrooms

2 tbsp sunflower oil

1 onion, sliced

1½ cups snow peas

1½ cups bamboo shoots

3 tbsp sweet chili sauce

5 cups fish or vegetable stock

3 tbsp light soy sauce

2 tbsp fresh cilantro, plus extra to garnish

1 lb cod fillet, skinned and cubed

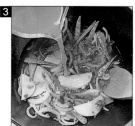

1 Place the mushrooms in a large bowl. Pour over enough boiling water to cover and leave to stand for 5 minutes. Drain the mushrooms thoroughly in a colander. Using a sharp knife, roughly chop the mushrooms.

2 Heat the sunflower oil in a preheated wok or large skillet. Add the sliced onion to the wok and stir-fry for 5 minutes, or until softened.

3 Add the snow peas, bamboo shoots, chili sauce, stock, and soy sauce to the wok and bring to a boil.

4 Add the cilantro and cod and leave to simmer for 5 minutes, or until the fish is cooked through.

5 Transfer the soup to warm bowls, garnish with extra cilantro, if wished, and serve hot.

COOK'S TIP

Cod is used in this recipe as it is a meaty white fish. For real luxury, use monkfish tail instead.

There are many different varieties of dried mushrooms, but shiitake are best. They are not cheap, but a small amount will go a long way.

Shrimp Dumpling Soup

These small dumplings filled with shrimp and pork may be made slightly larger and served as dim sum on their own, if you prefer.

NUTRITIONAL INFORMATION

Calories	311	Sugars	........2g
Protein	........18g	Fat	..........8g
Carbohydrate	...41g	Saturates	.......2g

 20 MINS   10 MINS

SERVES 4

I N G R E D I E N T S

D U M P L I N G S

1⅝ cups all-purpose flour

¼ cup boiling water

⅛ cup cold water

1½ tsp vegetable oil

F I L L I N G

4½ oz ground pork

4½ oz cooked peeled shrimp, chopped

1¾ oz canned water chestnuts, drained, rinsed, and chopped

1 celery stalk, chopped

1 tsp cornstarch

1 tbsp sesame oil

1 tbsp light soy sauce

S O U P

3¾ cups fish stock

1¾ oz cellophane noodles

1 tbsp dry sherry

chopped chives, to garnish

1 To make the dumplings, mix together the flour, boiling water, cold water, and oil in a bowl until a pliable dough is formed.

2 Knead the dough on a lightly floured surface for 5 minutes. Cut the dough into 16 equal sized pieces.

3 Roll the dough pieces into rounds about 3 inches in diameter.

4 Mix the filling ingredients together in a large bowl.

5 Spoon a little of the filling mixture into the center of each round. Bring the edges of the dough together, scrunching them up to form a "moneybag" shape. Twist the gathered edges to seal.

6 Pour the fish stock into a large saucepan and bring to a boil.

7 Add the cellophane noodles, dumplings and dry sherry to the pan and cook for 4–5 minutes, until the noodles and dumplings are tender. Garnish with chopped chives and serve immediately.

Chicken Noodle Soup

Quick to make, this hot and spicy soup is hearty and warming. If you like your food really fiery, add a chopped dried or fresh chili with its seeds.

NUTRITIONAL INFORMATION

Calories	196	Sugars	........4g
Protein	........16g	Fat	..........11g
Carbohydrate	....8g	Saturates	.......2g

🥘 10 MINS   🕐 25 MINS

SERVES 4–6

I N G R E D I E N T S

1 sheet of dried egg noodles
from a 9 oz pack

1 tbsp oil

4 skinless, boneless
chicken thighs, diced

1 bunch green onions, sliced

2 garlic cloves, chopped

¾ inch piece fresh ginger, finely chopped

3¾ cups chicken stock

scant 1 cup coconut milk

3 tsp red curry paste

3 tbsp peanut butter

2 tbsp light soy sauce

1 small red bell pepper, chopped

½ cup frozen peas

salt and pepper

VARIATION

Green curry paste can be
used instead of red curry paste
for a less fiery flavor.

1 Put the noodles in a shallow dish and soak in boiling water as the packet directs.

2 Heat the oil in a large preheated saucepan or wok.

3 Add the diced chicken to the pan or wok and fry for 5 minutes, stirring until lightly browned.

4 Add the white part of the green onions, the garlic, and ginger and fry for 2 minutes, stirring.

5 Stir in the chicken stock, coconut milk, red curry paste, peanut butter, and soy sauce.

6 Season with salt and pepper to taste. Bring to a boil, stirring, then simmer for 8 minutes, stirring occasionally.

7 Add the red bell pepper, peas, and green onion tops and cook for 2 minutes.

8 Add the drained noodles and heat through. Spoon the chicken noodle soup into warmed bowls and serve with a spoon and fork.

Spinach & Tofu Soup

This is a very colorful and delicious soup. If spinach is not in season, watercress or lettuce can be used instead.

NUTRITIONAL INFORMATION

Calories 33   Sugar 1g
Protein ....4g   Fat 2g
Carbohydrate ....1g   Saturates 0.2g

 3¹/₂ HOURS   10 MINS

SERVES 4

INGREDIENTS

1 cake tofu

4½ oz spinach leaves without stems

3 cups Chinese Stock (see page 30)
   or water

1 tbsp light soy sauce

salt and pepper

1 Using a sharp knife, cut the tofu into small pieces about ¼ inch thick.

2 Wash the spinach leaves thoroughly under cold, running water and drain thoroughly.

3 Cut the spinach leaves into small pieces or shreds, discarding any discolored leaves and tough stalks. (If possible, use fresh young spinach leaves, which have not yet developed tough ribs. Otherwise, it is important to cut out all the ribs and stems for this soup.) Set the spinach aside until required.

4 In a preheated wok or large skillet, bring the Chinese stock or water to a rolling boil.

5 Add the tofu cubes and light soy sauce, bring back to a boil, and simmer for about 2 minutes over a medium heat.

6 Add the shredded spinach leaves and simmer for 1 more minute, stirring gently. Skim the surface of the soup to make it clear, adjust the seasoning to taste.

7 Transfer the spinach and tofu soup to a warm soup tureen or individual serving bowls and serve with chopsticks, to pick up the pieces of food and a broad, shallow spoon for drinking the soup.

COOK'S TIP

Soup is an integral part of a Chinese meal; it is usually presented in a large bowl placed in the center of the table, and consumed as the meal progresses. It serves as a refresher between different dishes and as a beverage throughout the meal.

Peking Duck Soup

This is a hearty and robustly flavored soup, containing pieces of duck and vegetables cooked in a rich stock.

NUTRITIONAL INFORMATION

Calories 92   Sugars 3g
Protein . . . . .8g   Fat 5g
Carbohydrate . . . .3g   Saturates 1g

 5 MINS   35 MINS

SERVES 4

INGREDIENTS

4½ oz lean duck breast meat

8 oz Chinese cabbage

3¾ cups chicken or duck stock

1 tbsp dry sherry or rice wine

1 tbsp light soy sauce

2 garlic cloves, crushed

pinch of ground star anise

1 tbsp sesame seeds

1 tsp sesame oil

1 tbsp chopped fresh parsley

1 Remove the skin from the duck breast and finely dice the flesh.

2 Using a sharp knife, shred the Chinese cabbage.

3 Put the stock in a large saucepan and bring to a boil. Add the sherry or rice wine, soy sauce, diced duck meat, and shredded Chinese leaves and stir to mix thoroughly. Reduce the heat and leave to simmer gently for 15 minutes.

4 Stir in the garlic and star anise and cook over a low heat for 10–15 minutes more, or until the duck is tender.

5 Meanwhile, dry-fry the sesame seeds in a preheated, heavy-bottomed skillet or wok, stirring constantly.

6 Remove the sesame seeds from the pan and stir them into the soup, together with the sesame oil and chopped fresh parsley.

7 Spoon the soup into warm bowls and serve immediately.

VARIATION

If Chinese leaves (cabbage) are unavailable, use leafy green cabbage instead. You may wish to adjust the quantity to taste, as Western cabbage has a stronger flavor and odour than Chinese leaves (cabbage).

Shrimp Soup

This soup is an interesting mix of colors and textures. The egg may be made into a flat omelet and added as thin strips if preferred.

NUTRITIONAL INFORMATION

Calories 123   Sugars 0.2g
Protein ....13g   Fat 8g
Carbohydrate ....1g   Saturates 1g

 5 MINS   20 MINS

SERVES 4

I N G R E D I E N T S

2 tbsp sunflower oil

2 green onions, thinly sliced diagonally

1 carrot, coarsely grated

4½ oz large mushrooms, thinly sliced

4 cups fish or vegetable stock

½ tsp Chinese five-spice powder

1 tbsp light soy sauce

4½ oz peeled jumbo shrimp, defrosted if frozen

½ bunch watercress, trimmed and roughly chopped

1 egg, well beaten

salt and pepper

4 jumbo shrimp in shells, to garnish (optional)

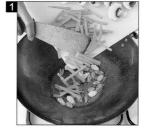 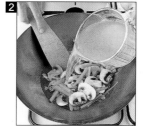 

1 Heat the oil in a wok, swirling it around until really hot. Add the green onions and stir-fry for a minute, then add the carrots and mushrooms and continue to cook for about 2 minutes.

2 Add the stock and bring to a boil, then season to taste with salt and pepper, five-spice powder, and soy sauce and simmer for 5 minutes.

3 If the shrimp are really large, cut them in half before adding to the wok and simmer for 3-4 minutes.

4 Add the watercress to the wok and mix well, then slowly pour in the beaten egg in a circular movement so that it cooks in threads in the soup. Adjust the seasoning and serve each portion topped with a whole shrimp.

COOK'S TIP

The large open mushrooms with black gills give the best flavor but they tend to spoil the color of the soup, making it very dark. Oyster mushrooms can also be used.

Clear Chicken & Egg Soup

This tasty chicken soup has the addition of poached eggs, making it both delicious and filling. Use fresh, home-made stock for a better flavor.

NUTRITIONAL INFORMATION

Calories 138   Sugars 1g
Protein ....16g   Fat 7g
Carbohydrate ....1g   Saturates 2g

 5 MINS   35 MINS

SERVES 4

INGREDIENTS

1 tsp salt

1 tbsp rice wine vinegar

4 eggs

3¾ cups chicken stock

1 leek, sliced

4½ oz broccoli florets

1 cup shredded cooked chicken

2 open-cap mushrooms, sliced

1 tbsp dry sherry

dash of chili sauce

chili powder, to garnish

VARIATION

You could use 4 dried Chinese mushrooms, rehydrated according to the pack instructions, instead of the open-cap mushrooms, if you prefer.

1 Bring a large saucepan of water to a boil and add the salt and rice wine vinegar.

2 Reduce the heat so that it is just simmering and carefully break the eggs into the water, one at a time. Poach the eggs for 1 minute.

3 Remove the poached eggs with a slotted spoon and set aside.

4 Bring the chicken stock to a boil in a separate pan and add the leek, broccoli, chicken, mushrooms, and sherry and season with chili sauce to taste. Cook for 10–15 minutes.

5 Add the poached eggs to the soup and cook for 2 minutes more. Carefully transfer the soup and poached eggs to 4 soup bowls. Dust with a little chili powder and serve immediately.

Curried Chicken & Corn Soup

Tender cooked chicken strips and baby corn-on-the-cob are the main flavors in this delicious clear soup, with just a hint of ginger.

NUTRITIONAL INFORMATION

Calories 206   Sugars 5g
Protein ....29g   Fat 5g
Carbohydrate ...13g   Saturates 1g

5 MINS   30 MINS

SERVES 4

INGREDIENTS

6 oz can corn kernels, drained

3¾ cups chicken stock

12 oz cooked, lean chicken, cut into strips

16 baby corn-on-the-cobs

1 tsp Chinese curry powder

½ inch piece fresh ginger, grated

3 tbsp light soy sauce

2 tbsp chopped chives

1 Place the canned corn in a food processor, together with ⅔ cup of the chicken stock and process until the mixture forms a smooth purée.

2 Sieve the corn purée through a fine strainer, pressing with the back of a spoon to remove any husks.

3 Pour the remaining chicken stock into a large saucepan and add the strips of cooked chicken. Stir in the corn purée.

4 Add the baby corn-on-the-cobs and bring the soup to a boil. Boil the soup for 10 minutes.

5 Add the Chinese curry powder, grated fresh ginger, and light soy sauce and cook for 10–15 minutes more.

6 Stir the chopped chives into the soup.

7 Transfer the curried chicken and corn soup to warm soup bowls and serve immediately.

COOK'S TIP

Prepare the soup up to 24 hours in advance without adding the chicken, cool, cover, and store in the refrigerator. Add the chicken and heat the soup through thoroughly before serving.

Fish & Vegetable Soup

A chunky fish soup with strips of vegetables, all flavored with ginger and lemon, makes a meal in itself.

NUTRITIONAL INFORMATION

Calories 88	Sugars 1g
Protein 12g	Fat 3g
Carbohydrate 3g	Saturates 0.5g

40 MINS   20 MINS

SERVES 4

INGREDIENTS

9 oz white fish fillets (cod, halibut, haddock, sole, etc.)

½ tsp ground ginger

½ tsp salt

1 small leek, trimmed

2-4 imitation crab/pollock sticks, defrosted if frozen (optional)

1 tbsp sunflower oil

1 large carrot, cut into julienne strips

8 canned water chestnuts, thinly sliced

5 cups fish or vegetable stock

1 tbsp lemon juice

1 tbsp light soy sauce

1 large zucchini, cut into julienne strips

black pepper

1 Remove any skin from the fish and cut into cubes, about 1 inch. Combine the ground ginger and salt and use to rub into the pieces of fish. Leave to marinate for at least 30 minutes.

2 Meanwhile, divide the green and white parts of the leek. Cut each part into 1 inch lengths and then into julienne strips down the length of each piece, keeping the two parts separate. Slice the crab sticks into ½ inch pieces.

3 Heat the oil in the wok, swirling it around so it is really hot. Add the white part of the leek and stir-fry for a couple of minutes, then add the carrots and water chestnuts and continue to cook for 1-2 minutes, stirring thoroughly.

4 Add the stock and bring to a boil, then add the lemon juice and soy sauce and simmer for 2 minutes.

5 Add the fish and continue to cook for about 5 minutes until the fish begins to break up a little, then add the green part of the leek and the zucchini and simmer for about 1 minute. Add the sliced crab sticks, if using, and season to taste with black pepper. Simmer for another minute or so and serve piping hot.

COOK'S TIP

To skin fish, place the fillet skin-side down and insert a sharp, flexible knife at one end between the flesh and the skin. Hold the skin tightly at the end and push the knife along, keeping the blade flat against the skin.

Three-Flavor Soup

Ideally, use raw shrimp in this soup. If that is not possible, add ready-cooked ones at the very last stage.

NUTRITIONAL INFORMATION

Calories 117	Sugars 0g
Protein 20g	Fat 3g
Carbohydrate 2g	Saturates 1g

  3½ HOURS   10 MINS

SERVES 4

I N G R E D I E N T S

4½ oz skinned, boned chicken breast

4½ oz raw peeled shrimp

salt

½ egg white, lightly beaten

2 tsp cornstarch paste
(see page 31)

4½ oz honey-roast ham

3 cups Chinese Stock
(see page 30) or water

finely chopped green onions, to garnish

1 Using a sharp knife or meat cleaver, thinly slice the chicken into small shreds. If the shrimp are large, cut each in half lengthwise, otherwise leave them whole.

2 Place the chicken and shrimps in a bowl and mix with a pinch of salt, the egg white and cornstarch paste until well coated. Set aside until required.

3 Cut the honey-roast ham into small thin slices roughly the same size as the chicken pieces.

4 In a preheated wok or large, heavy skillet, bring the Chinese stock or water to a rolling boil and add the chicken, the raw shrimp, and the ham.

5 Bring the soup back to a boil, and simmer for 1 minute.

6 Adjust the seasoning to taste, then pour the soup into four warmed individual serving bowls, garnish with the green onions and serve immediately.

COOK'S TIP

Soups such as this are improved enormously in flavor if you use a well-flavored stock. Either use a stock cube, or find time to make Chinese Stock—see the recipe on page 30. Better still, make double quantities and freeze some for future use.

Beef & Vegetable Noodle Soup

Thin strips of beef are marinated in soy sauce and garlic to form the basis of this delicious soup. Served with noodles, it is both filling and delicious.

NUTRITIONAL INFORMATION

Calories	186	Sugars	.........1g
Protein	........17g	Fat	...........5g
Carbohydrate	...20g	Saturates	.......1g

35 MINS   20 MINS

SERVES 4

INGREDIENTS

8 oz lean beef

1 garlic clove, crushed

2 green onions, chopped

3 tbsp soy sauce

1 tsp sesame oil

8 oz egg noodles

3¾ cups beef stock

3 baby corn-on-the-cobs, sliced

½ leek, shredded

4½ oz broccoli, cut into flowerets

pinch of chili powder

1 Using a sharp knife, cut the beef into thin strips and place in a bowl with the garlic, green onions, soy sauce, and sesame oil.

2 Mix together the ingredients in the bowl, turning the beef to coat. Cover and leave to marinate in the refrigerator for 30 minutes.

3 Cook the noodles in a saucepan of boiling water for 3–4 minutes. Drain the noodles thoroughly and set aside.

4 Put the beef stock in a large saucepan and bring to a boil. Add the beef, together with the marinade, the baby corn, leek, and broccoli. Cover and leave to simmer over a low heat for 7–10 minutes, or until the beef and vegetables are tender and cooked through.

5 Stir in the noodles and chili powder and cook for 2–3 minutes more.

6 Transfer the soup to bowls and serve immediately.

VARIATION

Vary the vegetables used, or use those available.

If preferred, use a few drops of chili sauce instead of chili powder, but remember it is very hot!

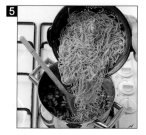

Chicken Soup with Almonds

This soup can also be made using pheasant breasts. For a really gamy flavor, make game stock from the carcass and use in the soup.

NUTRITIONAL INFORMATION

Calories 219	Sugars 2g	
Protein 18g	Fat 15g	
Carbohydrate 2g	Saturates 2g	

10 MINS   20 MINS

SERVES 4

INGREDIENTS

1 large or 2 small boneless skinned
  chicken breasts

1 tbsp sunflower oil

4 green onions, thinly sliced diagonally

1 carrot, cut into julienne strips

3 cups chicken stock

finely grated zest of ½ lemon

⅓ cup ground almonds

1 tbsp light soy sauce

1 tbsp lemon juice

¼ cup slivered almonds, toasted

salt and pepper

1 Cut each breast into 4 strips lengthwise, then slice very thinly across the grain to give shreds of chicken.

2 Heat the oil in a wok, swirling it around until really hot.

3 Add the green onions and cook for 2 minutes, then add the chicken and toss it for 3-4 minutes until sealed and almost cooked through, stirring all the time. Add the carrot strips and stir.

4 Add the stock to the wok and bring to a boil. Add the lemon zest, ground almonds, soy sauce, lemon juice, and plenty of seasoning. Bring back to a boil and simmer, uncovered, for 5 minutes, stirring from time to time.

5 Adjust the seasoning, add most of the toasted slivered almonds, and continue to cook for 1-2 minutes more.

6 Serve the soup very hot, in individual bowls, sprinkled with the remaining slivered almonds.

COOK'S TIP

To make game stock, break up a pheasant carcass and place in a pan with 8 cups water. Bring to a boil slowly, skimming off any scum. Add 1 bouquet garni, 1 peeled onion, and seasoning. Cover and simmer gently for 1½ hours. Strain, and skim off any surface fat.

Oriental Fish Soup

This is a deliciously different fish soup which can be made quickly and easily in a microwave.

NUTRITIONAL INFORMATION

Calories 105	Sugars 1g
Protein 13g	Fat 5g
Carbohydrate 1g	Saturates 1g

20 MINS   10 MINS

SERVES 4

INGREDIENTS

1 egg

1 tsp sesame seeds, toasted

1 celery stalk, chopped

1 carrot, cut into julienne strips

4 green onions, sliced on the diagonal

1 tbsp oil

1½ cups fresh spinach

3½ cups hot vegetable stock

4 tsp light soy sauce

9 oz haddock, skinned and cut into small chunks

salt and pepper

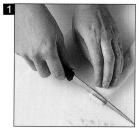

VARIATION

Instead of topping the soup with omelet shreds, you could pour the beaten egg, without the sesame seeds, into the hot stock at the end of the cooking time. The egg will set in pretty strands to give a flowery look.

1 Beat the egg with the sesame seeds and seasoning. Lightly oil a plate and pour on the egg mixture. Cook on HIGH power for 1½ minutes until just setting in the center. Leave to stand for a few minutes then remove from the plate. Roll up the egg and shred thinly.

2 Mix together the celery, carrot, green onions, and oil. Cover and cook on HIGH power for 3 minutes.

3 Wash the spinach thoroughly under cold, running water. Cut off and discard any long stalks and drain well. Shred the spinach finely.

4 Add the hot stock, soy sauce, spinach, and haddock to the vegetable mixture. Cover and cook on HIGH power for 5 minutes. Stir the soup and season to taste. Serve in warmed bowls with the shredded egg scattered over.

Mushroom Noodle Soup

A light, refreshing clear soup of mushrooms, cucumber and small pieces of rice noodles, flavored with soy sauce and a touch of garlic.

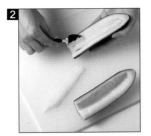

NUTRITIONAL INFORMATION

Calories	84	Sugars	. . . . .1g
Protein	. . . . .1g	Fat	. . . . .8g
Carbohydrate	. . . .3g	Saturates	. . . . . . .1g

 5 MINS   10 MINS

SERVES 4

I N G R E D I E N T S

4½ oz flat or open-cap
 mushrooms

½ cucumber

2 green onions

1 garlic clove

2 tbsp vegetable oil

¼ cup Chinese rice
 noodles

¾ tsp salt

1 tbsp soy sauce

1 Wash the mushrooms and pat dry on paper towel. Slice thinly. Do not remove the peel because this will add more flavor.

2 Halve the cucumber lengthwise. Scoop out the seeds, using a teaspoon, and slice the cucumber thinly.

3 Chop the green onions finely and cut the garlic clove into thin strips.

4 Heat the vegetable oil in a large saucepan or wok.

5 Add the green onions and garlic to the pan or wok and stir-fry for 30 seconds. Add the mushrooms and stir-fry for 2–3 minutes.

6 Stir in 2½ cups water. Break the noodles into short lengths and add to the soup. Bring to a boil, stirring occasionally.

7 Add the cucumber slices, salt, and soy sauce, and simmer for 2–3 minutes.

8 Serve the mushroom noodle soup in warmed bowls, distributing the noodles and vegetables evenly.

COOK'S TIP

Scooping the seeds out from the cucumber gives it a prettier effect when sliced, and also helps to reduce any bitterness, but if you prefer, you can leave them in.

Fish Soup with Wontons

This soup is topped with small wontons filled with shrimp, making it both very tasty and satisfying.

NUTRITIONAL INFORMATION

Calories	115	Sugars	0g
Protein	16g	Fat	5g
Carbohydrate	1g	Saturates	1g

10 MINS   15 MINS

SERVES 4

INGREDIENTS

4½ oz cooked, peeled jumbo shrimp

1 tsp chopped chives

1 small garlic clove, finely chopped

1 tbsp vegetable oil

12 wonton skins

1 small egg, beaten

3¾ cups fish stock

16 oz white fish fillet, diced

dash of chili sauce

sliced fresh red chili and chives, to garnish

1 Roughly chop a quarter of the shrimp and mix together with the chopped chives and garlic.

2 Heat the oil in a preheated wok or large skillet until it is really hot.

3 Stir-fry the shrimp mixture for 1–2 minutes. Remove from the heat and set aside to cool completely.

4 Spread out the wonton skins on a work counter. Spoon a little of the shrimp filling into the center of each skin. Brush the edges of the skins with beaten egg and press the edges together, scrunching them to form a "moneybag" shape. Set aside while you are preparing the soup.

5 Pour the fish stock into a large saucepan and bring to a boil. Add the diced white fish and the remaining shrimp and cook for 5 minutes.

6 Season to taste with the chili sauce. Add the wontons and cook for 5 minutes more.

7 Spoon into warmed serving bowls, garnish with sliced red chili and chives, and serve immediately.

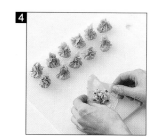

VARIATION

Replace the prawns (shrimp) with cooked crabmeat for an alternative flavor.

Chicken, Noodle & Corn Soup

The vermicelli gives this Chinese-style soup an Italian twist, but you can use egg noodles if you prefer.

NUTRITIONAL INFORMATION

Calories	.401	Sugars	.6g
Protein	.31g	Fat	.24g
Carbohydrate	.17g	Saturates	.13g

 5 MINS   25 MINS

SERVES 4

I'N G R E D I E N T S

1 lb boned chicken breasts,
   cut into strips

5 cups chicken stock

⅝ cup heavy cream

¾ cup dried vermicelli

1 tbsp cornstarch

3 tbsp milk

6 oz can corn kernels

salt and pepper

finely chopped green onions,
   to garnish (optional)

1 Put the chicken strips, chicken stock, and heavy cream into a large saucepan and bring to a boil over a low heat.

2 Reduce the heat slightly and simmer for about 20 minutes. Season the soup with salt and black pepper to taste.

3 Meanwhile, cook the vermicelli in lightly salted boiling water for 10-12 minutes, until just tender. Drain the pasta and keep warm.

4 In a small bowl, mix together the cornstarch and milk to make a

smooth paste. Stir the cornstarch paste into the soup until thickened.

5 Add the corn and vermicelli to the pan and heat through.

6 Transfer the soup to a warm tureen or individual soup bowls, garnish with green onions, if desired, and serve immediately.

VARIATION

For crab and corn soup, substitute 1 lb cooked crab meat for the chicken breasts. Flake the crab meat well before adding it to the saucepan and reduce the cooking time by 10 minutes.

Chicken & Coconut Soup

This fragrant soup combines citrus flavors with coconut and a hint of piquancy from chilies.

NUTRITIONAL INFORMATION

Calories	345	Sugars	.........2g
Protein	........28g	Fat	..........24g
Carbohydrate	....5g	Saturates	......18g

 2¼ HOURS   15 MINS

SERVES 4

INGREDIENTS

1¾ cups cooked, skinned chicken breast

1⅓ cups unsweetened shredded coconut

2 cups boiling water

2 cups Fresh Chicken Stock (see page 30)

4 green onions, white and green parts, sliced thinly

2 stalks lemon grass

1 lime

1 tsp grated fresh ginger

1 tbsp light soy sauce

2 tsp ground cilantro

2 large fresh red chilies

1 tbsp chopped fresh cilantro

1 tbsp cornstarch, mixed with 2 tbsp cold water

salt and white pepper

chopped red chili, to garnish

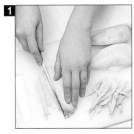

1 Using a sharp knife, slice the chicken into thin strips.

2 Place the coconut in a heatproof bowl and pour over the boiling water. Work the coconut mixture through a strainer. Pour the coconut water into a large saucepan and add the stock.

3 Add the green onions to the saucepan. Slice the base of each lemon grass and discard damaged leaves. Bruise the stalks and add to the saucepan.

4 Peel the rind from the lime in large strips. Extract the juice and add to the pan with the lime strips, ginger, soy sauce, and cilantro. Bruise the chilies with a fork, then add to the pan. Heat the pan to just below boiling point.

5 Add the chicken and fresh cilantro to the saucepan, bring to a boil, then simmer for 10 minutes.

6 Discard the lemon grass, lime rind and red chilies. Pour the blended cornstarch mixture into the saucepan and stir until slightly thickened. Season with salt and white pepper to taste and serve immediately, garnished with chopped red chili.

Pork & Szechuan Vegetable

Sold in cans, Szechuan preserved vegetable is pickled mustard root which is quite hot and salty, so rinse in water before use.

NUTRITIONAL INFORMATION

Calories	135	Sugars	.........1g
Protein	........14g	Fat	..........7g
Carbohydrate	....3g	Saturates	.......2g

 5 MINS   5 MINS

SERVES 4

I N G R E D I E N T S

9 oz pork tenderloin

2 tsp cornstarch paste
(see page 31)

4½ oz Szechuan preserved vegetable

3 cups Chinese stock (see page 30) or
water

salt and pepper

a few drops sesame oil (optional)

2-3 green onions, sliced,
to garnish

1 Preheat a wok or large, heavy-bottomed skillet.

2 Using a sharp knife, cut the pork across the grain into thin shreds.

3 Mix the pork with the cornstarch paste until the pork is completely coated in the mixture.

4 Thoroughly wash and rinse the Szechuan preserved vegetable, then pat dry on absorbent paper towels. Cut the Szechuan preserved vegetable into thin shreds the same size as the pork.

5 Pour the Chinese stock or water into the wok or skillet and bring to a rolling boil. Add the pork to the wok and stir to separate the shreds. Return to a boil.

6 Add the shredded Szechuan preserved vegetable and bring back to a boil once more.

7 Adjust the seasoning to taste and sprinkle with sesame oil. Serve hot, garnished with green onions.

COOK'S TIP

Szechuan preserved vegetable is actually mustard green root, pickled in salt and chilies. Available in cans from specialist Chinese supermarkets, it gives a crunchy, spicy taste to dishes. Rinse in cold water before use and store in the refrigerator.

Crab & Ginger Soup

Two classic ingredients in Chinese cooking are blended together in this recipe for a special soup.

NUTRITIONAL INFORMATION

Calories	32	Sugars	.........1g
Protein	.........6g	Fat	..........0.4g
Carbohydrate	....1g	Saturates	.......0g

10 MINS   25 MINS

SERVES 4

INGREDIENTS

1 carrot

1 leek

1 bay leaf

3¾ cups fish stock

2 medium-sized cooked crabs

1 inch piece fresh ginger, grated

1 tsp light soy sauce

½ tsp ground star anise

salt and pepper

1 Using a sharp knife, chop the carrot and leek into small pieces and place in a large saucepan with the bay leaf and fish stock.

2 Bring the mixture in the saucepan to a boil.

3 Reduce the heat, cover, and leave to simmer for about 10 minutes, or until the vegetables are nearly tender.

4 Remove all of the meat from the cooked crabs. Break off and reserve the claws, break the joints and remove the meat, using a fork or skewer.

5 Add the crabmeat to the pan of fish stock, together with the ginger, soy sauce, and star anise and bring to a boil. Leave to simmer for about 10 minutes, or until the vegetables are tender and the crab is heated through.

6 Season the soup then ladle into a warmed soup tureen or individual serving bowls and garnish with crab claws. Serve immediately.

VARIATION

If fresh crabmeat is unavailable, use drained canned crabmeat or thawed frozen crabmeat instead.

Crab & Corn Soup

Crab and corn are classic ingredients in Chinese cookery. Here egg noodles are added for a filling dish.

NUTRITIONAL INFORMATION

Calories	324	Sugars	.........6g
Protein	........27g	Fat	..........8g
Carbohydrate	...39g	Saturates	.......2g

 5 MINS   20 MINS

SERVES 4

INGREDIENTS

1 tbsp sunflower oil

1 tsp Chinese five-spice powder

8 oz carrots, cut into thin sticks

½ cup canned or frozen corn

¼ cup peas

6 green onions, trimmed and sliced

1 red chili, seeded and very thinly sliced

2 x 7 oz can white crab meat

6 oz egg noodles

7½ cups fish stock

3 tbsp soy sauce

1 Heat the sunflower oil in a large preheated wok or heavy-bottomed skillet.

2 Add the Chinese five-spice powder, carrots, corn, peas, green onions, and red chili to the wok and cook for about 5 minutes, stirring constantly.

3 Add the crab meat to the wok and stir-fry the mixture for 1 minute, distributing the crab meat evenly.

4 Roughly break up the egg noodles and add to the wok.

5 Pour the fish stock and soy sauce into the mixture in the wok and bring to a boil.

6 Cover the wok or skillet and leave the soup to simmer for 5 minutes.

7 Stir once more, then transfer the soup to a warm soup tureen or individual serving bowls and serve immediately.

COOK'S TIP

Chinese five-spice powder is a mixture of star anise, fennel, cloves, cinnamon, and Szechuan pepper. It has an unmistakeable flavor. Use it sparingly, as it is very pungent.

Hot & Sour Mushroom Soup

Hot and sour soups are found across South East Asia in different forms. Reduce the number of chilies added if you prefer a milder dish.

NUTRITIONAL INFORMATION

Calories	.87	Sugars	.7g
Protein	.4g	Fat	.5g
Carbohydrate	.8g	Saturates	.1g

10 MINS   20 MINS

SERVES 4

INGREDIENTS

2 tbsp tamarind paste

4 red chilies, very finely chopped

2 cloves garlic, crushed

1 inch piece of Thai ginger, peeled and very finely chopped

4 tbsp fish sauce

2 tbsp sugar

8 lime leaves, roughly torn

5 cups vegetable stock

3½ oz carrots, very thinly sliced

8 oz small mushrooms, halved

12 oz shredded white cabbage

3½ oz green beans, halved

3 tbsp fresh cilantro, roughly chopped

3½ oz cherry tomatoes, halved

COOK'S TIP

Tamarind is the dried fruit of the tamarind tree. Sold as a pulp or paste, it is used to give a special sweet and sour flavor to Oriental dishes.

1 Place the tamarind paste, red chilies, garlic, Thai ginger, fish sauce, sugar, lime leaves, and vegetable stock in a large, preheated wok or heavy-bottomed skillet. Bring the mixture to a boil, stirring occasionally.

2 Reduce the heat and add the carrots, mushrooms, white cabbage, and green beans. Leave the soup to simmer, uncovered, for about 10 minutes, or until the vegetables are just tender.

3 Stir the fresh cilantro and cherry tomatoes into the mixture in the wok and heat through for another 5 minutes.

4 Transfer the soup to a warm tureen or individual serving bowls and serve immediately.

Chinese Cabbage Soup

This is a piquant soup, which is slightly sweet-and-sour in flavor.
It can be served as a hearty meal or appetizer.

NUTRITIONAL INFORMATION

Calories	65	Sugars 7g
Protein	.........3g	Fat 0.5g
Carbohydrate	....11g	Saturates 0.1g

 5 MINS   30 MINS

SERVES 4

INGREDIENTS

1 lb bok choy

2½ cups vegetable stock

1 tbsp rice wine vinegar

1 tbsp light soy sauce

1 tbsp sugar

1 tbsp dry sherry

1 fresh red chili, thinly sliced

1 tbsp cornstarch

2 tbsp water

1 Wash the bok choy thoroughly under cold running water, rinse, and drain. Pat dry on paper towels.

2 Trim the stems of the bok choy and shred the leaves.

3 Heat the vegetable stock in a large saucepan. Add the bok choy and cook for 10–15 minutes.

4 Mix together the rice wine vinegar, soy sauce, sugar, and sherry in a small bowl. Add this mixture to the stock, together with the sliced chili.

5 Bring to a boil, lower the heat, and cook for 2–3 minutes.

6 Blend the cornstarch with the water to form a smooth paste.

7 Gradually stir the cornstarch mixture into the soup. Cook, stirring constantly, until it thickens. Cook for 4–5 minutes more.

8 Ladle the Chinese cabbage soup into individual warm serving bowls and serve immediately.

COOKS TIP

Bok choy, also known as pak choy or spoon cabbage, has long, white leaf stalks and fleshy, spoon-shaped, shiny green leaves. There are a number of varieties available, which differ mainly in size rather than flavor.

Mixed Vegetable Soup

Select 3 or 4 vegetables for this soup: the Chinese like to blend different colors, flavors, and textures to create harmony as well as contrast.

NUTRITIONAL INFORMATION

Calories	38	Sugars	........3g
Protein	.........3g	Fat	..........2g
Carbohydrate	....4g	Saturates	.....0.2g

 3½ HOURS   5 MINS

SERVES 4

I N G R E D I E N T S

about 1-2 oz each of mushrooms, carrots, asparagus, snow peas, bamboo shoots, baby corn-on-the-cob, cucumber, tomatoes, spinach, lettuce, Chinese cabbage, tofu, etc.

2 ½ cups Chinese Stock (see page 30)

1 tbsp light soy sauce

a few drops sesame oil (optional)

salt and pepper

finely chopped green onions, to garnish

1 Preheat a wok or large heavy-bottomed skillet.

2 Using a sharp knife or cleaver, cut your selection of vegetables into roughly uniform shapes and sizes (slices, shreds, or cubes).

3 Pour the Chinese stock into the wok or skillet and bring to a rolling boil.

4 Add the vegetables, bearing in mind that some require a longer cooking time than others: add carrots and baby corn-on-the-cob first, cook for 2 minutes, then add asparagus, mushrooms, Chinese cabbage, tofu, and cook for another minute.

5 Spinach, lettuce, watercress, cucumber and tomato are added last. Stir, and bring the soup back to a boil.

6 Add the soy sauce and the sesame oil, if wished, and adjust the seasoning to taste.

7 Transfer the mixed vegetable soup to warm serving bowls and serve hot, garnished with green onions.

COOK'S TIP

Sesame oil is a low-saturate oil widely used for its nutty, aromatic flavor. Made from toasted sesame seeds it is used as a seasoning, not as a cooking oil. Thick and dark, it burns easily, so it should be added at the last moment.

Chili & Watercress Soup

This delicious soup is a wonderful blend of colors and flavors. It is very hot, so if you prefer a milder taste, omit the seeds from the chilies.

NUTRITIONAL INFORMATION

Calories 90   Sugars 1g
Protein . . . . .7g   Fat 6g
Carbohydrate . . . .2g   Saturates 1g

  10 MINS   🕐 15 MINS

SERVES 4

I N G R E D I E N T S

1 tbsp sunflower oil

9 oz smoked tofu, sliced

1 cup shiitake mushrooms, sliced

2 tbsp chopped fresh cilantro

2 cups watercress

1 red chili, sliced finely, to garnish

S T O C K

1 tbsp tamarind pulp

2 dried red chilies, chopped

2 kaffir lime leaves, torn in half

1 inch piece fresh ginger, chopped

2 inch piece Thai ginger, chopped

1 stalk lemon grass, chopped

1 onion, quartered

4 cups cold water

1 Put all the ingredients for the stock into a saucepan and bring to a boil.

2 Simmer the stock for 5 minutes. Remove from the heat and strain, reserving the stock.

3 Heat the sunflower oil in a wok or large, heavy skillet and cook the tofu over a high heat for about 2 minutes, stirring constantly so that the tofu cooks evenly on both sides. Add the strained stock.

4 Add the mushrooms and cilantro and boil for 3 minutes.

5 Add the watercress and boil for 1 minute.

6 Serve immediately, garnished with red chili slices.

VARIATION

You might like to try a mixture of different types of mushroom. Oyster and straw mushrooms are all suitable.

Appetizers

Appetizers are often served as first courses in a Chinese meal. This chapter contains a range of old favorites and traditional Chinese dishes, and there is sure to be something to suit every occasion. One of the advantages of these dishes is that they can be prepared in advance. The Chinese usually serve a selection of appetizers

together as an assorted hors d'oeuvres. Remember not to have more than one type of the same food. The ingredients should be chosen for their harmony and balance in color, aroma, texture and flavor. A suitable selection might contain Crispy Seaweed, Sesame Shrimp Toasts, Spare Ribs and Spring Rolls. Many of these dishes would also make an attractive addition to a buffet, for example Filled Cucumber Cups and Eggplant Dipping Platter.

Spicy Salt & Pepper Shrimp

For best results, use raw jumbo shrimp in their shells. They are 3-4 inches long, and you should get about 10 in 10oz.

NUTRITIONAL INFORMATION

Calories	160	Sugars	.......0.2g
Protein	.........17g	Fat	..........10g
Carbohydrate	...0.5g	Saturates	.......1g

 35 MINS   20 MINS

SERVES 4

INGREDIENTS

9-10½ oz raw shrimp in their shells, defrosted if frozen

1 tbsp light soy sauce

1 tsp Chinese rice wine or dry sherry

2 tsp cornstarch

vegetable oil, for deep-frying

2-3 green onions, to garnish

SPICY SALT AND PEPPER

1 tbsp salt

1 tsp ground Szechuan peppercorns

1 tsp five-spice powder

1 Pull the soft legs off the shrimp, but keep the body shell on. Dry well on absorbent paper towels.

2 Place the shrimp in a bowl with the soy sauce, rice wine or sherry, and cornstarch. Turn the shrimp to coat thoroughly in the mixture and leave to marinate for about 25-30 minutes.

3 To make the Spicy Salt and Pepper, mix the salt, ground Szechuan peppercorns, and five-spice powder together. Place in a dry skillet and stir-fry for about 3-4 minutes over a low heat, stirring constantly to prevent the spices burning on the bottom of the pan. Remove from the heat and allow to cool.

4 Heat the vegetable oil in a preheated wok or large skillet until smoking, then deep-fry the shrimp in batches until golden brown. Remove the shrimp from the wok with a slotted spoon and drain on paper towels.

5 Place the green onions in a bowl, pour on 1 tablespoon of the hot oil and leave for 30 seconds. Serve the shrimp garnished with the green onions, and with the Spicy Salt and Pepper as a dip.

COOK'S TIP

The roasted spice mixture made with Szechuan peppercorns is used throughout China as a dip for deep-fried food. The peppercorns are sometimes roasted first and then ground. Dry-frying is a way of releasing the flavors of the spices.

Pork with Chili & Garlic

Any leftovers from this dish can be used for a number of other dishes, for example Twice-cooked Pork (see page 225).

see page 225

NUTRITIONAL INFORMATION

Calories	137	Sugars	.......0.1g
Protein	........16g	Fat	...........8g
Carbohydrate	....1g	Saturates	.......2g

5 HOURS   35 MINS

SERVES 4

INGREDIENTS

1 lb 2 oz leg of pork, boned but not skinned

SAUCE

1 tsp finely chopped garlic

1 tsp finely chopped green onions

2 tbsp light soy sauce

1 tsp red chili oil

½ tsp sesame oil

sprig of fresh cilantro,
   to garnish (optional)

1 Place the pork, tied together in one piece, in a large saucepan, add enough cold water to cover, and bring to a rolling boil over a medium heat.

2 Using a slotted spoon, skim off the froth that rises to the surface, cover the pan with a lid, and simmer gently for 25–30 minutes.

3 Leave the meat in the liquid to cool, under cover, for at least 1–2 hours.

4 Lift out the meat with 2 slotted spoons and leave to cool completely, skin-side up, for 2–3 hours.

5 To serve, cut off the skin, leaving a very thin layer of fat on top like a

ham joint. Cut the meat in small thin slices across the grain, and arrange on a plate in an overlapping pattern.

6 In a small bowl, mix together the sauce ingredients, and pour the sauce evenly over the pork.

7 Garnish the pork with a sprig of fresh cilantro, if wished, and serve immediately.

COOK'S TIP

This is a very simple dish, but beautifully presented. Make sure you slice the meat as thinly and evenly as possible to make an elegantly arranged dish.

Butterfly Shrimp

Use unpeeled, raw extra-large or jumbo shrimp, which are about 3-4 inches long.

NUTRITIONAL INFORMATION

Calories 157   Sugars 0.3g
Protein ....8g   Fat 9g
Carbohydrate ....11g Saturates 2g

🔔 25 MINS   🕐 10 MINS

SERVES 4

INGREDIENTS

12 raw jumbo shrimp in their shells

2 tbsp light soy sauce

1 tbsp Chinese rice wine or dry sherry

1 tbsp cornstarch

vegetable oil, for deep-frying

2 eggs, lightly beaten

8-10 tbsp breadcrumbs

salt and pepper

shredded lettuce leaves, to serve

chopped green onions,
  either raw or soaked for about
  30 seconds in hot oil, to garnish

1 Shell and devein the shrimp leaving the tails on. Split them in half from the underbelly about halfway along, leaving the tails still firmly attached. Mix together the salt, pepper, soy sauce, wine, and cornstarch, add the shrimp and turn to coat. Leave to marinate for 10-15 minutes.

2 Heat the oil in a preheated wok. Pick up each shrimp by the tail, dip it in the beaten egg then roll it in the breadcrumbs to coat well.

3 Deep-fry the shrimp in batches until golden brown. Remove them with a slotted spoon and drain on paper towels.

4 To serve, arrange the shrimp neatly on a bed of lettuce leaves and garnish with green onions.

COOK'S TIP

To devein shrimp, first remove the shell. Make a shallow cut about three-quarters of the way along the back of each shrimp, then pull out and discard the black intestinal vein.

Barbecue Spare Ribs

This is a simplified version of the half saddle of pork ribs seen hanging in the windows of Cantonese restaurants.

NUTRITIONAL INFORMATION

Calories 271   Sugars 4g
Protein . . . . .13g   Fat 22g
Carbohydrate . . . .5g   Saturates 8g

6½ HOURS   50 MINS

SERVES 4

INGREDIENTS

1 lb 2 oz pork "finger" spare ribs

1 tbsp sugar

1 tbsp light soy sauce

1 tbsp dark soy sauce

3 tbsp hoisin sauce

1 tbsp rice wine or dry sherry

4-5 tbsp water or Chinese Stock
  (see page 30)

mild chili sauce, to dip

cilantro leaves, to garnish

1 Using a sharp knife, trim off any excess fat from the spare ribs and cut into pieces. Place the ribs in a baking dish.

2 Mix together the sugar, light and dark soy sauce, hoisin sauce, and wine. Pour over the ribs in the baking dish. Turn to coat the ribs thoroughly in the mixture and leave to marinate for about 2-3 hours.

3 Add the water or Chinese stock to the ribs and spread them out in the dish. Roast in a preheated hot oven for 15 minutes.

4 Turn the ribs over, lower the oven temperature, and cook for 30-35 minutes longer.

5 To serve, chop each rib into 3-4 small, bite-sized pieces with a large knife or meat cleaver and arrange neatly on a serving dish.

6 Pour the sauce from the baking dish over the spare ribs and garnish with a few cilantro leaves. Place some mild chili sauce into a small dish and serve with the ribs as a dip. Serve immediately.

COOK'S TIP

Finger ribs are specially small, thin ribs. Ask your local butcher to cut some if you can't find the right size in the supermarket. Don't throw away any trimmings from the ribs – they can be used for soup or stock.

Spring Rolls

This classic Chinese dish is very popular in the West. Serve hot or chilled with a soy sauce or hoisin dip.

NUTRITIONAL INFORMATION

Calories 442   Sugars 4g
Protein . . . . .23g   Fat 21g
Carbohydrate . . .42g   Saturates 3g

45 MINS   45 MINS

SERVES 4

INGREDIENTS

6 oz cooked pork, chopped

2¾ oz cooked chicken, chopped

1 tsp light soy sauce

1 tsp light brown sugar

1 tsp sesame oil

1 tsp vegetable oil

8 oz bean sprouts

1 oz canned bamboo shoots, drained, rinsed, and chopped

1 green bell pepper, seeded and chopped

2 green onions, sliced

1 tsp cornstarch

2 tsp water

vegetable oil, for deep-frying

SKINS

1⅛ cups all-purpose flour

5 tbsp cornstarch

2 cups water

3 tbsp vegetable oil

1 Mix the pork, chicken, soy sauce, sugar, and sesame oil. Cover and marinate for 30 minutes.

2 Heat the vegetable oil in a preheated wok. Add the bean sprouts, bamboo shoots, bell pepper, and green onions to the wok and stir-fry for 2–3 minutes. Add the meat and the marinade to the wok and stir-fry for 2–3 minutes.

3 Blend the cornstarch with the water and stir the mixture into the wok. Set aside to cool completely.

4 To make the skins, mix the flour and cornstarch and gradually stir in the water, to make a smooth batter.

5 Heat a small, oiled skillet. Swirl one-eighth of the batter over the base and cook for 2–3 minutes. Repeat with the remaining batter. Cover the skins with a damp tea towel while frying the remaining skins.

6 Spread out the skins and spoon one-eighth of the filling along the center of each. Brush the edges with water and fold in the sides, then roll up.

7 Heat the oil for deep-frying in a wok to 350°F. Cook the spring rolls, in batches, for 2–3 minutes, or until golden and crisp. Remove from the oil with a slotted spoon, drain, and serve immediately.

Pot Sticker Dumplings

These dumplings obtain their name from the fact that they would stick to the pot when steamed if they were not fried crisply enough initially.

NUTRITIONAL INFORMATION

Calories 345	Sugar 3g
Protein 13g	Fat 17g
Carbohydrate ...36g	Saturates 2g

🍲 🍲 🍲 🍲

🍲 50 MINS 🕐 25 MINS

SERVES 4

I N G R E D I E N T S

DUMPLINGS

1½ cups all-purpose flour

pinch of salt

3 tbsp vegetable oil

6–8 tbsp boiling water

oil, for deep-frying

½ cup water, for steaming

sliced green onions and chives, to garnish

soy sauce or hoisin sauce, to serve

FILLING

5½ oz lean chicken, very finely chopped

1 oz canned bamboo shoots, drained and chopped

2 green onions, finely chopped

½ small red bell pepper, seeded and finely chopped

½ tsp Chinese curry powder

1 tbsp light soy sauce

1 tsp sugar

1 tsp sesame oil

 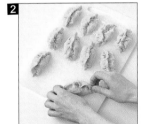 

1 To make the dumplings, mix together the flour and salt in a bowl. Make a well in the center, add the oil and water, and mix well to form a soft dough. Knead the dough on a lightly floured surface, wrap in plastic wrap, and let stand for 30 minutes. Meanwhile, mix all of the filling ingredients together in a large bowl.

2 Divide the dough into 12 equal-sized pieces and roll each piece into a 5 inch round. Spoon a portion of the filling onto one half of each round. Fold the dough over the filling to form a "pasty", pressing the edges together to seal.

3 Pour a little oil into a skillet and cook the dumplings, in batches, until browned and slightly crisp.

4 Return all of the dumplings to the pan and add about ½ cup water. Cover and steam for 5 minutes, or until the dumplings are cooked through. Remove with a slotted spoon and garnish with green onions and chives. Serve with soy sauce or hoisin sauce.

Pancake Rolls

This classic *dim sum* dish is adaptable to almost any filling of your choice. Here the traditional mixture of pork and bok choy is used.

NUTRITIONAL INFORMATION

Calories 488	Sugars 19g	
Protein 16g	Fat 24g	
Carbohydrate ...55g	Saturates 4g	

🐚 🐚 🐚 🐚

🍲 20 MINS   🕐 20 MINS

SERVES 4

INGREDIENTS

4 tsp vegetable oil

1–2 garlic cloves, crushed

8 oz ground pork

8 oz bok choy, shredded

4½ tsp light soy sauce

½ tsp sesame oil

8 spring roll skins, 10 inches square, thawed if frozen

oil, for deep-frying

CHILI SAUCE

¼ cup sugar

¼ cup rice vinegar

2 tbsp water

2 red chilies, finely chopped

1 Heat the oil in a preheated wok. Add the garlic and stir-fry for 30 seconds. Add the pork and stir-fry for 2–3 minutes, until lightly colored.

2 Add the bok choy, soy sauce, and sesame oil to the wok and stir-fry for 2–3 minutes. Remove from the heat and set aside to cool.

3 Spread out the spring roll skins on a work counter and spoon 2 tablespoons of the pork mixture along one edge of each. Roll the skin over once and

fold in the sides. Roll up completely to make a sausage shape, brushing the edges with a little water to seal. Set the pancake rolls aside for 10 minutes to seal firmly.

4 To make the chili sauce, heat the sugar, vinegar, and water in a small saucepan, stirring until the sugar dissolves. Bring the mixture to a boil and boil rapidly until a light syrup forms. Remove from the heat and stir in the

chopped red chilies. Leave the sauce to cool before serving.

5 Heat the oil for deep-frying in a wok until almost smoking. Reduce the heat slightly and fry the pancake rolls, in batches if necessary, for 3–4 minutes, until golden brown. Remove from the oil with a slotted spoon and drain on absorbent paper towels. Serve with the chili sauce.

Filled Cucumber Cups

These attractive little cups would make an impressive appetizer at a dinner party.

NUTRITIONAL INFORMATION

Calories 256   Sugars 7g
Protein . . . . .10g   Fat 21g
Carbohydrate . . . .8g   Saturates 4g

10 MINS   0 MINS

SERVES 4

I N G R E D I E N T S

1 cucumber

4 green onions,
  chopped finely

4 tbsp lime juice

2 small red chilies, seeded and
  chopped finely

3 tsp sugar

1¼ cups ground roasted peanuts

¼ tsp salt

3 shallots, sliced finely and deep-fried,
  to garnish

1 Wash the cucumber thoroughly and pat dry with absorbent paper towels.

2 To make the cucumber cups, cut the ends off the cucumber, and divide it into 3 equal lengths. Mark a line around the center of each one as a guide.

3 Make a zigzag cut all the way around the center of each section, always pointing the knife towards the center of the cucumber.

4 Pull apart the two halves. Scoop out the center of each cup with a melon baller or teaspoon, leaving a base on the bottom of each cup.

5 Put the green onions, lime juice, red chilies, sugar, ground roasted peanuts, and salt in a bowl and mix well to combine.

6 Divide the filling evenly between the 6 cucumber cups and arrange on a serving plate.

7 Garnish the cucumber cups with the deep-fried shallots and serve.

COOK'S TIP

Cherry tomatoes can also be hollowed out very simply with a melon baller and filled with this mixture. The two look very pretty arranged together on a serving dish.

Little Golden Parcels

These little parcels will draw admiring gasps from your guests, but they are fairly simple to prepare.

NUTRITIONAL INFORMATION

Calories 320	Sugars 1g	
Protein 6g	Fat 21g	
Carbohydrate ...28g	Saturates 5g	

🍚 35 MINS   🕐 35 MINS

SERVES 4

INGREDIENTS

1 garlic clove, crushed

1 tsp chopped cilantro root

1 tsp pepper

1 cup mashed potato

1 cup water chestnuts, chopped finely

1 tsp grated fresh ginger

2 tbsp ground roasted peanuts

2 tsp light soy sauce

½ tsp salt

½ tsp sugar

30 wonton skins, defrosted

1 tsp cornstarch, made into a paste with a little water

vegetable oil for deep-frying

fresh chives to garnish

sweet chili sauce, to serve

VARIATION

If wonton skins are not available, use spring roll skins or phyllo pastry, and cut the large squares down to about 4 inches square.

1 Mix together all the ingredients except the wonton skins, cornstarch, and oil.

2 Keeping the rest of the wonton skins covered with a damp cloth, lay 4 skins out on a work counter. Put a teaspoonful of the mixture on each. Make a line of the cornstarch paste around each skin, about ½ inch from the edge.

3 Bring all four corners to the center and press together to form little bags. Repeat with all the wonton skins.

4 Heat 2 inches of the oil in a pan until a light haze appears on top and fry the parcels, in batches of 3, until golden brown. Remove and drain on paper towels. Tie a chive around the neck of each bag to garnish, and serve with a sweet chili sauce for dipping.

 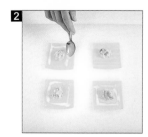 

Stuffed Zucchini

Hollow out some zucchini, fill them with a spicy beef mixture, and bake them in the oven for a delicious side dish.

NUTRITIONAL INFORMATION

Calories	208	Sugars	.........3g
Protein	........12g	Fat	...........9g
Carbohydrate	...20g	Saturates	.......4g

 45 MINS   35 MINS

SERVES 4

INGREDIENTS

8 medium zucchini

1 tbsp sesame or vegetable oil

1 garlic clove, crushed

2 shallots, chopped finely

1 small red chili, seeded and chopped finely

1 cup lean ground beef

1 tbsp fish sauce or oyster mushroom sauce

1 tbsp chopped fresh cilantro or basil

2 tsp cornstarch, blended with a little cold water

½ cup cooked long-grain rice

salt and pepper

TO GARNISH

sprigs of fresh cilantro or basil

carrot slices

1 Slice the zucchini in half horizontally and scoop out a channel down the middle, discarding all the seeds. Sprinkle with salt and set aside for 15 minutes.

2 Heat the oil in a wok or skillet and add the garlic, shallots, and chili. Stir-fry for 2 minutes, until golden. Add the ground beef and stir-fry briskly for about 5 minutes. Stir in the fish sauce or mushroom sauce, the chopped cilantro or basil, and the blended cornstarch, and cook for 2 minutes, stirring until thickened. Season with salt and pepper, then remove from the heat.

3 Rinse the zucchini in cold water and arrange them in a greased shallow ovenproof dish, cut side up. Mix the cooked rice into the ground beef, then use this mixture to stuff the zucchini.

4 Cover with foil and bake in a preheated oven at 375°F for 20–25 minutes, removing the foil for the last 5 minutes of cooking time.

5 Serve immediately, garnished with sprigs of fresh cilantro or basil, and carrot slices.

Spare Ribs

Another classic favorite in Chinese restaurants, these sticky ribs are best eaten with your fingers.

NUTRITIONAL INFORMATION

Calories 436   Sugars 3g
Protein ....21g   Fat 37g
Carbohydrate ....3g   Saturates 14g

1¼ HOURS   1 HOUR

SERVES 4

INGREDIENTS

2 lb pork spare ribs

2 tbsp dark soy sauce

3 tbsp hoisin sauce

1 tbsp Chinese rice wine or dry sherry

pinch of Chinese five-spice powder

2 tsp dark brown sugar

¼ tsp chili sauce

2 garlic cloves, crushed

cilantro sprigs, to garnish (optional)

1 Cut the spare ribs into separate pieces if they are joined together. If desired, you can chop them into 2 inch lengths, using a cleaver.

2 Mix together the soy sauce, hoisin sauce, Chinese rice wine or sherry, Chinese five-spice powder, dark brown sugar, chili sauce, and garlic in a large mixing bowl.

3 Place the ribs in a shallow dish and pour the mixture over them, turning to coat the ribs thoroughly. Cover with plastic wrap and leave to marinate in the refrigerator, turning the ribs from time to time, for at least 1 hour.

4 Remove the ribs from the marinade and arrange them in a single layer

on a wire rack placed over a roasting pan half-filled with warm water. Using a pastry brush, coat the ribs evenly with the marinade, reserving the remaining marinade.

5 Cook the ribs in a preheated oven at 350°F for 30 minutes. Remove the roasting pan from the oven and turn the ribs over. Brush with the remaining marinade and return to the oven for another 30 minutes, or until cooked through. Add more hot water to the

roasting pan during cooking, if required. Do not allow it to dry out as the water steams the ribs and aids in their cooking.

6 Transfer the ribs to a warmed serving dish, garnish with the cilantro sprigs (if using), and serve immediately.

Chinese Omelet

This is a fairly filling omelet, as it contains chicken and shrimp. It is cooked as a whole omelet and then sliced for serving.

NUTRITIONAL INFORMATION

Calories 309	Sugars 0g
Protein 34g	Fat 19g
Carbohydrate ...0.2g	Saturates 5g

5 MINS   5 MINS

SERVES 4

I N G R E D I E N T S

8 eggs

2 cups cooked chicken, shredded

12 jumbo shrimp,
    peeled and deveined

2 tbsp chopped chives

2 tsp light soy sauce

dash of chili sauce

2 tbsp vegetable oil

1 Lightly beat the eggs in a large mixing bowl.

2 Add the shredded chicken and jumbo shrimp to the eggs, mixing well.

3 Stir in the chopped chives, light soy sauce, and chili sauce, mixing well to combine all the ingredients.

4 Heat the vegetable oil in a large preheated skillet over a medium heat.

5 Add the egg mixture to the skillet, tilting the pan to coat the base completely.

6 Cook over a medium heat, gently stirring the omelet with a fork, until the surface is just set and the underside is a golden brown color.

7 When the omelet is set, slide it out of the pan, with the aid of a metal spatula.

8 Cut the Chinese omelet into squares or slices and serve immediately. Alternatively, serve the omelet as a main course for two people.

VARIATION

You could add extra flavor to the omelet by stirring in 3 tablespoons of finely chopped fresh cilantro or 1 teaspoon sesame seeds with the chives in step 3.

Shrimp Parcels

These small shrimp bites are packed with the flavor of lime and cilantro for a quick and tasty first course.

NUTRITIONAL INFORMATION

Calories	305	Sugars	.........2g
Protein	........15g	Fat	..........21g
Carbohydrate	...14g	Saturates	.......8g

15 MINS   20 MINS

SERVES 4

INGREDIENTS

1 tbsp sunflower oil

1 red bell pepper, seeded and very thinly sliced

¾ cup beansprouts

finely grated zest and juice of 1 lime

1 red chili, seeded and very finely chopped

½ inch piece of fresh ginger, peeled and grated

8 oz peeled shrimp

1 tbsp fish sauce

½ tsp arrowroot

2 tbsp chopped fresh cilantro

8 sheets phyllo pastry

2 tbsp butter

2 tsp sesame oil

oil, for frying

green onion tassels, to garnish

chili sauce, to serve

1 Heat the sunflower oil in a large preheated wok. Add the red bell pepper and bean sprouts and stir-fry for 2 minutes, or until the vegetables have softened.

2 Remove the wok from the heat and toss in the lime zest and juice, red chili, ginger, and shrimp, stirring the mixture well.

3 Mix the fish sauce with the arrowroot and stir the mixture into the wok juices. Return the wok to the heat and cook, stirring, for 2 minutes, or until the juices thicken. Toss in the cilantro and mix well.

4 Lay the sheets of phyllo pastry out on a board. Melt the butter and sesame oil and brush each pastry sheet with the mixture.

5 Spoon a little of the shrimp filling onto the top of each sheet, fold over each end, and roll up to enclose the filling.

6 Heat the oil in a large wok. Cook the parcels, in batches, for 2–3 minutes, or until crisp and golden. Garnish with green onion tassels and serve hot with a chili dipping sauce.

4

5

5

COOK'S TIP

If using cooked shrimp, cook for 1 minute only otherwise the shrimp will toughen.

Eggplant Dipping Platter

Dipping platters are a very sociable dish, bringing together all the diners at the table.

NUTRITIONAL INFORMATION

Calories	.81	Sugars	.4g
Protein	.4g	Fat	.5g
Carbohydrate	.5g	Saturates	.1g

15 MINS   10 MINS

SERVES 4

INGREDIENTS

1 eggplant, peeled and cut into 1 inch cubes

3 tbsp sesame seeds, roasted in a dry pan over a low heat

1 tsp sesame oil

grated zest and juice of ½ lime

1 small shallot, diced

1 tsp sugar

1 red chili, seeded and sliced

1¼ cups broccoli flowerets

2 carrots, cut into thin sticks

8 baby corn-on-the-cob, cut in half lengthwise

2 celery stalks, cut into thin sticks

1 baby red cabbage, cut into 8 wedges, the leaves of each wedge held together by the core

salt and pepper

  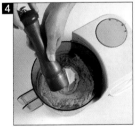

1 Cook the diced eggplant in a saucepan of boiling water for 7–8 minutes.

2 Meanwhile, grind the sesame seeds with the oil in a food processor or pestle and mortar.

3 Add the eggplant, lime zest and juice, shallot, ½ tsp salt, pepper, sugar, and chili in that order to the sesame seeds.

Process, or chop and mash by hand, until smooth.

4 Adjust the seasoning to taste then spoon the dip into a bowl.

5 Serve the eggplant dipping platter surrounded by the broccoli, carrots, baby corn-on-the-cob, celery, and red cabbage.

VARIATION

You can vary the selection of vegetables depending on your preference or whatever you have available. Other vegetables you could use are cauliflower flowerets and cucumber sticks.

Chili Fish Cakes

These small fish cakes are quick to make and are delicious served with a chili dip.

NUTRITIONAL INFORMATION

Calories 164   Sugars 1g
Protein . . . . .23g   Fat 6g
Carbohydrate . . . .6g   Saturates 1g

 5 MINS   40 MINS

SERVES 4

I N G R E D I E N T S

1 lb cod fillets, skinned

2 tbsp fish sauce

2 red chilies, seeded and very finely
    chopped

2 cloves garlic, crushed

10 lime leaves, very finely chopped

2 tbsp fresh cilantro,
    chopped

1 large egg

¼ cup all-purpose flour

3½ oz green beans,
    very finely sliced

peanut oil, for frying

chili dip, to serve

1 Using a sharp knife, roughly cut the cod fillets into bite-sized pieces.

2 Place the cod in a food processor together with the fish sauce, chilies, garlic, lime leaves, cilantro, egg, and flour. Process until finely chopped and transfer to a large mixing bowl.

3 Add the green beans to the cod mixture and combine.

4 Divide the mixture into small balls. Flatten the balls between the palms of your hands to form cakes.

5 Heat a little oil in a preheated wok or large skillet. Fry the fish cakes on both sides until brown and crispy on the outside.

6 Transfer the fish cakes to serving plates and serve hot with a chili dip.

VARIATION

Almost any kind of fish fillets and seafood can be used in this recipe – try haddock, crab meat, or lobster.

Honeyed Chicken Wings

Chicken wings are ideal for an appetizer because they are small and perfect for eating with the fingers.

NUTRITIONAL INFORMATION

Calories 131   Sugars 4g
Protein . . . . .10g   Fat 8g
Carbohydrate . . . .4g   Saturates 2g

5 MINS   40 MINS

SERVES 4

INGREDIENTS

1 lb chicken wings

2 tbsp peanut oil

2 tbsp light soy sauce

2 tbsp hoisin sauce

2 tbsp honey

2 garlic cloves, crushed

1 tsp sesame seeds

MARINADE

1 dried red chili

½–1 tsp chili powder

½–1 tsp ground ginger

finely grated zest of 1 lime

1 To make the marinade, crush the dried chili in a pestle and mortar. Mix together the crushed dried chili, chili powder, ground ginger, and lime zest in a small mixing bowl.

2 Thoroughly rub the spice mixture into the chicken wings with your fingertips. Set aside for at least 2 hours to allow the flavors to penetrate the chicken wings.

3 Heat the peanut oil in a large wok or skillet.

4 Add the chicken wings and fry, turning frequently, for about 10–12 minutes, until golden and crisp. Drain off any excess oil.

5 Add the soy sauce, hoisin sauce, honey, garlic, and sesame seeds to the wok, turning the chicken wings to coat.

6 Reduce the heat and cook for 20–25 minutes, turning the chicken wings frequently, until completely cooked through. Serve hot.

COOK'S TIP

Make the dish in advance and freeze the chicken wings. Defrost thoroughly, cover with foil, and heat right through in a moderate oven.

Lettuce-Wrapped Meat

Serve the ground meat and lettuce leaves on separate dishes: each guest then wraps his or her own.

NUTRITIONAL INFORMATION

Calories 159	Sugars 0.2g
Protein 14g	Fat 10g
Carbohydrates 1g	Saturates 2g

5 MINS   5 MINS

SERVES 4

I N G R E D I E N T S

9 oz ground pork or chicken

1 tbsp finely chopped Chinese mushrooms

1 tbsp finely chopped water chestnuts

pinch of sugar

1 tsp light soy sauce

1 tsp Chinese rice wine or dry sherry

1 tsp cornstarch

2-3 tbsp vegetable oil

½ tsp finely chopped fresh ginger

1 tsp finely chopped green onions

1 tbsp finely chopped Szechuan preserved
  vegetables (optional)

1 tbsp oyster sauce

a few drops of sesame oil

salt and pepper

8 crisp lettuce leaves, to serve

1 Mix the ground pork or chicken with the Chinese mushrooms, water chestnuts, salt, pepper, sugar, soy sauce, rice wine or sherry, and cornstarch. Blend well until all the ingredients are thoroughly combined.

2 Heat the vegetable oil in a preheated wok or large skillet.

3 Add the ginger and green onions to the wok or skillet, followed by the ground meat. Stir-fry for 1 minute.

4 Add the Szechuan preserved vegetables (if using) and continue stirring for 1 more minute.

5 Add the oyster sauce and sesame oil, blend well and cook for 1 more minute. Remove the mixture in the wok to a warmed serving dish.

6 To serve: place about 2-3 tablespoons of the mixture on a lettuce leaf and roll it up tightly to wrap. Eat with your fingers.

COOK'S TIP

Szechuan preserved vegetables are pickled mustard roots. Hot and salty with a peppery flavor, they are often used to intensify the spiciness of a dish. Once opened, store in the refrigerator in a tightly sealed jar.

Bang-Bang Chicken

The cooked chicken meat is tenderized by being beaten with a rolling pin, hence the name for this very popular Szechuan dish.

NUTRITIONAL INFORMATION

Calories	.82	Sugars	1g
Protein	13g	Fat	3g
Carbohydrate	.2g	Saturates	1g

1¼ HOURS   40 MINS

SERVES 4

INGREDIENTS

4 cups water

2 chicken quarters (breast half and leg)

1 cucumber, cut into thin shreds

SAUCE

2 tbsp light soy sauce

1 tsp sugar

1 tbsp finely chopped green onions, plus extra to garnish

1 tsp red chili oil

¼ tsp pepper

1 tsp white sesame seeds

2 tbsp peanut butter, creamed with a little sesame oil, plus extra to garnish

1 Bring the water to a rolling boil in a wok or a large saucepan. Add the chicken pieces, reduce the heat, cover, and cook for 30-35 minutes.

2 Remove the chicken from the wok or pan and immerse in a bowl of cold water for at least 1 hour to cool it, ready for shredding.

3 Remove the chicken pieces, drain, and dry on absorbent paper towels. Take the meat off the bone.

4 On a flat surface, pound the chicken with a rolling pin, then tear the meat

into shreds with 2 forks. Mix the chicken with the shredded cucumber and arrange in a serving dish.

5 To serve, mix together all the sauce ingredients until thoroughly combined and pour over the chicken and cucumber in the serving dish. Sprinkle some sesame seeds and chopped green onions over the sauce and serve.

COOK'S TIP

Take the time to tear the chicken meat into similar-sized shreds, to make an elegant-looking dish. You can do this quite efficiently with 2 forks, although Chinese cooks would do it with their fingers.

Shrimp Rolls

This variation of a spring roll is made with small shrimp, stir-fried with shallots, carrot, cucumber, bamboo shoots, and rice.

NUTRITIONAL INFORMATION

Calories	388	Sugars	.........2g
Protein	.........9g	Fat	..........25g
Carbohydrate	...33g	Saturates	.......6g

10 MINS   15 MINS

SERVES 4

I N G R E D I E N T S

2 tbsp vegetable oil

3 shallots, chopped very finely

1 carrot, cut into thin sticks

3 inch piece of cucumber, cut into thin sticks

½ cup bamboo shoots, shredded finely

½ cup peeled small shrimp

½ cup cooked long-grain rice

1 tbsp fish sauce or light soy sauce

1 tsp sugar

2 tsp cornstarch, blended in 2 tbsp cold water

8 × 10 inch spring roll skins

oil for deep-frying

salt and pepper

plum sauce, to serve

TO GARNISH

green onion brushes (see page 305)

sprigs of fresh cilantro

1 Heat the oil in a wok and add the shallots, carrot, cucumber, and bamboo shoots. Stir-fry briskly for 2–3 minutes. Add the shrimp and cooked rice, and cook for another 2 minutes. Season.

2 Mix together the fish sauce or soy sauce, sugar and blended cornstarch. Add to the stir-fry and cook, stirring constantly, for about 1 minute, until thickened. Leave to cool slightly.

3 Place spoonfuls of the shrimp and vegetable mixture on the spring roll skins. Dampen the edges and roll them up to enclose the filling completely.

4 Heat the oil for deep-frying and fry the spring rolls until crisp and golden brown. Drain on paper towels. Serve the rolls garnished with green onion brushes and fresh cilantro and accompanied by the plum sauce.

Spinach Meatballs

Balls of pork mixture are coated in spinach and steamed before being served with a sesame and soy sauce dip.

NUTRITIONAL INFORMATION

Calories 137	Sugars 2g
Protein 13g	Fat 7g
Carbohydrate 6g	Saturates 2g

  20 MINS   25 MINS

SERVES 4

INGREDIENTS

4½ oz pork

1 small egg

½ inch piece fresh ginger, chopped

1 small onion, finely chopped

1 tbsp boiling water

1 oz canned bamboo shoots, drained, rinsed, and chopped

2 slices smoked ham, chopped

2 tsp cornstarch

1 lb fresh spinach

2 tsp sesame seeds

SAUCE

⅔ cup vegetable stock

½ tsp cornstarch

1 tsp cold water

1 tsp light soy sauce

½ tsp sesame oil

1 tbsp chopped chives

1 Griind the pork very finely in a food processor. Lightly beat the egg in a bowl and stir into the pork.

2 Put the ginger and onion in a separate bowl, add the boiling water, and let stand for 5 minutes. Drain and add to the pork mixture with the bamboo shoots, ham, and cornstarch. Mix thoroughly and roll into 12 balls.

3 Wash the spinach and remove the stalks. Blanch in boiling water for 10 seconds, drain well, then slice into very thin strips and mix with the sesame seeds. Roll the meatballs in the mixture to coat.

4 Place the meatballs on a heatproof plate in the base of a steamer. Cover and steam for 8–10 minutes, until cooked through and tender.

5 Meanwhile, make the sauce. Put the stock in a saucepan and bring to a boil. Mix together the cornstarch and water to a smooth paste and stir it into the stock. Stir in the soy sauce, sesame oil, and chives. Transfer the cooked meatballs to a warm plate and serve with the sauce.

Rice Paper Parcels

These special rice paper skins are available in Chinese supermarkets and health stores. Do not use the rice paper sold for making cakes.

NUTRITIONAL INFORMATION

Calories	133	Sugars	.........2g
Protein	........10g	Fat	...........8g
Carbohydrate	....5g	Saturates	.......1g

 5 MINS · 15 MINS

SERVES 4

I N G R E D I E N T S

1 egg white

2 tsp cornstarch

2 tsp dry sherry

1 tsp sugar

2 tsp hoisin sauce

8 oz peeled, cooked shrimp

4 green onions, sliced

1 oz canned water chestnuts, drained, rinsed, and chopped

8 Chinese rice papers

vegetable oil, for deep-frying

hoisin sauce or plum sauce, to serve

1 Lightly beat the egg white in a bowl. Mix in the cornstarch, dry sherry, sugar, and hoisin sauce. Add the shrimp, green onions, and water chestnuts, mixing thoroughly.

COOK'S TIP

Use this filling inside wonton skins (see page 42) if the rice papers are unavailable.

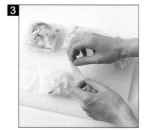

2 Soften the rice papers first by dipping them in a bowl of water one at a time. Spread them out on a clean work counter.

3 Using a dessert spoon, place a little of the shrimp mixture into the center of each rice paper. Carefully wrap the rice paper around the filling to make secure. Repeat to make 8 parcels.

4 Heat the oil in a wok until it is almost smoking. Reduce the heat slightly, add the parcels, in batches if necessary, and deep-fry for 4–5 minutes, until crisp. Remove from the oil with a slotted spoon and drain on absorbent paper towels.

5 Transfer the parcels to a warmed serving dish and serve immediately with a little hoisin or plum sauce.

Crispy Wontons

Mushroom-filled crispy wontons are served on skewers with a dipping sauce flavored with chilies.

NUTRITIONAL INFORMATION

Calories 302   Sugars 1g
Protein . . . . .3g   Fat 25
Carbohydrate . . .15g   Saturates 6g

  45 MINS   20 MINS

SERVES 4

INGREDIENTS

8 wooden skewers, soaked in cold water
for 30 minutes

1 tbsp vegetable oil

1 tbsp chopped onion

1 small garlic clove, chopped

½ tsp chopped fresh ginger

½ cup flat mushrooms,
chopped

16 wonton skins (see page 42)

vegetable oil, for deep-frying

salt

SAUCE

2 tbsp vegetable oil

2 green onions,
shredded thinly

1 red and 1 green chili, seeded and
shredded thinly

3 tbsp light soy sauce

1 tbsp vinegar

1 tbsp dry sherry

pinch of sugar

1 Heat the vegetable oil in a preheated wok or skillet.

2 Add the onion, garlic and fresh ginger to the wok or pan and stir-fry for 2 minutes. Stir in the mushrooms and fry for

another 2 minutes. Season well with salt and leave to cool.

3 Place 1 teaspoon of the cooled mushroom filling in the center of each wonton skin.

4 Bring two opposite corners of each wonton skin together to cover the mixture and pinch together to seal. Repeat with the remaining corners.

5 Thread 2 wontons onto each skewer. Heat enough oil in a large saucepan to deep-fry the wontons in batches until golden and crisp. Do not overheat the oil or the wontons will brown on the outside before they are fully cooked inside. Remove the wontons with a perforated spoon and drain on absorbent paper towels.

6 To make the sauce, heat the vegetable oil in a small saucepan until quite hot or until a small cube of bread dropped in the oil browns in a few seconds. Put the green onions and chilies in a bowl and pour the hot oil slowly on top. Mix in the remaining ingredients.

7 Transfer the crispy wontons to a serving dish and serve with the dipping sauce.

Salt & Pepper Shrimp

Szechuan peppercorns are very hot, adding heat and a red color to the shrimp. They are effectively offset by the sugar in this recipe.

NUTRITIONAL INFORMATION

Calories	174	Sugars	.........1g
Protein	........25g	Fat	...........8g
Carbohydrate	....1g	Saturates	.......1g

 5 MINS   10 MINS

SERVES 4

I N G R E D I E N T S

2 tsp salt

1 tsp black pepper

2 tsp Szechuan peppercorns

1 tsp sugar

1 lb peeled raw jumbo shrimp

2 tbsp peanut oil

1 red chili, seeded and finely chopped

1 tsp freshly grated ginger

3 cloves garlic, crushed

green onions, sliced, to garnish

oriental crackers, to serve

1 Grind the salt, black pepper and Szechuan peppercorns in a pestle and mortar.

2 Mix the salt and pepper mixture with the sugar and set aside until required.

3 Rinse the jumbo shrimp under cold running water and pat dry with absorbent paper towels.

4 Heat the oil in a preheated wok or large skillet.

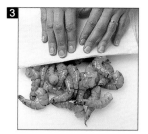

5 Add the shrimp, chopped red chili, ginger and garlic to the wok or skillet and stir-fry for 4–5 minutes, or until the shrimp are cooked through.

6 Add the salt and pepper mixture to the wok and stir-fry for 1 minute, stirring constantly so it does not burn on the base of the wok.

7 Transfer the shrimp to warm serving bowls and garnish with green onions. Serve hot with oriental crackers.

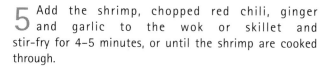
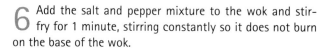

COOK'S TIP

Tiger shrimp (jumbo shrimp) are widely available and have a lovely meaty texture. If using cooked tiger shrimp, add them with the salt and pepper mixture in step 5 – if the cooked shrimp are added any earlier they will toughen up and be inedible.

Tofu Tempura

Crispy coated vegetables and tofu accompanied by a sweet, spicy dip give a real taste of the Orient in this Japanese-style dish.

NUTRITIONAL INFORMATION

Calories 582   Sugars 10g
Protein ....16g   Fat 27g
Carbohydrate ...65g   Saturates 4g

    15 MINS   20 MINS

SERVES 4

I N G R E D I E N T S

4½ oz baby zucchini

4½ oz baby carrots

4½ oz baby corn cobs

4½ oz baby leeks

2 baby eggplants

8 oz tofu

vegetable oil, for deep-frying

julienne strips of carrot, root ginger, and
   baby leek to garnish

noodles, to serve

B A T T E R

2 egg yolks

1¼ cups water

2 cups all-purpose flour

D I P P I N G   S A U C E

5 tbsp mirin or dry sherry

5 tbsp Japanese soy sauce

2 tsp clear honey

1 garlic clove, crushed

1 tsp grated ginger

1 Slice the zucchini and carrots in half lengthwise. Trim the corn. Trim the leeks at both ends. Quarter the eggplants. Cut the tofu into 1 inch cubes.

2 To make the batter, mix the egg yolks with the water. Sift in 1½ cups of the flour and beat with a balloon whisk to form a thick batter. Don't worry if there are any lumps. Heat the oil for deep-frying to 350°F or until a cube of bread browns in 30 seconds.

3 Place the remaining flour on a large plate and toss the vegetables and tofu until lightly coated.

4 Dip the bean curd in the batter and deep-fry for 2–3 minutes, until lightly golden. Drain on paper towels and keep warm.

5 Dip the vegetables in the batter and deep-fry, a few at a time, for 3–4 minutes, until golden. Drain and place on a warmed serving plate.

6 To make the dipping sauce, mix all the ingredients together. Serve with the vegetables and tofu, accompanied with noodles and garnished with julienne strips of vegetables.

Steamed Cabbage Rolls

These small cabbage packages are quick and easy to prepare and cook. They are ideal for a speedy first course.

NUTRITIONAL INFORMATION

Calories	162	Sugars	.......0.3g
Protein	........24g	Fat	...........7g
Carbohydrates	....2g	Saturates	.......1g

5 MINS   20 MINS

SERVES 4

I N G R E D I E N T S

8 cabbage leaves, trimmed

8 oz skinless, boneless chicken

6 oz peeled raw or cooked shrimp

1 tsp cornstarch

½ tsp chili powder

1 egg, lightly beaten

1 tbsp vegetable oil

1 leek, sliced

1 garlic clove, thinly sliced

sliced fresh red chili, to garnish

1 Blanch the cabbage for 2 minutes. Drain and pat dry with absorbent paper towels.

2 Grind the chicken and shrimp in a food processor. Place in a bowl with the cornstarch, chili powder, and egg. Mix well to combine all the ingredients.

3 Place 2 tablespoons of the chicken and shrimp mixture towards one end of each cabbage leaf. Fold the sides of the cabbage leaf around the filling and roll up.

4 Arrange the rolls, seam-side down, in a single layer on a heatproof plate and cook in a steamer for 10 minutes.

5 Meanwhile, sauté the leek and garlic in the oil for 1–2 minutes.

6 Transfer the cabbage rolls to warmed individual serving plates and garnish with red chili slices. Serve with the leek and garlic sauté.

COOK'S TIP

Use Chinese cabbage or savoy cabbage for this recipe, choosing leaves of a similar size for wrapping.

Chicken Spring Rolls

A cucumber dipping sauce tastes perfect with these delicious spring rolls, filled with chicken and fresh, crunchy vegetables.

NUTRITIONAL INFORMATION

Calories	367	Sugars	........18g
Protein	........13g	Fat	..........21g
Carbohydrate	...32g	Saturates	.......3g

 10 MINS   25 MINS

SERVES 4

I N G R E D I E N T S

2 tbsp vegetable oil

4 green onions, trimmed and sliced very finely

1 carrot, cut into thin sticks

1 small green or red bell pepper, cored, seeded, and sliced finely

⅔ cup small mushrooms, sliced

1 cup bean sprouts

1 cup cooked chicken, shredded

1 tbsp light soy sauce

1 tsp sugar

2 tsp cornstarch, blended in 2 tbsp cold water

12 × 8 inch spring roll skins

oil for deep-frying

salt and pepper

green onion brushes to garnish

S A U C E

¼ cup light malt vinegar

¼ cup light brown sugar

½ tsp salt

2 inch piece of cucumber, peeled and chopped finely

4 green onions, trimmed and sliced finely

1 small red or green chili, seeded and chopped very finely

1 Stir-fry the green onions, carrot, and bell pepper for 2–3 minutes. Add the mushrooms, bean sprouts, and chicken and cook for 2 minutes. Season. Mix the soy sauce, sugar and blended cornstarch. Add to the wok and stir-fry for 1 minute. Leave to cool slightly. Spoon the chicken and vegetable mixture onto the spring roll skins. Dampen the edges and roll them up to enclose the filling completely.

2 To make the sauce, heat the vinegar, water, sugar, and salt in a pan. Boil for 1 minute. Combine the cucumber, green onions, and chili and pour over the vinegar mixture. Leave to cool.

3 Heat the oil and fry the rolls until crisp and golden brown. Drain on paper towels, garnish with green onion brushes, and serve with the cucumber dipping sauce.

Sesame Shrimp Toasts

These are one of the most recognized and popular appetizers in Chinese restaurants in the Western world. They are also quick and easy to make.

NUTRITIONAL INFORMATION

Calories	237	Sugars	.........1g
Protein	........18g	Fat	..........12g
Carbohydrate	...15g	Saturates	.......2g

🐚 🐚

🦐 5 MINS 🕐 10 MINS

SERVES 4

I N G R E D I E N T S

4 slices medium, thick-sliced white bread

8 oz cooked peeled shrimp

1 tbsp soy sauce

2 cloves garlic, crushed

1 tbsp sesame oil

1 egg

2 tbsp sesame seeds

oil, for deep-frying

sweet chili sauce, to serve

1 Remove the crusts from the bread, if desired, then set aside until required.

2 Place the peeled shrimp, soy sauce, crushed garlic, sesame oil, and egg into a food processor and blend until a smooth paste has formed.

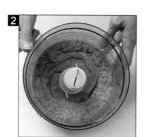  

3 Spread the shrimp paste evenly over the 4 slices of bread. Sprinkle the sesame seeds over the top of the shrimp mixture and press the seeds down with your hands so that they stick to the mixture. Cut each slice in half and in half again to form 4 triangles.

4 Heat the oil in a large wok or skillet and deep-fry the toasts, sesame seed-side up, for 4-5 minutes, or until golden and crispy.

5 Remove the toasts with a slotted spoon and transfer to absorbent paper towels and leave to drain thoroughly.

6 Serve the sesame shrimp toasts warm with sweet chili sauce for dipping.

VARIATION

Add 2 chopped green onions to the mixture in step 2 for added flavor and crunch.

Pork Dim Sum

These small steamed tidbits are traditionally served as an appetizer and are very adaptable to your favorite fillings.

NUTRITIONAL INFORMATION

Calories	478	Sugars 3g
Protein	........33g	Fat 29g
Carbohydrate	...21g	Saturates 9g

 10 MINS   15 MINS

SERVES 4

I N G R E D I E N T S

14 oz ground pork

2 green onions, chopped

1¾ oz canned bamboo shoots, drained, rinse, and chopped

1 tbsp light soy sauce

1 tbsp dry sherry

2 tsp sesame oil

2 tsp sugar

1 egg white, lightly beaten

4½ tsp cornstarch

24 wonton skins

1 Place the ground pork, green onions, bamboo shoots, soy sauce, dry sherry, sesame oil, sugar, and beaten egg white in a large mixing bowl and mix until all the ingredients are thoroughly combined.

2 Stir in the cornstarch, mixing until thoroughly incorporated with the other ingredients.

3 Spread out the wonton skins on a work counter. Place a spoonful of the pork and vegetable mixture in the center of each wonton skin and lightly brush the edges of the skins with water.

4 Bring the sides of the skins together in the center of the filling, pinching firmly together.

5 Line a steamer with a clean, damp tea towel and arrange the wontons inside.

6 Cover and steam for 5–7 minutes, until the dim sum are cooked through. Serve immediately.

COOK'S TIP

Bamboo steamers are designed to rest on the sloping sides of a wok above the water. They are available in a range of sizes.

Son-in-Law Eggs

This recipe is supposedly so called because it is an easy dish for a son-in-law to cook to impress his new mother-in-law!

NUTRITIONAL INFORMATION

Calories 229	Sugars 8g	
Protein 9g	Fat 18g	
Carbohydrate 8g	Saturates 3g	

15 MINS   15 MINS

SERVES 4

I N G R E D I E N T S

6 eggs, hard-cooked and shelled

4 tbsp sunflower oil

1 onion, sliced thinly

2 fresh red chilies, sliced

2 tbsp sugar

1 tbsp water

2 tsp tamarind pulp

1 tbsp liquid seasoning, such as Maggi

rice, to serve

1 Prick the hard-cooked eggs 2 or 3 times with a toothpick.

2 Heat the sunflower oil in a wok and fry the eggs until crispy and golden. Drain on absorbent paper towels.

3 Halve the eggs lengthwise and put on a serving dish.

4 Reserve one tablespoon of the oil, pour off the rest, then heat the tablespoonful in the wok. Cook the onion and chilies over a high heat until golden and slightly crisp. Drain on paper towels.

5 Heat the sugar, water, tamarind pulp, and liquid seasoning in the wok and simmer for 5 minutes until thickened.

6 Pour the sauce over the eggs and spoon over the onion and chilies. Serve immediately with rice.

COOK'S TIP

Tamarind pulp is sold in oriental stores, and is quite sour. If it is not available, use twice the amount of lemon juice in its place.

Chili & Peanut Shrimp

Peanut flavors are widely used in Far East and South East Asian cooking and complement many ingredients.

NUTRITIONAL INFORMATION

Calories	478	Sugars	........2g
Protein	........32g	Fat	..........30g
Carbohydrate	...19g	Saturates	......11g

15 MINS   10 MINS

SERVES 4

I N G R E D I E N T S

1 lb large shrimp (peeled apart from tail end)

3 tbsp crunchy peanut butter

1 tbsp chili sauce

10 sheets phyllo pastry

1 oz butter, melted

1¾ oz fine egg noodles

oil, for frying

1 Using a sharp knife, make a small horizontal slit across the back of each shrimp. Press down on the shrimp so that they lie flat.

2 Mix together the peanut butter and chili sauce in a small bowl until well blended. Using a pastry brush, spread a little of the sauce onto each shrimp so they are evenly coated.

3 Cut each phyllo sheet in half and brush with melted butter.

4 Wrap each shrimp in a piece of phyllo, tucking the edges under to fully enclose the shrimp.

5 Place the fine egg noodles in a bowl, pour over enough boiling water to cover, and leave to stand for 5 minutes. Drain the noodles thoroughly. Use 2–3

cooked noodles to tie around each shrimp pastry.

6 Heat the oil in a preheated wok. Cook the shrimp for 3–4 minutes, or until golden and crispy.

7 Remove the shrimp with a slotted spoon, transfer to absorbent kitchen paper, and leave to drain. Transfer to serving plates and serve warm.

COOK'S TIP

When using phyllo pastry, keep any unused pastry covered to prevent it drying out and becoming brittle.

Red Curry Fish Cakes

You can use almost any kind of fish fillets or seafood for these delicious fishcakes which can be eaten as an appetizer or a light meal.

NUTRITIONAL INFORMATION

Calories 203   Sugars 1g
Protein ....32g   Fat 8g
Carbohydrate ....1g   Saturates 1g

 15 MINS   15 MINS

SERVES 6

INGREDIENTS

2 lb 4 oz fish fillets or prepared seafood,
   such as cod, haddock, shrimp, crab meat,
   or lobster

1 egg, beaten

2 tbsp chopped fresh cilantro

Red Curry Paste (see page 184)

1 bunch green onions, finely chopped

vegetable oil, for deep-frying

chili flowers, to garnish

CUCUMBER SALAD

1 large cucumber, peeled and grated

2 shallots, peeled and grated

2 red chilies, seeded and very finely
   chopped

2 tbsp fish sauce

2 tbsp dried powdered shrimp

1½-2 tbsp lime juice

COOK'S TIP

When handling chilies be very careful not to touch your face or eyes: chili juice is a powerful irritant, and can be very painful on the skin. Always wash your hands after preparing chilies.

1 Place the fish in a blender or food processor with the egg, cilantro, and curry paste and purée until smooth and well blended.

2 Turn the mixture into a bowl, add the green onions, and mix well to combine.

3 Taking 2 tablespoons of the fish mixture at a time, shape into balls, then flatten them slightly with your fingers to make cakes.

4 Heat the vegetable oil in a preheated wok or skillet until hot.

5 Add a few of the fish cakes to the wok or pan and deep-fry for a few minutes until brown and cooked through. Remove with a slotted spoon and drain on absorbent paper towels. Keep warm while cooking the remaining fish cakes.

6 Meanwhile, to make the cucumber salad, mix the cucumber with the shallots, chilies, fish sauce, dried shrimp, and lime juice.

7 Serve the cucumber salad immediately, with the warm fish cakes.

Vegetable Spring Rolls

There are many different versions of spring rolls throughout the Far East, a vegetable filling being the classic.

NUTRITIONAL INFORMATION

Calories	189	Sugars	........4g
Protein	.........2g	Fat	..........16g
Carbohydrate	....11g	Saturates	......5g

10 MINS   15 MINS

SERVES 4

I N G R E D I E N T S

8 oz carrots

1 red bell pepper

1 tbsp sunflower oil, plus extra for frying

¾ cup bean sprouts

finely grated zest and juice of 1 lime

1 red chili, seeded and very finely chopped

1 tbsp soy sauce

½ tsp arrowroot

2 tbsp chopped fresh cilantro

8 sheets phyllo pastry

1 oz butter

2 tsp sesame oil

TO SERVE

chili sauce

green onion tassels

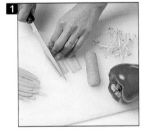  

1 Using a sharp knife, cut the carrots into thin sticks. Seed the bell pepper and cut into thin slices.

2 Heat the sunflower oil in a large preheated wok.

3 Add the carrot, red bell pepper, and bean sprouts and cook, stirring, for 2 minutes, or until softened. Remove the wok from the heat and toss in the lime zest and juice, and the red chili.

4 Mix the soy sauce with the arrowroot. Stir the mixture into the wok, return to the heat, and cook for 2 minutes or until the juices thicken.

5 Add the chopped fresh cilantro to the wok and mix well.

6 Lay the sheets of phyllo pastry out on a board. Melt the butter and sesame oil and brush each sheet with the mixture.

7 Spoon a little of the vegetable filling at the top of each sheet, fold over each long side, and roll up.

8 Add a little oil to the wok and cook the spring rolls in batches, for 2–3 minutes, or until crisp and golden.

9 Transfer the spring rolls to a serving dish, garnish, and serve hot with chili dipping sauce.

Crispy Seaweed

This tasty Chinese first course is not all that it seems – the "seaweed" is in fact bok choy which is then fried, salted, and tossed with pine nuts.

NUTRITIONAL INFORMATION

Calories	.214	Sugars	.14g
Protein	.6g	Fat	.15g
Carbohydrate	.15g	Saturates	.2g

  10 MINS   5 MINS

SERVES 4

INGREDIENTS

2 lb 4 oz bok choy

peanut oil, for deep-frying (about 3¾ cups)

1 tsp salt

1 tbsp sugar

2½ tbsp toasted pine nuts

1 Rinse the bok choy leaves under cold running water and then pat dry thoroughly with absorbent paper towels.

2 Discarding any tough outer leaves, roll each bok choy leaf up, then slice through thinly so that the leaves are finely

shredded. Alternatively, use a food processor to shred the bok choy.

3 Heat the peanut oil in a large wok or heavy-bottomed skillet.

4 Carefully add the shredded bok choy leaves to the wok or skillet and fry for about 30 seconds , or until they shrivel up and become crispy (you will probably need

to do this in several batches, depending on the size of the wok).

5 Remove the crispy seaweed from the wok with a slotted spoon and drain on absorbent paper towels.

6 Transfer the crispy seaweed to a large bowl and toss with the salt, sugar, and pine nuts. Serve immediately.

COOK'S TIP

The tough, outer leaves of bok choy are discarded as these will spoil the overall taste and texture of the dish.

Use savoy cabbage instead of the bok choy if it is unavailable, drying the leaves thoroughly before frying.

Money Bags

These traditional steamed dumplings can be eaten on their own or dipped in a mixture of soy sauce, sherry, and slivers of fresh ginger.

NUTRITIONAL INFORMATION

Calories	315	Sugars	........3g
Protein	.........8g	Fat	..........8g
Carbohydrate	...56g	Saturates	.......1g

 45 MINS   20 MINS

SERVES 4

INGREDIENTS

3 Chinese dried mushrooms
  (if unavailable, use thinly sliced
  open-cap mushrooms)

2 cups all-purpose flour

1 egg, beaten

⅓ cup water

1 tsp baking powder

¾ tsp salt

2 tbsp vegetable oil

2 green onions, chopped

½ cup corn kernels

½ red chili, seeded and chopped

1 tbsp brown bean sauce

1 Place the dried mushrooms in a small bowl, cover with warm water, and leave to soak for 20–25 minutes.

2 To make the skins, sift the all-purpose flour into a bowl. Add the beaten egg and mix in lightly. Stir in the water, baking powder, and salt. Mix to make a soft dough.

3 Knead the dough lightly on a floured board. Cover with a damp tea towel and set aside for 5–6 minutes. This allows the baking powder time to activate, so that the dumplings swell when steaming.

4 Drain the mushrooms, squeezing them dry. Remove the tough centers and chop the mushrooms.

5 Heat the vegetable oil in a wok or large skillet and stir-fry the mushrooms, green onions, corn, and chili for 2 minutes.

6 Stir in the brown bean sauce and remove from the heat.

7 Roll the dough into a large sausage and cut into 24 even-sized pieces. Roll each piece out into a thin round and place a teaspoonful of the filling in the center. Gather up the edges to a point, pinch together, and twist to seal.

8 Place the dumplings in an oiled steaming basket. Place over a saucepan of simmering water, cover, and steam for 12–14 minutes before serving.

Vegetable Dim Sum

Dim sum are small Chinese appetizers, which may be filled with any variety of fillings, steamed or fried, and served with a dipping sauce.

NUTRITIONAL INFORMATION

Calories ....295 Sugars 1g
Protein ....5g Fat 22g
Carbohydrate ...20g Saturates 6g

15 MINS   15 MINS

SERVES 4

I N G R E D I E N T S

2 green onions, chopped

1 oz green beans, chopped

½ small carrot, finely chopped

1 red chili, chopped

⅓ cup bean sprouts, chopped

⅓ cup small mushrooms, chopped

¼ cup unsalted cashews, chopped

1 small egg, beaten

2 tbsp cornstarch

1 tsp light soy sauce

1 tsp hoisin sauce

1 tsp sesame oil

32 wonton skins

oil, for deep-frying

1 tbsp sesame seeds

1 Mix all of the vegetables together in a bowl. Add the nuts, egg, cornstarch, soy sauce, hoisin sauce, and sesame oil to the bowl. Mix well.

2 Lay the wonton skins out on a cutting board and spoon small quantities of the mixture into the center of each. Gather the skin around the filling at the top, to make little pastries, leaving the top open.

3 Heat the oil for deep-frying in a wok to 350°F or until a cube of bread browns in 30 seconds. Fry the wontons, in batches, for 1–2 minutes or until golden brown. Drain on paper towels and keep warm while frying the remaining wontons.

4 Sprinkle the sesame seeds over the wontons. Serve the vegetable dim sum with a soy or plum dipping sauce.

COOK'S TIP

If preferred, arrange the wontons on a heatproof plate and then steam in a steamer for 5-7 minutes for a healthier cooking method.

Crispy Crab Wontons

These delicious wontons are a superb appetizer. Deep-fried until crisp and golden, they are delicious with a chili dipping sauce.

NUTRITIONAL INFORMATION

Calories	266	Sugars	.......0.4g
Protein	........10g	Fat	.........17g
Carbohydrate	...18g	Saturates	.......5g

 10 MINS   15 MINS

SERVES 4

INGREDIENTS

6 oz white crab meat, flaked

1¾ oz canned water chestnuts, drained, rinsed, and chopped

1 small fresh red chili, chopped

1 green onion, chopped

1 tbsp cornstarch

1 tsp dry sherry

1 tsp light soy sauce

½ tsp lime juice

24 wonton skins

vegetable oil, for deep-frying

sliced lime, to garnish

1 To make the filling, mix together the crab meat, water chestnuts, chili, green onion, cornstarch, sherry, soy sauce, and lime juice.

2 Spread out the wonton skins on a work counter and spoon one portion of the filling into the center of each wonton skin.

3 Dampen the edges of the wonton skins with a little water and fold them in half to form triangles. Fold the two pointed ends in towards the center, moisten with a little water to secure, and then pinch together to seal.

4 Heat the oil for deep-frying in a wok or deep-fryer to 350°F–375°F, or until a cube of bread browns in 30 seconds. Fry the wontons, in batches, for 2–3 minutes, until golden brown and crisp. Remove the wontons from the oil and leave to drain on paper towels.

5 Serve the wontons hot, garnished with slices of lime.

COOK'S TIP

Handle wonton skins carefully as they can be easily damaged. Make sure that the wontons are sealed well and secured before deep-frying to prevent the filling coming out and the wontons unwrapping.

Eggplant Satay

Eggplants and mushrooms are broiled on skewers and served with a satay sauce.

NUTRITIONAL INFORMATION

Calories	 155	Sugars	.... 2g
Protein	.... 4g	Fat	.... 14g
Carbohydrate	.... 3g	Saturates	.... 3g

2¼ HOURS   25 MINS

SERVES 4

I N G R E D I E N T S

2 eggplants, cut into 1 inch pieces

6 oz small chestnut mushrooms

M A R I N A D E

1 tsp cumin seeds

1 tsp coriander seeds

1 inch piece fresh ginger, grated

2 garlic cloves, crushed lightly

½ stalk lemon grass, chopped roughly

4 tbsp light soy sauce

8 tbsp sunflower oil

2 tbsp lemon juice

P E A N U T   S A U C E

½ tsp cumin seeds

½ tsp coriander seeds

3 garlic cloves

1 small onion, puréed in a food processor or chopped very finely by hand

1 tbsp lemon juice

1 tsp salt

½ red chili, seeded and sliced

½ cup coconut milk

1 cup crunchy peanut butter

1 cup water

1 Thread the vegetables onto eight metal or pre-soaked wooden skewers.

2 For the marinade, grind the cumin and coriander seeds, ginger, garlic, and lemon grass. Stir-fry over a high heat until fragrant. Remove from the heat and add the remaining marinade ingredients. Place the skewers in a dish and spoon the marinade over. Leave to marinate for at least 2 hours and up to 8 hours.

3 To make the sauce, grind the cumin and coriander seeds with the garlic. Add all the ingredients except the water. Transfer to a pan and stir in the water. Bring to a boil and cook until thick.

4 Cook the skewers under a preheated very hot broiler for 15–20 minutes. Brush with the marinade frequently and turn once. Serve with the peanut sauce.

Spicy Corn Fritters

Cornmeal can be found in most supermarkets or health food stores. Yellow in color, it acts as a binding agent in this recipe.

NUTRITIONAL INFORMATION

Calories 213   Sugars 6g
Protein . . . . .5g   Fat 8g
Carbohydrate . . .30g   Saturates 1g

 5 MINS   15 MINS

SERVES 4

I N G R E D I E N T S

¾ cup canned or frozen corn

2 red chilies, seeded and very finely chopped

2 cloves garlic, crushed

10 lime leaves, very finely chopped

2 tbsp fresh cilantro, chopped

1 large egg

½ cup cornmeal

3½ oz green beans, very finely sliced

peanut oil, for frying

1 Place the corn, chilies, garlic, lime leaves, cilantro, egg, and cornmeal in a large mixing bowl, and stir to combine.

2 Add the green beans to the ingredients in the bowl and mix well, using a wooden spoon.

3 Divide the mixture into small, evenly sized balls. Flatten the balls of mixture between the palms of your hands to form rounds.

4 Heat a little peanut oil in a preheated wok or large skillet until really hot. Cook the fritters, in batches, until brown and crispy on the outside, turning occasionally.

5 Leave the fritters to drain on absorbent paper towels while frying the remaining fritters.

6 Transfer the fritters to warm serving plates and serve immediately.

COOK'S TIP

Kaffir lime leaves are dark green, glossy leaves that have a lemony-lime flavor. They can be bought from Asian stores either fresh or dried. Fresh leaves impart the most delicious flavor.

Steamed Duck Buns

The dough used in this recipe may also be wrapped around chicken, pork, or shrimp, or sweet fillings as an alternative.

NUTRITIONAL INFORMATION

Calories 307	Sugars 11g	
Protein 17g	Fat 6g	
Carbohydrate . . .50g	Saturates 1g	

🐚 🐚 🐚 🐚

🍲 1½ HOURS   🕐 1 HOUR

SERVES 4

INGREDIENTS

DUMPLING DOUGH

2⅔ cups all-purpose flour

½ oz dried yeast

1 tsp sugar

2 tbsp warm water

¾ cup warm milk

FILLING

10½ oz duck breast

1 tbsp light brown sugar

1 tbsp light soy sauce

2 tbsp honey

1 tbsp hoisin sauce

1 tbsp vegetable oil

1 leek, finely chopped

1 garlic clove, crushed

½ inch piece fresh ginger, grated

1 Place the duck breast in a large bowl. Mix together the light brown sugar, soy sauce, honey, and hoisin sauce. Pour the mixture over the duck and marinate for 20 minutes.

2 Remove the duck from the marinade and cook on a wire rack set over a roasting pan in a preheated oven at 400°F for 35–40 minutes, or until cooked through. Leave to cool, remove the meat from the bones, and cut into small cubes.

3 Heat the vegetable oil in a preheated wok or skillet until really hot.

4 Add the leek, garlic, and ginger to the wok and fry for 3 minutes. Mix with the duck meat.

5 Sift the all-purpose flour into a large bowl. Mix the yeast, sugar, and warm water in a separate bowl and leave in a warm place for 15 minutes.

6 Pour the yeast mixture into the flour, together with the warm milk, mixing to form a firm dough. Knead the dough on a floured surface for 5 minutes. Roll into a sausage shape, 1 inch in diameter. Cut into 16 pieces, cover, and let stand for 20–25 minutes.

7 Flatten the dough pieces into 4 inch rounds. Place a spoonful of filling in the center of each, draw up the sides to form a "moneybag" shape, and twist to seal.

8 Place the dumplings on a clean, damp tea towel in the base of a steamer, cover, and steam for 20 minutes. Serve immediately.

Barbecue Pork (Char Siu)

Also called honey-roasted pork, these are the strips of reddish meat sometimes seen hanging in the windows of Cantonese restaurants.

NUTRITIONAL INFORMATION

Calories	250	Sugar	.........8g
Protein	........27g	Fat	..........10g
Carbohydrate	....9g	Saturates	.......3g

🍲 4¼ HOURS   🕐 30 MINS

SERVES 4

I N G R E D I E N T S

1 lb 2 oz pork tenderloin

⅔ cup boiling water

1 tbsp honey, dissolved with a little hot water

M A R I N A D E

1 tbsp sugar

1 tbsp crushed yellow bean sauce

1 tbsp light soy sauce

1 tbsp hoisin sauce

1 tbsp oyster sauce

½ tsp chili sauce

1 tbsp brandy or rum

1 tsp sesame oil

shredded lettuce, to serve

1 Using a sharp knife or meat cleaver, cut the pork into strips about 1 inch thick and 7-8 inches long and place in a large shallow dish. Mix the marinade ingredients together and pour over the pork, turning until well coated. Cover, and leave to marinate for at least 3-4 hours, turning occasionally.

2 Remove the pork strips from the dish with a slotted spoon, reserving the marinade. Arrange the pork strips on a rack over a baking pan. Place the pan in a preheated oven and pour in the boiling water. Roast the pork for about 10-15 minutes.

3 Lower the oven temperature. Baste the pork strips with the reserved marinade and turn over using metal tongs. Roast for another 10 minutes.

4 Remove the pork from the oven, brush with the honey syrup, and lightly brown under a medium hot broiler for about 3-4 minutes, turning once or twice.

5 To serve, allow the pork to cool slightly before cutting it. Cut across the grain into thin slices and arrange neatly on a bed of shredded lettuce. Make a sauce by boiling the marinade and the drippings in the baking pan for a few minutes, strain, and pour over the pork.

Fat Horses

A mixture of meats is flavored with coconut milk, fish sauce, and cilantro in this curious-sounding dish.

NUTRITIONAL INFORMATION

Calories ....195 Sugars 1g
Protein ....23g Fat 11g
Carbohydrate ....1g Saturates 6g

🥟 🥟 🥟

🍲 10 MINS   🕐 30 MINS

SERVES 4

INGREDIENTS

2 tbsp creamed coconut

4½ oz lean pork

4½ oz chicken breast, skin removed

½ cup canned crab meat, drained

2 eggs

2 garlic cloves, crushed

4 green onions, trimmed and chopped

1 tbsp fish sauce

1 tbsp chopped fresh cilantro leaves and stems

1 tbsp dark brown sugar

salt and pepper

TO GARNISH

finely sliced white radish (daikon) or turnip

chives

red chili

sprigs of fresh cilantro

1 Mix the coconut with 3 tbsp of hot water. Stir to dissolve the coconut.

2 Put the pork, chicken, and crab meat into a food processor or blender and process for 10–15 seconds until ground, or chop them finely by hand and put in a mixing bowl.

3 Add the coconut mixture to the food processor or blender with the eggs, garlic, green onions, fish sauce, cilantro, and sugar. Season to taste and process for a few more seconds. Alternatively, mix these ingredients into the chopped pork, chicken, and crab meat.

4 Grease 6 ramekin dishes with a little butter. Spoon in the ground mixture, leveling the surface. Place them in a steamer, then set the steamer over a pan of gently boiling water. Cook until set—about 30 minutes.

5 Lift out the dishes and leave to cool for a few minutes. Run a knife around the edge of each dish, then invert onto warmed plates. Serve garnished with finely sliced white radish (daikon) or turnip, chives, red chili, and sprigs of fresh cilantro.

Crispy-Fried Vegetables

A hot and sweet dipping sauce makes the perfect accompaniment to fresh vegetables coated in a light batter and deep-fried.

NUTRITIONAL INFORMATION

Calories	258	Sugars	........11g
Protein	.........6g	Fat	...........9g
Carbohydrate	...39g	Saturates	......11g

 40 MINS   10 MINS

SERVES 4

I N G R E D I E N T S

vegetable oil for deep-frying

1 lb 2 oz selection of vegetables, such as cauliflower, broccoli, mushrooms, zucchini, bell peppers and baby corn-on-the-cob, cut into even-sized pieces

B A T T E R

1 cup all-purpose flour

½ tsp salt

1 tsp sugar

1 tsp baking powder

3 tbsp vegetable oil

scant 1 cup warm water

S A U C E

6 tbsp light malt vinegar

2 tbsp fish sauce or light soy sauce

2 tbsp water

1 tbsp soft brown sugar

pinch of salt

2 garlic cloves, crushed

2 tsp grated fresh ginger

2 red chilies, seeded and chopped finely

2 tbsp chopped fresh cilantro

1 To make the batter, sift the flour, salt, sugar, and baking powder into a bowl. Add the oil and most of the water. Whisk together to make a smooth batter, adding extra water to give it the consistency of light cream. Chill for 20–30 minutes.

2 Meanwhile, make the sauce. Heat the vinegar, fish sauce or soy sauce, water, sugar, and salt until boiling. Remove from the heat and leave to cool.

3 Mix together the garlic, ginger, chilies, and cilantro. Add the cooled vinegar mixture and stir well to combine.

4 Heat the oil for deep-frying in a wok. Dip the vegetables in the batter and fry, in batches, until crisp and golden—about 2 minutes. Drain on paper towels. Serve the vegetables accompanied by the dipping sauce.

Pork Satay

Small pieces of tender pork are skewered on bamboo satay sticks, broiled or grilled, then served with a delicious peanut sauce.

NUTRITIONAL INFORMATION

Calories	397	Sugars	.........8g
Protein	........35g	Fat	..........24g
Carbohydrate	....11g	Saturates	.......6g

 10 MINS   15 MINS

SERVES 4

INGREDIENTS

8 bamboo satay sticks, soaked in warm water

1 lb 2 oz pork tenderloin

SAUCE

1 cup unsalted peanuts

2 tsp hot chili sauce

¾ cup coconut milk

2 tbsp soy sauce

1 tbsp ground coriander

pinch of ground turmeric

1 tbsp dark brown sugar

salt

TO GARNISH

fresh flat leaved (Italian) parsley or cilantro

cucumber leaves

red chilies

1 To make the sauce, scatter the peanuts on a cookie sheet and toast under a preheated broiler until golden brown, turning them once or twice. Leave to cool, then grind them in a food processor, blender or food mill. Alternatively, chop the peanuts very finely.

2 Put the ground peanuts into a small saucepan with the hot chili sauce, coconut milk, soy sauce, coriander, turmeric, sugar, and salt. Heat gently, stirring constantly and taking care not to burn the sauce on the bottom of the pan. Reduce the heat to very low and cook gently for 5 minutes.

3 Meanwhile, trim any fat from the pork. Cut the pork into small cubes and thread it onto the bamboo satay sticks. Place the kabobs on a rack covered with foil in a broiler pan.

4 Put half the peanut sauce into a small serving bowl. Brush the skewered pork with the remaining satay sauce and place under a preheated broiler for about 10 minutes, turning and basting frequently, until cooked.

5 Serve the pork with the reserved peanut sauce and garnish with flat leaved parsley or cilantro leaves, cucumber leaves, and red chilies.

COOK'S TIP

To make cucumber leaves, slice a thick chunk from the side of a cucumber, and cut to shape. Cut grooves in the cucumber flesh in the shape of leaf veins.

Sweet & Sour Pork Ribs

Here I have used the spare rib, the traditional Chinese-style rib. Baby back ribs and loin ribs are also suitable in this recipe.

NUTRITIONAL INFORMATION

Calories ....565 Sugars 29g
Protein ....24g Fat 37g
Carbohydrate ...32g Saturates 14g

2¼ HOURS   50 MINS

SERVES 4

INGREDIENTS

2 garlic cloves, crushed

2 inch piece ginger, grated

⅔ cup soy sauce

2 tbsp sugar

4 tbsp sweet sherry

4 tbsp tomato paste

2 cups pineapple, cubed

4 lb 8 oz pork spare ribs

3 tbsp honey

5 pineapple rings, fresh or canned, to serve

1 Mix together the garlic, ginger, soy sauce, sugar, sherry, tomato paste, and cubed pineapple in a glass dish.

2 Put the spare ribs into the dish and make sure that they are coated completely with the marinade.

3 Cover the dish with plastic wrap.

4 Leave the ribs to marinate at room temperature for 2 hours only.

5 Cook the ribs over a medium grill for 30–40 minutes, brushing with the honey after 20–30 minutes.

6 Baste the spare ribs with the reserved marinade frequently until cooked.

7 Cook the pineapple rings over the grill for about 10 minutes, turning once.

8 Transfer the sweet & sour ribs to a serving dish and serve with the grilled pineapple rings on the side.

COOK'S TIP

If a marinade contains soy sauce, the marinating time should be limited, usually to 2 hours. If allowed to marinate for too long, the meat will dry out and become tough.

Lentil Balls with Sauce

Crisp golden lentil balls are served in a sweet and sour sauce with bell peppers and pineapple chunks.

NUTRITIONAL INFORMATION

Calories	384	Sugars	........15g
Protein	........17g	Fat	..........14g
Carbohydrate	...49g	Saturates	.......2g

15 MINS   35 MINS

SERVES 4

I N G R E D I E N T S

1 cup red lentils

scant 2 cups water

½ green chili, seeded and chopped

4 green onions, chopped finely

1 garlic clove, crushed

1 tsp salt

4 tbsp pineapple juice from can

1 egg, beaten

vegetable oil for deep-frying

rice or noodles, to serve

S A U C E

3 tbsp white wine vinegar

2 tbsp sugar

2 tbsp tomato paste

1 tsp sesame oil

1 tsp cornstarch

½ tsp salt

6 tbsp water

2 tbsp vegetable oil

½ red bell pepper, cut into chunks

½ green bell pepper, cut into chunks

2 canned pineapple rings, cut into chunks

1 Wash the lentils, then place in a saucepan with the water, and bring to a boil. Skim and boil rapidly for 10 minutes, uncovered. Reduce the heat and simmer for 5 minutes until you have a fairly dry mixture, stirring occasionally.

2 Remove from the heat and stir in the chili, green onions, garlic, salt, and pineapple juice. Leave to cool for 10 minutes.

3 To make the sauce, mix together the vinegar, sugar, tomato paste, sesame oil, cornstarch, salt, and water, and set aside.

4 Add the beaten egg to the lentil mixture. Heat the oil in a large pan or wok and deep-fry tablespoonfuls of the mixture in batches until crisp and golden. Remove with a perforated spoon and drain on paper towels.

5 Heat the 2 tablespoons oil in a wok or skillet. Stir-fry the bell peppers for 2 minutes. Add the sauce mixture with the pineapple chunks. Bring to a boil, then reduce the heat and simmer for 1 minute, stirring constantly, until the sauce has thickened. Add the lentil balls and heat thoroughly, being careful not to break them up. Serve with rice or noodles.

Shrimp Omelet

This is called *Foo Yung* in China and is a classic dish which may be flavored with any ingredients you have available.

NUTRITIONAL INFORMATION

Calories	320	Sugars	.........1g
Protein	........31g	Fat	..........18g
Carbohydrate	....8g	Saturates	.......4g

 5 MINS   🕐 10 MINS

SERVES 4

I N G R E D I E N T S

3 tbsp sunflower oil

2 leeks, trimmed and sliced

12 oz raw jumbo shrimp

4 tbsp cornstarch

1 tsp salt

6 oz mushrooms, sliced

1½ cups bean sprouts

6 eggs

deep-fried leeks, to garnish (optional)

1 Heat the sunflower oil in a preheated wok or large skillet. Add the sliced leeks and stir-fry for 3 minutes.

2 Rinse the shrimp under cold running water and then pat dry with absorbent paper towels.

3 Mix together the cornstarch and salt in a large bowl.

4 Add the shrimp to the cornstarch and salt mixture and toss to coat all over.

5 Add the shrimp to the wok or skillet and stir-fry for 2 minutes, or until the shrimp are almost cooked through.

6 Add the mushrooms and bean sprouts to the wok and stir-fry for 2 minutes.

7 Beat the eggs with 3 tablespoons of cold water. Pour the egg mixture into the wok and cook until the egg sets, carefully turning over once. Turn the omelet out onto a clean board, divide into 4, and serve hot, garnished with deep-fried leeks (if using).

VARIATION

If you like, divide the mixture into 4 once the initial cooking has taken place in step 6 and cook 4 individual omelets.

Chicken or Beef Satay

In this dish, strips of chicken or beef are threaded onto skewers, broiled, and served with a spicy peanut sauce.

NUTRITIONAL INFORMATION

Calories	314	Sugars	.........8g
Protein	........32g	Fat	..........16g
Carbohydrate	...10g	Saturates	.......4g

  2¼ HOURS   15 MINS

SERVES 6

I N G R E D I E N T S

4 boneless, skinned chicken breasts or
  1 lb 10 oz rump steak, trimmed

M A R I N A D E

1 small onion, finely chopped

1 garlic clove, crushed

1 inch piece fresh ginger, peeled
  and grated

2 tbsp dark soy sauce

2 tsp chili powder

1 tsp ground coriander

2 tsp dark brown sugar

1 tbsp lemon or lime juice

1 tbsp vegetable oil

S A U C E

1¼ cups coconut milk

⅓ cup crunchy peanut butter

1 tbsp fish sauce

1 tsp lemon or lime juice

salt and pepper

1 Using a sharp knife, trim any fat from the chicken or beef then cut into thin strips, about 3 inches long.

2 To make the marinade, place all the ingredients in a shallow dish and mix well. Add the chicken or beef strips and turn in the marinade until well coated.

 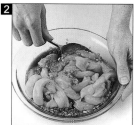 

Cover with plastic wrap and leave to marinate for 2 hours or place overnight in the refrigerator.

3 Remove the meat from the marinade and thread the pieces, accordian style, on pre-soaked bamboo or thin wooden skewers.

4 Broil the chicken and beef satays for 8-10 minutes, turning and brushing

occasionally with the marinade, until cooked through.

5 Meanwhile, to make the sauce, mix the coconut milk with the peanut butter, fish sauce, and lemon or lime juice in a saucepan. Bring to a boil and cook for 3 minutes. Season to taste.

6 Transfer the sauce to a serving bowl and serve with the cooked satays.

Vegetable Rolls

In this recipe a mixed vegetable stuffing is wrapped in Chinese cabbage and steamed until tender.

NUTRITIONAL INFORMATION

Calories 69	Sugars 1g	
Protein 2g	Fat 5g	
Carbohydrate 3g	Saturates 1g	

 10 MINS   20 MINS

SERVES 4

INGREDIENTS

8 large Chinese cabbage

FILLING

2 baby corn-on-the-cob, sliced

1 carrot, finely chopped

1 celery stalk, chopped

4 green onions, chopped

4 water chestnuts, chopped

2 tbsp unsalted cashews, chopped

1 garlic clove, chopped

1 tsp grated fresh ginger

1 oz canned bamboo shoots, drained, rinsed and chopped

1 tsp sesame oil

2 tsp soy sauce

1 Place the Chinese cabbage in a large bowl and pour over boiling water to soften them. Leave to stand for 1 minute and drain thoroughly.

2 Mix together the baby corn-on-the-cob, chopped carrot, celery, green onions, water chestnuts, cashews, ginger, garlic, and bamboo shoots in a large bowl.

3 In a separate bowl, mix together the sesame oil and soy sauce. Add this mixture to the vegetables, mixing well until the vegetables are thoroughly coated in the mixture.

4 Spread out the Chinese cabbage on a cutting board and spoon an equal quantity of the filling mixture onto each leaf.

5 Roll the Chinese cabbage up, folding in the sides neatly. Secure the rolls with toothpicks.

6 Place the filled rolls in a small heatproof dish in a steamer, cover, and cook for 15–20 minutes, until the rolls are cooked.

7 Transfer the vegetable rolls to a warm serving dish and serve with a soy or chili sauce.

Crudites with Shrimp Sauce

In this recipe, fruit and vegetable crudités are served with a spicy, garlicky shrimp sauce.

NUTRITIONAL INFORMATION

Calories . . . . .85 Sugars 11g
Protein . . . . .7g Fat 1g
Carbohydrate . . .12g Saturates 0.2g

12¼ HOURS   0 MINS

SERVES 4

I N G R E D I E N T S

about 1 lb10 oz prepared
    raw fruit and vegetables, such
    as broccoli, cauliflower, apple,
    pineapple, cucumber, celery, bell
    peppers, and mushrooms

S A U C E

2 oz dried shrimp

½ inch cube shrimp paste

3 garlic cloves, crushed

4 red chilies, seeded and chopped

6 stems fresh cilantro,
    coarsely chopped

juice of 2 limes

fish sauce, to taste

brown sugar, to taste

1 Soak the dried shrimp in warm water for 10 minutes.

2 To make the sauce, place the shrimp paste, drained shrimp, garlic, chilies, and cilantro in a food processor or blender and process until well chopped but not smooth.

3 Turn the sauce mixture into a bowl and add the lime juice, mixing well.

4 Add fish sauce and brown sugar to taste to the sauce. Mix well.

5 Cover the bowl tightly and chill the sauce in the refrigerator for at least 12 hours, or overnight.

6 To serve, arrange the fruit and vegetables attractively on a large serving plate. Place the prepared sauce in the center for dipping.

COOK'S TIP

Hard-cooked quail's eggs
are often added to this
traditional fruit and vegetable
platter and certainly would be
offered on a special occasion.

Asparagus Parcels

These small parcels are ideal as part of a main meal and irresistible as a quick snack with extra plum sauce for dipping.

NUTRITIONAL INFORMATION

Calories 194	Sugars 2g
Protein 3g	Fat 16g
Carbohydrate 11g	Saturates 4g

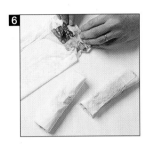

 5 MINS   25 MINS

SERVES 4

I N G R E D I E N T S

3½ oz thin asparagus

1 red bell pepper, seeded and thinly sliced

½ cup bean sprouts

2 tbsp plum sauce

1 egg yolk

8 sheets phyllo pastry

oil, for deep-frying

1 Place the asparagus, bell pepper, and bean sprouts in a large mixing bowl.

2 Add the plum sauce to the vegetables and mix until well-combined.

3 Beat the egg yolk and set aside until required.

4 Lay the sheets of phyllo pastry out onto a clean work counter.

5 Place a little of the asparagus and red bell pepper filling at the top end of each phyllo pastry sheet. Brush the edges of the pastry with a little of the beaten egg yolk.

6 Roll up the phyllo pastry, tucking in the ends and enclosing the filling like a spring roll. Repeat with the remaining phyllo sheets.

7 Heat the oil for deep-frying in a large preheated wok. Carefully cook the parcels, 2 at a time, in the hot oil for 4–5 minutes or until crispy.

8 Remove the parcels with a slotted spoon and leave to drain on absorbent paper towels.

9 Transfer the parcels to warm serving plates and serve immediately.

COOK'S TIP

Be sure to use thin-tipped asparagus as it is more tender than the larger stems.

Chicken Wontons

These deliciously crispy nibbles make an ideal introduction to a Chinese meal. Here they are filled with a chicken and mushroom mixture.

NUTRITIONAL INFORMATION

Calories 285   Sugars 1g
Protein . . . . .16g   Fat 19g
Carbohydrate . . .14g   Saturates 5g

20 MINS   35 MINS

SERVES 4

I N G R E D I E N T S

9 oz boneless chicken breast, skinned

⅔ cup mushrooms

1 garlic clove

2 shallots

1 tbsp fish sauce or oyster mushroom
   sauce

1 tbsp chopped fresh cilantro

2 tbsp vegetable oil

about 50 wonton skins

oil, for deep-frying

salt and pepper

sliced green onion, to garnish

sweet chili sauce, to serve

1 Put the chicken, mushrooms, garlic, shallots, fish sauce or mushroom sauce, and cilantro into a blender or food processor. Blend for 10–15 seconds. Alternatively, chop all the ingredients finely and mix together well.

2 Heat the vegetable oil in a wok or skillet and add the chicken mixture. Stir-fry for about 8 minutes, breaking up the mixture as it cooks, until it browns. Transfer to a bowl and leave to cool for 10–15 minutes.

3 Place the wonton skins on a clean, damp tea towel. Layering 2 skins

together at a time, place teaspoonfuls of the chicken mixture into the middle. Dampen the edges with water, then make small pouches, pressing the edges together to seal. Repeat with the remaining skins until all the mixture is used.

4 Heat the oil for deep-frying in a wok or deep fat fryer. Fry the wontons, a few at a time, for about 2–3 minutes until golden brown. Remove the wontons

from the oil with a perforated spoon and drain on paper towels. Keep warm while frying the remaining wontons.

5 Transfer the wontons to a warmed serving platter and garnish with the sliced green onion. Serve immediately, accompanied by some sweet chili sauce.

Deep-fried Chili Corn Balls

These small corn balls have a wonderful hot and sweet flavor, offset by the pungent cilantro.

NUTRITIONAL INFORMATION

Calories 248	Sugars 6g
Protein 6g	Fat 12
Carbohydrate ...30g	Saturates 5g

 15 MINS   30 MINS

SERVES 4

INGREDIENTS

6 green onions, sliced

3 tbsp fresh cilantro, chopped

8 oz canned corn kernels

1 tsp mild chili powder

1 tbsp sweet chili sauce

¼ cup shredded coconut

1 egg

⅓ cup cornmeal

oil, for deep-frying

extra sweet chili sauce, to serve

1 In a large bowl, mix together the green onions, cilantro, corn, chili powder, chili sauce, coconut, egg, and cornmeal until well blended.

2 Cover the bowl with plastic wrap and leave to stand for about 10 minutes.

3 Heat the oil for deep-frying in a large preheated wok or skillet to 350°F or until a cube of bread browns in 30 seconds.

4 Carefully drop spoonfuls of the chili and cornmeal mixture into the hot oil. Deep-fry the chili corn balls, in batches, for 4–5 minutes or until crispy and a deep golden brown color.

5 Remove the chili corn balls with a slotted spoon, transfer to absorbent paper towels, and leave to drain thoroughly.

6 Transfer the chili corn balls to serving plates and serve with an extra sweet chili sauce for dipping.

COOK'S TIP

For safe deep-frying in a round-bottomed wok, place it on a wok rack so that it rests securely. Only half-fill the wok with oil. Never leave the wok unattended over a high heat.

Sesame Ginger Chicken

Chunks of chicken breast are marinated in a mixture of lime juice, garlic, sesame oil, and fresh ginger to give them a great flavor.

NUTRITIONAL INFORMATION

Calories	204	Sugars	.........0g
Protein	........28g	Fat	..........10g
Carbohydrate	....1g	Saturates	.......2g

   2¼ HOURS   10 MINS

SERVES 4

INGREDIENTS

4 wooden satay sticks, soaked in
    warm water

1 lb 2 oz boneless chicken breasts

sprigs of fresh mint, to garnish

MARINADE

1 garlic clove, crushed

1 shallot, chopped very finely

2 tbsp sesame oil

1 tbsp fish sauce or light soy sauce

finely grated zest of 1 lime or
    ½ lemon

2 tbsp lime juice or lemon juice

1 tsp sesame seeds

2 tsp finely grated fresh ginger

2 tsp chopped fresh mint

salt and pepper

1 To make the marinade, put the crushed garlic, chopped shallot, sesame oil, fish sauce or soy sauce, lime or lemon zest and juice, sesame seeds, grated fresh ginger, and chopped mint into a large non-metallic bowl. Season with a little salt and pepper and mix together until all the ingredients are thoroughly combined.

2 Remove the skin from the chicken breasts and cut the flesh into chunks.

3 Add the chicken to the marinade, stirring to coat the chicken completely in the mixture. Cover with plastic wrap and chill in the refrigerator for at least 2 hours so the flavors are absorbed.

4 Thread the chicken onto wooden satay sticks. Place them on the rack of a broiler pan and baste with the marinade.

5 Place the kabobs under a preheated broiler for about 8–10 minutes. Turn them frequently, basting them with the remaining marinade.

6 Serve the chicken skewers immediately, garnished with sprigs of fresh mint.

COOK'S TIP

The kabobs taste delicious if dipped into an accompanying bowl of hot chili sauce.

Deep-Fried Spare Ribs

The spare ribs should be chopped into small bite-sized pieces before or after cooking.

NUTRITIONAL INFORMATION

Calories 177	Sugars 0.2g
Protein 6g	Fat 14g
Carbohydrate 6g	Saturates 4g

5 MINS

2¼ HOURS

SERVES 4

INGREDIENTS

8-10 finger spare ribs

1 tsp five-spice powder or 1 tbsp mild curry powder

1 tbsp rice wine or dry sherry

1 egg

2 tbsp flour

vegetable oil, for deep-frying

1 tsp finely shredded green onions

1 tsp finely shredded fresh green or red hot chilies, seeded

salt and pepper

Spicy Salt and Pepper (see page 76), to serve

1 Chop the ribs into 3-4 small pieces. Place the ribs in a bowl with salt, pepper, five-spice or curry powder, and the wine. Turn to coat the ribs in the spices and leave to marinate for 1-2 hours.

2 Mix the egg and flour together to make a batter. Dip the ribs in the batter one by one to coat well.

3 Heat the oil in a preheated wok until smoking. Deep-fry the ribs for 4-5 minutes, then remove with chopsticks or a slotted spoon and drain on paper towels.

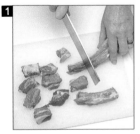

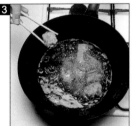

4 Reheat the oil over a high heat and deep-fry the ribs once more for another minute. Remove and drain again on paper towels.

5 Pour 1 tablespoon of the hot oil over the green onions and chilies and leave for 30-40 seconds. Serve the ribs with Spicy Salt and Pepper, garnished with the shredded green onions and chilies.

COOK'S TIP

To make finger ribs, cut the sheet of spare ribs into individual ribs down each side of the bones. These ribs are then chopped into bite-sized pieces for deep-frying.

Crab Ravioli

These small packages are made from wonton skins, filled with mixed vegetables and crab meat for a melt-in-the-mouth first course.

NUTRITIONAL INFORMATION

Calories 292   Sugars 1g
Protein ....25g   Fat 17g
Carbohydrate ....11g Saturates 5g

20 MINS   25 MINS

SERVES 4

INGREDIENTS

1 lb crab meat (fresh or canned and drained)

½ red bell pepper, seeded and finely diced

4½ oz Chinese cabbage, shredded

1 oz bean sprouts, roughly chopped

1 tbsp light soy sauce

1 tsp lime juice

16 wonton skins

1 small egg, beaten

2 tbsp peanut oil

1 tsp sesame oil

salt and pepper

1 Mix together the crab meat, bell pepper, Chinese cabbage, bean sprouts, soy sauce and lime juice. Season and leave to stand for 15 minutes.

2 Spread out the wonton skins on a work counter. Spoon a little of the crab meat mixture into the center of each skin. Brush the edges with egg and fold in half, pushing out any air. Press the edges together to seal.

3 Heat the peanut oil in a preheated wok or skillet. Fry the ravioli, in batches, for 3–4 minutes, turning, until browned. Remove with a slotted spoon and drain on paper towels.

4 Heat any remaining filling in the wok or skillet over a gentle heat until hot. Serve the ravioli with the hot filling and sprinkled with sesame oil.

COOK'S TIP

Make sure that the edges of the ravioli are sealed well and that all of the air is pressed out to prevent them from opening during cooking.

Pork Sesame Toasts

This classic Chinese appetizer makes a great nibble for serving at parties—but be sure to make plenty!

NUTRITIONAL INFORMATION

Calories	...... .674	Sugars	.... .2g
Protein	........33g	Fat	.... .46g
Carbohydrate	...33g	Saturates	.... .7g

5 MINS   35 MINS

SERVES 4

I N G R E D I E N T S

9 oz lean pork

⅔ cup uncooked peeled shrimp, deveined

4 green onions, trimmed

1 garlic clove, crushed

1 tbsp chopped fresh cilantro leaves and stems

1 tbsp fish sauce

1 egg

8–10 slices of thick-cut white bread

3 tbsp sesame seeds

⅔ cup vegetable oil

salt and pepper

T O   G A R N I S H

sprigs of fresh cilantro

red bell pepper, sliced finely

1 Put the pork, shrimp, green onions, garlic, cilantro, fish sauce, egg, and seasoning into a food processor or blender. Process for a few seconds until the ingredients are finely chopped. Transfer the mixture to a bowl. Alternatively, chop the pork, shrimp, and green onions very finely, and mix with the garlic, cilantro, fish sauce, beaten egg, and seasoning until all the ingredients are well combined.

2 Spread the pork and shrimp mixture thickly over the bread so that it reaches right up to the edges. Cut off the crusts and slice each piece of bread into 4 squares or triangles.

3 Sprinkle the topping liberally with sesame seeds.

4 Heat the oil in a wok or skillet. Fry a few pieces of the bread, topping side down first so that it sets the egg, for about 2 minutes or until golden brown. Turn the pieces over to cook on the other side, about 1 minute.

5 Drain the pork and shrimp toasts and place them on paper towels. Fry the remaining pieces. Serve garnished with sprigs of fresh cilantro and strips of red bell pepper.

Seven Spice Eggplant

This is a really simple dish which is perfect served with a chili dip.

NUTRITIONAL INFORMATION

Calories 169	Sugars 2g	
Protein 2g	Fat 12g	
Carbohydrate ...15g	Saturates 1g	

 35 MINS   20 MINS

SERVES 4

I N G R E D I E N T S

1 lb eggplants, wiped

1 egg white

3½ tbsp cornstarch

1 tsp salt

1 tbsp seven spice seasoning

oil, for deep-frying

1 Using a sharp knife, thinly slice the eggplants. Place the eggplant in a colander, sprinkle with salt, and leave to stand for 30 minutes. This will remove all the bitter juices.

2 Rinse the eggplant thoroughly and pat dry with absorbent paper towels.

3 Place the egg white in a small bowl and whip until light and foamy.

4 Using a spoon, mix together the cornstarch, salt, and seven spice powder on a large plate.

5 Heat the oil for deep-frying in a large preheated wok or heavy-bottomed skillet.

6 Dip the eggplants into the egg white, and then into the cornstarch and seven spice mixture to coat evenly.

7 Deep-fry the coated eggplant slices, in batches, for 5 minutes, or until pale golden and crispy.

8 Transfer the eggplants to absorbent paper towels and leave to drain. Transfer the seven spice eggplants to serving plates and serve hot.

COOK'S TIP

The best oil to use for deep-frying is peanut oil which has a high smoke point and mild flavor, so it will neither burn or taint the food. About 1 pint oil is sufficient.

Chinese Potato Sticks

These potato sticks are a variation of the great Western favorite, being flavored with soy sauce and chili.

NUTRITIONAL INFORMATION

Calories	326	Sugars	.........1g
Protein	.........4g	Fat	.........22g
Carbohydrate	...29g	Saturates	.......3g

  10 MINS   15 MINS

SERVES 4

INGREDIENTS

1 lb 7 oz medium-size potatoes

8 tbsp vegetable oil

1 fresh red chili, halved

1 small onion, quartered

2 garlic cloves, halved

2 tbsp soy sauce

pinch of salt

1 tsp wine vinegar

1 tbsp coarse sea salt

pinch of chili powder

1 Peel the potatoes and cut into thin slices along their length. Cut the slices into thin sticks.

2 Bring a saucepan of water to a boil and blanch the potato sticks for 2 minutes, drain, rinse under cold water, and drain well again. Pat the potato sticks thoroughly dry with absorbent paper towels.

3 Heat the oil in a preheated wok until it is almost smoking. Add the chili, onion, and garlic and stir-fry for 30 seconds. Remove and discard the chili, onion, and garlic.

4 Add the potato sticks to the oil and fry for 3–4 minutes, or until golden.

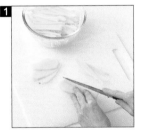  

5 Add the soy sauce, salt and vinegar to the wok, reduce the heat, and fry for 1 minute, or until the potatoes are crisp.

6 Remove the potatoes with a slotted spoon and leave to drain on absorbent paper towels.

7 Transfer the potato sticks to a serving dish, sprinkle with the sea salt and chili powder, and serve.

VARIATION

Sprinkle other flavorings over the cooked potato sticks, such as curry powder, or serve with a chili dip.

Rice Cubes with Sauce

Plain rice cubes are a good contrast to any piquant dipping sauce, and they are often served with satay, to complement the dipping sauce.

NUTRITIONAL INFORMATION

Calories 317   Sugars 3g
Protein . . . . .10g   Fat 10g
Carbohydrate . . .49g   Saturates 2g

🐷 🐷 🐷 🐷

🍲 8¼ HOURS   🕐 25 MINS

SERVES 4

INGREDIENTS

1½ cups jasmine rice

5 cups water

CILANTRO DIPPING SAUCE

1 garlic clove

2 tsp salt

1 tbsp black peppercorns

1 cup washed cilantro, including roots and stem

3 tbsp lemon juice

¾ cup coconut milk

2 tbsp peanut butter

2 green onions, chopped roughly

1 red chili, seeded and sliced

1 Grease and line a 8 x 4 x 1 inch pan.

2 To make the sauce, grind together the garlic, salt, peppercorns, cilantro, and lemon juice in a pestle and mortar or blender.

3 Add the coconut milk, peanut butter, green onions, and chili. Grind finely. Transfer to a saucepan and bring to a boil. Leave to cool.

4 To cook the rice, do not rinse. Bring the water to a boil and add the rice.

 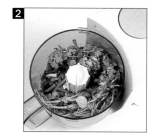 

Stir and return to a medium boil. Cook, uncovered, for 14–16 minutes until very soft. Drain thoroughly.

5 Put ²/₃ cup of the cooked rice in a blender and purée until smooth. Alternatively, grind to a paste in a pestle and mortar.

6 Stir into the remaining cooked rice and spoon into the lined pan. Level the

surface and cover with plastic wrap. Compress the rice by using either a smaller-sized pan or a small cutting board, and weigh this down with cans. Chill in the refrigerator for at least 8 hours or preferably overnight.

7 Invert the pan onto a board. Cut the rice into cubes with a wet knife. Serve with the cilantro dipping sauce.

Sweet & Sour Shrimp

Shrimp are marinated in a soy sauce mixture then coated in a light batter, fried, and served with a delicious sweet-and-sour dip.

NUTRITIONAL INFORMATION

Calories	294	Sugars	.......11g
Protein	........14g	Fat	..........12g
Carbohydrate	...34g	Saturates	.......2g

40 MINS   20 MINS

SERVES 4

INGREDIENTS

16 large raw shrimp, peeled

1 tsp grated fresh ginger

1 garlic clove, crushed

2 green onions, sliced

2 tbsp dry sherry

2 tsp sesame oil

1 tbsp light soy sauce

vegetable oil, for deep-frying

shredded green onion, to garnish

BATTER

4 egg whites

4 tbsp cornstarch

2 tbsp all-purpose flour

SAUCE

2 tbsp tomato paste

3 tbsp white wine vinegar

4 tsp light soy sauce

2 tbsp lemon juice

3 tbsp light brown sugar

1 green bell pepper, seeded and cut into thin sticks

½ tsp chili sauce

1¼ cups vegetable stock

2 tsp cornstarch

1 Using tweezers, devein the shrimp, then flatten them with a large knife.

2 Place the shrimp in a dish and add the ginger, garlic, green onions, dry sherry, sesame oil, and soy sauce. Cover with plastic wrap and leave to marinate for 30 minutes.

3 Make the batter by beating the egg whites until thick. Fold in the cornstarch and all-purpose flour to form a light batter.

4 Place all of the sauce ingredients in a saucepan and bring to a boil. Reduce the heat and leave to simmer for 10 minutes.

5 Remove the shrimp from the marinade and dip them into the batter to coat.

6 Heat the vegetable oil in a preheated wok or large skillet until almost smoking. Reduce the heat and fry the shrimp for 3–4 minutes, until crisp and golden brown.

7 Garnish the shrimp with shredded green onion and serve with the sauce.

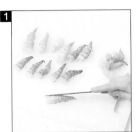

Salads & Pickles

Vegetables play an important part of the Chinese diet and although salads, as we know them in the West, do not feature greatly on the Chinese menu, many lightly cooked

vegetable dishes can be classified as salads when allowed to cool and are lightly tossed in dressing. The freshest vegetables and brief cooking ensure the necessary balance of texture and flavor, while dressings add a touch of sharpness and acidity. Pickled vegetables are very popular in China. They are often served as snacks and hors d'eouvres, and can also be served with cold meat dishes. Once made, they will keep in the refrigerator for up to 2 weeks.

Shrimp Salad

Noodles and bean sprouts form the basis of this refreshing salad which combines the flavors of fruit and shrimp.

NUTRITIONAL INFORMATION

Calories 359	Sugars 4g
Protein 31g	Fat 15g
Carbohydrate . . .25g	Saturates 2g

 15 MINS   5 MINS

SERVES 4

I N G R E D I E N T S

9 oz fine egg noodles

3 tbsp sunflower oil

1 tbsp sesame oil

1 tbsp sesame seeds

1½ cups bean sprouts

1 ripe mango, sliced

6 green onions, sliced

2¾ oz radish, sliced

12 oz peeled cooked shrimp

2 tbsp light soy sauce

1 tbsp sherry

1 Place the egg noodles in a large bowl and pour over enough boiling water to cover. Leave to stand for 10 minutes.

2 Drain the noodles thoroughly and pat dry with paper towels.

COOK'S TIP

If fresh mango is unavailable, use canned mango slices, rinsed and drained, instead.

3 Heat the sunflower oil in a large wok or skillet and stir-fry the noodles for 5 minutes. tossing frequently.

4 Remove the wok from the heat and add the sesame oil, sesame seeds, and bean sprouts, tossing to mix well.

5 In a separate bowl, mix together the sliced mango, green onions, radish and shrimp. Stir in the light soy sauce and sherry and mix until thoroughly combined.

6 Toss the shrimp mixture with the noodles and transfer to a serving dish. Alternatively, arrange the noodles around the edge of a serving plate and pile the shrimp mixture into the center. Serve immediately because this salad is best eaten warm.

Sweet & Sour Tofu Salad

Tofu is a delicious, healthy alternative to meat. Mixed with crisp stir-fried vegetables it makes an ideal light meal or first course.

NUTRITIONAL INFORMATION

Calories	262	Sugars	........15g
Protein	........16g	Fat	..........14g
Carbohydrate	...19g	Saturates	.......2g

   10 MINS   15 MINS

SERVES 4

I N G R E D I E N T S

2 tbsp vegetable oil

1 garlic clove, crushed

1 lb 2 oz tofu, cubed

1 onion, sliced

1 carrot, cut into julienne strips

1 stalk celery, sliced

2 small red bell peppers, cored, seeded, and sliced

9 oz snow peas, trimmed and halved

4½ oz broccoli, trimmed and divided into flowerets

4½ oz green beans, halved

2 tbsp oyster sauce

1 tbsp tamarind concentrate

1 tbsp fish sauce

1 tbsp tomato paste

1 tbsp light soy sauce

1 tbsp chili sauce

2 tbsp sugar

1 tbsp white vinegar

pinch of ground star anise

1 tsp cornstarch

1¼ cups water

1 Heat the vegetable oil in a large, heavy-bottomed skillet or wok until hot.

2 Add the crushed garlic to the wok or pan and cook for a few seconds.

3 Add the tofu, in batches, and stir-fry over a gentle heat, until golden on all sides. Remove with a slotted spoon and keep warm.

4 Add the onion, carrot, celery, red bell pepper, snow peas, broccoli, and green beans to the pan and stir-fry for about 2-3 minutes or until tender-crisp.

5 Add the oyster sauce, tamarind concentrate, fish sauce, tomato paste, soy sauce, chili sauce, sugar, vinegar, and star anise, mixing well to blend. Stir-fry for 2 minutes longer.

6 Mix the cornstarch with the water and add to the pan with the fried tofu. Stir-fry gently until the sauce boils and thickens slightly.

7 Transfer the sweet and sour tofu salad to warm serving plates and serve immediately.

Chicken & Papaya Salad

Try this recipe with a selection of different fruits, for an equally tasty salad.

NUTRITIONAL INFORMATION

Calories 408	Sugars 8g
Protein 30g	Fat 28g
Carbohydrate . . .10g	Saturates 5g

  5 MINS   15 MINS

SERVES 4

I N G R E D I E N T S

4 skinless, boneless chicken breasts

1 red chili, seeded and chopped

1⅔ tbsp red wine vinegar

⅓ cup olive oil

1 papaya, peeled

1 avocado, peeled

4½ oz alfalfa sprouts

4½ oz bean sprouts

salt and pepper

T O   G A R N I S H

diced red bell pepper

diced cucumber

1 Poach the chicken breasts in boiling water for about 15 minutes or until cooked through.

2 Remove the chicken with a slotted spoon and set aside to cool.

3 To make the dressing, combine the chili, red wine vinegar, and olive oil, season well with salt and pepper, and set aside.

4 Place the chicken breasts on a cutting board. Using a very sharp knife, cut the chicken breasts across the grain into thin diagonal slices. Set aside.

5 Slice the papaya and avocado to the same thickness as the chicken.

6 Arrange the slices of papaya and avocado, together with the chicken, in an alternating pattern on four serving plates.

7 Arrange the alfalfa sprouts and bean sprouts on the serving plates and garnish with the diced red bell pepper and cucumber. Serve the salad with the dressing.

VARIATION

Try this recipe with peaches or nectarines instead of papaya.

Hot & Sour Duck Salad

This is a lovely tangy salad, drizzled with a lime juice and fish sauce dressing. It makes a splendid first course or a light main course dish.

NUTRITIONAL INFORMATION

Calories	236	Sugars	.........3g
Protein	........27g	Fat	..........10g
Carbohydrate	...10g	Saturates	.......3g

🍲 40 MINS   🕐 5 MINS

SERVES 4

INGREDIENTS

2 heads crisp salad lettuce, washed and separated into leaves

2 shallots, thinly sliced

4 green onions, chopped

1 celery stalk, finely sliced into julienne strips

2 inch piece cucumber, cut into julienne strips

4½ oz bean sprouts

1 x 7 oz can water chestnuts, drained and sliced

4 duck breast fillets, roasted and sliced (see page 183)

orange slices, to serve

DRESSING

3 tbsp fish sauce

1½ tbsp lime juice

2 garlic cloves, crushed

1 red chili pepper, seeded and very finely chopped

1 green chili pepper, seeded and very finely chopped

1 tsp brown sugar

1 Place the lettuce leaves into a large mixing bowl. Add the sliced shallots, chopped green onions, celery strips, cucumber strips, bean sprouts, and sliced water chestnuts. Toss well to mix. Place the mixture on a large serving platter.

2 Arrange the duck breast slices on top of the salad in an attractive overlapping pattern.

3 To make the dressing, put the fish sauce, lime juice, garlic, chilies, and sugar into a small saucepan. Heat gently, stirring constantly. Taste and adjust the piquancy if liked by adding more lime juice, or add more fish sauce to reduce the sharpness.

4 Drizzle the warm salad dressing over the duck salad and serve immediately with orange slices.

Oriental Salad

This colorful crisp salad has a fresh orange dressing and is topped with crunchy vermicelli.

NUTRITIONAL INFORMATION

Calories 139	Sugars 8g	
Protein 5g	Fat 7g	
Carbohydrate ...15g	Saturates 1g	

 10 MINS   5 MINS

SERVES 4

I N G R E D I E N T S

¼ cup dried vermicelli

½ head Chinese cabbage

2 cups bean sprouts

6 radishes

4½ oz snow peas

1 large carrot

4½ oz sprouting beans

D R E S S I N G

juice of 1 orange

1 tbsp sesame seeds, toasted

1 tsp honey

1 tsp sesame oil

1 tbsp hazelnut oil

1 Break the vermicelli into small strands. Heat a wok and dry-fry the vermicelli until lightly golden.

COOK'S TIP

Make your own sprouting beans by soaking mung and aduki beans overnight in cold water, then drain and rinse. Place in a large jar covered with cheesecloth to secure it. Lay the jar on its side and place in indirect light. For the next 3 days, rinse the beans once a day in cold water until they are ready to eat.

2 Remove from the pan with a slotted spoon and set aside until required.

3 Using a sharp knife or food processor, shred the Chinese cabbage and wash with the bean sprouts. Drain thoroughly and place the leaves and bean sprouts in a large mixing bowl.

4 Thinly slice the radishes. Trim the snow peas and cut each into 3 pieces.

Cut the carrot into thin sticks. Add the sprouting beans and prepared vegetables to the bowl.

5 Place all the dressing ingredients in a screw-top jar and shake until well-blended. Pour over the salad and toss.

6 Transfer the salad to a serving bowl and sprinkle over the reserved vermicelli before serving.

Papaya Salad

Choose firm papayas—or paw-paws as they are sometimes called—for this delicious salad.

NUTRITIONAL INFORMATION

Calories	193	Sugars	........11g
Protein	.........3g	Fat	.........15g
Carbohydrate	...12g	Saturates	.......2g

10 MINS   0 MINS

SERVES 4

I N G R E D I E N T S

D R E S S I N G

4 tbsp olive oil

1 tbsp fish sauce or light soy sauce

2 tbsp lime or lemon juice

1 tbsp dark brown sugar

1 tsp finely chopped fresh red or
   green chili

S A L A D

1 crisp lettuce

¼ small white cabbage

2 papayas

2 tomatoes

¼ cup roasted peanuts,
   chopped roughly

4 green onions, trimmed
   and sliced thinly

basil leaves, to garnish

1 To make the dressing, whisk together the oil, fish sauce or soy sauce, lime or lemon juice, sugar and chili. Set aside, stirring occasionally to dissolve the sugar.

2 Shred the lettuce and white cabbage, then toss together and arrange on a large serving plate.

3 Peel the papayas and slice them in half. Scoop out the seeds, then slice the flesh thinly. Arrange on top of the lettuce and cabbage.

4 Soak the tomatoes in a bowl of boiling water for 1 minute, then lift out and peel. Remove the seeds and chop the flesh. Arrange on the salad leaves.

5 Scatter the peanuts and green onions over the top. Whisk the dressing and pour over the salad. Garnish with basil leaves and serve immediately.

COOK'S TIP

Choose plain, unsalted peanuts and toast them under the broiler until golden to get the best flavor. Be careful not to burn them—they brown very quickly.

Chicken & Noodle Salad

Strips of chicken are coated in a delicious spicy mixture, then stir-fried with noodles and served on a bed of salad.

NUTRITIONAL INFORMATION

Calories	..217	Sugars	...1g
Protein	...21g	Fat	...11g
Carbohydrate	..9g	Saturates	...2g

 10 MINS   10 MINS

SERVES 4

I N G R E D I E N T S

1 tsp finely grated fresh ginger

½ tsp Chinese five-spice powder

1 tbsp all-purpose flour

½ tsp chili powder

12 oz boned chicken breast, skinned and sliced thinly

2 oz rice noodles

1½ cups Chinese cabbage or hard white cabbage, shredded finely

3 inch piece of cucumber, sliced finely

1 large carrot, pared thinly

1 tbsp olive oil

2 tbsp lime or lemon juice

2 tbsp sesame oil

salt and pepper

T O   G A R N I S H

lemon or lime slices

fresh cilantro leaves

1 Mix together the ginger, five-spice powder, flour, and chili powder in a shallow mixing bowl. Season with salt and pepper. Add the strips of chicken and roll in the mixture until well coated.

2 Put the noodles into a large bowl and cover with warm water. Leave to soak for about 5 minutes, then drain them well.

3 Mix together the Chinese cabbage or white cabbage, cucumber, and carrot, and arrange in a salad bowl. Whisk together the olive oil and lime or lemon juice, season with a salt and pepper, and use to dress the salad.

4 Heat the sesame oil in a wok or skillet and add the chicken. Stir-fry for 5–6 minutes until well-browned and crispy on the outside. Remove from the wok or skillet with a perforated spoon and drain on absorbent paper towels.

5 Add the noodles to the wok or skillet and stir-fry for 3–4 minutes until heated through. Remove from the wok, mix with the chicken, and pile the mixture on top of the salad. Serve garnished with lime or lemon slices and cilantro leaves.

Chinese Hot Salad

This salad can also be eaten cold—add 3-4 tablespoons French dressing as the vegetables cool, toss well and serve cold or chilled.

NUTRITIONAL INFORMATION

Calories	192	Sugars 13g
Protein	.........5g	Fat 9g
Carbohydrate	...20g	Saturates 1g

5 MINS   10 MINS

SERVES 4

INGREDIENTS

1 tbsp dark soy sauce

1½-2 tsp bottled sweet chili sauce

2 tbsp sherry

1 tbsp brown sugar

1 tbsp wine vinegar

2 tbsp sunflower oil

1 garlic clove, crushed

4 green onions, thinly sliced diagonally

9 oz zucchini, cut into julienne strips about 1½ inches long

9 oz carrots, cut into julienne strips about 1½ inches long

1 red or green bell pepper, cored, seeded, and thinly sliced

1 x 14 ½oz can bean sprouts, well drained

4½ oz green beans, cut into 2 inch lengths

1 tbsp sesame oil

salt and pepper

1-2 tsp sesame seeds, to garnish

1 Combine the soy sauce, chili sauce, sherry, sugar, vinegar, and seasoning.

2 Heat the 2 tablespoons of sunflower oil in a wok or large, heavy-bottomed skillet, swirling it around until it is really hot.

3 Add the garlic and green onions to the wok and stir-fry for 1-2 minutes.

4 Add the zucchini, carrots, and bell peppers and stir-fry for 1-2 minutes, then add the soy sauce mixture and bring to a boil.

5 Add the bean sprouts and green beans and stir-fry for 1-2 minutes, making sure all the vegetables are thoroughly coated with the sauce.

6 Drizzle the sesame oil over the vegetables in the wok and stir-fry for about 30 seconds.

7 Serve the salad hot, sprinkled with sesame seeds.

Potato & Chicken Salad

The spicy peanut dressing served with this salad may be prepared in advance and left to chill a day before required.

NUTRITIONAL INFORMATION

Calories	802	Sugars	........15g
Protein	........35g	Fat	..........55g
Carbohydrate	...45g	Saturates	......10g

5 MINS   15 MINS

SERVES 4

I N G R E D I E N T S

4 large waxy (boiling) potatoes

10½ oz fresh pineapple, diced

2 carrots, grated

6 oz bean sprouts

1 bunch green onions, sliced

1 large zucchini, cut into thin sticks

3 celery stalks, cut into thin sticks

6 oz unsalted peanuts

2 cooked chicken breast fillets, about 4½ oz each, sliced

D R E S S I N G

6 tbsp crunchy peanut butter

6 tbsp olive oil

2 tbsp light soy sauce

1 red chili, seeded and chopped

2 tsp sesame oil

4 tsp lime juice

COOK'S TIP

Unsweetened canned pineapple may be used instead of the fresh pineapple for convenience. If only sweetened canned pineapple is available, drain it and rinse under cold running water before using.

1 Using a sharp knife, cut the potatoes into small dice. Bring a saucepan of water to a boil.

2 Cook the diced potatoes in a saucepan of boiling water for 10 minutes or until tender. Drain and leave to cool until required.

3 Transfer the cooled potatoes to a salad bowl.

4 Add the pineapple, carrots, bean sprouts, green onions, zucchini, celery, peanuts, and sliced chicken to the potatoes. Toss well to mix all the salad ingredients together.

5 To make the dressing, put the peanut butter in a small mixing bowl and gradually whisk in the olive oil and light soy sauce.

6 Stir in the chopped red chili, sesame oil, and lime juice. Mix until well combined.

7 Pour the spicy dressing over the salad and toss lightly to coat all of the ingredients. Serve the potato and chicken salad immediately.

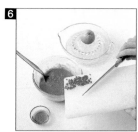

Gado Gado Salad

The vegetables in this salad can either be arranged in individual piles on the serving platter or mixed together.

NUTRITIONAL INFORMATION

Calories 450	Sugars 11g
Protein 19g	Fat 28g
Carbohydrate ...29g	Saturates 6g

20 MINS   25 MINS

SERVES 4

INGREDIENTS

9 oz new potatoes, scrubbed

4½ oz green beans

4½ oz cauliflower, broken into small flowerets

1½ cups shredded white cabbage

1 carrot, cut into thin sticks

¼ cucumber, cut into chunks

2 cups bean sprouts

2 hard-boiled eggs, shelled

SAUCE

6 tbsp crunchy peanut butter

1¼ cups cold water

1 garlic clove, crushed

1 fresh red chili, seeded and finely chopped

2 tbsp soy sauce

1 tbsp dry sherry

2 tsp sugar

1 tbsp lemon juice

1 Halve the potatoes and place in a saucepan of lightly salted water. Bring to a boil and then simmer for 12–15 minutes, or until cooked through.

2 Drain and plunge into cold water to cool. Set aside until required.

3 Bring another pan of lightly salted water to a boil. Add the green beans, cauliflower, and cabbage, and cook for 3 minutes. Drain and plunge the vegetables into cold water to cool and prevent any more cooking.

4 Drain the potatoes and other cooked vegetables. Arrange in piles on a large serving platter with the carrot, cucumber, and bean sprouts.

5 Cut the hard-boiled eggs into quarters and arrange on the salad. Cover and set aside.

6 To make the sauce, place the peanut butter in a bowl and blend in the water gradually, followed by the remaining ingredients.

7 Uncover the salad and drizzle some sauce over each serving.

Beef & Peanut Salad

This recipe looks stunning if you arrange the ingredients rather than toss them together.

NUTRITIONAL INFORMATION

Calories	194	Sugars	.........3g
Protein	........21g	Fat	..........10g
Carbohydrate	....5g	Saturates	.......3g

10 MINS   10 MINS

SERVES 4

INGREDIENTS

½ head Chinese cabbage

1 large carrot

4 oz radishes

3½ oz baby corn-on-the-cob

1 tbsp peanut oil

1 red chili, seeded and chopped finely

1 clove garlic, chopped finely

12 oz lean beef (such as fillet, sirloin, or rump), trimmed and shredded finely

1 tbsp dark soy sauce

1 oz fresh peanuts (optional)

red chili, sliced, to garnish

DRESSING

1 tbsp smooth peanut butter

1 tsp sugar

2 tbsp light soy sauce

1 tbsp sherry vinegar

salt and pepper

VARIATION

If preferred, use chicken, turkey, lean pork, or even strips of venison instead of beef in this recipe. Cut off all visible fat before you begin.

1 Finely shred the Chinese cabbage and arrange on a platter.

2 Peel the carrot and cut into thin, matchstick-like strips. Wash, trim, and quarter the radishes, and halve the baby corn lengthwise. Arrange these ingredients around the edge of the dish and set aside.

3 Heat the peanut oil in a non-stick wok or large skillet until really hot.

4 Add the red chili, garlic, and beef to the wok or skillet and stir-fry for 5 minutes.

5 Add the dark soy sauce and stir-fry for 1–2 minutes more, until tender and cooked through.

6 Meanwhile, make the dressing. Place all of the ingredients in a small bowl and blend them together until smooth.

7 Place the hot cooked beef in the center of the salad ingredients. Spoon over the dressing and sprinkle with a few peanuts, if using. Garnish with slices of red chili and serve immediately.

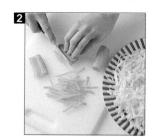

Carrot & Cilantro Salad

This tangy, crunchy salad makes an ideal accompaniment to Eggplant Satay (see page 112).

NUTRITIONAL INFORMATION

Calories	50	Sugars 4g
Protein	.........1g	Fat 3g
Carbohydrate	....5g	Saturates 0.4g

 5 MINS   0 MINS

SERVES 4

INGREDIENTS

4 large carrots

2 celery stalks, cut into
  thin sticks

2 tbsp roughly chopped fresh
  cilantro

DRESSING

1 tbsp sesame oil

1½ tbsp rice vinegar

½ tsp sugar

½ tsp salt

1 To create flower-shaped carrot slices, as shown, cut several grooves length-wise along each carrot before slicing it.

2 Slice each carrot into very thin slices, using the slicing cutter of a grater.

3 Combine the carrot, celery, and cilantro in a bowl.

4 To make the dressing, combine the sesame oil, rice vinegar, sugar, and salt in a bowl.

5 Just before serving, toss the carrot, celery, and cilantro mixture in the dressing and transfer to a serving dish.

Noodle & Mango Salad

Fruit combines well with the peanut dressing, bell peppers, and chili in this delicous hot salad.

NUTRITIONAL INFORMATION

Calories	368	Sugars	........11g
Protein	........11g	Fat	..........26g
Carbohydrate	...24g	Saturates	.......5g

15 MINS   5 MINS

SERVES 4

INGREDIENTS

9 oz thread egg noodles

2 tbsp peanut oil

4 shallots, sliced

2 cloves garlic, crushed

1 red chili, seeded and sliced

1 red bell pepper, seeded and sliced

1 green bell pepper, seeded and sliced

1 ripe mango, sliced into thin strips

¼ cup salted peanuts, chopped

DRESSING

4 tbsp peanut butter

⅓ cup coconut milk

1 tbsp tomato paste

1 Place the egg noodles in a large dish or bowl. Pour over enough boiling water to cover the noodles and leave to stand for 10 minutes.

COOK'S TIP

If preferred, gently heat the peanut dressing before pouring over the noodle salad.

2 Heat the peanut oil in a large preheated wok or skillet.

3 Add the shallots, crushed garlic, chili and bell pepper slices to the wok or skillet and stir-fry for 2–3 minutes.

4 Drain the egg noodles thoroughly in a colander. Add the drained noodles and mango slices to the wok or skillet and heat through for about 2 minutes.

5 Transfer the noodle and mango salad to warmed serving dishes and scatter with chopped peanuts.

6 To make the dressing, mix together the peanut butter, coconut milk, and tomato paste, then spoon over the noodle salad. Serve immediately.

Duck & Radish Salad

Juicy duck breasts are coated with sesame seeds, then cooked, thinly sliced and served with a crisp salad.

NUTRITIONAL INFORMATION

Calories	328	Sugars	.......0.2g
Protein	........22g	Fat	.........24g
Carbohydrate	....7g	Saturates	.......4g

5 MINS   10 MINS

SERVES 4

I N G R E D I E N T S

12 oz boneless duck breasts, skinned

2 tbsp all-purpose flour

1 egg

2 tbsp water

2 tbsp sesame seeds

3 tbsp sesame oil

½ head Chinese cabbage, shredded

3 celery stalks, sliced finely

8 radishes, trimmed and halved

salt and pepper

fresh basil leaves, to garnish

D R E S S I N G

finely grated zest of 1 lime

2 tbsp lime juice

2 tbsp olive oil

1 tbsp light soy sauce

1 tbsp chopped fresh basil

3 Beat the egg and water together in a shallow bowl, then sprinkle the sesame seeds on a separate plate.

4 Dip the duck breasts first into the seasoned flour, then into the egg mixture, and finally into the sesame seeds, to coat the duck evenly.

5 Heat the sesame oil in a preheated wok or large skillet.

6 Fry the duck breasts over a medium heat for about 8 minutes, turning once. To test whether they are cooked, insert a sharp knife into the thickest part —the juices should run clear. Lift them out and drain on paper towels.

7 To make the dressing for the salad, whisk together the lime zest and juice, olive oil, soy sauce, and chopped basil. Season with a little salt and pepper.

8 Arrange the Chinese cabbage, celery, and radish on a serving plate. Slice the duck breasts thinly and place on top of the salad.

9 Drizzle with the dressing and garnish with fresh basil leaves. Serve immediately.

1 Put each duck breast between sheets of baking parchment or plastic wrap. Use a meat mallet or rolling pin to flatten them slightly.

2 Sprinkle the flour onto a large plate and season with salt and pepper.

Cucumber Salad

This is a very refreshing accompaniment to any main dish and is an excellent "cooler" for curries.

NUTRITIONAL INFORMATION

Calories	33	Sugars	.........8g
Protein	........0.2g	Fat	...........0g
Carbohydrate	....9g	Saturates	.......0g

  10 MINS   0 MINS

SERVES 4

INGREDIENTS

½ cucumber

1 tbsp rice vinegar

2 tbsp sugar

½ tsp salt

2 tbsp hot water

1 small shallot

1 Wash the cucumber thoroughly and pat dry with paper towels.

2 Peel the cucumber, halve it lengthwise, and seed it, using a teaspoon or a melon baller.

3 Using a sharp knife, slice the cucumber thinly.

4 Arrange the cucumber slices in an attractive pattern on a serving plate.

5 To make the dressing, mix together the rice vinegar, sugar, and salt in a bowl. Pour on the hot water and stir until the sugar has dissolved. Leave the dressing to cool slightly.

6 Pour the dressing evenly over the cucumber slices.

7 Using a sharp knife, thinly slice the shallot and sprinkle over the cucumber.

8 Cover the cucumber salad with plastic wrap and leave to chill in the refrigerator before serving. Serve as a cooling accompaniment to spicy curries.

COOK'S TIP

Some people dislike the bitter taste that cucumbers can have—I find that peeling off the skin and deseeding the cucumber often eliminates this problem. Using a melon baller is the neatest method of deseeding a cucumber.

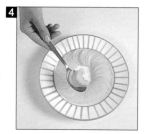

Hot & Sweet Salad

This salad is made by mixing fruit and vegetables with the sharp, sweet and fishy flavors of the dressing.

NUTRITIONAL INFORMATION

Calories 169   Sugars 8g
Protein ....14g   Fat 8g
Carbohydrate ....11g   Saturates 1g

15 MINS   0 MINS

SERVES 4

INGREDIENTS

9 oz white cabbage, finely shredded

2 tomatoes, skinned, seeded, and chopped

9 oz cooked green beans, halved if large

4½ oz peeled shrimp

1 papaya, peeled, seeded, and chopped

1-2 fresh red chilies, seeded and very finely sliced

scant ⅓ cup roasted salted peanuts, crushed

handful of lettuce or baby spinach leaves, shredded or torn into small pieces

DRESSING

4 tbsp lime juice

2 tbsp fish sauce

sugar, to taste

pepper

1 Mix the white cabbage with the tomatoes, green beans, shrimp, three-quarters of the papaya, and half of the chilies in a large mixing bowl.

2 Stir in two-thirds of the crushed peanuts and mix well.

3 Line the rim of a large serving plate with the lettuce or spinach leaves and pile the salad mixture into the center of the leaves.

4 To make the dressing, beat the lime juice with the fish sauce and add sugar and pepper to taste. Drizzle over the salad.

5 Scatter the top with the remaining papaya, chilies, and crushed peanuts. Serve immediately.

COOK'S TIP

To skin tomatoes, make a cross at the base with a very sharp knife, then immerse in a bowl of boiling water for a few minutes. Remove with a slotted spoon and peel off the skin.

Hot Rice Salad

Nutty brown rice combines well with peanuts and a sweet and sour mixture of fruit and vegetables in this tangy combination.

NUTRITIONAL INFORMATION

Calories 464   Sugars 17g
Protein . . . . .15g   Fat 24g
Carbohydrate . . .52g   Saturates 4g

 5 MINS   30 MINS

SERVES 4

I N G R E D I E N T S

1½ cups brown rice

1 bunch green onions

1 red bell pepper

4½ oz radishes

15 oz can pineapple pieces in natural juice, drained

2 cups bean sprouts

¾ cup dry-roasted peanuts

D R E S S I N G

2 tbsp crunchy peanut butter

1 tbsp peanut oil

2 tbsp light soy sauce

2 tbsp white wine vinegar

2 tsp honey

1 tsp chili powder

½ tsp garlic salt

pepper

1 Put the rice in a pan and cover with water. Bring to a boil, then cover and simmer for 30 minutes until tender.

2 Meanwhile, chop the onions, using a sharp knife. Seed and chop the red bell pepper and thinly slice the radishes.

3 To make the dressing, place the crunchy peanut butter, peanut oil, light soy sauce, white wine vinegar, honey, chili powder, garlic salt, and pepper in a small bowl and whisk for a few seconds until well combined.

4 Drain the rice thoroughly and place in a heatproof bowl.

5 Heat the dressing in a small saucepan for 1 minute and then toss into the rice and mix well.

6 Working quickly, stir the pineapple pieces, green onions, bell pepper, bean sprouts, and peanuts into the mixture in the bowl.

7 Pile the hot rice salad into a warmed serving dish.

8 Arrange the radish slices around the outside of the salad and serve immediately.

Oriental Chicken Salad

Mirin, soy sauce, and sesame oil give an oriental flavor to this delicious salad.

NUTRITIONAL INFORMATION

Calories	.361	Sugars	.2g
Protein	.34g	Fat	.16g
Carbohydrate	.17g	Saturates	.3g

 5 MINS   35 MINS

SERVES 4

I N G R E D I E N T S

4 skinless, boneless chicken breasts

⅓ cup mirin or sweet sherry

⅓ cup light soy sauce

1 tbsp sesame oil

3 tbsp olive oil

1 tbsp red wine vinegar

1 tbsp Dijon mustard

9 oz egg noodles

9 oz bean sprouts

9 oz Chinese cabbage, shredded

2 green onions, sliced

4½ oz mushrooms, sliced

1 fresh red chili, finely sliced,
   to garnish

1 Pound the chicken breasts out to an even thickness between two sheets of plastic wrap with a rolling pin or cleaver.

2 Put the chicken breasts in a roasting pan. Combine the mirin and soy sauce and brush the mixture over the chicken.

3 Place the chicken in a preheated oven at 400°F for 20–30 minutes, basting regularly.

4 Remove the chicken from the oven and allow to cool slightly.

5 Meanwhile, combine the sesame oil, olive oil, and red wine vinegar with the mustard.

6 Cook the noodles according to the instructions on the pack. Rinse under cold running water, then drain.

7 Toss the noodles in the dressing until the noodles are completely coated.

8 Toss the bean sprouts, Chinese cabbage, green onions, and mushrooms with the noodles.

9 Slice the cooked chicken very thinly and stir into the noodles. Garnish the salad with the chili slices and serve.

Mango Salad

This is an unusual combination but works well as long as the mango is very unripe. Papaya can be used instead, if you prefer.

NUTRITIONAL INFORMATION

Calories	26	Sugars	........3g
Protein	.........1g	Fat	..........0.2g
Carbohydrate	....6g	Saturates	.......0g

    10 MINS   0 MINS

SERVES 4

INGREDIENTS

1 large unripe mango, peeled and
   cut into long thin shreds

1 small red chili, seeded and
   chopped finely

2 shallots, chopped finely

2 tbsp lemon juice

1 tbsp light soy sauce

6 roasted canned chestnuts,
   quartered

1 melon, to serve

1 lollo biondo lettuce, or any crunchy
   lettuce

½ oz cilantro leaves

1 Soak the mango briefly in cold water, in order to remove any syrup. Meanwhile, combine the chili, shallots, lemon juice, and soy sauce. Drain the mango and combine with the chestnuts.

2 To make the melon basket, stand the watermelon on one end on a level surface. Holding a knife level and in one place, turn the watermelon on its axis so the knife marks an even line all around the middle. Mark a 1 inch wide handle across the top and through the center stem, joining the middle line at either end. (If you prefer a zigzag finish, mark the shape to be cut at this point before any cuts are made, to make sure the zigzags are even.)

3 Take a sharp knife and, following the marks made for the handle, make the first vertical cut. Then cut down the other side of the handle. Now follow the middle line and make your straight or zigzag cut, making sure that the knife is always pointing towards the center of the watermelon, and is level with the work counter, so when you reach the handle cuts, the cut out piece of melon will pull away cleanly.

4 Hollow out the flesh with a spoon, leaving a clean edge and line with the lettuce and cilantro. Fill with the salad, pour over the dressing, and serve.

COOK'S TIP

A relative of the onion, though less pungent, shallots come in round and elongated varieties. When buying shallots, choose firm, dry-skinned ones which show no signs of wrinkling. Fresh shallots can be stored in the refrigerator for up to a week.

Chinese Salad Nests

Crisp fried potato nests are perfect as an edible salad bowl and delicious when filled with a colorful Chinese-style salad of vegetables and fruit.

NUTRITIONAL INFORMATION

Calories . . . . . . .272 Sugars 11g
Protein . . . . .4g Fat 4g
Carbohydrate . . .59g Saturates 0.4g

15 MINS   15 MINS

SERVES 4

INGREDIENTS

POTATO NESTS

1 lb mealy potatoes, grated

1 cup cornstarch

vegetable oil, for frying

fresh chives, to garnish

SALAD

14½ oz pineapple, cubed

1 green bell pepper, cut into strips

1 carrot, cut into thin strips

1¾ oz snow peas, sliced thickly

4 baby corn-on-the-cobs, halved lengthwise

1 oz beansprouts

2 green onions, sliced

DRESSING

1 tbsp honey

1 tsp light soy sauce

1 garlic clove, crushed

1 tsp lemon juice

1 To make the nests, rinse the potatoes several times in cold water. Drain well on paper towels so they are completely dry. This is to prevent the potatoes spitting when they are cooked in the fat. Place the potatoes in a mixing bowl. Add the cornstarch, mixing well to coat the potatoes.

2 Half fill a wok with vegetable oil and heat until smoking. Line a 6 inch diameter wire strainer with a quarter of the potato mixture and press another strainer of the same size on top.

3 Lower the strainers into the oil and cook for 2 minutes until the potato nest is golden brown and crisp. Remove from the wok, allowing the excess oil to drain off.

4 Repeat 3 more times to use up all of the mixture and make a total of 4 nests. Leave to cool.

5 Mix the salad ingredients together then spoon into the potato baskets.

6 Mix the dressing ingredients together in a bowl. Pour the dressing over the salad, garnish with chives, and serve immediately.

Bean Sprout Salad

This is a very light dish and is ideal on its own for a summer meal or as an appetizer.

NUTRITIONAL INFORMATION

Calories 70	Sugars 5g	
Protein 4g	Fat 3g	
Carbohydrate 7g	Saturates 0.5g	

  10 MINS   5 MINS

SERVES 4

I N G R E D I E N T S

1 green bell pepper, seeded

1 carrot

1 celery stalk

2 tomatoes, finely chopped

12 oz bean sprouts

1 small cucumber

1 garlic clove, crushed

dash of chili sauce

2 tbsp light soy sauce

1 tsp wine vinegar

2 tsp sesame oil

16 fresh chives

1 Using a sharp knife, cut the green bell pepper, carrot, and celery into thin sticks and finely chop the tomatoes.

2 Blanch the bean sprouts in boiling water for 1 minute. Drain well and rinse under cold water. Drain thoroughly again.

3 Cut the cucumber in half lengthwise. Scoop out the seeds with a teaspoon and discard. Cut the flesh into thin sticks.

4 Mix the cucumber with the bean sprouts, green bell pepper, carrot, tomatoes, and celery.

5 To make the dressing, mix together the garlic, chili sauce, soy sauce, wine vinegar, and sesame oil in a small bowl.

6 Pour the dressing over the vegetables, tossing well to coat.

7 Spoon the bean sprout salad into a serving dish or on to 4 individual serving plates. Garnish the salad with fresh chives and serve.

VARIATION

Substitute 12 oz cooked, cooled green beans or snow peas for the cucumber. Vary the bean sprouts for a different flavor. Try adzuki bean or alfalfa sprouts, as well as the better-known mung and soya bean sprouts.

Chinese Chicken Salad

This is a refreshing dish suitable for a summer meal or light lunch.

NUTRITIONAL INFORMATION

Calories	162	Sugars	.........3g
Protein	........15g	Fat	..........10g
Carbohydrate	....5g	Saturates	.......2g

 25 MINS   10 MINS

SERVES 4

INGREDIENTS

8 oz skinless, boneless chicken breasts

2 tsp light soy sauce

1 tsp sesame oil

1 tsp sesame seeds

2 tbsp vegetable oil

14½ oz bean sprouts

1 red bell pepper, seeded and thinly sliced

1 carrot, cut into thin sticks

3 baby corn-on-the-cobs, sliced

snipped chives and thin carrot sticks,
  to garnish

SAUCE

2 tsp rice wine vinegar

1 tbsp light soy sauce

dash of chili oil

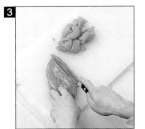

1 Place the chicken breasts in a shallow glass dish.

2 Mix together the soy sauce and sesame oil and pour over the chicken. Sprinkle with the sesame seeds and let stand for 20 minutes, turning the chicken over occasionally.

3 Remove the chicken from the marinade and cut the meat into thin slices.

4 Heat the vegetable oil in a preheated wok or large skillet. Add the chicken and fry for 4-5 minutes, until cooked through and golden brown on both sides. Carefully remove the chicken from the wok with a slotted spoon, set aside, and leave to cool.

5 Add the bean sprouts, bell pepper, carrot, and baby corn-on-the-cobs to the wok and stir-fry for 2–3 minutes.

Remove from the wok with a slotted spoon, set aside, and leave to cool.

6 To make the sauce, mix together the rice wine vinegar, light soy sauce, and chili oil.

7 Arrange the chicken and vegetables together on a serving plate. Spoon the sauce over the salad, garnish with chives and carrot sticks, and serve.

Sweet & Sour Fish Salad

This refreshing blend of pink and white fish mixed with fresh pineapple and bell peppers would make an interesting first course or a light meal.

NUTRITIONAL INFORMATION

Calories	168	Sugars	.........5g
Protein	........24g	Fat	...........6g
Carbohydrate	....5g	Saturates	.......1g

  🌀 🌀 🌀

🍲 25 MINS 🕐 10 MINS

SERVES 4

I N G R E D I E N T S

8 oz trout fillets

8 oz white fish fillets (such as haddock or cod)

1¼ cups water

1 stalk lemon grass

2 lime leaves

1 large red chili

1 bunch green onions, trimmed and shredded

4 oz fresh pineapple flesh, diced

1 small red bell pepper, seeded and diced

1 bunch watercress, washed and trimmed

fresh snipped chives, to garnish

D R E S S I N G

1 tbsp sunflower oil

1 tbsp rice wine vinegar

pinch of chili powder

1 tsp honey

salt and pepper

1 Rinse the fish, place in a skillet, and pour over the water.

2 Bend the lemon grass in half to bruise it and add to the pan with the lime leaves. Prick the chili with a fork and add to the pan. Bring to a boil and simmer for 7–8 minutes. Leave to cool.

3 Drain the fish, flake the flesh away from the skin, and place in a bowl.

Gently stir in the green onions, pineapple, and bell pepper.

4 Arrange the washed watercress on 4 serving plates, spoon the cooked fish mixture on top, and set aside.

5 To make the dressing, mix all the ingredients together and season well. Spoon over the fish and serve garnished with chives.

Broccoli & Almond Salad

This is a colorful, crunchy salad with a delicious dressing. It is better left overnight if possible for the flavors to mingle.

NUTRITIONAL INFORMATION

Calories	181	Sugars	.........7g
Protein	.........9g	Fat	..........12g
Carbohydrate	....9g	Saturates	.......2g

  4¹/₂ HOURS   10 MINS

SERVES 4

INGREDIENTS

1 lb small broccoli flowerets

1¾ oz baby corn-on-the-cobs, halved lengthwise

1 red bell pepper, seeded and cut into thin strips

1¾ oz blanched almonds

DRESSING

1 tbsp sesame seeds

1 tbsp peanut oil

2 garlic cloves, crushed

2 tbsp light soy sauce

1 tbsp honey

2 tsp lemon juice

pepper

lemon zest, to garnish (optional)

1 Blanch the broccoli and baby corn cobs in boiling water for 5 minutes. Drain well, rinse, and drain again.

2 Transfer the broccoli and baby corn cobs to a large mixing bowl and add the bell pepper and almonds.

3 To make the dressing, heat a wok and add the sesame seeds. Dry-fry, stirring constantly, for about 1 minute, or until the sesame seeds are lightly browned and are giving off a delicious aroma.

4 Mix the peanut oil, garlic, soy sauce, honey, lemon juice, and pepper to taste. Add the sesame seeds and mix well.

5 Pour the dressing over the salad, cover, and set aside in the refrigerator for a minimum of 4 hours and preferably overnight.

6 Garnish the salad with lemon zest (if using) and serve.

COOK'S TIP

Be careful when browning the sesame seeds because they will quickly burn. Dry-fry over a low heat and stir constantly.

Pickled Cucumber

The pickling takes minutes rather than days—but the longer you leave it, the better the result.

NUTRITIONAL INFORMATION

Calories 29	Sugars 3g	
Protein 0.2g	Fat 2g	
Carbohydrate 3g	Saturates 0.3g	

 35 MINS   0 MINS

SERVES 4

I N G R E D I E N T S

1 slender cucumber, about
   12 inches long

1 tsp salt

2 tsp sugar

1 tsp rice vinegar

1 tsp red chili oil

a few drops sesame oil

1 Wash and halve the cucumber, leaving it unpeeled, lengthwise.

2 Scrape out the seeds from the cucumber using a knife or a teaspoon and discard. Cut the cucumber across into thick chunks.

3 Sprinkle the cucumber chunks with the salt and mix well.

4 Leave the cucumber chunks to marinate for at least 20-30 minutes, longer if possible, then pour the juice away. Drain and rinse the cucumber, then pat dry.

5 Transfer the cucumber chunks to a serving dish.

6 Add the sugar, rice vinegar, and chili oil to the cucumber chunks in the dish and mix thoroughly until the cucumber is completely coated in the mixture.

7 Sprinkle the pickled cucumber with the sesame oil just before serving.

8 Serve as a snack or appetizer, or as an accompaniment to cold meat dishes.

COOK'S TIP

Pickled vegetables and fruits are very popular with the Chinese. Usually, the vegetables are allowed to stay in the marinade for 3-4 days. Once made, they will keep in the refrigerator for up to 2 weeks.

Green Sesame Salad

A very elegant and light salad which will complement rice and noodle dishes beautifully.

NUTRITIONAL INFORMATION

Calories	78	Sugars	.........8g
Protein	.........3g	Fat	..........3g
Carbohydrate	....3g	Saturates	.....0.5g

10 MINS   0 MINS

SERVES 4

I N G R E D I E N T S

2 cups bean sprouts

1½ tbsp chopped fresh cilantro

3 tbsp fresh lime juice

½ tsp mild chili powder

1 tsp sugar

½ tsp salt

3 celery stalks

1 large green bell pepper, seeded

1 large Granny Smith apple

2 tbsp toasted sesame seeds,
    to garnish

1 Soak the bean sprouts and drain thoroughly.

2 Pick over the bean sprouts, removing any that seem a little brown or limp—it is essential that they are fresh and crunchy for this recipe.

3 To make the dressing, combine the cilantro, lime juice, chili powder, sugar, and salt in a small bowl and mix thoroughly.

4 Using a sharp knife, cut the celery into 1 inch pieces. Cut the bell pepper into small pieces and the Granny Smith apple into small chunks.

5 Place the chopped celery, bell pepper, and apple into the bowl containing the bean sprouts and stir gently to mix.

6 Just before serving, pour the dressing over the salad, tossing well to mix.

7 Garnish the green sesame salad with the toasted sesame seeds and serve with rice or noodle dishes.

COOK'S TIP

Keeping each ingredient as fresh and crunchy as possible will make all the difference to the appearance and taste of this elegant salad. To prevent the apples from going brown, soak the slices briefly in a little lemon juice and water as soon as you have cut them.

Sweet & Sour Cucumber

Chunks of cucumber are marinated in vinegar and sweetened with honey to make a sweet and sour appetizer.

NUTRITIONAL INFORMATION

Calories	45	Sugars	. . . . .2g
Protein	. . . . .1g	Fat	. . . . .3g
Carbohydrate	. . . .4g	Saturates	. . . . .0.4g

 50 MINS   0 MINS

SERVES 4

INGREDIENTS

1 cucumber

1 tsp salt

2 tsp honey

2 tbsp rice vinegar

3 tbsp chopped fresh cilantro

2 tsp sesame oil

¼ tsp crushed red peppercorns

strips of red and yellow bell pepper,
   to garnish

1 Peel thin strips off the cucumber, along the length, to give a pretty striped effect. Cut the cucumber in quarters lengthwise and then into 1 inch long pieces. Place in a colander. Sprinkle with salt and leave to stand for 30 minutes to allow the salt to draw out the excess water from the cucumber.

2 Wash the cucumber thoroughly to remove the salt, drain, and pat dry with paper towels.

3 Place the cucumber pieces in a large mixing bowl.

4 Combine the honey with the vinegar and pour over the cucumber. Mix together and marinate for 15 minutes.

5 Stir in the chopped fresh cilantro and sesame oil, and place in a serving bowl.

6 Sprinkle over the crushed red peppercorns. Serve garnished with strips of red and yellow bell pepper.

COOK'S TIP

Rice vinegar is a common Chinese cooking ingredient. White rice vinegar is made from rice wine, whereas red rice vinegar is made from fermented rice. Both have a distinctive flavor, but the white version tends to be used more often, as it will not colour the food.

Stir-Fried Chili Cucumber

Warm cucumbers are absolutely delicious, especially when combined with the heat of chili and the flavor of ginger.

NUTRITIONAL INFORMATION

Calories ....67 Sugars 4g
Protein ....1g Fat 5g
Carbohydrate ....5g Saturates 1g

 30 MINS   5 MINS

SERVES 4

INGREDIENTS

2 medium cucumbers

2 tsp salt

1 tbsp vegetable oil

2 garlic cloves, minced

½-inch fresh gingerroot, grated

2 fresh red chilies, chopped

2 scallions, chopped

1 tsp yellow bean sauce

1 tbsp honey

½ cup water

1 tsp sesame oil

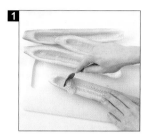

1 Peel the cucumbers and cut in half lengthways. Scrape the seeds from the center with a teaspoon or melon baller and discard.

2 Cut the cucumber into strips and place on a plate. Sprinkle the salt over the cucumber strips and set aside for 20 minutes. Rinse well under cold running water and pat dry with absorbent paper towels.

3 Heat the vegetable oil in a preheated wok or large skillet until it is almost smoking. Lower the heat slightly and add the garlic, ginger, chilies, and scallions and stir-fry for 30 seconds.

4 Add the cucumbers to the wok, together with the yellow bean sauce and honey, and stir-fry for 30 seconds.

5 Add the water and cook over a high heat until most of the water has evaporated.

6 Sprinkle the sesame oil over the stir-fry. Transfer to a warm serving dish and serve immediately.

COOK'S TIP

The cucumber is sprinkled with salt and left to stand in order to draw out the excess water, thus preventing a soggy meal!

Poultry

Second to pork, poultry is one of the most popular foods throughout China. It also plays an important symbolic role in Chinese cooking. The cock symbolizes the male, positiveness, and aggression, while the duck represents happiness and fidelity. Being uniformly tender, poultry is ideal for Chinese cooking methods which rely on the rapid

cooking of small, even-sized pieces of meat. Poultry can be cut into wafer-thin slices, thin matchstick strips or cubes, and can be quickly cooked without any loss of moisture or tenderness. This chapter contains dishes which are stir-fried, braised, steamed, and roasted and contains old favorites such as Lemon Chicken and Aromatic & Crispy Duck, as well as more unusual dishes such as Duck with Lime & Kiwi Fruit and Honey & Soy Chicken.

Chicken Chop Suey

Chop suey is a well known and popular dish based on bean sprouts and soy sauce with a meat or vegetable flavoring.

NUTRITIONAL INFORMATION

Calories 337	Sugars 7g
Protein 32g	Fat 18g
Carbohydrate ...14g	Saturates 3g

25 MINS   15 MINS

SERVES 4

INGREDIENTS

4 tbsp light soy sauce

2 tsp light brown sugar

1 lb 2 oz skinless, boneless chicken breasts

3 tbsp vegetable oil

2 onions, quartered

2 garlic cloves, crushed

12 oz bean sprouts

3 tsp sesame oil

1 tbsp cornstarch

3 tbsp water

2 cups chicken stock

shredded leek, to garnish

1 Mix the soy sauce and sugar together, stirring until the sugar has dissolved.

2 Trim any fat from the chicken and cut into thin strips. Place the meat in a shallow dish and spoon the soy mixture over them, turning to coat. Marinate in the refrigerator for 20 minutes.

3 Heat the oil in a wok and stir-fry the chicken for 2–3 minutes, until golden brown. Add the onions and garlic and cook for 2 minutes more. Add the bean sprouts, cook for 4–5 minutes, then add the sesame oil.

4 Mix the cornstarch and water to form a smooth paste. Pour the stock into the wok, add the cornstarch paste and bring to a boil, stirring until the sauce is thickened and clear. Serve, garnished with shredded leek.

VARIATION

This recipe may be made with strips of lean steak, pork, or with mixed vegetables. Change the type of stock accordingly.

Cashew Chicken

Yellow bean sauce is available from large supermarkets. Try to buy a chunky sauce rather than a smooth sauce for texture.

NUTRITIONAL INFORMATION

Calories	398	Sugars	........2g
Protein	........31g	Fat	.........27g
Carbohydrate	....8g	Saturates	.......4g

10 MINS   15 MINS

SERVES 4

INGREDIENTS

1 lb boneless chicken breasts

2 tbsp vegetable oil

1 red onion, sliced

1½ cups flat mushrooms, sliced

⅓ cup cashews

2¾ oz jar yellow bean sauce

fresh cilantro, to garnish

egg fried rice or plain boiled rice,
   to serve

1 Using a sharp knife, remove the excess skin from the chicken breasts, if desired. Cut the chicken into small, bite-sized chunks.

2 Heat the vegetable oil in a preheated wok or skillet.

3 Add the chicken to the wok and stir-fry for 5 minutes.

4 Add the red onion and mushrooms to the wok and continue to stir-fry for 5 minutes more.

5 Place the cashews on a cookie sheet and toast under a preheated medium broiler until just browning – toasting nuts brings out their flavor.

6 Toss the toasted cashews into the wok together with the yellow bean sauce and heat through.

7 Allow the sauce to bubble for 2–3 minutes.

8 Transfer the chop suey to warm serving bowls and garnish with fresh cilantro. Serve hot with egg fried rice or plain boiled rice.

VARIATION

Chicken thighs could be used instead of the chicken breasts for a more economical dish.

Lemon Chicken

This is on everyone's list of favorite Chinese dishes, and it is so simple to make. Serve with stir-fried vegetables for a truly delicious meal.

NUTRITIONAL INFORMATION

Calories . . . . . . .272 Sugars 1g
Protein . . . . .36g Fat 11g
Carbohydrate . . . .5g Saturates 2g

5 MINS   15 MINS

SERVES 4

INGREDIENTS

vegetable oil, for deep-frying

1 lb 7 oz skinless, boneless chicken, cut into strips

lemon slices and shredded green onion, to garnish

SAUCE

1 tbsp cornstarch

6 tbsp cold water

3 tbsp fresh lemon juice

2 tbsp sweet sherry

½ tsp sugar

1 Heat the oil for deep-frying in a preheated wok or skillet to 350°F or until a cube of bread browns in 30 seconds.

2 Reduce the heat and stir-fry the chicken strips for 3–4 minutes, until cooked through.

3 Remove the chicken with a slotted spoon, set aside, and keep warm. Drain the oil from the wok.

4 To make the sauce, mix the cornstarch with 2 tablespoons of the water to form a paste.

5 Pour the lemon juice and remaining water into the mixture in the wok.

6 Add the sweet sherry and sugar and bring to a boil, stirring until the sugar has completely dissolved.

7 Stir in the cornstarch mixture and return to a boil. Reduce the heat and simmer, stirring constantly, for 2-3 minutes, until the sauce is thickened and clear.

8 Transfer the chicken to a warm serving plate and pour the sauce over the top.

9 Garnish the chicken with the lemon slices and shredded green onion and serve immediately.

COOK'S TIP

If you would prefer to use chicken portions rather than strips, cook them in the oil, covered, over a low heat for about 30 minutes, or until cooked through.

Celery & Cashew Chicken

Stir-fry yellow bean sauce gives this quick and easy Chinese dish a really authentic taste. Pecans can be used instead of the cashews.

NUTRITIONAL INFORMATION

Calories 549   Sugars 24g
Protein ....41g   Fat 31g
Carbohydrate ...28g   Saturates 5g

5 MINS   10 MINS

SERVES 4

I N G R E D I E N T S

3-4 boneless, skinned chicken breasts, about 1 lb 6 oz

2 tbsp sunflower or vegetable oil

1 cup cashews (unsalted)

4-6 green onions, thinly sliced diagonally

5-6 celery stalks, thinly sliced diagonally

1 x 6 oz jar stir-fry yellow bean sauce

salt and pepper

celery leaves, to garnish (optional)

plain boiled rice, to serve

1 Using a sharp knife or metal cleaver, cut the chicken into thin slices across the grain.

2 Heat the oil in a preheated wok or large skillet, swirling it around until it is really hot.

3 Add the cashews and stir-fry until they begin to brown but do not allow them to burn.

4 Add the chicken and stir-fry until well sealed and almost cooked through.

5 Add the green onions and celery and continue to stir-fry for 2–3 minutes, stirring the food well around the wok.

6 Add the stir-fry yellow bean sauce to the wok or skillet and season lightly with salt and pepper.

7 Toss the mixture in the wok until the chicken and vegetables are thoroughly coated with the sauce and piping hot.

8 Serve with plain boiled rice, garnished with celery leaves, if liked.

VARIATION

This recipe can be adapted to use turkey fillets or steaks, or pork fillet or boneless steaks. Cut the turkey or pork lengthwise first, then slice thinly across the grain. Alternatively, cut into ½ inch cubes.

Aromatic & Crispy Duck

Because it is time-consuming to make the pancakes, buy ready-made ones from Oriental stores, or use crisp lettuce leaves as the wrapper.

NUTRITIONAL INFORMATION

Calories 169	Sugars 1g
Protein 7g	Fat 11g
Carbohydrate 7g	Saturates 3g

9¹/₄ HOURS   3¹/₄ HOURS

SERVES 4

INGREDIENTS

2 large duckling quarters

1 tsp salt

3-4 pieces star anise

1 tsp Szechuan red peppercorns

1 tsp cloves

2 cinnamon sticks, broken into pieces

2-3 green onions, cut into short sections

4-5 small slices fresh ginger

3-4 tbsp rice wine or dry sherry

vegetable oil, for deep-frying

TO SERVE

12 ready-made pancakes or 12 crisp
  lettuce leaves

hoisin or plum sauce

¼ cucumber, thinly shredded

3-4 green onions, thinly shredded

1 Rub the duck with the salt and arrange the star anise, peppercorns, cloves, and cinnamon on top. Sprinkle with the green onions, ginger, and wine and marinate for at least 3-4 hours.

2 Arrange the duck pieces on a plate that will fit inside a bamboo steamer. Pour some hot water into a wok, place the bamboo steamer on top, sitting on a trivet. Add the duck and cover with the bamboo lid. Steam the duck over a high heat for 2-3 hours, until tender and cooked through. Add more hot water from time to time as required. Remove the duck and leave to cool for at least 4-5 hours so the duck becomes crispy.

3 Pour off the water and wipe the wok dry. Pour in the oil and heat until smoking. Deep-fry the duck pieces, skin-side down, for 4-5 minutes or until crisp and brown. Remove and drain.

4 To serve, scrape the meat off the bone, place about 1 teaspoon of hoisin or plum sauce on the center of a pancake (or lettuce leaf), add a few pieces of cucumber and green onion with a portion of the duck meat. Wrap up to form a small parcel and eat with your fingers.

Stir-Fried Ginger Chicken

The oranges add color and piquancy to this refreshing dish, which complements the chicken well.

NUTRITIONAL INFORMATION

Calories 289   Sugars 15g
Protein . . . . .20g   Fat 9g
Carbohydrate . . .17g   Saturates 2g

5 MINS   20 MINS

SERVES 4

INGREDIENTS

2 tbsp sunflower oil

1 onion, sliced

6 oz carrots, cut into thin sticks

1 clove garlic, crushed

12 oz boneless skinless chicken breasts

2 tbsp fresh ginger, peeled and grated

1 tsp ground ginger

4 tbsp sweet sherry

1 tbsp tomato paste

1 tbsp brown sugar

⅓ cup orange juice

1 tsp cornstarch

1 orange, peeled and segmented

fresh snipped chives, to garnish

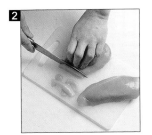

1 Heat the oil in a large preheated wok. Add the onion, carrots, and garlic and stir-fry over a high heat for 3 minutes or until the vegetables begin to soften.

2 Slice the chicken into thin strips. Add to the wok with the fresh and ground ginger. Stir-fry for 10 minutes more, or until the chicken is well cooked through and golden in color.

3 Mix together the sherry, tomato paste, sugar, orange juice, and cornstarch in a bowl. Stir the mixture into the wok and heat through until the mixture bubbles and the juices start to thicken.

4 Add the orange segments and carefully toss to mix.

5 Transfer the stir-fried chicken to warm serving bowls and garnish with freshly snipped chives. Serve immediately.

COOK'S TIP

Make sure that you do not continue cooking the dish once the orange segments have been added in step 4, otherwise they will break up.

Grilled Chicken Legs

Just the thing to put on the grill – chicken legs, coated with a spicy, curry-like butter, then grilled until crispy and golden.

NUTRITIONAL INFORMATION

Calories	660	Sugars	.........4g
Protein	........34g	Fat	..........57g
Carbohydrate	....4g	Saturates	......30g

5 MINS   20 MINS

SERVES 4

INGREDIENTS

12 chicken drumsticks

SPICED BUTTER

¾ cup butter

2 garlic cloves, crushed

1 tsp grated fresh ginger

2 tsp ground turmeric

4 tsp cayenne pepper

2 tbsp lime juice

3 tbsp mango chutney

TO SERVE

crisp green seasonal salad

boiled rice

VARIATION

This spicy butter mixture would be equally effective on grilled chicken or turkey breast fillets. Skin before coating with the mixture.

1 To make the Spiced Butter mixture, beat the butter with the garlic, ginger, turmeric, cayenne pepper, lime juice, and chutney until well blended.

2 Using a sharp knife, slash each chicken leg to the bone 3-4 times.

3 Cook the drumsticks over a moderate grill for about 12-15 minutes or until almost cooked. Alternatively, broil the

chicken for about 10-12 minutes until almost cooked, turning halfway through.

4 Spread the chicken legs liberally with the butter mixture and continue to cook for a further 5-6 minutes, turning and basting frequently with the butter until golden and crisp. Serve the chicken legs hot or cold with a crisp green salad and rice.

Braised Chicken

This is a delicious way to cook a whole chicken. It has a wonderful glaze, which is served as a sauce.

NUTRITIONAL INFORMATION

Calories 294	Sugars 9g	
Protein 31g	Fat 15g	
Carbohydrate ...10g	Saturates 3g	

5 MINS   1¼ HOURS

SERVES 4

I N G R E D I E N T S

3 lb 5 oz chicken

3 tbsp vegetable oil

1 tbsp peanut oil

2 tbsp dark brown sugar

5 tbsp dark soy sauce

⅔ cup water

2 garlic cloves, crushed

1 small onion, chopped

1 fresh red chili, chopped

celery leaves and chives,
    to garnish

1 Preheat a large wok or large skillet.

2 Clean the chicken inside and out with damp paper towels.

3 Put the vegetable oil and peanut oil in the wok, add the dark brown sugar, and heat gently until the sugar caramelizes.

4 Stir the soy sauce into the wok. Add the chicken and turn it in the mixture to coat thoroughly on all sides.

5 Add the water, garlic, onion, and chili. Cover and simmer, turning the chicken occasionally, for about 1 hour, or

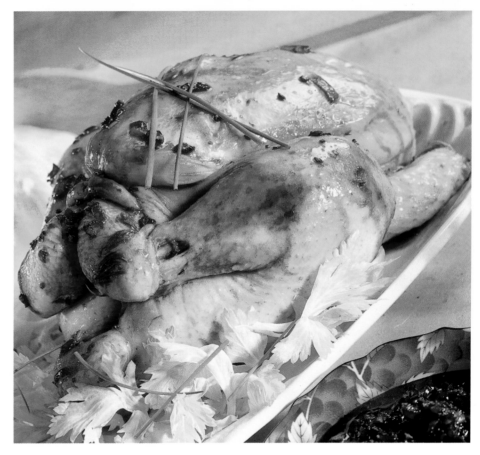

until cooked through. Test by piercing a thigh with the point of a knife or a skewer – the juices will run clear when the chicken is cooked.

6 Remove the chicken from the wok and set aside. Increase the heat and reduce the sauce in the wok until thickened. Transfer the chicken to a serving plate, garnish with celery leaves and chives, and serve with the sauce.

COOK'S TIP

For a spicier sauce, add 1 tbsp finely chopped fresh ginger and 1 tbsp ground Szechuan peppercorns with the chili in step 5.

Yellow Bean Chicken

Ready-made yellow bean sauce is available from large supermarkets and Chinese food stores. It is made from yellow soya beans and is quite salty.

NUTRITIONAL INFORMATION

Calories	234	Sugars	.........1g
Protein	........26g	Fat	..........12g
Carbohydrate	....6g	Saturates	.......2g

  25 MINS 10 MINS

SERVES 4

INGREDIENTS

1 lb skinless, boneless chicken breasts

1 egg white, beaten

1 tbsp cornstarch

1 tbsp rice wine vinegar

1 tbsp light soy sauce

1 tsp sugar

3 tbsp vegetable oil

1 garlic clove, crushed

½ inch piece fresh ginger, grated

1 green bell pepper, seeded and diced

2 large mushrooms, sliced

3 tbsp yellow bean sauce

yellow or green bell pepper strips, to garnish

1 Trim any fat from the chicken and cut the meat into 1 inch cubes.

2 Mix the egg white and cornstarch in a shallow bowl. Add the chicken and turn in the mixture to coat. Set aside for 20 minutes.

3 Mix the rice wine vinegar, soy sauce, and sugar in a bowl.

4 Remove the chicken from the egg white mixture.

5 Heat the oil in a preheated wok, add the chicken, and stir-fry for 3–4 minutes, until golden brown. Remove the chicken from the wok with a slotted spoon, set aside and keep warm.

6 Add the garlic, ginger, bell pepper, and mushrooms to the wok and stir-fry for 1–2 minutes.

7 Add the yellow bean sauce and cook for 1 minute. Stir in the vinegar mixture and return the chicken to the wok. Cook for 1–2 minutes and serve hot, garnished with bell pepper strips.

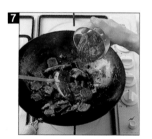

VARIATION

Black bean sauce would work equally well with this recipe. Although this would affect the appearance of the dish because it is much darker in color, the flavors would be compatible.

Kung Po Chicken

In this recipe, cashew nuts are used but peanuts, walnuts, or almonds can be substituted, if preferred.

NUTRITIONAL INFORMATION

Calories	294	Sugars	.........3g
Protein	........21g	Fat	..........18g
Carbohydrate	...10g	Saturates	.......4g

10 MINS   5 MINS

SERVES 4

INGREDIENTS

9-10½ oz chicken meat, boned and skinned

¼ tsp salt

⅓ egg white

1 tsp cornstarch paste (see page 31)

1 medium green bell pepper, cored and seeded

4 tbsp vegetable oil

1 scallion, cut into short sections

a few small slices of gingerroot

4-5 small dried red chilies, soaked, seeded, and shredded

2 tbsp crushed yellow bean sauce

1 tsp rice wine or dry sherry

4½ oz roasted cashew nuts

a few drops of sesame oil

boiled rice, to serve

1 Cut the chicken into small cubes about the size of sugar lumps. Place the chicken in a small bowl and mix with a pinch of salt, the egg white, and the cornstarch paste, in that order.

2 Cut the green bell pepper into cubes or triangles about the same size as the chicken pieces.

3 Heat the oil in a wok, add the chicken and stir-fry for 1 minute. Remove with a draining spoon and keep warm.

4 Add the scallion, ginger, chilies, and green bell pepper. Stir-fry for 1 minute, then add the chicken with the yellow bean sauce and wine. Blend well and stir-fry for another minute. Finally stir in the cashew nuts and sesame oil. Serve hot with boiled rice.

VARIATION

Any nuts can be used in place of the cashew nuts, if preferred. The important point is the crunchy texture, which is very much a feature of Szechuan cooking.

Fruity Duck Stir-fry

The pineapple and plum sauce add a sweetness and fruity flavor to this colorful recipe which blends well with the duck.

NUTRITIONAL INFORMATION

Calories	241	Sugars	.........7g
Protein	........26g	Fat	...........8g
Carbohydrate	...16g	Saturates	.......2g

🍲 5 MINS   🕐 25 MINS

SERVES 4

INGREDIENTS

4 duck breasts

1 tsp Chinese five-spice powder

1 tbsp cornstarch

1 tbsp chili oil

8 oz baby onions, peeled

2 cloves garlic, crushed

1 cup baby corn-on-the-cobs

1¼ cups canned pineapple chunks

6 green onions, sliced

1 cup bean sprouts

2 tbsp plum sauce

1 Remove any skin from the duck breasts. Cut the duck into thin slices.

2 Mix the five-spice powder and the cornstarch. Toss the duck in the mixture until well coated.

3 Heat the oil in a preheated wok. Stir-fry the duck for 10 minutes, or until just beginning to crisp around the edges. Remove from the wok and set aside.

4 Add the onions and garlic to the wok and stir-fry for 5 minutes, or until softened. Add the baby corn-on-the-cobs and stir-fry for 5 minutes more. Add the pineapple, green onions, and bean sprouts and stir-fry for 3–4 minutes. Stir in the plum sauce.

5 Return the cooked duck to the wok and toss until well mixed. Transfer to warm serving dishes and serve hot.

COOK'S TIP

Buy pineapple chunks in natural juice rather than syrup for a fresher flavor. If you can only obtain pineapple in syrup, rinse it in cold water and drain thoroughly before using.

Green Chicken Stir-Fry

Tender chicken is mixed with a selection of spring greens and flavored with yellow bean sauce in this crunchy stir-fry.

NUTRITIONAL INFORMATION

Calories ....297 Sugars 5g
Protein ....30g Fat 16g
Carbohydrate ....8g Saturates 3g

5 MINS   15 MINS

SERVES 4

I N G R E D I E N T S

2 tbsp sunflower oil

1 lb skinless, boneless chicken breasts

2 cloves garlic, crushed

1 green bell pepper

1½ cups snow peas

6 green onions, sliced, plus
    extra to garnish

8 oz spring greens or cabbage, shredded

5¾ oz jar yellow bean sauce

3 tbsp roasted cashews

1 Heat the sunflower oil in a large preheated wok.

2 Slice the chicken into thin strips and add to the wok together with the garlic. Stir-fry for about 5 minutes or until the chicken is sealed on all sides and beginning to turn golden.

3 Using a sharp knife, seed the green bell pepper and cut into thin strips.

4 Add the snow peas, green onions, green bell pepper strips, and spring greens or cabbage to the wok. Stir-fry for 5 minutes more or until the vegetables are just tender.

5 Stir in the yellow bean sauce and heat through for about 2 minutes or until the mixture starts to bubble.

6 Scatter the roasted cashews into the wok.

7 Transfer the stir-fry to warm serving plates and garnish with extra green onions, if desired. Serve the stir-fry immediately.

COOK'S TIP

Do not add salted cashews to this dish otherwise the dish will be too salty.

Chicken with Bean Sprouts

This is the basic Chicken Chop Suey to be found in almost every Chinese restaurant and takeout all over the world.

NUTRITIONAL INFORMATION

Calories 153   Sugars 4g
Protein ....9g   Fat 10g
Carbohydrate ....8g   Saturates 1g

3¹/₂ HOURS   10 MINS

SERVES 4

INGREDIENTS

4½ oz chicken breast fillet, skinned

1 tsp salt

¼ egg white, lightly beaten

2 tsp cornstarch paste
  (see page 31)

about 1¼ cups vegetable oil

1 small onion, thinly shredded

1 small green bell pepper, cored, seeded,
  and thinly shredded

1 small carrot, thinly shredded

4½ oz fresh bean sprouts

½ tsp sugar

1 tbsp light soy sauce

1 tsp rice wine or dry sherry

2-3 tbsp Chinese Stock (see page 30)

a few drops of sesame oil

chili sauce, to serve

1 Using a sharp knife or meat cleaver, cut the chicken into thin shreds and place in a bowl.

2 Add a pinch of the salt, the egg white and cornstarch paste to the chicken and mix well.

3 Heat the vegetable oil in a preheated wok or large skillet.

4 Add the chicken and stir-fry for about 1 minute, stirring to separate the shreds. Remove with a slotted spoon and drain on paper towels.

5 Pour off the oil, leaving about 2 tablespoons in the wok. Add the onion, green bell pepper, and carrot and stir-fry for about 2 minutes.

6 Add the bean sprouts and stir-fry for a few seconds.

7 Add the chicken with the remaining salt, sugar, soy sauce, and rice wine or dry sherry, blend well and add the Chinese stock or water.

8 Sprinkle the stir-fry with the sesame oil and serve with the chili sauce.

COOK'S TIP

Chop Suey actually originated in San Francisco at the turn of the century when Chinese immigrants were first settling there, and was first devised as a handy dish for using up leftovers.

Chili Coconut Chicken

This tasty dish combines the flavors of lime, peanut, coconut, and chili. You'll find coconut cream in most supermarkets or delicatessens.

NUTRITIONAL INFORMATION

Calories	348	Sugars	.........2g
Protein	........36g	Fat	..........21g
Carbohydrate	....3g	Saturates	.......8g

5 MINS   15 MINS

SERVES 4

INGREDIENTS

⅔ cup hot chicken stock

⅓ cup coconut cream

1 tbsp sunflower oil

8 skinless, boneless chicken thighs, cut into long, thin strips

1 small red chili, sliced thinly

4 green onions, sliced thinly

4 tbsp smooth or crunchy peanut butter

finely grated zest and juice of 1 lime

1 fresh red chili and green onion tassel, to garnish

boiled rice, to serve

1 Pour the chicken stock into a measuring jug or small bowl. Crumble the coconut cream into the chicken stock and stir the mixture until the coconut cream dissolves.

2 Heat the oil in a preheated wok or large heavy pan.

3 Add the chicken strips and cook, stirring, until the chicken turns a golden color.

4 Stir in the chopped red chili and green onions and cook gently for a few minutes.

5 Add the peanut butter, coconut cream and chicken stock mixture, lime zest, lime juice and simmer, uncovered, for about 5 minutes, stirring frequently to prevent the mixture sticking to the base of the wok or pan.

6 Transfer the chili coconut chicken to a warm serving dish, garnish with the red chili and green onion tassel and serve with boiled rice.

COOK'S TIP

Serve jasmine rice with this spicy dish. It has a fragrant aroma that is well-suited to the flavors in this dish.

Chicken with Black Bean Sauce

This tasty chicken stir-fry is quick and easy to make and is full of fresh flavors and crunchy vegetables.

NUTRITIONAL INFORMATION

Calories 205	Sugars 4g	
Protein 25g	Fat 9g	
Carbohydrate 6g	Saturates 2g	

40 MINS   10 MINS

SERVES 4

INGREDIENTS

15 oz chicken breasts,
    sliced thinly

pinch of salt

pinch of cornstarch

2 tbsp oil

1 garlic clove, crushed

1 tbsp black bean sauce

1 each small red and green bell pepper, cut
    into strips

1 red chili, chopped finely

1 cup mushrooms, sliced

1 onion, chopped

6 green onions, chopped

salt and pepper

SEASONING

½ tsp salt

½ tsp sugar

3 tbsp chicken stock

1 tbsp dark soy sauce

2 tbsp beef stock

2 tbsp rice wine

1 tsp cornstarch, blended
    with a little rice wine

1 Put the chicken strips in a bowl. Add a pinch of salt and a pinch of cornstarch and cover with water. Leave to stand for 30 minutes.

2 Heat 1 tablespoon of the oil in a wok or deep-sided skillet and stir-fry the chicken for 4 minutes.

3 Remove the chicken to a warm serving dish and clean the wok.

4 Add the remaining oil to the wok and add the garlic, black bean sauce, green and red bell peppers, chili, mushrooms, onion, and green onions. Stir-fry for 2 minutes then return the chicken to the wok.

5 Add the seasoning ingredients, fry for 3 minutes and thicken with a little of the cornstarch blend. Serve with fresh noodles.

Duck with Ginger & Lime

Just the thing for a lazy summer day – roasted duck sliced and served with a dressing made of ginger, lime juice, sesame oil, and fish sauce.

NUTRITIONAL INFORMATION

Calories	529	Sugars	.........3g
Protein	........38g	Fat	..........41g
Carbohydrate	....3g	Saturates	.......6g

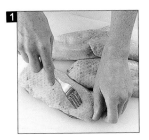

20 MINS   25 MINS

SERVES 4

I N G R E D I E N T S

3 boneless duck breasts, about
  9 oz each

salt

D R E S S I N G

½ cup olive oil

2 tsp sesame oil

2 tbsp lime juice

grated zest and juice of 1 orange

2 tsp fish sauce

1 tbsp grated fresh ginger

1 garlic clove, crushed

2 tsp light soy sauce

3 green onions, finely chopped

1 tsp sugar

about 9 oz assorted salad leaves

orange slices, to garnish (optional)

1 Wash the duck breasts, dry on paper towels, then cut in half. Prick the skin all over with a fork and season well with salt. Place the duck pieces, skin-side down, on a wire rack or trivet over a roasting pan.

2 Cook the duck in a preheated oven for 10 minutes, then turn over and cook for 12–15 minutes more, or until the duck is cooked, but still pink in the center, and the skin is crisp.

3 To make the dressing, beat the olive oil and sesame oil with the lime juice, orange zest and juice, fish sauce, grated fresh ginger, garlic, light soy sauce, green onions, and sugar until well blended.

4 Remove the duck from the oven, and allow to cool. Using a sharp knife, cut the duck into thick slices.

5 Add a little of the dressing to moisten and coat the duck.

6 To serve, arrange assorted salad leaves on a serving dish. Top with the sliced duck breasts and drizzle with the remaining salad dressing.

7 Garnish with orange slices, if using, then serve immediately.

Red Chicken Curry

The chicken is cooked with a curry paste using red chilies. It is a fiery hot sauce—for a milder version, reduce the number of chilies used.

NUTRITIONAL INFORMATION

Calories	331	Sugars	. . . . .5g
Protein	. . . . .36g	Fat	. . . . .17g
Carbohydrate	. . . .7g	Saturates	. . . . . . .3g

10 MINS   10 MINS

SERVES 4

I N G R E D I E N T S

4 tbsp vegetable oil

2 garlic cloves, crushed

1¾ cups coconut milk

6 chicken breast fillets, skinned and
    cut into bite-sized pieces

½ cup chicken stock

2 tbsp fish sauce

sliced red and green chilies,
    to garnish

boiled rice, to serve

R E D   C U R R Y   P A S T E

8 dried red chilies, seeded
    and chopped

1 inch Thai ginger or fresh ginger, peeled
    and sliced

3 stalks lemon grass, chopped

1 garlic clove, peeled

2 tsp shrimp paste

1 kaffir lime leaf, chopped

1 tsp ground coriander

¾ tsp ground cumin

1 tbsp chopped fresh cilantro

1 tsp salt and black pepper

1 To make the red curry paste, place all the ingredients in a food processor or blender and process until smooth.

2 Heat the vegetable oil in a large, heavy-bottomed pan or wok. Add the garlic and cook for 1 minute or until it turns golden.

3 Stir in the red curry paste and cook for 10–15 seconds.

4 Gradually add the coconut milk, stirring constantly (don't worry if the mixture starts to look curdled at this stage).

5 Add the chicken pieces and turn in the sauce mixture to coat. Cook gently for about 3–5 minutes or until almost tender.

6 Stir in the chicken stock and fish sauce, mixing well, then cook for 2 minutes more.

7 Transfer the chicken curry to a warmed serving dish and garnish with sliced red and green chilies. Serve with rice.

Grilled Duckling

The sweet, spicy marinade used in this recipe gives the duckling a subtle flavor of the Orient.

NUTRITIONAL INFORMATION

Calories	249	Sugars	........20g
Protein	........27g	Fat	...........6g
Carbohydrate	...23g	Saturates	.......2g

6¼ HOURS   30 MINS

SERVES 4

I N G R E D I E N T S

3 cloves garlic, crushed

⅔ cup light soy sauce

5 tbsp light brown sugar

1 inch piece fresh ginger, grated

1 tbsp chopped, fresh cilantro

1 tsp five-spice powder

4 duckling breasts

sprig of fresh cilantro,
    to garnish (optional)

1 To make the marinade, mix together the garlic, soy sauce, sugar, grated ginger, chopped cilantro, and five-spice powder in a small bowl until well combined.

2 Place the duckling breasts in a shallow, non-metallic dish and pour over the marinade. Carefully turn over the duckling so that it is fully coated with the marinade on both sides.

3 Cover the bowl with plastic wrap and leave to marinate for 1–6 hours, turning the duckling once or twice so that the marinade is fully absorbed.

4 Remove the duckling from the marinade, reserving the marinade for basting.

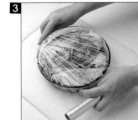

5 Grill the duckling breasts over hot coals for about 20–30 minutes, turning and basting frequently with the reserved marinade, using a pastry brush.

6 Cut the duckling into slices and transfer to warm serving plates. Serve the grilled duckling garnished with a sprig of fresh cilantro, if using.

COOK'S TIP

Duckling is quite a fatty meat so there is no need to add oil to the marinade. However, you must remember to oil the grill rack to prevent the duckling from sticking. Oil the rack well away from the grill to avoid any danger of a flare-up.

Garlic & Lime Chicken

Garlic and cilantro flavor the chicken breasts which are served with a caramelized sauce, sharpened with lime juice.

NUTRITIONAL INFORMATION

Calories	280	Sugars	.........7g
Protein	........26g	Fat	..........17g
Carbohydrate	....7g	Saturates	.......8g

🐔 🐔 🐔

🍗 10 MINS   🕐 25 MINS

SERVES 4

I N G R E D I E N T S

4 large skinless, boneless
  chicken breasts

3 tbsp garlic butter, softened

3 tbsp chopped fresh cilantro

1 tbsp sunflower oil

finely grated zest and juice of 2 limes,
  plus extra zest, to garnish

4 tbsp sugar or brown sugar

T O   S E R V E

boiled rice

lemon wedges

1 Place each chicken breast between 2 sheets of plastic wrap and pound with a rolling pin until flattened to about ½ inch thick.

2 Mix together the garlic butter and cilantro and spread over each flattened chicken breast. Roll up and secure with a toothpick.

3 Heat the sunflower oil in a preheated wok or heavy-bottomed skillet.

4 Add the chicken rolls to the wok or pan and cook, turning, for 15–20 minutes or until cooked through.

5 Remove the chicken from the wok and transfer to a board. Cut each chicken roll into slices.

6 Add the lime zest, juice and sugar to the wok and heat gently, stirring, until the sugar has dissolved. Raise the heat and allow to bubble for 2 minutes.

7 Arrange the chicken on warmed serving plates and spoon the pan juices over to serve.

8 Garnish the garlic and lime chicken with extra lime zest, if desired.

COOK'S TIP

Be sure to check that the chicken is cooked through before slicing and serving. Cook over a gentle heat so as not to overcook the outside, while the inside remains raw.

Orange Chicken Stir-Fry

Chicken thighs are inexpensive, meaty portions which are easily available. Although not as tender as breast, it is perfect for stir-frying.

NUTRITIONAL INFORMATION

Calories	267	Sugars	........11g
Protein	........23g	Fat	..........11g
Carbohydrate	...15g	Saturates	.......2g

10 MINS   15 MINS

SERVES 4

INGREDIENTS

3 tbsp sunflower oil

12 oz boneless chicken thighs, skinned, and cut into thin strips

1 onion, sliced

1 clove garlic, crushed

1 red bell pepper, seeded and sliced

1¼ cups snow peas

4 tbsp light soy sauce

4 tbsp sherry

1 tbsp tomato paste

finely grated zest and juice of 1 orange

1 tsp cornstarch

2 oranges

1 cup bean sprouts

cooked rice or noodles, to serve

1 Heat the oil in a large preheated wok. Add the chicken and stir-fry for 2–3 minutes or until sealed on all sides.

2 Add the onion, garlic, bell pepper, and snow peas to the wok. Stir-fry for 5 minutes more, or until the vegetables are just tender and the chicken is completely cooked through.

3 Mix together the soy sauce, sherry, tomato paste, orange zest and juice, and the cornstarch. Add to the wok and cook, stirring, until the juices start to thicken.

4 Using a sharp knife, peel and segment the oranges. Add the segments to the mixture in the wok with the bean sprouts and heat through for 2 minutes more.

5 Transfer the stir-fry to serving plates and serve immediately with cooked rice or noodles.

COOK'S TIP

Bean sprouts are sprouting mung beans and are a regular ingredient in Chinese cooking. They require very little cooking and may even be eaten raw, if wished.

Sweet Mango Chicken

The sweet, scented flavor of mango gives this dish its characteristic sweetness.

NUTRITIONAL INFORMATION

Calories	244	Sugars	........18g
Protein	........27g	Fat	...........7g
Carbohydrate	...2.1g	Saturates	.......2g

10 MINS   15 MINS

SERVES 4

I N G R E D I E N T S

1 tbsp sunflower oil

6 skinless, boneless chicken thighs

1 ripe mango

2 cloves garlic, crushed

8 oz leeks, shredded

1 cup bean sprouts

⅔ cup mango juice

1 tbsp white wine vinegar

2 tbsp honey

2 tbsp tomato ketchup

1 tsp cornstarch

COOK'S TIP

Mango juice is avaialable in jars from most supermarkets and is quite thick and sweet. If it is unavailable, purée and strain a ripe mango and add a little water to make up the required quantity.

1 Heat the sunflower oil in a large preheated wok.

2 Cut the chicken into bite-sized cubes, add to the wok, and stir-fry over a high heat for 10 minutes, tossing frequently until the chicken is cooked through and golden in color.

3 Peel and slice the mango and add to the wok with the garlic, leeks, and bean sprouts. Stir-fry for 2–3 minutes more, or until softened.

4 Mix together the mango juice, white wine vinegar, honey, tomato ketchup and cornstarch. Pour into the wok and stir-fry for 2 minutes more, or until the juices start to thicken.

5 Transfer to a warmed serving dish and serve immediately.

Peking Duck

No Chinese cookery book would be complete without this famous recipe in which crisp-skinned duck is served with pancakes and a tangy sauce.

NUTRITIONAL INFORMATION

Calories 357   Sugars 48g
Protein . . . . .20g   Fat 10g
Carbohydrate . . .49g   Saturates 2g

  6¼ HOURS   1½ HOURS

SERVES 4

INGREDIENTS

4 lb duck

7½ cups boiling water

4 tbsp honey

2 tsp dark soy sauce

2 tbsp sesame oil

½ cup hoisin sauce

⅔ cup sugar

½ cup water

carrot strips, to garnish

Chinese pancakes, raw cucumber
    sticks, and sliced green onions, to serve

4 Brush the mixture over the skin and inside the duck. Reserve the remaining glaze. Set the duck aside for 1 hour, until the glaze has dried.

5 Coat the duck with another layer of glaze. Let dry and repeat until all of the glaze is used.

6 Heat the sesame oil in a saucepan and add the hoisin sauce, sugar, and water. Simmer for 2–3 minutes, until thickened. Leave to cool and then refrigerate until required.

7 Cook the duck in a preheated oven at 375°F for 30 minutes. Turn the duck over and cook for 20 minutes. Turn the duck again and cook for 20–30 minutes, or until cooked through and the skin is crisp.

8 Remove the duck from the oven and set aside for 10 minutes.

9 Meanwhile, heat the pancakes in a steamer for 5–7 minutes or according to the instructions on the pack. Cut the skin and duck meat into strips, garnish with the carrot strips, and serve with the pancakes, sauce, cucumber and green onions.

1 Place the duck on a rack set over a roasting pan and pour 5 cups of the boiling water over it.

2 Remove the duck and rack and discard the water. Pat dry with absorbent paper towels, replace the duck and the rack, and set aside for several hours.

3 In a small bowl, mix together the honey, remaining boiling water, and dark soy sauce, until they are thoroughly combined.

Szechuan Chili Chicken

In China, the chicken pieces are chopped through the bone for this dish, but if you do not possess a meat cleaver, use filleted chicken meat.

NUTRITIONAL INFORMATION

Calories 218   Sugars 4g
Protein . . . . .23g   Fat 9g
Carbohydrate . . . .8g   Saturates 2g

 4 HOURS   15 MINS

SERVES 4

I N G R E D I E N T S

1 lb 2 oz chicken thighs

¼ tsp pepper

1 tbsp sugar

2 tsp light soy sauce

1 tsp dark soy sauce

1 tbsp rice wine or dry sherry

2 tsp cornstarch

2-3 tbsp vegetable oil

1-2 garlic cloves, crushed

2 green onions, cut into
   short sections, with the green
   and white parts separated

4-6 small dried red chilies, soaked and
   seeded

2 tbsp crushed yellow bean sauce

⅔ cup Chinese Stock (see page 30) or water

1 Cut or chop the chicken thighs into bite-sized pieces and marinate with the pepper, sugar, soy sauce, wine, and cornstarch for 25-30 minutes.

2 Heat the oil in a pre-heated wok and stir-fry the chicken for about 1–2 minutes until lightly brown. Remove with a slotted spoon, transfer to a warm dish, and reserve. Add the garlic, the white parts of the green onions, the chilies, and yellow bean sauce to the wok and stir-fry for about 30 seconds.

3 Return the chicken to the wok, stirring constantly for about 1-2 minutes, then add the stock or water, bring to a boil, and cover. Braise over a medium heat for 5-6 minutes, stirring once or twice. Garnish with the green parts of the green onions and serve immediately.

COOK'S TIP

One of the striking features of Szechuan cooking is the quantity of chilies used. Food generally in this region is much hotter than elsewhere in China—people tend to keep a string of dry chilies hanging from the eaves of their houses.

Chicken with Mushrooms

Dried Chinese mushrooms (shiitake) should be used for this dish—otherwise use black rather than white fresh mushrooms.

NUTRITIONAL INFORMATION

Calories 125   Sugars 0.3g
Protein ....20g   Fat 3g
Carbohydrates ....3g   Saturates 1g

  1¼ HOURS   20 MINS

SERVES 4

INGREDIENTS

10½-12 oz chicken, boned and skinned

½ tsp sugar

1 tbsp light soy sauce

1 tsp rice wine or dry sherry

2 tsp cornstarch

4-6 dried Chinese mushrooms, soaked in warm water

1 tbsp finely shredded fresh ginger

salt and pepper

a few drops of sesame oil

cilantro leaves, to garnish

1 Using a sharp knife or meat cleaver, cut the chicken into small bite-sized pieces and place in a bowl.

2 Add the sugar, light soy sauce, wine or sherry and cornstarch to the chicken, toss to coat, and leave to marinate for 25-30 minutes.

3 Drain the mushrooms and dry on absorbent paper towels. Slice the mushrooms into thin shreds, discarding any hard pieces of stem.

4 Place the chicken pieces on a heat-proof dish that will fit inside a bamboo steamer. Arrange the mushroom slices and ginger shreds on top of the chicken and sprinkle with salt, pepper and sesame oil.

5 Place the dish on the rack inside a hot steamer or on a rack in a wok filled with hot water and steam over a high heat for 20 minutes.

6 Serve hot, garnished with fresh cilantro leaves.

COOK'S TIP

Do not throw away the soaking water from the dried Chinese mushrooms. It is very useful because it can be added to soups and stocks to give extra flavor.

Chicken with Vegetables

Coconut adds a creamy texture and delicious flavor to this stir-fry, which is spiked with green chili.

NUTRITIONAL INFORMATION

Calories	330	Sugars	.........4g
Protein	........23g	Fat	..........24g
Carbohydrate	....6g	Saturates	......10g

 10 MINS   10 MINS

SERVES 4

INGREDIENTS

3 tbsp sesame oil

12 oz chicken breast,
    sliced thinly

8 shallots, sliced

2 garlic cloves, finely chopped

1 inch piece fresh ginger, grated

1 green chili, finely chopped

1 each red and green bell pepper,
    sliced thinly

3 zucchini, thinly sliced

2 tbsp ground almonds

1 tsp ground cinnamon

1 tbsp oyster sauce

¼ cup creamed coconut, grated

salt and pepper

1 Heat the sesame oil in a preheated wok or large skillet.

2 Add the chicken slices to the wok or skillet, season with salt and pepper and stir fry for about 4 minutes.

3 Add the shallots, garlic, ginger, and chili and stir-fry for 2 minutes.

4 Add the red and green bell peppers and zucchini and cook for about 1 minute.

5 Finally, add the ground almonds, cinnamon, oyster sauce, and coconut. Stir fry for 1 minute.

6 Transfer to a warm serving dish and serve immediately.

VARIATION

You can vary the vegetables in this dish according to seasonal availability or whatever you have at hand. Try broccoli flowerets or baby corn-on-the-cobs.

Duck in Spicy Sauce

Chinese five-spice powder gives a lovely flavor to this sliced duck, and the chili adds a little subtle heat.

NUTRITIONAL INFORMATION

Calories	162	Sugars	.........2g
Protein	........20g	Fat	..........7g
Carbohydrate	....3g	Saturates	.......2g

5 MINS   25 MINS

SERVES 4

INGREDIENTS

1 tbsp vegetable oil

1 tsp grated fresh ginger

1 garlic clove, crushed

1 fresh red chili, chopped

12 oz skinless, boneless duck meat, cut into strips

4½ oz cauliflower, cut into flowerets

2 oz snow peas

2 oz baby corn-on-the-cobs, halved lengthwise

1¼ cups chicken stock

1 tsp Chinese five-spice powder

2 tsp Chinese rice wine or dry sherry

1 tsp cornstarch

2 tsp water

1 tsp sesame oil

1 Heat the oil in a wok. Lower the heat slightly, add the ginger, garlic, chili, and duck and stir-fry for 2-3 minutes. Remove from the wok and set aside.

2 Add the vegetables to the wok and stir-fry for 2-3 minutes. Pour off any excess oil from the wok and push the vegetables to one side.

3 Return the duck to the wok and pour in the stock. Sprinkle the Chinese five-spice powder over the top, stir in the wine or sherry and cook over a low heat for 15 minutes, or until the duck is tender.

4 Blend the cornstarch with the water to form a paste and stir into the wok with the sesame oil. Bring to a boil, stirring until the sauce has thickened and cleared. Transfer the duck and spicy sauce to a warm serving dish and serve immediately.

COOK'S TIP

Omit the chili for a milder dish, or seed the chili before adding it to remove some of the heat.

Cumin-spiced Chicken

Cumin seeds are more frequently associated with Indian cooking, but they are used in this Chinese recipe for their earthy flavor.

NUTRITIONAL INFORMATION

Calories	245	Sugars	.........9g
Protein	........28g	Fat	..........10g
Carbohydrate	....11g	Saturates	.......2g

5 MINS   15 MINS

SERVES 4

I N G R E D I E N T S

1 lb boneless, skinless chicken breasts

2 tbsp sunflower oil

1 clove garlic, crushed

1 tbsp cumin seeds

1 tbsp grated fresh ginger

1 red chili, seeded and sliced

1 red bell pepper, seeded and sliced

1 green bell pepper, seeded and sliced

1 yellow bell pepper, seeded and sliced

1 cup bean sprouts

12 oz bok choy or other green leaves

2 tbsp sweet chili sauce

3 tbsp light soy sauce

deep-fried crispy ginger, to garnish (see Cook's Tip)

COOK'S TIP

To make the deep-fried ginger garnish, peel and thinly slice a large piece of fresh ginger. Carefully lower the slices of ginger into a wok or small pan of hot oil and cook for about 30 seconds. Transfer to paper towels and leave to drain thoroughly.

1 Using a sharp knife, slice the chicken breasts into thin strips.

2 Heat the oil in a large preheated wok.

3 Add the chicken to the wok and stir-fry for 5 minutes.

4 Add the garlic, cumin seeds, ginger, and chili to the wok, stirring to mix.

5 Add all the bell peppers to the wok and stir-fry for 5 minutes more.

6 Toss in the bean sprouts and bok choy together with the sweet chili sauce and soy sauce and continue to cook until the bok choy leaves start to wilt.

7 Transfer to warm serving bowls and garnish with deep-fried ginger (see Cook's Tip).

Spicy Peanut Chicken

This quick dish has many variations, but this version includes the classic combination of peanuts, chicken, and chilies.

NUTRITIONAL INFORMATION

Calories	342	Sugars	........3g
Protein	........25g	Fat	.........24g
Carbohydrate	....6g	Saturates	.......5g

5 MINS   10 MINS

SERVES 4

I N G R E D I E N T S

10½ oz skinless, boneless
   chicken breast

2 tbsp peanut oil

1 cup shelled peanuts

1 fresh red chili, sliced

1 green bell pepper, seeded and
   cut into strips

fried rice, to serve

S A U C E

⅔ cup chicken stock

1 tbsp Chinese rice wine or
   dry sherry

1 tbsp light soy sauce

1½ tsp light brown sugar

2 garlic cloves, crushed

1 tsp grated fresh ginger

1 tsp rice wine vinegar

1 tsp sesame oil

1 Trim any fat from the chicken and cut the meat into 1 inch cubes. Set aside until required.

2 Heat the peanut oil in a preheated wok or skillet.

3 Add the peanuts to the wok and stir-fry for 1 minute. Remove the peanuts with a slotted spoon and set aside.

4 Add the chicken to the wok and cook for 1–2 minutes.

5 Stir in the chili and green bell pepper and cook for 1 minute. Remove from the wok with a slotted spoon and set aside.

6 Put half of the peanuts in a food processor and process until almost smooth. If necessary, add a little stock to form a softer paste. Alternatively, place them in a plastic bag and crush them with a rolling pin.

7 To make the sauce, add the chicken stock, Chinese rice wine or dry sherry, light soy sauce, light brown sugar, crushed garlic cloves, grated fresh ginger, and rice wine vinegar to the wok.

8 Heat the sauce without boiling and stir in the peanut purée, remaining peanuts, chicken, sliced red chili, and green bell pepper strips. Mix well until all the ingredients are thoroughly combined.

9 Sprinkle the sesame oil into the wok, stir and cook for 1 minute. Transfer the spicy peanut chicken to a warm serving dish and serve hot with fried rice.

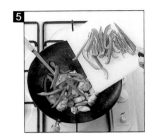

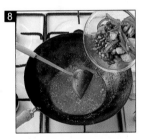

Duck with Leek & Cabbage

Duck is a strongly flavored meat which benefits from the added citrus peel to counteract the rich taste.

NUTRITIONAL INFORMATION

Calories	192	Sugars	.........5g
Protein	........26g	Fat	..........7g
Carbohydrate	....6g	Saturates	.......2g

🥄 10 MINS   ⏱ 40 MINS

SERVES 4

INGREDIENTS

4 duck breasts

12 oz green cabbage,
  thinly shredded

8 oz leeks, sliced

finely grated zest of 1 orange

6 tbsp oyster sauce

1 tsp toasted sesame seeds,
  to serve

1 Heat a large wok and dry-fry the duck breasts, with the skin on, for about 5 minutes on each side (you may need to do this in 2 batches).

2 Remove the duck breasts from the wok and transfer to a clean board.

3 Using a sharp knife, cut the duck breasts into thin slices.

4 Remove all but 1 tablespoon of the fat from the duck left in the wok; discard the rest.

5 Using a sharp knife, thinly shred the green cabbage.

6 Add the leeks, green cabbage and orange zest to the wok and stir-fry for about 5 minutes, or until the vegetables have softened.

7 Return the duck to the wok and heat through for 2–3 minutes.

8 Drizzle the oyster sauce over the mixture in the wok, toss well until all the ingredients are combined, and then heat through.

9 Scatter the stir-fry with toasted sesame seeds, transfer to a warm serving dish, and serve hot.

VARIATION

Use Chinese cabbage for a lighter, sweeter flavor instead of the green cabbage, if you prefer.

Peppered Chicken

Crushed mixed peppercorns coat tender, thin strips of chicken which are cooked with green and red bell peppers for a really colorful dish.

NUTRITIONAL INFORMATION

Calories . . . . .219 Sugars 6g
Protein . . . . .22g Fat 10g
Carbohydrate . . . .11g Saturates 2g

5 MINS   15 MINS

SERVES 4

INGREDIENTS

2 tbsp tomato ketchup

2 tbsp soy sauce

1 lb boneless, skinless chicken breasts

2 tbsp crushed mixed peppercorns

2 tbsp sunflower oil

1 red bell pepper

1 green bell pepper

2½ cups sugar snap peas

2 tbsp oyster sauce

1 Mix the tomato ketchup with the soy sauce in a bowl.

2 Using a sharp knife, slice the chicken into thin strips.

3 Toss the chicken in the tomato ketchup and soy sauce mixture until the chicken is well coated.

4 Sprinkle the crushed peppercorns on to a plate. Dip the coated chicken in the peppercorns until evenly coated.

5 Heat the sunflower oil in a preheated wok or large skillet, until the oil is smoking.

6 Add the chicken to the wok and stir-fry for 5 minutes.

7 Using a sharp knife, seed and slice the bell peppers.

8 Add the bell peppers to the wok together with the sugar snap peas and stir-fry for 5 minutes more.

9 Add the oyster sauce and allow to bubble for 2 minutes. Transfer the peppered chicken to serving bowls and serve immediately.

VARIATION

Use snow peas instead of the sugar snap peas, if you prefer.

Turkey with Cranberry Glaze

Traditional Christmas ingredients are given a Chinese twist in this stir-fry which contains cranberries, ginger, chestnuts, and soy sauce!

NUTRITIONAL INFORMATION

Calories 167	Sugars 11g	
Protein 8g	Fat 7g	
Carbohydrate ...20g	Saturates 1g	

 5 MINS   15 MINS

SERVES 4

INGREDIENTS

1 turkey breast

2 tbsp sunflower oil

2 tbsp stem ginger

½ cup fresh or frozen cranberries

¼ cup canned chestnuts

4 tbsp cranberry sauce

3 tbsp light soy sauce

salt and pepper

1 Remove any skin from the turkey breast. Using a sharp knife, thinly slice the turkey breast.

2 Heat the sunflower oil in a large preheated wok or heavy-bottomed skillet.

3 Add the turkey to the wok and stir-fry for 5 minutes, or until cooked through.

4 Using a sharp knife, finely chop the stem ginger.

5 Add the ginger and the cranberries to the wok or skillet and stir-fry for 2–3 minutes or until the cranberries have softened.

6 Add the chestnuts, cranberry sauce and soy sauce, season to taste with salt and pepper, and allow to bubble for 2–3 minutes.

7 Transfer the turkey stir-fry to warm serving dishes and serve immediately.

COOK'S TIP

It is very important that the wok is very hot before you stir-fry. Test by holding your hand flat about 3 inches above the base of the interior—you should be able to feel the heat radiating from it.

Chicken & Corn Sauté

This quick and healthy dish is stir-fried, which means you need use only the minimum of fat.

NUTRITIONAL INFORMATION

Calories 280   Sugars 7g
Protein . . . . .31g   Fat 11g
Carbohydrate . . . .9g   Saturates 2g

5 MINS   10 MINS

SERVES 4

I N G R E D I E N T S

4 skinless, boneless chicken breasts

1⅓ cups baby corn-on-the-cob

9 oz snow peas

2 tbsp sunflower oil

1 tbsp sherry vinegar

1 tbsp honey

1 tbsp light soy sauce

1 tbsp sunflower seeds

pepper

rice or Chinese egg noodles, to serve

1 Using a sharp knife, slice the chicken breasts into long, thin strips.

2 Cut the baby corn in half lengthwise and top and tail the mangetout (snow peas).

3 Heat the sunflower oil in a preheated wok or a wide skillet.

4 Add the chicken and fry over a fairly high heat, stirring, for 1 minute.

5 Add the baby corn-on-the-cob and snow peas and stir-fry over a moderate heat for 5–8 minutes, until evenly cooked. The vegetables should still be slightly crunchy.

6 Mix together the sherry vinegar, honey and soy sauce in a small bowl.

7 Stir the vinegar mixture into the pan with the sunflower seeds.

8 Season well with pepper. Cook, stirring, for 1 minute.

9 Serve the chicken & corn sauté hot with rice or Chinese egg noodles.

VARIATION

Rice vinegar or balsamic vinegar makes a good substitute for the sherry vinegar.

Duck with Lime & Kiwi Fruit

Tender breasts of duck served in thin slices, with a sweet but very tangy lime and wine sauce, full of pieces of kiwi fruit.

NUTRITIONAL INFORMATION

Calories 264   Sugars 20g
Protein ....20g   Fat 10g
Carbohydrate ...21g   Saturates 2g

1¼ HOURS   15 MINS

SERVES 4

INGREDIENTS

4 boneless or part-boned
 duck breasts

grated zest and juice of 2 large limes

2 tbsp sunflower oil

4 green onions, thinly sliced diagonally

4½ oz carrots, cut into thin sticks

6 tbsp dry white wine

¼ cup white sugar

2 kiwi fruit, peeled, halved, and sliced

salt and pepper

parsley sprigs and lime halves tied in knots
 (see Cook's Tip), to garnish

1 Trim any fat from the duck, then prick the skin all over with a fork and lay in a shallow dish. Add half the grated lime and half the juice to the duck breasts, rubbing in thoroughly. Leave to stand in a cool place for at least 1 hour, turning the breasts at least once.

2 Drain the duck breasts, reserving the marinade. Heat 1 tbsp of oil in a wok. Add the duck and fry quickly to seal all over, then lower the heat and continue to cook for about 5 minutes, turning several times until just cooked through and well browned all over. Remove and keep warm.

3 Wipe the wok clean with paper towels and heat the remaining oil. Add the green onions and carrots and stir-fry for 1 minute, then add the remaining lime marinade, wine, and sugar. Bring to a boil and simmer for 2-3 minutes until slightly syrupy.

4 Add the duck breasts to the sauce, season and add the kiwi fruit. Stir-fry for a minute or until really hot and both the duck and kiwi fruit are well coated in the sauce.

5 Cut each duck breast into slices, leaving a "hinge'" at one end, open out into a fan shape and arrange on plates. Spoon the sauce over the duck, sprinkle with the remaining pieces of lime peel, garnish, and serve.

COOK'S TIP

To make the garnish, trim a piece off the base of each lime half so they stand upright. Pare off a thin strip of zest from the top of the lime halves, about ¼ inch thick, but do not detach it. Tie the strip into a knot with the end bending over the cut surface of the lime.

Chicken with Bell Peppers

Red bell pepper or celery can also be used in the recipe; the method is the same.

NUTRITIONAL INFORMATION

Calories	113	Sugars	.........1g
Protein	........17g	Fat	...........3g
Carbohydrate	....4g	Saturates	.......1g

🍲 5 MINS   🕐 5 MINS

SERVES 4

I N G R E D I E N T S

10½ oz boned, skinned chicken breast

1 tsp salt

½ egg white

2 tsp cornstarch paste (see page 31)

1 medium green bell pepper, cored and seeded

1¼ cups vegetable oil

1 green onion, finely shredded

a few strips of fresh ginger, thinly shredded

1-2 red chilies, seeded and thinly shredded

½ tsp sugar

1 tbsp rice wine or dry sherry

a few drops of sesame oil

1 Cut the chicken breast into strips. Mix the chicken with a pinch of the salt, the egg white and cornstarch.

2 Cut the green bell pepper into fairly thin shreds.

3 Heat the oil in a preheated wok, and deep-fry the chicken strips in batches for about 1 minute, or until the chicken changes color. Remove the chicken strips with a slotted spoon, pat dry on paper towels and keep warm.

4 Pour off the excess oil from the wok, leaving about 1 tablespoon. Add the green onion, ginger, chilies, and green bell pepper and stir-fry for 1 minute.

5 Return the chicken to the wok with the remaining salt, the sugar, and wine or sherry. Stir-fry for another minute, sprinkle with sesame oil, and serve immediately.

COOK'S TIP

Rice wine is used everywhere in China for both cooking and drinking. Made from glutinous rice, it is known as "yellow wine" because of its rich amber color. Sherry is the best substitute as a cooking ingredient.

Duck with Broccoli & Peppers

This is a colorful dish using different colored bell peppers and broccoli to make it both tasty and appealing to the eye.

NUTRITIONAL INFORMATION

Calories	.261	Sugars	.3g
Protein	.26g	Fat	.13g
Carbohydrate	.11g	Saturates	.2g

35 MINS   15 MINS

SERVES 4

INGREDIENTS

1 egg white

2 tbsp cornstarch

1 lb skinless, boneless duck meat

vegetable oil, for deep-frying

1 red bell pepper, seeded and diced

1 yellow bell pepper, seeded and diced

4½ oz small broccoli flowerets

1 garlic clove, crushed

2 tbsp light soy sauce

2 tsp Chinese rice wine or dry sherry

1 tsp light brown sugar

½ cup chicken stock

2 tsp sesame seeds

1 In a mixing bowl, beat together the egg white and cornstarch.

2 Using a sharp knife, cut the duck into 1 inch cubes and stir into the egg white mixture. Leave to stand for 30 minutes.

3 Heat the oil for deep-frying in a preheated wok or heavy-bottomed skillet until almost smoking.

4 Remove the duck from the egg white mixture, add to the wok and fry in the oil for 4–5 minutes, until crisp. Remove the duck from the oil with a slotted spoon and drain on paper towels.

5 Add the bell peppers and broccoli to the wok and fry for 2–3 minutes. Remove with a slotted spoon and drain on paper towels.

6 Pour all but 2 tablespoons of the oil from the wok and return to the heat. Add the garlic and stir-fry for 30 seconds.

Stir in the soy sauce, Chinese rice wine or sherry, sugar, and chicken stock and bring to a boil.

7 Stir in the duck and reserved vegetables and cook for 1–2 minutes.

8 Carefully spoon the duck and vegetables on to a warmed serving dish and sprinkle with the sesame seeds. Serve immediately.

Honey & Soy Chicken

Honey is often added to Chinese recipes for sweetness. It combines well with the saltiness of the soy sauce.

NUTRITIONAL INFORMATION

Calories	279	Sugars	........10g
Protein	........38g	Fat	..........8g
Carbohydrate	...12g	Saturates	.......2g

 35 MINS   25 MINS

SERVES 4

INGREDIENTS

2 tbsp honey

3 tbsp light soy sauce

1 tsp Chinese five-spice powder

1 tbsp sweet sherry

1 clove garlic, crushed

8 chicken thighs

1 tbsp sunflower oil

1 red chili

1¼ cups baby corn-on-the-cobs, halved

8 green onions, sliced

1½ cups bean sprouts

1 Mix together the honey, soy sauce, Chinese five-spice powder, sherry, and garlic in a large bowl.

2 Using a sharp knife, make 3 slashes in the skin of each chicken thigh. Brush the honey and soy marinade over the chicken thighs, cover, and leave to stand for at least 30 minutes.

3 Heat the oil in a large preheated wok. Add the chicken and cook over a fairly high heat for 12–15 minutes, or until the chicken browns and the skin begins to crisp. Remove the chicken with a slotted spoon and keep warm until required.

4 Using a sharp knife, seed and very finely chop the chili.

5 Add the chili, corns, green onions, and bean sprouts to the wok and stir-fry for 5 minutes.

6 Return the chicken to the wok and mix all of the ingredients together until completely heated through. Transfer to serving plates and serve immediately.

COOK'S TIP

Chinese five-spice powder is found in most large supermarkets and is a blend of star anise, fennel seeds, cloves, cinnamon bark, and Szechuan pepper.

Roast Game Hens

Game hens are stuffed with lemon grass and lime leaves, coated with a spicy marinade, then roasted until crisp and golden.

NUTRITIONAL INFORMATION

Calories 183	Sugars 1g	
Protein 30g	Fat 7g	
Carbohydrate 1g	Saturates 2g	

🍲 10 MINS   🕐 55 MINS

SERVES 4

INGREDIENTS

4 small game hens, weighing about
  12 oz-1 lb 2 oz each

cilantro leaves and lime
  wedges, to garnish

a mixture of wild rice and Basmati rice,
  to serve

MARINADE

4 garlic cloves, peeled

2 fresh cilantro roots

1 tbsp light soy sauce

salt and pepper

STUFFING

4 blades lemon grass

4 kaffir lime leaves

4 slices fresh ginger

about 6 tbsp coconut milk, to brush

1 Wash the game hens and dry on paper towels.

2 Place all the ingredients for the marinade in a small blender and purée until smooth. Alternatively, grind to a paste in a pestle and mortar. Season to taste with salt and pepper.

3 Rub this marinade mixture into the skin of the game hens, using the back of a spoon to spread it evenly over the skins.

4 Place a blade of lemon grass, a lime leaf and a piece of ginger in the cavity of each hen.

5 Place the game hens in a roasting pan and brush lightly with the coconut milk. Roast for about 30 minutes in a preheated oven.

6 Remove from the oven, brush again with coconut milk, return to the oven

and cook for 15-25 minutes more, until golden and cooked through, depending upon the size of the game hens. The game hens are cooked when the juices from the thigh run clear and are not tinged at all with pink.

7 Serve the game hens with the pan juices poured over. Garnish with cilantro leaves and lime wedges, and serve with rice.

Duck with Mangoes

Use fresh mangoes in this recipe for a terrific flavor and color. If they are unavailable, use canned mangoes and rinse them before using.

NUTRITIONAL INFORMATION

Calories 235   Sugars 6g
Protein ....23g   Fat 14g
Carbohydrate ....6g   Saturates 2g

5 MINS   35 MINS

SERVES 4

INGREDIENTS

2 medium-size ripe mangoes

1¼ cups chicken stock

2 garlic cloves, crushed

1 tsp grated fresh ginger

3 tbsp vegetable oil

2 large skinless duck breasts, about 8 oz each

1 tsp wine vinegar

1 tsp light soy sauce

1 leek, sliced

freshly chopped parsley, to garnish

1 Peel the mangoes and cut the flesh from each side of the pits. Cut the flesh into strips.

2 Put half of the mango pieces and the chicken stock in a food processor and process until smooth. Alternatively, press half of the mangoes through a fine strainer and mix with the stock.

3 Rub the garlic and ginger over the duck. Heat the vegetable oil in a preheated wok and cook the duck breasts, turning, until sealed. Reserve the oil in the wok and remove the duck.

4 Place the duck on a rack set over a roasting pan and cook in a preheated oven at 425°F for 20 minutes, until the duck is cooked through.

5 Meanwhile, place the mango and stock mixture in a saucepan and add the wine vinegar and light soy sauce.

6 Bring the mixture in the saucepan to a boil and cook over a high heat, stirring, until reduced by half.

7 Heat the oil reserved in the wok and stir-fry the sliced leek and remaining mango for 1 minute. Remove from the wok, transfer to a serving dish, and keep warm until required.

8 Slice the cooked duck breasts and arrange the slices on top of the leek and mango mixture. Pour the sauce over the duck slices, garnish, and serve.

Chicken & Vegetables

This is a popular dish in Chinese restaurants in the West, although nothing beats making it yourself.

NUTRITIONAL INFORMATION

Calories	298	Sugars	.........4g
Protein	........22g	Fat	..........19g
Carbohydrate	....11g	Saturates	.......4g

🍲 30 MINS   🕐 15 MINS

SERVES 4

INGREDIENTS

10½ oz boneless, skinless chicken breasts

1 tbsp cornstarch

1 tsp sesame oil

1 tbsp hoisin sauce

1 tsp light soy sauce

3 garlic cloves, crushed

2 tbsp vegetable oil

¾ cup unsalted cashews

1 oz snow peas

1 celery stalk, sliced

1 onion, cut into 8 pieces

2 oz bean sprouts

1 red bell pepper, seeded and diced

SAUCE

2 tsp cornstarch

2 tbsp hoisin sauce

⅞ cup chicken stock

1 Trim any fat from the chicken breasts and cut the meat into thin strips. Place the chicken in a mixing bowl. Sprinkle with the cornstarch and toss to coat the chicken, shaking off any excess. Mix together the sesame oil, hoisin sauce, soy sauce, and 1 garlic clove. Pour this mixture over the chicken, turning to coat. Leave to marinate for 20 minutes.

2 Heat half of the vegetable oil in a preheated wok. Add the cashews and stir-fry for 1 minute, until browned.

3 Add the snow peas, celery, the remaining garlic, the onion, bean sprouts, and red bell pepper and cook, stirring occasionally, for 2–3 minutes. Remove the vegetables from the wok with a slotted spoon, set aside and keep warm.

4 Heat the remaining oil in the wok. Remove the chicken from the marinade and stir-fry for 3–4 minutes. Return the vegetables to the wok.

5 To make the sauce, mix the cornstarch, hoisin sauce, and chicken stock together and pour into the wok. Bring to a boil, stirring until thickened and clear. Tranfer the stir-fry to a warm serving dish and serve.

Peanut Sesame Chicken

Sesame seeds and peanuts give extra crunch and flavor to this stir-fry and the fruit juice glaze gives a lovely shiny coating to the sauce.

NUTRITIONAL INFORMATION

Calories	435	Sugars	........10g
Protein	........38g	Fat	..........26g
Carbohydrate	...14g	Saturates	.......4g

 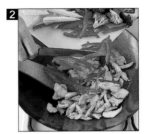 

10 MINS

15 MINS

SERVES 4

INGREDIENTS

2 tbsp vegetable oil

2 tbsp sesame oil

1 lb 2 oz boneless, skinned chicken breasts, sliced into strips

9 oz broccoli, divided into small flowerets

9 oz baby corn-on-the-cob, halved if large

1 small red bell pepper, cored, seeded, and sliced

2 tbsp soy sauce

1 cup orange juice

2 tsp cornstarch

2 tbsp toasted sesame seeds

⅓ cup roasted, shelled, unsalted peanuts

rice or noodles, to serve

1 Heat the vegetable oil and sesame oil in a large, heavy-bottomed skillet or wok until smoking. Add the chicken strips and stir-fry until browned, about 4-5 minutes.

2 Add the broccoli, corn, and red bell pepper and stir-fry for 1-2 minutes more.

3 Meanwhile, mix the soy sauce with the orange juice and cornstarch. Stir into the chicken and vegetable mixture, stirring constantly until the sauce has slightly thickened and a glaze develops.

4 Stir in the sesame seeds and peanuts, mixing well. Heat the stir-fry for 3-4 minutes more.

5 Transfer the stir-fry to a warm serving dish and serve with rice or noodles.

COOK'S TIP

Make sure you use the unsalted variety of peanuts or the dish will be too salty. The soy sauce adds saltiness.

Chicken Fu-Yung

Although commonly described as an omelet, a foo-yung ("white lotus petals") should use egg whites only to create a very delicate texture.

NUTRITIONAL INFORMATION

Calories	220	Sugars	.........1g
Protein	........16g	Fat	..........14g
Carbohydrate	....7g	Saturates	.......3g

5 MINS   5 MINS

SERVES 4

INGREDIENTS

6 oz chicken breast fillet, skinned

½ tsp salt

pepper

1 tsp rice wine or dry sherry

1 tbsp cornstarch

3 eggs

½ tsp finely chopped green onions

3 tbsp vegetable oil

4½ oz green peas

1 tsp light soy sauce

salt

few drops of sesame oil

1 Cut the chicken across the grain into very small, paper-thin slices, using a cleaver. Place the chicken slices in a shallow dish.

2 In a small bowl, mix together ½ teaspoon salt, pepper, rice wine or dry sherry, and cornstarch.

3 Pour the mixture over the chicken slices in the dish, turning the chicken until well coated.

4 Beat the eggs in a small bowl with a pinch of salt and the green onions.

5 Heat the vegetable oil in a preheated wok, add the chicken slices and stir-fry for about 1 minute, making sure that the slices are kept separated.

6 Pour the beaten eggs over the chicken, and lightly scramble until set. Do not stir too vigorously, or the mixture will break up in the oil. Stir the oil from the bottom of the wok so that the foo-yung rises to the surface.

7 Add the peas, light soy sauce, and salt to taste and blend well. Transfer to warm serving dishes, sprinkle with sesame oil, and serve.

COOK'S TIP

If available, chicken *goujons* can be used for this dish: these are small, delicate strips of chicken which require no extra cutting and are very tender.

Coconut Chicken Curry

Okra, or ladies fingers, are slightly bitter in flavor. The pineapple and coconut in this recipe offsets them in both color and flavor.

NUTRITIONAL INFORMATION

Calories ....456 Sugars 21g
Protein ....29g Fat 29g
Carbohydrate ...22g Saturates 17g

 5 MINS   45 MINS

SERVES 4

INGREDIENTS

2 tbsp sunflower oil

1 lb boneless, skinless chicken thighs or breasts

1 cup okra

1 large onion, sliced

2 cloves garlic, crushed

3 tbsp mild curry paste

2¼ cups chicken stock

1 tbsp fresh lemon juice

½ cup creamed coconut, coarsely grated

1¼ cups fresh or canned pineapple, cubed

⅔ cup thick, unsweetened, plain yogurt

2 tbsp chopped fresh cilantro

freshly boiled rice, to serve

TO GARNISH

lemon wedges

fresh cilantro sprigs

1 Heat the oil in a wok. Cut the chicken into bite-sized pieces, add to the wok and stir-fry until evenly browned.

2 Using a sharp knife, trim the okra. Add the onion, garlic and okra to the wok and cook for 2–3 minutes more, stirring constantly.

3 Mix the curry paste with the chicken stock and lemon juice and pour into the wok. Bring to a boil, cover, and leave to simmer for 30 minutes.

4 Stir the grated coconut into the curry and cook for about 5 minutes.

5 Add the pineapple, yogurt, and cilantro and cook for 2 minutes, stirring. Garnish and serve.

COOK'S TIP

Score around the top of the okra with a knife before cooking to release the sticky glue-like substance which is bitter in taste.

Crispy Chicken

In this recipe, the chicken is brushed with a syrup and deep-fried until golden. It is a little time consuming, but well worth the effort.

NUTRITIONAL INFORMATION

Calories 283   Sugars 8g
Protein . . . . .29g   Fat 15g
Carbohydrate . . . .8g   Saturates 3g

🍲 15 HOURS   🕐 35 MINS

SERVES 4

INGREDIENTS

3 lb 5 oz oven-ready chicken

2 tbsp honey

2 tsp Chinese five-spice powder

2 tbsp rice wine vinegar

3¾ cups vegetable oil,
   for deep-frying

chili sauce, to serve

1 Rinse the chicken inside and out under cold running water and pat dry with paper towels.

2 Bring a large saucepan of water to a boil and remove from the heat. Place the chicken in the water, cover and set aside for 20 minutes.

3 Remove the chicken from the water and pat dry with absorbent paper towels. Cool and leave to chill in the refrigerator overnight.

4 To make the glaze, mix the honey, Chinese five-spice powder, and rice wine vinegar.

5 Brush some of the glaze all over the chicken and return to the refrigerator for 20 minutes.

6 Repeat this process of glazing and refrigerating the chicken until all of the glaze has been used up. Return the chicken to the refrigerator for at least 2 hours after the final coating.

7 Using a cleaver or heavy kitchen knife, open the chicken by splitting it through the center through the breast and then cut each half into 4 pieces.

8 Heat the oil for deep-frying in a wok until almost smoking. Reduce the heat and fry each piece of chicken for 5–7 minutes, until golden and cooked through. Remove from the oil with a slotted spoon and drain on absorbent paper towels.

9 Transfer to a serving dish and serve hot with a little chili sauce.

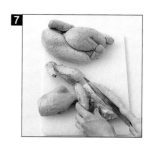

COOK'S TIP

If it is easier, use chicken portions instead of a whole chicken. You could also use chicken legs for this recipe, if you prefer.

Duck with Pineapple

For best results, use ready-cooked duck meat, widely available from Chinese restaurants and takeouts.

NUTRITIONAL INFORMATION

Calories 187   Sugars 7g
Protein ....10g   Fat 12g
Carbohydrate ....11g   Saturates 2g

25 MINS   10 MINS

SERVES 4

INGREDIENTS

4½–6 oz cooked duck meat

3 tbsp vegetable oil

1 small onion, thinly shredded

2-3 slices fresh ginger, thinly shredded

1 green onion, thinly shredded

1 small carrot, thinly shredded

4½ oz canned pineapple, cut into small slices

½ tsp salt

1 tbsp red rice vinegar

2 tbsp syrup from the pineapple

1 tbsp cornstarch paste (see page 31)

black bean sauce, to serve (optional)

1 Using a sharp knife or metal cleaver, cut the cooked duck meat into thin even-sized strips and set aside until required.

2 Heat the oil in a preheated wok or large heavy-bottomed skillet.

3 Add the shredded onion and stir-fry until the shreds are opaque.

4 Add the slices of fresh ginger, green onion shreds, and carrot shreds to the wok and stir-fry for about 1 minute.

5 Add the duck shreds and pineapple to the wok together with the salt, rice vinegar, and the pineapple syrup. Stir until the mixture is well blended.

6 Add the cornstarch paste and stir for 1–2 minutes until the sauce has thickened.

7 Transfer to a serving dish and serve with black bean sauce, if desired.

COOK'S TIP

Red rice vinegar is made from fermented rice. It has a distinctive dark color and depth of flavor. If unavailable, use red wine vinegar, which is similar in flavor.

Red Chicken with Tomatoes

This is a really colorful dish, the red of the tomatoes perfectly complementing the orange sweet potato.

NUTRITIONAL INFORMATION

Calories 316	Sugars 5g
Protein 28g	Fat 19g
Carbohydrate 8g	Saturates 3g

 5 MINS   35 MINS

SERVES 4

INGREDIENTS

1 tbsp sunflower oil

1 lb boneless, skinless chicken

2 cloves garlic, crushed

2 tbsp red curry paste

2 tbsp fresh grated Thai ginger or
   fresh ginger

1 tbsp tamarind paste

4 lime leaves

8 oz sweet potato

2½ cups coconut milk

8 oz cherry tomatoes, halved

3 tbsp chopped fresh cilantro

cooked jasmine or fragrant rice,
   to serve

1 Heat the sunflower oil in a large preheated wok or heavy-bottomed skillet.

COOK'S TIP

Thai ginger, or galangal, is a spice very similar to ginger but not as pungent. It can be bought fresh from Oriental food stores but is also available dried and as a powder. The fresh root needs to be peeled before slicing to use.

2 Using a sharp knife, thinly slice the chicken. Add the chicken to the wok or skillet and stir-fry for 5 minutes until lightly browned.

3 Add the garlic, curry paste, Thai ginger or fresh ginger, tamarind paste, and lime leaves to the wok and stir-fry for 1 minute.

4 Using a sharp knife, peel and dice the sweet potato.

5 Add the coconut milk and sweet potato to the mixture in the wok and bring to a boil. Allow to bubble over a medium heat for 20 minutes, or until the juices start to thicken and reduce.

6 Add the cherry tomatoes and cilantro to the curry and cook for 5 minutes more, stirring occasionally. Transfer to serving plates and serve hot with cooked jasmine or fragrant rice.

Chili Chicken

This is quite a hot dish, using fresh chilies. If you prefer a milder dish, halve the number of chilies used.

NUTRITIONAL INFORMATION

Calories	265	Sugars	.........3g
Protein	........21g	Fat	..........14g
Carbohydrate	....11g	Saturates	.......2g

 10 MINS   🕐 10 MINS

SERVES 4

I N G R E D I E N T S

12 oz skinless, boneless
   lean chicken

½ tsp salt

1 egg white, lightly beaten

2 tbsp cornstarch

4 tbsp vegetable oil

2 garlic cloves, crushed

½-inch piece fresh ginger,
   grated

1 red bell pepper, seeded and diced

1 green bell pepper, seeded and diced

2 fresh red chilies, chopped

2 tbsp light soy sauce

1 tbsp dry sherry or Chinese rice wine

1 tbsp wine vinegar

1 Cut the chicken into cubes and place in a mixing bowl.

2 Mix together the salt, egg white, cornstarch and 1 tablespoon of the oil and pour over the chicken. Turn the chicken in the mixture to coat thoroughly.

3 Heat the remaining oil in a preheated wok or large skillet.

4 Add the garlic and ginger and stir-fry for 30 seconds.

5 Add the chicken pieces to the wok and stir-fry for 2–3 minutes, or until browned.

6 Stir in the red and green bell peppers, chilies, soy sauce, sherry or Chinese rice wine, and wine vinegar and cook for 2–3 minutes more, until the chicken is cooked through. Transfer the chili chicken to a warm serving dish and serve immediately.

COOK'S TIP

When preparing chilies, wear rubber gloves to prevent the juices from burning and irritating your hands. Be careful not to touch your face, especially your lips or eyes, until you have washed your hands.

Lemon & Sesame Chicken

Sesame seeds have a strong flavor which adds nuttiness to recipes. They are perfect for coating these thin chicken strips.

NUTRITIONAL INFORMATION

Calories	273	Sugars	.........5g
Protein	........29g	Fat	..........13g
Carbohydrate	....11g	Saturates	.......3g

10 MINS   10 MINS

SERVES 4

I N G R E D I E N T S

4 boneless, skinless chicken breasts

1 egg white

2 tbsp sesame seeds

2 tbsp vegetable oil

1 onion, sliced

1 tbsp brown sugar

finely grated zest and juice of
    1 lemon

3 tbsp lemon curd

7 oz can water chestnuts,
    drained

lemon zest, to garnish

COOK'S TIP

Water chestnuts are commonly added to Chinese recipes for their crunchy texture but they do not have a great deal of flavor.

1 Place the chicken breasts between 2 sheets of plastic wrap and pound with a rolling pin to flatten. Slice the chicken into thin strips.

2 Whisk the egg white until light and foamy. Dip the chicken strips into the egg white, then coat in the sesame seeds.

3 Heat the oil in a wok and stir-fry the onion for 2 minutes until softened.

4 Add the chicken to the wok and stir-fry for 5 minutes, or until the chicken turns golden.

5 Mix the sugar, lemon zest, lemon juice, and lemon curd and add to the wok. Allow it to bubble slightly.

6 Slice the water chestnuts thinly, add to the wok and cook for 2 minutes. Garnish with lemon zest and serve hot.

Honey-glazed Duck

The honey and soy glaze gives a wonderful sheen and flavor to the duck skin. Such a simple recipe, yet the result is out of this world.

NUTRITIONAL INFORMATION

Calories 176   Sugars 8g
Protein ....22g   Fat 5g
Carbohydrate ...10g   Saturates 1g

2¼ HOURS   30 MINS

SERVES 4

INGREDIENTS

1 tsp dark soy sauce

2 tbsp honey

1 tsp garlic vinegar

2 garlic cloves, crushed

1 tsp ground star anise

2 tsp cornstarch

2 tsp water

2 large boneless duck breasts, about 8 oz each

celery leaves, cucumber wedges, and snipped chives, to garnish

1 Mix together the soy sauce, honey, garlic vinegar, garlic, and star anise.

2 Blend the cornstarch with the water to form a smooth paste and stir it into the soy sauce mixture.

3 Place the duck breasts in a shallow ovenproof dish. Brush with the soy marinade, turning to coat them completely. Cover and leave to marinate in the refrigerator for at least 2 hours, or overnight if possible.

4 Remove the duck from the marinade and cook in a preheated oven at 425°F for 20–25 minutes, basting frequently with the glaze.

5 Remove the duck from the oven and transfer to a preheated broiler. Broil for about 3–4 minutes to caramelize the top.

6 Remove the duck from the broiler pan and cut into thin slices. Arrange the duck slices in a warm serving dish, garnish with celery leaves, cucumber wedges, and snipped chives, and serve immediately.

COOK'S TIP

If the duck begins to burn slightly while it is cooking in the oven, cover with foil. Check that the duck breasts are cooked through by inserting the point of a sharp knife into the thickest part of the flesh – the juices should run clear.

Chicken with Peanut Sauce

A tangy stir-fry with a strong peanut flavor. Serve with freshly boiled rice or noodles.

NUTRITIONAL INFORMATION

Calories	538	Sugars	........5g
Protein	........45g	Fat	.........36g
Carbohydrate	...10g	Saturates	......16g

10 MINS   10 MINS

SERVES 4

I N G R E D I E N T S

4 boneless, skinned chicken breasts,
  about 1 lb 6 oz

4 tbsp soy sauce

4 tbsp sherry

3 tbsp crunchy peanut butter

12 oz zucchini, trimmed

2 tbsp sunflower oil

4-6 green onions, thinly
  sliced diagonally

1 x 9 oz can bamboo shoots,
  well drained and sliced

salt and pepper

4 tbsp shredded coconut, toasted

1 Cut the chicken into thin strips across the grain and season lightly with salt and pepper.

2 Stir the soy sauce in a bowl with the sherry and peanut butter until smooth and well blended.

3 Cut the zucchini into 2 inch lengths and then cut into sticks about ¼ inch thick.

4 Heat the oil in a preheated wok, swirling it around until it is really hot.

5 Add the green onions and stir-fry for 1 minute or so, then add the chicken strips and stir-fry for 3-4 minutes until well sealed and almost cooked.

6 Add the zucchini and bamboo shoots and continue to stir-fry for 1-2 minutes.

7 Add the peanut butter mixture and heat thoroughly, stirring all the time so everything is coated in the sauce as it thickens.

8 Adjust the seasoning to taste and serve the chicken very hot, sprinkled with toasted coconut.

VARIATION

This dish can also be made with turkey fillet or pork fillet.

For coconut lovers dissolve 1 oz creamed coconut in 2-3 tablespoons boiling water and add to the soy sauce mixture before adding to the wok.

Chicken with Chili & Basil

Chicken drumsticks are cooked in a delicious sauce and served with deep-fried basil for color and flavor.

NUTRITIONAL INFORMATION

Calories	196	Sugars	.........2g
Protein	........23g	Fat	..........10g
Carbohydrate	....3g	Saturates	.......2g

5 MINS   30 MINS

SERVES 4

INGREDIENTS

8 chicken drumsticks

2 tbsp soy sauce

1 tbsp sunflower oil

1 red chili

3½ oz carrots, cut into thin sticks

6 celery stalks, cut into sticks

3 tbsp sweet chili sauce

oil, for frying

about 50 fresh basil leaves

1 Remove the skin from the chicken drumsticks if desired. Make 3 slashes in each drumstick. Brush the drumsticks with the soy sauce.

2 Heat the sunflower oil in a preheated wok and fry the drumsticks for 20 minutes, turning frequently, until they are cooked through.

3 Seed and finely chop the chili. Add the chili, carrots, and celery to the wok and cook for 5 minutes more. Stir in the chili sauce, cover, and allow to bubble gently while preparing the basil leaves.

4 Heat a little oil in a heavy-bottomed pan. Carefully add the basil leaves – stand well away from the pan and protect your hand with a tea towel as they may spit a little. Cook the basil leaves for about 30 seconds or until they begin to curl up but not brown. Leave the leaves to drain on absorbent paper towels.

5 Arrange the cooked chicken, vegetables and pan juices onto a warm serving plate, garnish with the deep-fried crispy basil leaves, and serve immediately.

COOK'S TIP

Basil has a very strong flavor which is perfect with chicken and Chinese flavorings. You could use baby spinach instead of the basil, if you prefer.

Meat

Pork is the most popular meat in China because it is tender and suitable for all Chinese cooking methods. Lamb is popular in northern China where religious laws forbid the eating of pork. Beef, although it is used in some dishes, is less popular than pork. This is partly because of economic and religious reasons, but also because it is less versatile in

cooking. One of the favorite cooking methods in China is stir-frying because it is a simple and easy way of preparing meat, as well as being healthy and economical. Stir-frying gives a dry, chewy texture, whereas braising and steaming, which are other popular cooking methods, ensure a tender result. This is also true of double-cooking in which the meat is first tenderized by long, slow simmering in water, followed by a quick crisping or stir-frying in a sauce.

Beef & Broccoli Stir-fry

This is a great combination of ingredients in terms of color and flavor, and it is so simple and quick to prepare.

NUTRITIONAL INFORMATION

Calories	232	Sugars	.........1g
Protein	........12g	Fat	..........19g
Carbohydrate	....4g	Saturates	.......6g

4¼ HOURS   15 MINS

SERVES 4

INGREDIENTS

8 oz lean steak, trimmed

2 garlic cloves, crushed

dash of chili oil

½ inch piece fresh ginger, grated

½ tsp Chinese five-spice powder

2 tbsp dark soy sauce

2 tbsp vegetable oil

5½ oz broccoli flowerets

1 tbsp light soy sauce

⅔ cup beef stock

2 tsp cornstarch

4 tsp water

carrot strips, to garnish

1 Using a sharp knife, cut the steak into thin strips and place in a shallow glass dish.

2 Mix together the garlic, chili oil, grated ginger, Chinese five-spice powder, and dark soy sauce in a small bowl and pour over the beef, tossing to coat the strips evenly.

3 Cover the bowl and leave the meat to marinate in the refrigerator for several hours to allow the flavors to develop fully.

4 Heat 1 tablespoon of the vegetable oil in a preheated wok or large skillet. Add the broccoli and stir-fry over a medium heat for 4–5 minutes. Remove from the wok with a slotted spoon and set aside until required.

5 Heat the remaining oil in the wok. Add the steak together with the marinade, and stir-fry for 2-3 minutes, until the steak is browned and sealed.

6 Return the broccoli to the wok and stir in the light soy sauce and stock.

7 Blend the cornstarch with the water to form a smooth paste and stir into the wok. Bring to a boil, stirring, until thickened and clear. Cook for 1 minute. Transfer the beef & broccoli stir-fry to a warm serving dish, arrange the carrot strips in a lattice on top, and serve immediately.

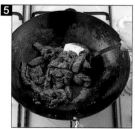

Pork with White Radish

Pork and white radish (daikon) are a perfect combination, especially with the added heat of the sweet chili sauce.

NUTRITIONAL INFORMATION

Calories	280	Sugars	.........1g
Protein	........25g	Fat	..........19g
Carbohydrate	....2g	Saturates	.......4g

10 MINS   15 MINS

SERVES 4

I N G R E D I E N T S

4 tbsp vegetable oil

1 lb pork tenderloin

1 eggplant

8 oz white radish (daikon)

2 cloves garlic, crushed

3 tbsp soy sauce

2 tbsp sweet chili sauce

boiled rice or noodles, to serve

1 Heat 2 tablespoons of the vegetable oil in a large preheated wok or skillet.

2 Using a sharp knife, thinly slice the pork into even-size pieces.

3 Add the slices of pork to the wok or skillet and stir-fry for about 5 minutes.

4 Using a sharp knife, trim and dice the eggplant. Peel and slice the white radish (daikon).

5 Add the remaining vegetable oil to the wok.

6 Add the diced eggplant to the wok or skillet together with the garlic and stir-fry for 5 minutes.

7 Add the white radish (daikon) to the wok and stir-fry for about 2 minutes.

8 Stir the soy sauce and sweet chili sauce into the mixture in the wok and cook until heated through.

9 Transfer the pork and white radish (daikon) to warm serving bowls and serve immediately with boiled rice or noodles.

COOK'S TIP

White radish are long white vegetables common in Chinese cooking. Usually grated, they have a milder flavor than red radish. They are available in many large supermarkets.

Beef with Bamboo Shoots

Tender beef, marinated in a soy and tomato sauce, is stir-fried with crisp bamboo shoots and snow peas in this simple recipe.

NUTRITIONAL INFORMATION

Calories 275	Sugars 3g	
Protein 21g	Fat 19g	
Carbohydrate 6g	Saturates 6g	

1¼ HOURS   10 MINS

SERVES 4

INGREDIENTS

12 oz rump steak

3 tbsp dark soy sauce

1 tbsp tomato ketchup

2 cloves garlic, crushed

1 tbsp fresh lemon juice

1 tsp ground coriander

2 tbsp vegetable oil

2¾ cups snow peas

7 oz can bamboo shoots

1 tsp sesame oil

COOK'S TIP

Leave the meat to marinate for at least 1 hour in order for the flavors to penetrate and increase the tenderness of the meat. If possible, leave for a little longer for a fuller flavor to develop.

1 Thinly slice the meat and place in a non-metallic dish together with the dark soy sauce, tomato ketchup, garlic, lemon juice, and ground coriander. Mix well so that all of the meat is coated in the marinade, cover, and leave for at least 1 hour.

2 Heat the vegetable oil in a preheated wok. Add the meat to the wok and stir-fry for 2–4 minutes (depending on how well cooked you like your meat) or until cooked through.

3 Add the snow peas and bamboo shoots to the mixture in the wok and stir-fry over a high heat, tossing frequently, for another 5 minutes.

4 Drizzle with the sesame oil and toss well to combine. Transfer to serving dishes and serve hot.

Lamb with Garlic Sauce

This dish contains Szechuan pepper which is quite hot and may be replaced with black pepper, if preferred.

NUTRITIONAL INFORMATION

Calories	320	Sugars	.........2g
Protein	........25g	Fat	..........21g
Carbohydrate	....4g	Saturates	.......6g

 35 MINS   10 MINS

SERVES 4

INGREDIENTS

1 lb lamb loin

2 tbsp dark soy sauce

2 tsp sesame oil

2 tbsp Chinese rice wine or dry sherry

½ tsp Szechuan pepper

4 tbsp vegetable oil

4 garlic cloves, crushed

2 oz water chestnuts, quartered

1 green bell pepper, seeded and sliced

1 tbsp wine vinegar

1 tbsp sesame oil

rice or noodles, to serve

1 Cut the lamb into 1 inch pieces and place in a shallow dish.

2 Mix together 1 tablespoon of the soy sauce, the sesame oil, Chinese rice wine or sherry, and Szechuan pepper. Pour the mixture over the lamb, turning to coat, and leave to marinate for 30 minutes.

3 Heat the vegetable oil in a preheated wok. Remove the lamb from the marinade and add to the wok, together with the garlic. Stir-fry for 2–3 minutes.

4 Add the water chestnuts and bell pepper to the wok and stir-fry for 1 minute.

5 Add the remaining soy sauce and the wine vinegar, mixing together well.

6 Add the sesame oil and cook, stirring constantly, for 1–2 minutes, or until the lamb is cooked through.

7 Transfer the lamb and garlic sauce to a warm serving dish and serve immediately with rice or noodles.

COOK'S TIP

Chinese chives, also known as garlic chives, would make an appropriate garnish for this dish.

Sesame oil is used as a flavoring, rather than for frying, as it burns readily, so it is added at the end of cooking.

Pork with Vegetables

This is a basic "meat and veg" recipe—the meat can be pork, chicken, beef, or lamb, and the vegetables can be varied according to the season.

NUTRITIONAL INFORMATION

Calories ....227 Sugars 4g
Protein ....15g Fat 16g
Carbohydrate ....7g Saturates 3g

3¾ HOURS   10 MINS

SERVES 4

INGREDIENTS

9 oz pork tenderloin

1 tsp sugar

1 tbsp light soy sauce

1 tsp rice wine or dry sherry

1 tsp cornstarch paste (see page 31)

1 small carrot

1 small green bell pepper, cored and seeded

about 6 oz Chinese cabbage

4 tbsp vegetable oil

1 green onion, cut into short sections

a few small slices of peeled fresh ginger

1 tsp salt

2-3 tbsp Chinese Stock (see page 30) or water

a few drops of sesame oil

VARIATION

This dish can be made with other meats, as mentioned in the introduction. If using chicken strips, reduce the initial cooking time in the wok.

1 Thinly slice the pork tenderloin into small pieces and place in a shallow dish.

2 In a small bowl, mix together half the sugar and the soy sauce, the wine or sherry, and cornstarch paste. Pour the mixture over the pork, stir well to coat the meat, and leave in the refrigerator to marinate for 10-15 minutes.

3 Cut the carrot, green bell pepper, and Chinese cabbage into thin slices roughly the same length and width as the pork pieces.

4 Heat the oil in a preheated wok and stir-fry the pork for about 1 minute to seal in the flavor. Remove with a slotted spoon and keep warm.

5 Add the carrot, bell pepper, Chinese cabbage, green onion, and ginger and stir-fry for about 2 minutes.

6 Add the salt and remaining sugar, followed by the pork and remaining soy sauce, and the Chinese stock or water. Blend well and stir for another 1-2 minutes until hot. Sprinkle the stir-fry with the sesame oil and serve immediately.

Twice-cooked Pork

Twice-cooked is a popular way of cooking meat in China. The meat is first boiled to tenderize it, then cut into strips or slices and stir-fried.

NUTRITIONAL INFORMATION

Calories ....199 Sugars 3g
Protein ....15g Fat 13g
Carbohydrate ....4g Saturates 3g

3¼ HOURS   30 MINS

SERVES 4

INGREDIENTS

9-10½ oz shoulder or leg of pork, in one piece

1 small green bell pepper, cored and seeded

1 small red bell pepper, cored and seeded

4½ oz canned sliced bamboo shoots, rinsed and drained

3 tbsp vegetable oil

1 green onion, cut into short sections

1 tsp salt

½ tsp sugar

1 tbsp light soy sauce

1 tsp chili bean sauce or freshly minced chili

1 tsp rice wine or dry sherry

a few drops of sesame oil

1 Immerse the pork in a pot of boiling water to cover. Return to a boil and skim the surface. Reduce the heat, cover, and simmer for 15-20 minutes. Turn off the heat and leave the pork in the water to cool for at least 2-3 hours.

2 Remove the pork and drain well. Trim off any excess fat, then cut into small, thin slices. Cut the bell peppers into pieces about the same size as the pork and the sliced bamboo shoots.

3 Heat the vegetable oil in a preheated wok and add the vegetables together with the green onion. Stir-fry for about 1 minute.

4 Add the pork, followed by the salt, sugar, light soy sauce, chili bean sauce, and wine or sherry. Blend well and continue stirring for another minute. Transfer the stir-fry to a warm serving dish, sprinkle with sesame oil, and serve.

COOK'S TIP

For ease of handling, buy a boned piece of meat, and roll into a compact shape. Tie securely with string before placing in the boiling water.

Hot Lamb

This is a spicy dish, using 2 chilies in the sauce. Halve the number of chilies to reduce the heat or seed the chilies before using if desired.

NUTRITIONAL INFORMATION

Calories ....323 Sugars 4g
Protein ....26g Fat 22g
Carbohydrate ....5g Saturates 7g

 25 MINS   15 MINS

SERVES 4

INGREDIENTS

1 lb lean, boneless lamb

2 tbsp hoisin sauce

1 tbsp dark soy sauce

1 garlic clove, crushed

2 tsp grated fresh ginger

2 tbsp vegetable oil

2 onions, sliced

1 fennel bulb, sliced

4 tbsp water

SAUCE

1 large fresh red chili, cut into thin strips

1 fresh green chili, cut into thin strips

2 tbsp rice wine vinegar

2 tsp light brown sugar

2 tbsp peanut oil

1 tsp sesame oil

VARIATION

Use beef, pork, or duck instead of the lamb and vary the vegetables, using leeks or celery instead of the onion and fennel.

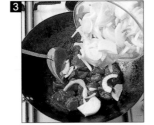

1 Cut the lamb into 1 inch cubes and place in a glass dish.

2 Mix together the hoisin sauce, soy sauce, garlic, and ginger and pour over the lamb, turning to coat well. Leave to marinate for 20 minutes.

3 Heat the oil in a preheated wok and stir-fry the lamb for 1–2 minutes. Add the onions and fennel and cook for

another 2 minutes, or until they are just beginning to brown. Stir in the water, cover, and cook for 2–3 minutes.

4 To make the sauce, place all the ingredients in a pan and cook over a low heat for 3-4 minutes, stirring.

5 Transfer the lamb and onions to a serving dish, toss lightly in the sauce, and serve immediately.

Lamb with Satay Sauce

This recipe demonstrates the classic serving of lamb satay—lamb marinated in chili and coconut and threaded onto wooden skewers.

NUTRITIONAL INFORMATION

Calories 501	Sugars 6g	
Protein 34g	Fat 37g	
Carbohydrate 9g	Saturates 10g	

 35 MINS 25 MINS

SERVES 4

INGREDIENTS

1 lb lamb loin

1 tbsp mild curry paste

⅔ cup coconut milk

2 cloves garlic, crushed

½ tsp chili powder

½ tsp cumin

SATAY SAUCE

1 tbsp corn oil

1 onion, diced

6 tbsp crunchy peanut butter

1 tsp tomato paste

1 tsp fresh lime juice

1⅓ cup cold water

1 Using a sharp knife, thinly slice the lamb and place in a large dish.

2 Mix together the curry paste, coconut milk, garlic, chili powder, and cumin in a bowl. Pour over the lamb, toss well, cover, and marinate for 30 minutes.

3 To make the satay sauce. Heat the oil in a large wok and stir-fry the onion for 5 minutes, then reduce the heat and cook for 5 minutes.

4 Stir in the peanut butter, tomato paste, lime juice, and water.

5 Thread the lamb onto wooden skewers, reserving the marinade.

6 Broil the lamb skewers under a hot broiler for 6–8 minutes, turning once.

7 Add the reserved marinade to the wok, bring to a boil and cook for 5 minutes. Serve the lamb skewers with the satay sauce.

COOK'S TIP

Soak the wooden skewers in cold water for 30 minutes before broiling to prevent the skewers from burning.

Stir-Fried Beef & Vegetables

Fillet of beef is perfect for stir-frying as it is so tender and lends itself to quick cooking.

NUTRITIONAL INFORMATION

Calories	521	Sugars	. . . . .7g
Protein	. . . . .31g	Fat	. . . . .35g
Carbohydrate	. . .18g	Saturates	. . . . . . .8g

10 MINS   20 MINS

SERVES 4

INGREDIENTS

2 tbsp sunflower oil

12 oz fillet of beef, sliced

1 red onion, sliced

6 oz zucchini

6 oz carrots, thinly sliced

1 red bell pepper, seeded and sliced

1 small head Chinese cabbage, shredded

1½ cups bean sprouts

8 oz can bamboo shoots, drained

½ cup cashews, toasted

SAUCE

3 tbsp medium sherry

3 tbsp light soy sauce

1 tsp ground ginger

1 clove garlic, crushed

1 tsp cornstarch

1 tbsp tomato paste

1 Heat the sunflower oil in a large preheated wok. Add the sliced beef and red onion to the wok and stir-fry for about 4–5 minutes or until the onion begins to soften and the meat is just browning.

2 Trim the zucchini and slice diagonally.

3 Add the carrots, bell pepper, and zucchini and stir-fry for 5 minutes.

4 Toss in the Chinese cabbage, bean sprouts, and bamboo shoots and heat through for 2–3 minutes, or until the leaves are just beginning to wilt.

5 Scatter the cashews over the stir-fry and toss well to mix.

6 To make the sauce, mix together the sherry, soy sauce, ground ginger, garlic, cornstarch, and tomato paste until well combined.

7 Pour the sauce over the stir-fry and toss to mix. Allow the sauce to bubble for 2–3 minutes or until the juices thicken.

8 Transfer to warm serving dishes and serve immediately.

Crispy Shredded Beef

A very popular Szechuan dish served in most Chinese restaurants all over the world.

NUTRITIONAL INFORMATION

Calories	.341	Sugars	.17g
Protein	.20g	Fat	.17g
Carbohydrate	.29g	Saturates	.4g

3½ HOURS   15 MINS

SERVES 4

INGREDIENTS

10½-12 oz steak

2 eggs

¼ tsp salt

4-5 tbsp all-purpose flour

vegetable oil, for deep-frying

2 medium carrots, finely shredded

2 green onions, thinly shredded

1 garlic clove, finely chopped

2-3 small fresh green or red chilies, seeded and thinly shredded

4 tbsp sugar

3 tbsp rice vinegar

1 tbsp light soy sauce

2-3 tbsp Chinese Stock (see page 30) or water

1 tsp cornstarch paste (see page 31)

1 Cut the steak across the grain into thin strips. Beat the eggs in a bowl with the salt and flour, adding a little water if necessary. Add the beef strips to the batter and mix well until coated.

2 Heat the oil in a preheated wok until smoking. Add the beef strips and deep-fry for 4-5 minutes, stirring to separate the shreds. Remove with a slotted spoon and drain on absorbent paper towels.

3 Add the carrots to the wok and deep-fry for about 1-1½ minutes, then remove with a slotted spoon and drain.

4 Pour off the excess oil, leaving about 1 tablespoon in the wok. Add the green onions, garlic, chilies, and carrots and stir-fry for 1 minute.

5 Add the sugar, rice vinegar, light soy sauce, and Chinese stock or water to the wok, blend well, and bring to a boil.

6 Stir in the cornstarch paste and simmer for a few minutes to thicken the sauce.

7 Return the beef to the wok and stir until the shreds of meat are well coated with the sauce. Serve hot.

Sweet & Sour Pork

In this classic Chinese dish, tender pork pieces are fried and served in a crunchy sauce. This dish is perfect served with plain rice.

NUTRITIONAL INFORMATION

Calories	357	Sugars	........25g
Protein	........28g	Fat	..........14g
Carbohydrate	...30g	Saturates	.......4g

 10 MINS   20 MINS

SERVES 4

INGREDIENTS

1 lb pork tenderloin

2 tbsp sunflower oil

8 oz zucchini

1 red onion, cut into thin wedges

2 cloves garlic, crushed

8 oz carrots, cut into thin sticks

1 red bell pepper, seeded and sliced

1 cup baby corn-on-the-cobs

3½ oz small mushrooms, halved

1¼ cups fresh pineapple, cubed

1 cup bean sprouts

⅔ cup pineapple juice

1 tbsp cornstarch

2 tbsp soy sauce

3 tbsp tomato ketchup

1 tbsp white wine vinegar

1 tbsp honey

COOK'S TIP

If you prefer a crisper coating, toss the pork in a mixture of cornstarch and egg white and deep fry in the wok in step 2.

1 Using a sharp knife, thinly slice the pork tenderloin into even-size pieces.

2 Heat the sunflower oil in a large preheated wok. Add the pork to the wok and stir-fry for 10 minutes, or until the pork is completely cooked through and beginning to turn crispy at the edges.

3 Meanwhile, cut the zucchini into thin sticks.

4 Add the onion, garlic, carrots, zucchini, bell pepper, baby corn-on-the-cobs, and mushrooms to the wok and stir-fry for another 5 minutes.

5 Add the pineapple cubes and bean sprouts to the wok and stir-fry for 2 minutes.

6 Mix together the pineapple juice, cornstarch, soy sauce, tomato ketchup, white wine vinegar, and honey.

7 Pour the sweet and sour mixture into the wok and cook over a high heat, tossing frequently, until the juices thicken. Transfer the sweet and sour pork to serving bowls and serve hot.

Beef & Beans

The green of the beans complements the dark color of the beef, served in a rich sauce.

NUTRITIONAL INFORMATION

Calories	381	Sugars	3g
Protein	25g	Fat	27g
Carbohydrate	10g	Saturates	8g

35 MINS   15 MINS

SERVES 4

INGREDIENTS

1 lb steak, cut into 1 inch pieces

MARINADE

2 tsp cornstarch

2 tbsp dark soy sauce

2 tsp peanut oil

SAUCE

2 tbsp vegetable oil

3 garlic cloves, crushed

1 small onion, cut into 8

8 oz green beans, halved

¼ cup unsalted cashews

1 oz canned bamboo shoots, drained and rinsed

2 tsp dark soy sauce

2 tsp Chinese rice wine or dry sherry

½ cup beef stock

2 tsp cornstarch

4 tsp water

salt and pepper

1 To make the marinade, mix together the cornstarch, soy sauce, and peanut oil.

2 Place the steak in a shallow glass bowl. Pour the marinade over the steak, turn to coat thoroughly, cover, and leave to marinate in the refrigerator for at least 30 minutes.

3 To make the sauce, heat the oil in a preheated wok. Add the garlic, onion, beans, cashews, and bamboo shoots and stir-fry for 2–3 minutes.

4 Remove the steak from the marinade, drain, add to the wok, and stir-fry for 3–4 minutes.

5 Mix the soy sauce, Chinese rice wine or sherry and beef stock together. Blend the cornstarch with the water and add to the soy sauce mixture, mixing to combine.

6 Stir the mixture into the wok and bring the sauce to a boil, stirring until thickened and clear. Reduce the heat and leave to simmer for 2–3 minutes. Season to taste and serve immediately.

Pork with Plums

Plum sauce is often used in Chinese cooking with duck or rich, fattier meat to counteract the flavor.

NUTRITIONAL INFORMATION

Calories 281   Sugars 6g
Protein . . . . .25g   Fat 14g
Carbohydrate . . .10g   Saturates 4g

 35 MINS   25 MINS

SERVES 4

INGREDIENTS

1 lb pork tenderloin

1 tbsp cornstarch

2 tbsp light soy sauce

2 tbsp Chinese rice wine

4 tsp light brown sugar

pinch of ground cinnamon

5 tsp vegetable oil

2 garlic cloves, crushed

2 green onions, chopped

4 tbsp plum sauce

1 tbsp hoisin sauce

⅔ cup water

dash of chili sauce

fried plum quarters and green onions, to garnish

1 Cut the pork tenderloin into thin slices.

2 Combine the cornstarch, soy sauce, rice wine, sugar, and cinnamon in a small bowl.

3 Place the pork in a shallow dish and pour the cornstarch mixture over it. Toss the meat in the marinade until it is completely coated. Cover and leave to marinate for at least 30 minutes.

4 Remove the pork from the dish, reserving the marinade.

5 Heat the oil in a preheated wok or large skillet. Add the pork and stir-fry for 3–4 minutes, until a light golden color.

6 Stir in the garlic, green onions, plum sauce, hoisin sauce, water, and chili sauce. Bring the sauce to a boil. Reduce the heat, cover, and leave to simmer for 8–10 minutes, or until the pork is cooked through and tender.

7 Stir in the reserved marinade and cook, stirring, for about 5 minutes.

8 Transfer the pork stir-fry to a warm serving dish and garnish with fried plum quarters and green onions. Serve immediately.

Deep-fried Pork Fritters

Small pieces of pork are coated in a light batter and deep-fried in this recipe—they are delicious dipped in a soy and honey sauce.

NUTRITIONAL INFORMATION

Calories 528   Sugars 12g
Protein ....32g   Fat 22g
Carbohydrate ...52g   Saturates 6g

🥘 10 MINS   🕐 15 MINS

SERVES 4

I N G R E D I E N T S

1 lb pork tenderloin

2 tbsp peanut oil

1¾ cups all-purpose flour

2 tsp baking powder

1 egg, beaten

1 cup milk

pinch of chili powder

vegetable oil, for deep-frying

S A U C E

2 tbsp dark soy sauce

3 tbsp honey

1 tbsp wine vinegar

1 tbsp chopped chives

1 tbsp tomato paste

chives, to garnish

1 Using a sharp knife, cut the pork into 1 inch cubes.

2 Heat the peanut oil in a preheated wok. Add the pork to the wok and stir-fry for 2-3 minutes, until sealed.

3 Remove the pork with a slotted spoon and set aside until required.

4 Sift the flour and baking powder into a mixing bowl and make a well in the center. Gradually beat in the egg, milk, and chili powder to make a thick batter.

5 Heat the oil for deep-frying in a wok until almost smoking, then reduce the heat slightly.

6 Toss the pork pieces in the batter to coat thoroughly. Add the pork to the wok and deep-fry until golden brown and cooked through. Remove with a slotted spoon and drain well on absorbent paper towels.

7 Meanwhile, mix together the soy sauce, honey, wine vinegar, chives, and tomato paste and spoon into a small serving bowl.

8 Transfer the pork fritters to serving dishes, garnish with chives, and serve with the sauce.

Lamb with Mushroom Sauce

Use a lean cut of lamb, such as fillet, for this recipe for both flavor and tenderness.

NUTRITIONAL INFORMATION

Calories 219   Sugars 1g
Protein . . . . .21g   Fat 14g
Carbohydrate . . . .4g   Saturates 4g

5 MINS   10 MINS

SERVES 4

INGREDIENTS

12 oz lean boneless lamb, such as loin

2 tbsp vegetable oil

3 garlic cloves, crushed

1 leek, sliced

6 oz large mushrooms, sliced

½ tsp sesame oil

fresh red chilies, to garnish

SAUCE

1 tsp cornstarch

4 tbsp light soy sauce

3 tbsp Chinese rice wine or dry sherry

3 tbsp water

½ tsp chili sauce

1 Using a sharp knife or meat cleaver, cut the lamb into thin strips.

2 Heat the vegetable oil in a preheated wok or large skillet.

3 Add the lamb strips, garlic, and leek and stir-fry for about 2-3 minutes.

4 To make the sauce, mix together the cornstarch, soy sauce, Chinese rice wine or dry sherry, water, and chili sauce and set aside.

5 Add the sliced mushrooms to the wok and stir-fry for 1 minute.

6 Stir in the prepared sauce and cook for 2–3 minutes, or until the lamb is cooked through and tender.

7 Sprinkle the sesame oil over the top and transfer the lamb and mushrooms to a warm serving dish. Garnish with red chilies and serve immediately.

VARIATION

The lamb can be replaced with lean steak or pork tenderloin in this classic recipe from Beijing. You could also use 2–3 green onions, 1 shallot, or 1 small onion instead of the leek, if you prefer.

Sesame Lamb Stir-Fry

This is a very simple, but delicious dish, in which lean pieces of lamb are cooked in sugar and soy sauce and then sprinkled with sesame seeds.

NUTRITIONAL INFORMATION

Calories	276	Sugars	.........4g
Protein	........25g	Fat	..........18g
Carbohydrate	....5g	Saturates	.......6g

🍲 5 MINS   🕐 10 MINS

SERVES 4

I N G R E D I E N T S

1 lb boneless lean lamb

2 tbsp peanut oil

2 leeks, sliced

1 carrot, cut into thin sticks

2 garlic cloves, crushed

⅓ cup lamb or vegetable stock

2 tsp light brown sugar

1 tbsp dark soy sauce

4½ tsp sesame seeds

1 Using a sharp knife, cut the lamb into thin strips.

2 Heat the peanut oil in a preheated wok or large skillet until it is really hot.

3 Add the lamb and stir-fry for 2–3 minutes. Remove the lamb from the wok with a slotted spoon and set aside until required.

4 Add the leeks, carrot, and garlic to the wok or skillet and stir-fry in the remaining oil for 1–2 minutes.

5 Remove the vegetables from the wok with a slotted spoon and set aside.

6 Drain any remaining oil from the wok. Place the lamb or vegetable stock,

light brown sugar, and dark soy sauce in the wok and add the lamb. Cook, stirring constantly to coat the lamb, for 2–3 minutes.

7 Sprinkle the sesame seeds over the top, turning the lamb to coat.

8 Spoon the leek, carrot, and garlic mixture onto a warm serving dish and top with the lamb. Serve immediately.

COOK'S TIP

Be careful not to burn the sugar in the wok when heating and coating the meat, otherwise the flavor of the dish will be spoiled.

Beef & Bok Choy

In this recipe, a colorful selection of vegetables is stir-fried with tender strips of steak.

NUTRITIONAL INFORMATION

Calories	369	Sugars	.........9g
Protein	........29g	Fat	..........23g
Carbohydrate	...12g	Saturates	.......8g

15 MINS   5 MINS

SERVES 4

INGREDIENTS

1 large head of bok choy, about
   9-9½ oz, torn into large pieces

2 tbsp vegetable oil

2 garlic cloves, crushed

1 lb 2 oz steak,
   cut into thin strips

5½ oz snow peas, trimmed

5½ oz baby corn-on-the-cobs

6 green onions, chopped

2 red bell peppers, cored, seeded,
   and thinly sliced

2 tbsp oyster sauce

1 tbsp fish sauce

1 tbsp sugar

rice or noodles, to serve

1 Steam the bok choy over boiling water until just tender. Keep warm.

2 Heat the oil in a large, heavy-bottomed skillet or wok, add the garlic and steak strips, and stir-fry until just browned, about 1-2 minutes.

3 Add the snow peas, baby corn, green onions, red bell pepper, oyster sauce, fish sauce, and sugar to the pan, mixing well. Stir-fry for another 2-3 minutes until the vegetables are tender, but still crisp.

4 Arrange the bok choy leaves in the base of a heated serving dish and spoon the beef and vegetable mixture into the center.

5 Serve the stir-fry immediately, with rice or noodles.

COOK'S TIP

Bok choy is one of the most important ingredients in this dish. If unavailable, use Chinese cabbage or kai choy (mustard leaves).

Lamb with Lime Leaves

Peanut oil is used here for flavor—it is a common oil used for stir-frying.

NUTRITIONAL INFORMATION

Calories	302	Sugars	........15g
Protein	........24g	Fat	..........16g
Carbohydrate	...17g	Saturates	.......6g

  5 MINS   35 MINS

SERVES 4

I N G R E D I E N T S

2 red chilies

2 tbsp peanut oil

2 cloves garlic, crushed

4 shallots, chopped

2 stalks lemon grass, sliced

6 lime leaves

1 tbsp tamarind paste

2 tbsp brown sugar

1 lb lean lamb (leg or loin)

2½ cups coconut milk

6 oz cherry tomatoes, halved

1 tbsp chopped fresh cilantro

fragrant rice, to serve

1 Using a sharp knife, seed and very finely chop the red chilies.

2 Heat the oil in a large preheated wok or skillet.

3 Add the garlic, shallots, lemon grass, lime leaves, tamarind paste, brown sugar, and chilies to the wok and stir-fry for about 2 minutes.

4 Using a sharp knife, cut the lamb into thin strips or cubes. Add the lamb to the wok or skillet and stir-fry for about 5 minutes, tossing well so that the lamb is evenly coated in the spice mixture.

5 Pour the coconut milk into the wok and bring to a boil. Reduce the heat and leave to simmer for 20 minutes.

6 Add the tomatoes and cilantro to the wok and leave to simmer for 5 minutes. Transfer to serving plates and serve hot with fragrant rice.

COOK'S TIP

When buying fresh cilantro, look for bright green, unwilted leaves. To store it, wash and dry the leaves, leaving them on the stem. Wrap the leaves in damp paper towels and keep them in a plastic bag in the refrigerator.

Beef & Black Bean Sauce

It is not necessary to use the expensive cuts of beef steak for this recipe: the meat will be tender as it is cut into small thin slices and marinated.

NUTRITIONAL INFORMATION

Calories	392	Sugars 2g
Protein	........13g	Fat 36g
Carbohydrate	....3g	Saturates 7g

🥘 3¼ HOURS   🕐 10 MINS

SERVES 4

INGREDIENTS

9-10½ oz steak (such as rump)

1 small onion

1 small green bell pepper, cored and seeded

about 1¼ cups vegetable oil

1 green onion, cut into short sections

a few small slices of fresh ginger

1-2 small green or red chilies, seeded and sliced

2 tbsp crushed black bean sauce

MARINADE

½ tsp baking soda or baking powder

½ tsp sugar

1 tbsp light soy sauce

2 tsp rice wine or dry sherry

2 tsp cornstarch paste (see page 31)

2 tsp sesame oil

1 Using a sharp knife or meat cleaver, cut the beef into small thin strips.

2 To make the marinade, mix together all the ingredients in a shallow dish. Add the beef strips, turn to coat, and leave to marinate for at least 2-3 hours.

3 Cut the onion and green bell pepper into small cubes.

4 Heat the vegetable oil in a pre-heated wok or large skillet. Add the beef strips and stir-fry for about 1 minute, or until the color changes. Remove the beef strips with a slotted spoon and drain on absorbent paper towels. Keep warm and set aside until required.

5 Pour off the excess oil, leaving about 1 tablespoon in the wok. Add the green onion, ginger, chilies, onion, and green bell pepper and stir-fry for about 1 minute.

6 Add the black bean sauce and stir until smooth. Return the beef strips to the wok, blend well, and stir-fry for another minute. Transfer the stir-fry to a warm serving dish and serve hot.

Spicy Pork & Rice

Pork is coated in a spicy mixture before being fried until crisp in this recipe and then stirred into a delicious egg rice for a very filling meal.

NUTRITIONAL INFORMATION

Calories ....599 Sugars 11g
Protein ....30g Fat 22g
Carbohydrate ...76g Saturates 7g

🥩 10 MINS   🕐 35 MINS

SERVES 4

INGREDIENTS

1¼ cups long-grain white rice

2½ cups cold water

12 oz pork tenderloin

2 tsp Chinese five-spice powder

24 tbsp cornstarch

3 large eggs, beaten

2 tbsp brown sugar

2 tbsp sunflower oil

1 onion

2 cloves garlic, crushed

3½ oz carrots, diced

1 red bell pepper, seeded and diced

1¾ cup peas

12 tbsp butter

salt and pepper

a sharp knife or meat cleaver. Set the pork strips aside until required.

3 Whisk together the Chinese five-spice powder, cornstarch, 1 egg, and the brown sugar. Toss the pork in the mixture until coated.

4 Heat the sunflower oil in a large wok or skillet. Add the pork and cook over a high heat until the pork is cooked through and crispy. Remove the pork from the wok with a slotted spoon and set aside until required.

5 Using a sharp knife, cut the onion into dice.

6 Add the onion, garlic, carrots, bell pepper, and peas to the wok and stir-fry for 5 minutes.

7 Return the pork to the wok together with the cooked rice and stir-fry for 5 minutes.

8 Heat the butter in a skillet. Add the remaining beaten eggs and cook until set. Turn out onto a clean board and slice thinly. Toss the strips of egg into the rice mixture and serve immediately.

1 Rinse the rice under cold running water. Place the rice in a large saucepan, add the cold water and a pinch of salt. Bring to a boil, cover, then reduce the heat and leave to simmer for about 9 minutes, or until all of the liquid has been absorbed and the rice is tender.

2 Meanwhile, slice the pork tenderloin into very thin even-sized pieces, using

Fish-flavored Pork

"Fish-flavored" is a Szechuan cookery term meaning that the dish is prepared with seasonings normally used in fish dishes.

NUTRITIONAL INFORMATION

Calories 183   Sugars 0.2g
Protein ....14g   Fat 13g
Carbohydrate ....3g   Saturates 3g

 25 MINS   10 MINS

SERVES 4

INGREDIENTS

about 2 tbsp dried wood ears

9-10½ oz pork tenderloin

1 tsp salt

2 tsp cornstarch paste
  (see page 31)

3 tbsp vegetable oil

1 garlic clove, finely chopped

½ tsp finely chopped fresh ginger

2 green onions, finely chopped, with the
  white and green parts separated

2 celery stalks, thinly sliced

½ tsp sugar

1 tbsp light soy sauce

1 tbsp chili bean sauce

2 tsp rice vinegar

1 tsp rice wine or dry sherry

a few drops of sesame oil

COOK'S TIP

Also known as cloud ears,
this is a dried grey-black fungus
widely used in Szechuan cooking.
It is always soaked in warm water
before using. Wood ears have a
crunchy texture and a mild flavor.

1 Soak the wood ears in warm water for about 20 minutes, then rinse in cold water until the water is clear. Drain well, then cut into thin shreds.

2 Cut the pork into thin shreds, then mix in a bowl with a pinch of salt and about half the cornstarch paste until well coated.

3 Heat 1 tablespoon of vegetable oil in a preheated wok. Add the pork strips and stir-fry for about 1 minute, or until the color changes, then remove with a slotted spoon and set aside until required.

4 Heat the remaining oil in the wok. Add the garlic, ginger, the white parts of the green onions, the wood ears, and celery and stir-fry for about 1 minute.

5 Return the pork strips together with the salt, sugar, soy sauce, chili bean sauce, vinegar, and wine or sherry. Blend well and continue stirring for another minute.

6 Finally add the green parts of the green onions and blend in the remaining cornstarch paste and sesame oil. Stir until the sauce has thickened. Transfer the fish-flavored pork to a warm serving dish and serve immediately.

Oyster Sauce Beef

Like Stir-fried Pork with Vegetables (see page 224), the vegetables used in this recipe can be varied as you like.

NUTRITIONAL INFORMATION

Calories 462   Sugars 2g
Protein . . . . .16g   Fat 42g
Carbohydrate . . . .4g   Saturates 8g

4 HOURS   10 MINS

SERVES 4

I N G R E D I E N T S

10½ oz steak

1 tsp sugar

1 tbsp light soy sauce

1 tsp rice wine or dry sherry

1 tsp cornstarch paste
(see page 31)

½ small carrot

2 oz snow peas

2 oz canned bamboo shoots

2 oz canned straw mushrooms

about 1¼ cups vegetable oil

1 green onion, cut into short sections

2-3 small slices fresh ginger

½ tsp salt

2 tbsp oyster sauce

2-3 tbsp Chinese Stock (see page 30) or
water

1 Cut the beef into small, thin slices. Place in a shallow dish with the sugar, soy sauce, wine, and cornstarch paste and leave to marinate for 25-30 minutes.

2 Slice the carrot, snow peas, bamboo shoots, and straw mushrooms into roughly the same size pieces as each other.

3 Heat the oil in a wok and add the beef slices. Stir-fry for 1 minute, then remove and keep warm.

4 Pour off the oil, leaving about 1 tablespoon in the wok. Add the sliced vegetables with the green onion and ginger and stir-fry for about 2 minutes. Add the salt, beef, and oyster sauce with stock or water. Blend well until heated through and serve.

VARIATION

You can use whatever vegetables are available for this dish, but it is important to get a good contrast of color—don't use all red or all green for example.

Spicy Pork Balls

These small meatballs are packed with flavor and cooked in a crunchy tomato sauce for a very quick dish.

NUTRITIONAL INFORMATION

Calories . . . . . . .299 Sugars 3g
Protein . . . . .28g Fat 15g
Carbohydrate . . .14g Saturates 4g

10 MINS   40 MINS

SERVES 4

INGREDIENTS

1 lb ground pork

2 shallots, finely chopped

2 cloves garlic, crushed

1 tsp cumin seeds

½ tsp chili powder

½ cup wholewheat breadcrumbs

1 egg, beaten

2 tbsp sunflower oil

14 oz can chopped tomatoes, flavored with chili

2 tbsp soy sauce

7 oz can water chestnuts, drained

3 tbsp chopped fresh cilantro

COOK'S TIP

Add a few teaspoons of chili sauce to a can of chopped tomatoes, if you can't find the flavored variety.

1 Place the ground pork in a large mixing bowl. Add the shallots, garlic, cumin seeds, chili powder, breadcrumbs, and beaten egg and mix together well.

2 Form the mixture into balls between the palms of your hands.

3 Heat the oil in a large preheated wok. Add the pork balls and stir-fry, in

batches, over a high heat for about 5 minutes or until sealed on all sides.

4 Add the tomatoes, soy sauce, and water chestnuts and bring to a boil. Return the pork balls to the wok, reduce the heat, and leave to simmer for 15 minutes.

5 Scatter with chopped fresh cilantro and serve hot.

Pork with Bell Peppers

This is a really simple yet colorful dish, the trio of bell peppers offsetting the pork and sauce wonderfully.

NUTRITIONAL INFORMATION

Calories	459	Sugars	.........5g
Protein	........19g	Fat	..........39g
Carbohydrate	....8g	Saturates	......13g

30 MINS   25 MINS

SERVES 4

INGREDIENTS

½ oz Chinese dried mushrooms

1 lb pork steaks

2 tbsp vegetable oil

1 onion, sliced

1 red bell pepper, seeded and diced

1 green bell pepper, seeded and diced

1 yellow bell pepper, seeded and diced

4 tbsp oyster sauce

1 Place the mushrooms in a large bowl. Pour over enough boiling water to cover, and leave to stand for 20 minutes.

2 Using a sharp knife, trim any excess fat from the pork steaks. Cut the pork into thin strips.

3 Bring a large saucepan of water to a boil. Add the pork to the boiling water and cook for 5 minutes.

4 Remove the pork from the pan with a slotted spoon and leave to drain thoroughly.

5 Heat the oil in a large preheated wok. Add the pork to the wok and stir-fry for about 5 minutes.

6 Remove the mushrooms from the water and leave to drain thoroughly. Roughly chop the mushrooms.

7 Add the mushrooms, onion, and the bell peppers to the wok and stir-fry for 5 minutes.

8 Stir in the oyster sauce and cook for 2-3 minutes. Serve immediately.

COOK'S TIP

Use open-cap mushrooms, sliced, instead of Chinese mushrooms, if you prefer.

Spare Ribs with Chili

For best results, chop the spare ribs into small bite-size pieces.

NUTRITIONAL INFORMATION

Calories	497	Sugars	.........3g
Protein	........13g	Fat	..........47g
Carbohydrate	....4g	Saturates	......11g

4¼ HOURS   20 MINS

SERVES 4

INGREDIENTS

1 lb 2 oz pork spare ribs

1 tsp sugar

1 tbsp light soy sauce

1 tsp rice wine or dry sherry

1 tsp cornstarch

about 2½ cups vegetable oil

1 garlic clove, finely chopped

1 green onion, cut into short sections

1 small hot chili (green or red), thinly sliced

2 tbsp black bean sauce

about ⅔ cup Chinese Stock (see page 30) or water

1 small onion, diced

1 medium green bell pepper, cored, seeded, and diced

COOK'S TIP

Be very careful when handling and cutting chilies because their juice can cause irritation of the skin. Be sure to wash your hands after handling, and keep well away from face and eyes. The seeds of the chili are the hottest part—remove seeds if you want a milder dish.

1 Trim any excess fat from the ribs. Using a sharp knife or meat cleaver, chop each rib into 3-4 bite-sized pieces and place in a shallow dish.

2 Mix together the sugar, soy sauce, wine, and cornstarch and pour the mixture over the pork ribs. Leave to marinate for 35-45 minutes.

3 Heat the vegetable oil in a large preheated wok or skillet.

4 Add the spare ribs to the wok and deep-fry for 2-3 minutes until light brown. Remove with a slotted spoon and drain on absorbent paper towels.

5 Pour off the oil, leaving about 1 tablespoon in the wok. Add the garlic, green onion, chili, and black bean sauce and stir-fry for 30-40 seconds.

6 Add the spare ribs, blend well, then add the stock or water. Bring to a boil, then reduce the heat, cover, and braise for 8-10 minutes, stirring once or twice.

7 Add the onion and green bell pepper, increase the heat to high, and stir uncovered for about 2 minutes to reduce the sauce a little. Serve hot.

Stir-Fried Lamb with Orange

Oranges and lamb are a great combination because the citrus flavor offsets the fattier, fuller flavor of the lamb.

NUTRITIONAL INFORMATION

Calories	209	Sugars	.........4g
Protein	........25g	Fat	..........10g
Carbohydrate	....5g	Saturates	.......5g

5 MINS   30 MINS

SERVES 4

INGREDIENTS

1 lb ground lamb

2 cloves garlic, crushed

1 tsp cumin seeds

1 tsp ground coriander

1 red onion, sliced

finely grated zest and juice of
    1 orange

2 tbsp soy sauce

1 orange, peeled and segmented

salt and pepper

snipped fresh chives, to garnish

1 Heat a wok or large, heavy-bottomed skillet, without adding any oil.

2 Add the ground lamb to the wok. Dry fry the ground lamb for 5 minutes, or until the lamb is evenly browned. Drain away any excess fat from the wok.

3 Add the garlic, cumin seeds, coriander, and red onion to the wok and stir-fry for another 5 minutes.

4 Stir in the finely grated orange zest and juice and the soy sauce, mixing until thoroughly combined. Cover, reduce the heat, and leave to simmer, stirring occasionally, for 15 minutes.

5 Remove the lid, increase the heat, and add the oranges. Stir to mix.

6 Season with salt and pepper to taste and heat through for another 2–3 minutes.

7 Transfer the stir-fry to warm serving plates and garnish with snipped fresh chives. Serve immediately.

COOK'S TIP

If you wish to serve wine with your meal, try light, dry white wines and lighter Burgundy-style red wines as they blend well with Oriental food.

Lamb & Ginger Stir-fry

Slices of lamb cooked with garlic, ginger, and shiitake mushrooms make a quick and easy supper. It is best served with Chinese egg noodles.

NUTRITIONAL INFORMATION

Calories	347	Sugars	.........2g
Protein	........31g	Fat	..........21g
Carbohydrate	....7g	Saturates	.......7g

 10 MINS   5 MINS

SERVES 4

INGREDIENTS

1 lb 2 oz lamb loin

2 tbsp sunflower oil

1 tbsp chopped fresh ginger

2 garlic cloves, chopped

6 green onions, white and
green parts diagonally sliced

6 oz shiitake mushrooms, sliced

6 oz sugar snap peas

1 tsp cornstarch

2 tbsp dry sherry

1 tbsp light soy sauce

1 tsp sesame oil

1 tbsp sesame seeds, toasted

Chinese egg noodles to serve

1 Using a sharp knife or meat cleaver, cut the lamb into ¹/₂ inch slices.

2 Heat the sunflower oil in a large preheated wok or skillet.

3 Add the lamb to the wok or skillet and stir-fry for 2 minutes.

4 Add the chopped fresh ginger, chopped garlic cloves, sliced green onions, mushrooms, and sugar snap peas and stir-fry for 2 minutes.

5 Blend the cornstarch with the sherry and stir into the wok.

6 Add the light soy sauce and sesame oil and cook, stirring, for 1 minute until thickened.

7 Sprinkle over the sesame seeds, transfer the lamb and ginger stir-fry to a warm serving dish, and serve the stir-fry with Chinese egg noodles.

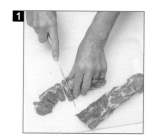

COOK'S TIP

Shiitake mushrooms are much used in Chinese cooking. They have a slightly meaty flavor and can be bought both fresh and dried. Their powerful flavor will permeate more bland mushrooms. Cook them briefly or they begin to toughen.

Pork Ribs with Plum Sauce

Pork ribs are always very popular for grilling, and you can flavor them with a number of spicy bastes.

NUTRITIONAL INFORMATION

Calories 590   Sugars 1g
Protein . . . . .26g   Fat 51g
Carbohydrate . . . .3g   Saturates 17g

35 MINS   45 MINS

SERVES 4

INGREDIENTS

2 lb pork spare ribs

2 tbsp sunflower oil

1 tsp sesame oil

2 cloves garlic, crushed

1 inch piece fresh ginger, grated

⅔ cup plum sauce

2 tbsp dry sherry

2 tbsp hoisin sauce

2 tbsp soy sauce

4–6 green onions, to garnish (optional)

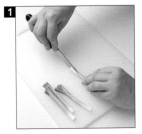  

1 To prepare the garnish, trim the green onions to about 3 inches long. Slice both ends into thin strips, leaving the onion intact in the center.

2 Put the green onions into a bowl of iced water for at least 30 minutes until the ends start to curl up. Leave them in the water and set aside until required.

3 If you buy the spare ribs in a single piece, cut them into individual ribs. Bring a large pan of water to a boil and add the ribs. Cook for 5 minutes, then drain thoroughly.

4 Heat the oils in a pan, add the garlic and ginger, and cook gently for 1–2 minutes. Stir in the plum sauce, sherry, hoisin, and soy sauce and heat through.

5 Brush the sauce over the pork ribs. Grill over hot coals for 5–10 minutes, then move to a cooler part of the grill for another 15–20 minutes, basting with the remaining sauce. Garnish and serve hot.

COOK'S TIP

Par-cooking the ribs in boiling water removes excess fat, which helps prevent the ribs from spitting during cooking. Do not be put off by the large quantity—there is only a little meat on each, but they are quite cheap to buy.

Pork Satay Stir-Fry

Satay sauce is easy to make and is one of the best known and loved sauces in Oriental cooking. It is perfect with beef, chicken, or pork.

NUTRITIONAL INFORMATION

Calories 506	Sugars 11g
Protein 31g	Fat 36g
Carbohydrate ...15g	Saturates 8g

 10 MINS   15 MINS

SERVES 4

INGREDIENTS

5½ oz carrots

2 tbsp sunflower oil

12 oz pork neck fillet, thinly sliced

1 onion, sliced

2 cloves garlic, crushed

1 yellow bell pepper, seeded and sliced

2⅓ cups snow peas

1½ cups thin asparagus

chopped salted peanuts, to serve

SATAY SAUCE

6 tbsp crunchy peanut butter

6 tbsp coconut milk

1 tsp chili flakes

1 clove garlic, crushed

1 tsp tomato paste

COOK'S TIP

Cook the sauce just before serving as it tends to thicken very quickly and will not be spoonable if you cook it too much ahead of time.

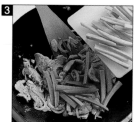

1 Using a sharp knife, slice the carrots into thin sticks.

2 Heat the oil in a large, preheated wok. Add the pork, onion, and garlic and stir-fry for 5 minutes or until the lamb is cooked through.

3 Add the carrots, bell pepper, snow peas, and asparagus to the wok and stir-fry for 5 minutes.

4 To make the satay sauce, place the peanut butter, coconut milk, chili flakes, garlic, and tomato paste in a small pan and heat gently, stirring, until well combined. Be careful not to let the sauce stick to the bottom of the pan.

5 Transfer the stir-fry to warm serving plates. Spoon the satay sauce over the stir-fry and scatter with chopped peanuts. Serve immediately.

Marinated Beef

This dish is quick to cook, but benefits from lengthy marinating, as this tenderizes and flavors the meat.

NUTRITIONAL INFORMATION

Calories	195	Sugars	.........1g
Protein	........12g	Fat	..........15g
Carbohydrate	....3g	Saturates	.......4g

🍖 🍖 🍖

🍲 1¼ HOURS   🕐 10 MINS

SERVES 4

I N G R E D I E N T S

8 oz lean steak

1 tbsp light soy sauce

1 tsp sesame oil

2 tsp Chinese rice wine or dry sherry

1 tsp sugar

2 tsp hoisin sauce

1 garlic clove, crushed

½ tsp cornstarch

green bell pepper slices, to garnish

rice or noodles, to serve

S A U C E

2 tbsp dark soy sauce

1 tsp sugar

½ tsp cornstarch

3 tbsp oyster sauce

8 tbsp water

2 tbsp vegetable oil

3 garlic cloves, crushed

½ inch piece fresh ginger, grated

8 baby corn-on-the-cob, halved lengthwise

½ green bell pepper, seeded and thinly sliced

1 oz bamboo shoots, drained and rinsed

1 Using a sharp knife or meat cleaver, cut the steak into 1 inch cubes and place in a shallow dish.

2 Mix together the soy sauce, sesame oil, Chinese rice wine or sherry, sugar, hoisin sauce, garlic, and cornstarch and pour over the steak, turning it to coat completely. Cover and marinate for at least 1 hour, or preferably overnight in the refrigerator for a fuller flavor.

3 Meanwhile, make the sauce. Mix together the dark soy sauce with the sugar, cornstarch, oyster sauce, and water.

4 Heat the oil in a preheated wok. Add the steak, together with the marinade, and stir-fry for 2–3 minutes, until sealed and lightly browned.

5 Add the garlic, ginger, baby corn-on-the-cob, bell pepper, and bamboo shoots. Stir in the oyster sauce mixture and bring to a boil. Reduce the heat and cook for 2–3 minutes.

6 Transfer to a warm serving dish, garnish with green bell pepper slices, and serve immediately with rice or noodles.

Peppered Beef Cashew

A simple but stunning dish of tender strips of beef mixed with crunchy cashews, coated in a hot sauce. Serve with rice noodles.

NUTRITIONAL INFORMATION

Calories	403	Sugars	.........7g
Protein	........26g	Fat	..........29g
Carbohydrate	....11g	Saturates	.......9g

10 MINS   10 MINS

SERVES 4

INGREDIENTS

1 tbsp peanut or sunflower oil

1 tbsp sesame oil

1 onion, sliced

1 garlic clove, crushed

1 tbsp grated fresh ginger

1 lb 2 oz fillet or rump steak, cut into thin strips

2 tsp brown sugar

2 tbsp light soy sauce

1 small yellow bell pepper, cored, seeded, and sliced

1 red bell pepper, cored, seeded, and sliced

4 green onions, chopped

2 celery stalks, chopped

4 large open-cap mushrooms, sliced

4 tbsp roasted cashews

3 tbsp stock or white wine

1 Heat the oils in a large, heavy-bottomed skillet or wok. Add the onion, garlic, and ginger and stir-fry for about 2 minutes until softened.

2 Add the steak strips and stir-fry for another 2-3 minutes, until the meat has browned.

3 Add the sugar and soy sauce, stirring to mix well.

4 Add the bell peppers, green onions, celery, mushrooms, and cashews, mixing well.

5 Add the stock or white wine and stir-fry for 2-3 minutes until the beef is cooked through and the vegetables are tender-crisp.

6 Serve the stir-fry immediately with rice noodles.

COOK'S TIP

Most American peanut oils are mild-flavored, whereas Chinese peanut oils are stronger. Buy the Chinese variety if you like a very distictive peanut flavor.

Beef Teriyaki

This Japanese-style teriyaki sauce complements grilled beef, but it can also be used to accompany chicken or salmon.

NUTRITIONAL INFORMATION

Calories	184	Sugars 6g
Protein	........24g	Fat 5g
Carbohydrate	....8g	Saturates 2g

 2¼ HOURS   🕐 15 MINS

SERVES 4

I N G R E D I E N T S

1 lb extra thin lean beef steaks

8 scallions, trimmed and cut into short
  lengths

1 yellow bell pepper, seeded and cut into
  chunks

green salad, to serve

S A U C E

1 tsp cornstarch

2 tbsp dry sherry

2 tbsp white wine vinegar

3 tbsp soy sauce

1 tbsp dark muscovado sugar

1 clove garlic, minced

½ tsp ground cinnamon

½ tsp ground ginger

1 Place the meat in a shallow, nonmetallic dish.

2 To make the sauce, combine the cornstarch with the sherry, then stir in the remaining sauce ingredients. Pour the sauce over the meat and leave to marinate for at least 2 hours.

3 Remove the meat from the sauce. Pour the sauce into a small saucepan.

4 Cut the meat into thin strips and thread these, concertina-style, on to pre-soaked wooden skewers, alternating each strip of meat with the prepared pieces of scallion and bell pepper.

5 Gently heat the sauce until it is just simmering, stirring occasionally.

6 Grill the kabobs over hot coals for 5–8 minutes, turning and basting the

beef and vegetables occasionally with the reserved teriyaki sauce.

7 Arrange the skewers on serving plates and pour the remaining sauce over the kabobs. Serve with a green salad.

Lamb Meatballs

These small meatballs are made with ground lamb and flavored with chili, garlic, parsley, and Chinese curry powder.

NUTRITIONAL INFORMATION

Calories	320	Sugars	.........1g
Protein	........28g	Fat	..........20g
Carbohydrate	....8g	Saturates	.......6g

5 MINS   20 MINS

SERVES 4

INGREDIENTS

1 lb ground lamb

3 garlic cloves, crushed

2 green onions, finely chopped

½ tsp chili powder

1 tsp Chinese curry powder

1 tbsp chopped fresh parsley

½ cup fresh white breadcrumbs

1 egg, beaten

3 tbsp vegetable oil

4½ oz Chinese cabbage, shredded

1 leek, sliced

1 tbsp cornstarch

2 tbsp water

1¼ cups lamb stock

1 tbsp dark soy sauce

shredded leek, to garnish

VARIATION

Use ground pork or beef instead of the lamb as an alternative.

1 Mix the lamb, garlic, green onions, chili powder, Chinese curry powder, parsley, and breadcrumbs together in a bowl. Work the egg into the mixture, bringing it together to form a firm mixture. Roll into 16 small, even-sized balls.

2 Heat the oil in a preheated wok. Add the Chinese cabbage and leek and stir-fry for 1 minute. Remove from the wok with a slotted spoon and set aside.

3 Add the meatballs to the wok and fry in batches, turning gently, for 3-4 minutes, or until golden brown all over.

4 Mix the cornstarch and water together to form a smooth paste and set aside. Pour the lamb stock and soy sauce into the wok and cook for 2–3 minutes. Stir in the cornstarch paste. Bring to a boil and cook, stirring constantly, until the sauce is thickened and clear.

5 Return the Chinese cabbage and leek to the wok and cook for 1 minute, until heated through. Arrange the Chinese cabbage and leek on a warm serving dish, top with the meatballs, garnish with shredded leek, and serve immediately.

Pork Fry with Vegetables

This is a very simple dish which lends itself to almost any combination of vegetables that you have available.

NUTRITIONAL INFORMATION

Calories 216	Sugars 3g	
Protein 19g	Fat 12g	
Carbohydrate 5g	Saturates 3g	

  5 MINS   15 MINS

SERVES 4

I N G R E D I E N T S

12 oz pork tenderloin

2 tbsp vegetable oil

2 garlic cloves, crushed

½ inch piece fresh ginger, cut into slivers

1 carrot, cut into thin strips

1 red bell pepper, seeded and diced

1 fennel bulb, sliced

1 oz water chestnuts, halved

2 ¾ oz bean sprouts

2 tbsp Chinese rice wine

1¼ cups pork or chicken stock

pinch of dark brown sugar

1 tsp cornstarch

2 tsp water

1 Cut the pork into thin slices. Heat the oil in a preheated wok. Add the garlic, ginger, and pork and stir-fry for 1–2 minutes, until the meat is sealed.

2 Add the carrot, bell pepper, fennel, and water chestnuts to the wok and stir-fry for about 2–3 minutes.

3 Add the bean sprouts and stir-fry for 1 minute. Remove the pork and vegetables from the wok and keep warm.

4 Add the Chinese rice wine, pork or chicken stock, and sugar to the wok. Blend the cornstarch to a smooth paste with the water and stir it into the sauce. Bring to a boil, stirring constantly until thickened and clear.

5 Return the meat and vegetables to the wok and cook for 1–2 minutes, until heated through and coated with the sauce. Serve immediately.

VARIATION

Use dry sherry instead of the Chinese rice wine if you have difficulty obtaining it.

Garlic Lamb with Soy Sauce

The long marinating time allows the garlic to really penetrate the meat, creating a much more flavorful dish.

NUTRITIONAL INFORMATION

Calories	309	Sugars	.......0.2g
Protein	........25g	Fat	.........21g
Carbohydrate	....3g	Saturates	.......9g

  1¼ HOURS   15 MINS

SERVES 4

INGREDIENTS

1 lb lamb loin

2 cloves garlic

2 tbsp peanut oil

3 tbsp dry sherry or rice wine

3 tbsp dark soy sauce

1 tsp cornstarch

2 tbsp cold water

2 tbsp butter

1 Using a sharp knife, make small slits in the flesh of the lamb.

2 Carefully peel the cloves of garlic and cut them into slices, using a sharp knife.

3 Push the slices of garlic into the slits in the lamb. Place the garlic-infused lamb in a shallow dish.

4 In a small bowl, mix together 1 tablespoon each of the peanut oil, dry sherry or rice wine, and dark soy sauce. Drizzle this mixture over the lamb, cover with plastic wrap, and leave to marinate for at least 1 hour, preferably overnight.

5 Using a sharp knife or meat cleaver, thinly slice the marinated lamb.

6 Heat the remaining oil in a preheated wok or large skillet. Add the marinated lamb and stir-fry for 5 minutes.

7 Add the marinade juices and the remaining sherry and soy sauce to the wok and allow the juices to bubble for 5 minutes.

8 Blend the cornstarch to a smooth paste with the cold water. Add the cornstarch mixture to the wok and cook, stirring occasionally, until the juices start to thicken.

9 Cut the butter into small pieces. Add the butter to the wok or skillet and stir until the butter melts. Transfer the lamb to serving dishes and serve immediately.

COOK'S TIP

Adding the butter at the end of the recipe gives a glossy, rich sauce which is ideal with the lamb.

Soy & Sesame Beef

Soy sauce and sesame seeds are classic ingredients in Chinese cookery. Use a dark soy sauce for fuller flavor and richness.

NUTRITIONAL INFORMATION

Calories	324	Sugars	.........2g
Protein	........25g	Fat	..........22g
Carbohydrate	....3g	Saturates	.......6g

5 MINS   10 MINS

SERVES 4

INGREDIENTS

2 tbsp sesame seeds

1 lb fillet steak

2 tbsp vegetable oil

1 green bell pepper, seeded and thinly sliced

4 cloves garlic, crushed

2 tbsp dry sherry

4 tbsp soy sauce

6 green onions, sliced

noodles, to serve

1 Heat a large wok or heavy-bottomed skillet until it is very hot.

2 Add the sesame seeds to the wok or skillet and dry fry, stirring, for 1–2 minutes or until they just begin to brown. Remove the sesame seeds from the wok and set aside until required.

3 Using a sharp knife or meat cleaver, thinly slice the beef.

4 Heat the vegetable oil in the wok or skillet. Add the beef and stir-fry for 2–3 minutes or until sealed on all sides.

5 Add the sliced bell pepper and crushed garlic to the wok and continue stir-frying for 2 minutes.

6 Add the dry sherry and soy sauce to the wok together with the green onions. Allow the mixture in the wok to bubble, stirring occasionally, for about 1 minute, but do not let the mixture burn.

7 Transfer the garlic beef stir-fry to warm serving bowls and scatter over the dry-fried sesame seeds. Serve hot with boiled noodles.

COOK'S TIP

You can spread the sesame seeds out on a cookie sheet and toast them under a preheated broiler until browned all over, if you prefer.

Five-spice Lamb

Chinese five-spice powder is a blend of cinnamon, fennel, star anise, ginger, and cloves, all finely ground together.

NUTRITIONAL INFORMATION

Calories 361	Sugars 3g
Protein 35g	Fat 22g
Carbohydrate 5g	Saturates 8g

1¼ HOURS   10 MINS

SERVES 4

INGREDIENTS

1 lb 6 oz lean boneless lamb

2 tsp Chinese five-spice powder

3 tbsp sunflower oil

1 red bell pepper, cored, seeded, and thinly sliced

1 green bell pepper, cored, seeded, and thinly sliced

1 yellow or orange bell pepper, cored, seeded, and thinly sliced

4-6 green onions, thinly sliced diagonally

16 oz green beans, cut into 1½ inch lengths

2 tbsp soy sauce

4 tbsp sherry

salt and pepper

Chinese noodles, to serve

TO GARNISH

strips of red and yellow bell pepper

fresh cilantro leaves

1 Cut the lamb into narrow strips, about 1½ inches long, across the grain. Place in a bowl, add the five-spice powder and ¼ teaspoon salt, mix well and leave to marinate, covered, in a cool place for at least an hour and up to 24 hours.

2 Heat half the oil in the wok, swirling it around until really hot. Add the lamb and stir-fry briskly for 3-4 minutes until almost cooked through. Remove from the pan and set aside.

3 Add the remaining oil to the wok and when hot add the bell peppers and green onions. Stir-fry for 2-3 minutes, then add the beans and stir for a minute or so.

4 Add the soy sauce and sherry to the wok and when hot return the lamb and any juices to the wok. Stir-fry for 1-2 minutes until the lamb is really hot again and thoroughly coated in the sauce. Season to taste.

5 Serve the Five-spice Lamb with Chinese noodles, garnished with strips of red and green bell pepper and fresh cilantro.

Sweet & Sour Pork

This dish is a popular choice in Western diets, and must be one of the best known of Chinese recipes.

NUTRITIONAL INFORMATION

Calories 471	Sugars 47g
Protein 16g	Fat 13g
Carbohydrate . . .77g	Saturates 2g

 10 MINS 20 MINS

SERVES 4

I N G R E D I E N T S

⅔ cup vegetable oil, for
    deep-frying

8 oz pork tenderloin, cut into ½ inch cubes

1 onion, sliced

1 green bell pepper, seeded and sliced

8 oz pineapple pieces

1 small carrot, cut into thin strips

1 oz canned bamboo shoots,
    drained, rinsed, and halved

rice or noodles, to serve

B A T T E R

1 cup all-purpose flour

1 tbsp cornstarch

1½ tsp baking powder

1 tbsp vegetable oil

S A U C E

⅔ cup light brown sugar

2 tbsp cornstarch

½ cup white wine vinegar

2 garlic cloves, crushed

4 tbsp tomato paste

6 tbsp pineapple juice

1 To make the batter, sift the all-purpose flour into a mixing bowl, together with the cornstarch and baking powder. Add the vegetable oil and stir in enough water to make a thick, smooth batter (about ¾ cup).

2 Pour the vegetable oil into a preheated wok and heat until almost smoking.

3 Dip the cubes of pork into the batter, and cook in the hot oil, in batches, until the pork is cooked through. Remove the pork from the wok with a slotted spoon and drain on absorbent paper towels. Set aside and keep warm until required.

4 Drain all but 1 tablespoon of oil from the wok and return it to the heat. Add the onion, bell pepper, pineapple pieces, carrot, and bamboo shoots and stir-fry for 1–2 minutes. Remove from the wok with a slotted spoon and set aside.

5 Mix all of the sauce ingredients together and pour into the wok. Bring to a boil, stirring until thickened and clear. Cook for 1 minute, then return the pork and vegetables to the wok. Cook for another 1–2 minutes, then transfer to a serving plate and serve with rice or noodles.

Sweet Potato & Coconut Beef

This is a truly aromatic dish, blending the heat of red curry paste with the aroma and flavor of the lime leaves and coconut.

NUTRITIONAL INFORMATION

Calories 322	Sugars 9g
Protein 18g	Fat 18g
Carbohydrate ...24g	Saturates 6g

 10 MINS   25 MINS

SERVES 4

I N G R E D I E N T S

2 tbsp vegetable oil

2 cloves garlic

1 onion

12 oz rump steak

12 oz sweet potato

2 tbsp red curry paste

1¼ cups coconut milk

3 lime leaves

cooked jasmine rice, to serve

1 Heat the vegetable oil in a large preheated wok or large heavy-bottomed skillet.

2 Peel the garlic cloves and crush them in a pestle and mortar. Thinly slice the onions.

3 Using a sharp knife, thinly slice the beef. Add the beef to the wok and stir-fry for about 2 minutes or until sealed on all sides.

4 Add the garlic and the onion to the wok and stir-fry for another 2 minutes.

5 Using a sharp knife, peel and dice the sweet potato.

6 Add the sweet potato to the wok with the red curry paste, coconut milk, and lime leaves and bring to a rapid boil. Reduce the heat, cover, and leave to simmer for about 15 minutes or until the potatoes are tender.

7 Remove and discard the lime leaves and transfer the stir-fry to warm serving bowls. Serve hot with cooked jasmine rice.

VARIATION

If you cannot obtain lime leaves, use grated lime zest instead.

Oyster Sauce Lamb

This really is a speedy dish, lamb leg steaks being perfect for the short cooking time.

NUTRITIONAL INFORMATION

Calories ....243 Sugars 0.4g
Protein ....26g Fat 14
Carbohydrate ....3g Saturates 5g

5 MINS   10 MINS

SERVES 4

I N G R E D I E N T S

1 lb lamb leg steaks

1 tsp ground Szechuan peppercorns

1 tbsp peanut oil

2 cloves garlic, crushed

8 green onions, sliced

2 tbsp dark soy sauce

6 tbsp oyster sauce

16 oz Chinese cabbage

Oriental crackers, to serve
  (optional)

1 Using a sharp knife, remove any excess fat from the lamb. Slice the lamb thinly.

2 Sprinkle the ground Szechuan peppercorns over the meat and toss together until well combined.

3 Heat the peanut oil in a preheated wok or large heavy-bottomed skillet.

4 Add the lamb to the wok or skillet and then stir-fry for about 5 minutes.

5 Meanwhile, crush the garlic cloves in a pestle and mortar and slice the green onions. Add the garlic and green onions to the wok together with the dark soy sauce and stir-fry for 2 minutes.

6 Add the oyster sauce and Chinese cabbage and stir-fry for another 2 minutes, or until the leaves have wilted and the juices are bubbling.

7 Transfer the stir-fry to warm serving bowls and serve hot with the Oriental crackers (if using).

COOK'S TIP

Oyster sauce is made from oysters which are cooked in brine and soy sauce. Sold in bottles, it will keep in the refrigerator for months.

Red Spiced Beef

A spicy stir-fry flavored with paprika, chili, and tomato, with a crisp bite to it from the celery strips.

NUTRITIONAL INFORMATION

Calories	431	Sugars	........0g
Protein	........32g	Fat	.........28g
Carbohydrate	...14g	Saturates	......10g

40 MINS   10 MINS

SERVES 4

INGREDIENTS

1 lb 6 oz sirloin or rump steak

2 tbsp paprika

2-3 tsp mild chili powder

½ tsp salt

6 celery stalks

4 tomatoes, peeled, seeded, and sliced

6 tbsp stock or water

2 tbsp tomato paste

2 tbsp honey

3 tbsp wine vinegar

1 tbsp Worcestershire sauce

2 tbsp sunflower oil

4 green onions, thinly sliced diagonally

1-2 garlic cloves, crushed

Chinese noodles, to serve

celery leaves, to garnish (optional)

1 Using a sharp knife or meat cleaver, cut the steak across the grain into narrow strips ½ inch thick and place in a bowl.

2 Combine the paprika, chili powder, and salt, add to the beef and mix thoroughly until the meat strips are evenly coated with the spices. Leave the beef to marinate in a cool place for at least 30 minutes.

3 Cut the celery into 2 inch lengths, then cut the lengths into strips about ¼ inches thick.

4 Combine the stock, tomato paste, honey, wine vinegar and Worcestershire sauce and set aside.

5 Heat the oil in the wok until really hot. Add the green onions, celery, and garlic and stir-fry for about 1 minute until the vegetables are beginning to soften, then add the steak strips. Stir-fry over a high heat for 3-4 minutes until the meat is well sealed.

6 Add the sauce to the wok and continue to stir-fry briskly until thoroughly coated and sizzling.

7 Serve with noodles and garnish with celery leaves, if liked.

Pork Balls with Mint Sauce

Made with lean minced pork the balls are first stir-fried, then braised in the wok with stock and pickled walnuts to give a tangy flavor.

NUTRITIONAL INFORMATION

Calories 318	Sugars 2g	
Protein 30g	Fat 20g	
Carbohydrate 6g	Saturates 5g	

5 MINS   25 MINS

SERVES 4

I N G R E D I E N T S

1 lb 2 oz lean ground pork

¾ cup fine fresh white breadcrumbs

½ tsp ground allspice

1 garlic clove, crushed

2 tbsp freshly chopped mint

1 egg, beaten

2 tbsp sunflower oil

1 red bell pepper, cored, seeded, and thinly sliced

1 cup chicken stock

4 pickled walnuts, sliced

salt and pepper

rice or Chinese noodles, to serve

fresh mint, to garnish

1 Mix together the ground pork, breadcrumbs, seasoning, allspice, garlic, and half the chopped mint in a mixing bowl, then bind together with the beaten egg.

2 Shape the meat mixture into 20 small balls with your hands, damping your hands if it is easier for shaping.

3 Heat the sunflower oil in the wok or heavy-bottomed skillet, swirling the

oil around until really hot, then stir-fry the pork balls for about 4-5 minutes, or until browned all over.

4 Remove the pork balls from the wok with a slotted spoon as they are ready and drain on absorbent paper towels.

5 Pour off all but 1 tablespoon of fat and oil from the wok or skillet then add the red bell pepper slices and stir-fry for 2-3 minutes, or until they begin to soften, but not color.

6 Add the chicken stock and bring to a boil. Season well with salt and pepper and return the pork balls to the wok, stirring well to coat in the sauce. Simmer for 7-10 minutes, turning the pork balls from time to time.

7 Add the remaining chopped mint and the pickled walnuts to the wok and continue to simmer for 2-3 minutes, turning the pork balls regularly to coat them in the sauce.

8 Adjust the seasoning and serve the pork balls with rice or Chinese noodles, or with a stir-fried vegetable dish, garnished with sprigs of fresh mint.

Meatballs in Peanut Sauce

Choose very lean ground beef to make these meatballs—or better still, buy some lean beef and grind it yourself.

NUTRITIONAL INFORMATION

Calories 553   Sugars 10g
Protein . . . . .32g   Fat 43g
Carbohydrate . . .21g   Saturates 12g

 5 MINS   30 MINS

SERVES 4

I N G R E D I E N T S

2 cups lean ground beef

2 tsp finely grated fresh ginger

1 small red chili, seeded and chopped finely

1 tbsp chopped fresh basil or cilantro

1 tbsp sesame oil

1 tbsp vegetable oil

salt and pepper

S A U C E

2 tbsp red curry paste

1¼ cups coconut milk

1 cup ground peanuts

1 tbsp fish sauce

T O   G A R N I S H

chopped fresh basil

sprigs of fresh basil or cilantro

VARIATION

Ground lamb makes a delicious alternative to beef. If you do use lamb, try substituting ground almonds for the peanuts and fresh mint for the basil.

1 Put the beef, ginger, chili, and basil or cilantro into a food processor or blender. Add ½ teaspoon of salt and plenty of pepper. Process for about 10–15 seconds until finely chopped. Alternatively, chop the ingredients finely and mix together.

2 Form the beef mixture into about 12 balls. Heat the sesame oil and vegetable oil in a wok or skillet and fry the meatballs over a medium-high heat until well browned on all sides, about 10 minutes. Lift them out and drain on paper towels.

3 To make the sauce, stir-fry the red curry paste in the wok or skillet for 1 minute. Add the coconut milk, peanuts, and fish sauce. Heat, stirring, until just simmering.

4 Return the meatballs to the wok or skillet and cook gently in the sauce for 10–15 minutes. If the sauce begins to get too thick, add a little extra coconut milk or water. Season with a little salt and pepper, according to taste.

5 Serve garnished with chopped fresh basil and sprigs of fresh basil or cilantro.

Roast Red Pork

Pork tenderloin is given a marvelous flavor and distinctive red color in this excellent recipe.

NUTRITIONAL INFORMATION

Calories	305	Sugars	........4g
Protein	........40g	Fat	.........13g
Carbohydrate	....5g	Saturates	.......5g

12¼ HOURS   40 MINS

SERVES 4

INGREDIENTS

1 lb 10 oz pork tenderloin

1 tsp red food coloring

4 garlic cloves, crushed

1 tsp Chinese five-spice powder

1 tbsp light soy sauce

1 tbsp fish sauce

1 tbsp dry sherry

1 tbsp dark brown sugar

1 tbsp sesame oil

1 tbsp finely grated fresh ginger

TO GARNISH

lettuce

green onions, finely sliced

1   Rinse the pork and trim off any fat. Place in a large clear plastic food bag or freezer bag and add the red food coloring. Roll the pork around in the bag to coat it in the coloring.

2   Mix all the remaining ingredients together and add the mixture to the pork in the plastic bag. Secure the opening and chill overnight, or for at least 12 hours, turning the bag over occasionally.

3   Place the pork on a rack over a roasting pan. Cook in a preheated oven at 425°F for 15 minutes. Remove from the oven and baste with the remaining marinade.

4   Reduce the oven temperature to 350°F and roast the pork for another 25 minutes, basting with any remaining marinade. Leave to cool for at least 10 minutes before slicing.

5   Slice thinly, arrange on a serving platter, garnish, and serve.

COOK'S TIP

Putting the pork in a plastic bag helps to prevent your hands from turning red from the food coloring.

Lamb with Black Bean Sauce

Red onions add great color to recipes and are perfect in this dish, combining with the colors of the bell peppers.

NUTRITIONAL INFORMATION

Calories 328   Sugars 5g
Protein . . . . .26g   Fat 20g
Carbohydrate . . .12g   Saturates 6g

10 MINS   15 MINS

SERVES 4

INGREDIENTS

1 lb lamb neck steak or boneless chops

1 egg white, lightly beaten

4 tbsp cornstarch

1 tsp Chinese five spice powder

3 tbsp sunflower oil

1 red onion

1 red bell pepper, seeded and sliced

1 green bell pepper, seeded and sliced

1 yellow or orange bell pepper, seeded and sliced

5 tbsp black bean sauce

boiled rice or noodles, to serve

1 Using a sharp knife, slice the lamb into very thin strips.

2 Mix together the egg white, cornstarch, and Chinese five-spice powder. Toss the lamb strips in the mixture until evenly coated.

3 Heat the oil in a wok and stir-fry the lamb over a high heat for 5 minutes or until it crisps around the edges.

4 Slice the red onion. Add the onion and bell pepper slices to the wok and stir-fry for 5–6 minutes, or until the vegetables just begin to soften.

5 Stir the black bean sauce into the mixture in the wok and heat through.

6 Transfer the lamb and sauce to warm serving plates and serve hot with freshly boiled rice or noodles.

COOK'S TIP

Be careful when frying the lamb because the cornstarch mixture may cause it to stick to the wok. Move the lamb around the wok constantly during stir-frying.

Caramelized Beef

Brown sugar is used in this recipe to give the beef a slightly caramelized flavor.

NUTRITIONAL INFORMATION

Calories 335	Sugars 8g	
Protein 23g	Fat 21g	
Carbohydrate ...14g	Saturates 7g	

1¼ HOURS   10 MINS

SERVES 4

INGREDIENTS

1 lb fillet steak

2 tbsp soy sauce

1 tsp chili oil

1 tbsp tamarind paste

2 tbsp brown sugar

2 cloves garlic, crushed

2 tbsp sunflower oil

8 oz baby onions

2 tbsp chopped fresh cilantro, to garnish

1 Using a sharp knife or meat cleaver, thinly slice the beef.

2 Place the slices of beef in a large, shallow non-metallic dish.

3 Mix together the soy sauce, chili oil, tamarind paste, brown sugar, and garlic in a mixing bowl.

4 Spoon the sugar mixture over the beef. Toss well to coat the beef in the mixture, cover with plastic wrap, and leave to marinate for at least 1 hour, the longer the better.

5 Heat the oil in a preheated wok or large skillet.

6 Peel the onions and cut them in half. Add the onion pieces to the wok and stir-fry for 2–3 minutes, or until just browning.

7 Add the beef and marinade juices to the wok and stir-fry over a high heat for about 5 minutes.

8 Scatter with chopped fresh cilantro and serve immediately.

COOK'S TIP

Use the chili oil carefully because it is very hot and could easily spoil the dish if too much is added.

Curried Lamb with Potatoes

This dish is very filling, only requiring a simple vegetable accompaniment or bread.

NUTRITIONAL INFORMATION

Calories 375   Sugars 6g
Protein ....26g   Fat 19g
Carbohydrate ...27g   Saturates 6g

10 MINS   1 HOUR

SERVES 4

I N G R E D I E N T S

1 lb potatoes, diced

1 lb lean lamb, cubed

2 tbsp medium hot curry paste

3 tbsp sunflower oil

1 onion, sliced

1 eggplant, diced

2 cloves garlic, crushed

1 tbsp grated fresh ginger

⅔ cup lamb or beef stock

salt

2 tbsp chopped fresh cilantro,
  to garnish

1 Bring a large saucepan of lightly salted water to a boil. Add the potatoes and cook for 10 minutes. Remove the potatoes from the saucepan with a slotted spoon and drain thoroughly.

COOK'S TIP

The wok is an ancient Chinese invention, the name coming from the Cantonese, meaning a 'cooking vessel'.

2 Meanwhile, place the lamb cubes in a large mixing bowl. Add the curry paste and mix well until the lamb is evenly coated in the paste.

3 Heat the sunflower oil in a large preheated wok.

4 Add the onion, eggplant, garlic, and ginger to the wok and stir-fry for about 5 minutes.

5 Add the lamb to the wok and stir-fry for another 5 minutes.

6 Add the stock and cooked potatoes to the wok, bring to a boil and leave to simmer for 30 minutes, or until the lamb is tender and cooked through.

7 Transfer the stir-fry to warm serving dishes and scatter with chopped fresh cilantro. Serve immediately.

Spicy Beef

In this recipe beef is marinated in a five-spice and chili marinade for a spicy flavor.

NUTRITIONAL INFORMATION

Calories 246   Sugars 2g
Protein . . . . .21g   Fat 13g
Carbohydrate . . .10g   Saturates 3g

1¼ HOURS   10 MINS

SERVES 4

INGREDIENTS

8 oz fillet steak

2 garlic cloves, crushed

1 tsp powdered star anise

1 tbsp dark soy sauce

green onion tassels, to garnish

SAUCE

2 tbsp vegetable oil

1 bunch green onions, halved lengthwise

1 tbsp dark soy sauce

1 tbsp dry sherry

¼ tsp chili sauce

⅔ cup water

2 tsp cornstarch

4 tsp water

1 Cut the steak into thin strips and place in a shallow dish.

2 Mix together the garlic, star anise, and dark soy sauce in a bowl.

3 Pour the sauce mixture over the steak strips, turning them to coat thoroughly. Cover and leave to marinate in the refrigerator for at least 1 hour.

4 To make the sauce, heat the oil in a preheated wok or large skillet. Reduce the heat and stir-fry the green onions for 1-2 minutes.

5 Remove the green onions from the wok with a slotted spoon, drain on absorbent paper towels, and set aside until required.

6 Add the beef to the wok, together with the marinade, and stir-fry for 3-4 minutes. Return the green onions to the wok and add the soy sauce, sherry, chili sauce, and two thirds of the water.

7 Blend the cornstarch with the remaining water and stir into the wok. Bring to a boil, stirring until the sauce thickens and clears.

8 Transfer to a warm serving dish, garnish, and serve immediately.

Beef with Green Peas

This recipe is the perfect example of quick stir-frying ingredients for a delicious, crisp, colorful dish.

NUTRITIONAL INFORMATION

Calories 325   Sugars 2g
Protein ....26g   Fat 22g
Carbohydrate ....8g   Saturates 7g

🍰 5 MINS   🕐 10 MINS

SERVES 4

I N G R E D I E N T S

1 lb rump steak

2 tbsp sunflower oil

1 onion

2 cloves garlic

1 cup fresh or frozen peas

5¾ oz jar black bean sauce

15½ oz Chinese cabbage, shredded

1 Using a sharp knife, trim away any fat from the beef. Cut the beef into thin slices.

2 Heat the sunflower oil in a large preheated wok.

3 Add the beef to the wok and stir-fry for 2 minutes.

4 Using a sharp knife, peel and slice the onion and crush the garlic cloves in a pestle and mortar.

5 Add the onion, garlic, and peas to the wok and stir-fry for 5 minutes.

6 Add the black bean sauce and Chinese cabbage to the wok.

7 Heat the mixture in the wok for another 2 minutes until the Chinese cabbage have wilted.

8 Transfer to warm serving bowls then serve immediately.

COOK'S TIP

Buy a chunky black bean sauce if you can for the best texture and flavor.

Chinese cabbage are now widely available. They look like a pale, elongated head of lettuce with light green, tightly packed crinkly leaves.

Stir-fried Pork & Cabbage

Rustle up this quick dish in a matter of moments. Assemble all your ingredients first, then everything is ready as you start to stir-fry.

NUTRITIONAL INFORMATION

Calories	226	Sugars	........2g
Protein	........21g	Fat	..........12g
Carbohydrate	....4g	Saturates	......3g

5 MINS   10 MINS

SERVES 4

INGREDIENTS

13 oz pork tenderloin

8 green onions, trimmed

½ small white cabbage

½ cucumber

2 tsp finely grated fresh ginger

1 tbsp fish sauce or light soy sauce

2 tbsp dry sherry

2 tbsp water

2 tsp cornstarch

1 tbsp chopped fresh mint or cilantro

2 tbsp sesame oil

salt and pepper

TO GARNISH

sprigs of fresh mint or cilantro

1 chili flower (see Cook's Tip, right)

1 Slice the pork very thinly. Shred the green onions and cabbage, and cut the cucumber into thin sticks.

2 Mix together the ginger, fish sauce or soy sauce, sherry, water, cornstarch, and chopped mint or cilantro until blended.

3 Heat the sesame oil in a wok and add the pork. Stir-fry briskly over a high heat until browned, about 4–5 minutes.

4 Add the green onions, cabbage, and cucumber and stir-fry for another 2 minutes. Add the cornstarch mixture and continue to cook for about 1 minute, until slightly thickened. Season to taste.

5 Transfer the stir-fry to a warmed dish and serve immediately, garnished with sprigs of fresh mint or cilantro and a chili flower.

COOK'S TIP

To make chili flowers, hold the stem of the chili and cut down its length several times with a sharp knife. Place in a bowl of chilled water and chill so that the "petals" turn out. Remove the chili seeds when the "petals" have opened.

Fish & Seafood

China's many miles of coastline, rivers, and lakes offer an enormous variety of fresh and saltwater fish and seafood. Among the most popular are carp, bass, bream, clams, crab,

crawfish and shrimp. Dishes which include shark's fins, abalone, squid and edible seaweed are also common. When buying fish and seafood for Chinese cooking, freshness is imperative to flavor so be sure to buy it and use it as soon as possible, preferably the same day. Chinese chefs buy live fish which are kept alive until just before cooking. Favorite cooking methods for fish are steaming and quick poaching in boiling water or stock.

Shrimp Fu Yong

The classic ingredients of this popular dish are eggs, carrots, and small shrimps. Add extra ingredients such as peas or crab meat, if desired.

NUTRITIONAL INFORMATION

Calories 240	Sugars 1g
Protein 22g	Fat 16g
Carbohydrate 1g	Saturates 3g

5 MINS   10 MINS

SERVES 4

I N G R E D I E N T S

2 tbsp vegetable oil

1 carrot, grated

5 eggs, beaten

8 oz raw small shrimp, peeled

1 tbsp light soy sauce

pinch of Chinese five-spice powder

2 green onions, chopped

2 tsp sesame seeds

1 tsp sesame oil

COOK'S TIP

If only cooked shrimp are available, add them just before the end of cooking, but make sure they are fully incorporated into the fu yong. They only need heating through. Overcooking will make them chewy and tasteless.

1 Heat the vegetable oil in a preheated wok or skillet, swirling it around until the oil is really hot.

2 Add the grated carrot and stir-fry for 1–2 minutes.

3 Push the carrot to one side of the wok or skillet and add the beaten eggs. Cook, stirring gently, for 1–2 minutes.

4 Stir the shrimp, light soy sauce, and five-spice powder into the mixture in the wok. Stir-fry the mixture for 2–3 minutes, or until the shrimp changes color and the mixture is almost dry.

5 Turn the shrimp fu yong out onto a warm plate and sprinkle the green onions, sesame seeds and sesame oil on top. Serve immediately.

Fried Shrimp with Cashews

Cashews are delicious as part of a stir-fry with almost any other ingredient. Use the unsalted variety in cooking.

NUTRITIONAL INFORMATION

Calories 406	Sugar 3g	
Protein 31g	Fat 25g	
Carbohydrate ...13g	Saturates 4g	

🍤 5 MINS   🕐 5 MINS

SERVES 4

INGREDIENTS

2 garlic cloves, crushed

1 tbsp cornstarch

pinch of sugar

1 lb raw jumbo shrimp

4 tbsp vegetable oil

1 leek, sliced

4½ oz broccoli flowerets

1 orange bell pepper, seeded
   and diced

¾ cup unsalted cashews

SAUCE

¾ cup fish stock

1 tbsp cornstarch

dash of chili sauce

2 tsp sesame oil

1 tbsp Chinese rice wine

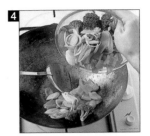

1 Mix together the garlic, cornstarch, and sugar in a bowl.

2 Peel and devein the shrimp. Stir the shrimp into the mixture to coat thoroughly.

3 Heat the vegetable oil in a preheated wok and add the shrimp mixture. Stir-fry over a high heat for 20–30 seconds until the shrimp turn pink. Remove the shrimp from the wok with a slotted spoon, drain on absorbent paper towels and set aside until required.

4 Add the leek, broccoli, and bell pepper to the wok and stir-fry for 2 minutes.

5 To make the sauce, place the fish stock, cornstarch, chili sauce to taste, the sesame oil and Chinese rice wine in a small bowl. Mix until thoroughly combined.

6 Add the sauce to the wok, together with the cashews. Return the shrimp to the wok and cook for 1 minute to heat through.

7 Transfer the shrimp stir-fry to a warm serving dish and serve immediately.

Szechuan White Fish

Szechuan pepper is quite hot and should be used sparingly to avoid making the dish unbearably spicy.

NUTRITIONAL INFORMATION

Calories 225   Sugars 3g
Protein . . . . .20g   Fat 8g
Carbohydrate . . .17g   Saturates 1g

5 MINS   20 MINS

SERVES 4

I N G R E D I E N T S

12 oz white fish fillets

1 small egg, beaten

3 tbsp all-purpose flour

4 tbsp dry white wine

3 tbsp light soy sauce

vegetable oil, for frying

1 garlic clove, cut into slivers

½-inch piece fresh ginger, finely chopped

1 onion, finely chopped

1 celery stalk, chopped

1 fresh red chili, chopped

3 green onions, chopped

1 tsp rice wine vinegar

½ tsp ground Szechuan pepper

¾ cup fish stock

1 tsp sugar

1 tsp cornstarch

2 tsp water

1 Cut the fish into 1½ inch cubes. Beat together the egg, flour, wine, and 1 tablespoon of soy sauce to make a batter. Dip the cubes of fish into the batter to coat well.

2 Heat the oil in a wok, reduce the heat slightly and cook the fish, in batches, for 2–3 minutes, until golden brown. Remove with a slotted spoon, drain on paper towels, set aside, and keep warm.

3 Pour all but 1 tablespoon of oil from the wok and return to the heat. Add the garlic, ginger, onion, celery, chili, and green onions and stir-fry for 1–2 minutes. Stir in the remaining soy sauce and the vinegar.

4 Add the Szechuan pepper, fish stock, and sugar to the wok. Mix the cornstarch with the water to form a smooth paste and stir it into the stock. Bring to a boil and cook, stirring, for 1 minute, until the sauce thickens and clears.

5 Return the fish cubes to the wok and cook for 1–2 minutes. Serve immediately.

Fish with Black Bean Sauce

Steaming is one of the preferred methods of cooking whole fish in China as it maintains both the flavor and the texture.

NUTRITIONAL INFORMATION

Calories 292	Sugars 3g
Protein 44g	Fat 7g
Carbohydrate 6g	Saturates 0.4g

 10 MINS   10 MINS

SERVES 4

I N G R E D I E N T S

2 lb whole snapper, cleaned and scaled

3 garlic cloves, crushed

2 tbsp black bean sauce

1 tsp cornstarch

2 tsp sesame oil

2 tbsp light soy sauce

2 tsp sugar

2 tbsp dry sherry

1 small leek, shredded

1 small red bell pepper, seeded and cut into thin strips

shredded leek and lemon wedges, to garnish

boiled rice or noodles, to serve

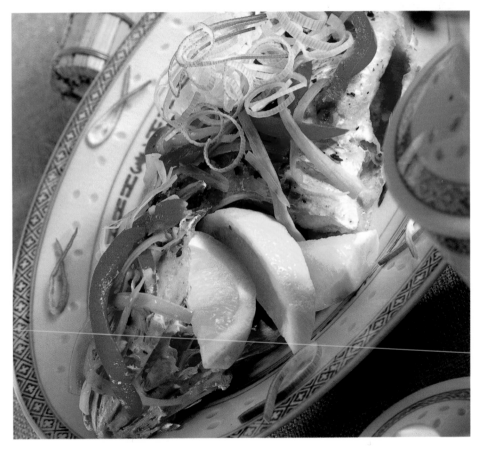

1 Rinse the fish inside and out with cold running water and pat dry with paper towels.

2 Make 2-3 diagonal slashes in the flesh on each side of the fish, using a sharp knife. Rub the garlic into the fish.

3 Mix together the black bean sauce, cornstarch, sesame oil, light soy sauce, sugar, and dry sherry.

4 Place the fish in a shallow heatproof dish and pour the sauce mixture over the top. Sprinkle the shredded leek and bell pepper strips on top of the sauce.

5 Place the dish in the top of a steamer, cover and steam for 10 minutes, or until the fish is cooked through.

6 Transfer the fish to a serving dish, garnish with shredded leek and lemon wedges and serve with boiled rice or noodles.

COOK'S TIP

Insert the point of a sharp knife into the fish to test if it is cooked. The fish is cooked through if the knife goes into the flesh easily.

Stir-fried Salmon with Leeks

Salmon is marinated in a deliciously rich, sweet sauce, stir-fried and served on a bed of crispy leeks.

NUTRITIONAL INFORMATION

Calories 360   Sugars 9g
Protein . . . . .24g   Fat 25
Carbohydrate . . . .11g   Saturates 4g

35 MINS   15 MINS

SERVES 4

INGREDIENTS

1 lb salmon fillet, skinned

2 tbsp sweet soy sauce

2 tbsp tomato ketchup

1 tsp rice wine vinegar

1 tbsp brown sugar

1 clove garlic, crushed

4 tbsp corn oil

1 lb leeks, thinly shredded

finely chopped red chilies,
   to garnish

1 Using a sharp knife, cut the salmon into slices. Place the slices of salmon in a shallow non-metallic dish.

2 Mix together the soy sauce, tomato ketchup, rice wine vinegar, sugar, and garlic.

3 Pour the mixture over the salmon, toss well, and leave to marinate for about 30 minutes.

4 Meanwhile, heat 3 tablespoons of the corn oil in a large preheated wok.

5 Add the leeks to the wok and stir-fry over a medium-high heat for about 10 minutes, or until the leeks become crispy and tender.

6 Using a slotted spoon, carefully remove the leeks from the wok and transfer to warmed serving plates.

7 Add the remaining oil to the wok. Add the salmon and the marinade to the wok and cook for 2 minutes.

8 Remove the salmon from the wok and spoon over the leeks, garnish with finely chopped red chilies and serve immediately.

VARIATION

You can use a fillet of beef instead of the salmon, if you prefer.

Sweet & Sour Shrimp

Use raw shrimp if possible. Omit steps 1 and 2 if cooked ones are used.

NUTRITIONAL INFORMATION

Calories 373   Sugars 11g
Protein ....13g   Fat 26g
Carbohydrate ...19g   Saturates 3g

3¹/₂ HOURS   10 MINS

SERVES 4

INGREDIENTS

6-9 oz peeled raw jumbo shrimp

pinch of salt

1 tsp egg white

1 tsp cornstarch paste (see page 31)

1¼ cups vegetable oil

SAUCE

1 tbsp vegetable oil

½ small green bell pepper, cored, seeded, and thinly sliced

½ small carrot, thinly sliced

4½ oz canned water chestnuts, drained and sliced

½ tsp salt

1 tbsp light soy sauce

2 tbsp sugar

3 tbsp rice or sherry vinegar

1 tsp rice wine or dry sherry

1 tbsp ketchup

½ tsp chili sauce

3-4 tbsp Chinese Stock (see page 30) or water

2 tsp cornstarch paste (see page 31)

a few drops sesame oil

 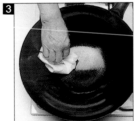 

1 Mix together the shrimp with the salt, egg white, and cornstarch paste.

2 Heat the oil in a preheated wok and stir-fry the shrimp for 30-40 seconds only. Remove and drain on paper towels.

3 Pour off the oil and wipe the wok clean with paper towels. To make the sauce, first heat the tablespoon of oil. Add the vegetables and stir-fry for about 1 minute, then add the seasonings with the stock or water and bring to a boil.

4 Add the shrimp and stir until blended well. Thicken the sauce with the cornstarch paste and stir until smooth. Sprinkle with sesame oil and serve hot.

Fried Squid Flowers

The addition of green bell pepper and black bean sauce to the squid makes a colorful and delicious dish from the Cantonese school.

NUTRITIONAL INFORMATION

Calories 172   Sugars 1g
Protein ....13g   Fat 13g
Carbohydrate ....2g   Saturates 1g

 10 MINS   5 MINS

SERVES 4

I N G R E D I E N T S

12-14 oz prepared and cleaned squid (see Cook's Tip, below)

1 medium green bell pepper, cored and seeded

3-4 tbsp vegetable oil

1 garlic clove, finely chopped

¼ tsp finely chopped fresh ginger

2 tsp finely chopped green onions

½ tsp salt

2 tbsp crushed black bean sauce

1 tsp Chinese rice wine or dry sherry

a few drops sesame oil

boiled rice, to serve

1 If ready-prepared squid is not available, prepare as instructed in the Cook's Tip, below.

2 Open up the squid and, using a meat cleaver or sharp knife, score the inside of the flesh in a criss-cross pattern.

3 Cut the squid into pieces about the size of a rectangular postage stamp.

4 Blanch the squid pieces in a bowl of boiling water for a few seconds. Remove and drain; dry well on absorbent paper towels.

5 Cut the bell pepper into small triangular pieces. Heat the oil in a preheated wok or large skillet and stir-fry the bell pepper for about 1 minute.

6 Add the garlic, ginger, green onion, salt, and squid. Continue stirring for another minute.

7 Finally add the black bean sauce and Chinese rice wine or dry sherry, and blend well.

8 Transfer the squid flowers to a serving dish, sprinkle with sesame oil, and serve with boiled rice.

COOK'S TIP

Clean the squid by first cutting off the head. Cut off the tentacles and reserve. Remove the small soft bone at the base of the tentacles and the transparent backbone, as well as the ink bag. Peel off the thin skin, then wash and dry well.

Fish & Seafood **279**

Fish with Saffron Sauce

White fish cooked in a bamboo steamer over the wok and served with a light creamy saffron sauce with a real bite to it.

NUTRITIONAL INFORMATION

Calories	254	Sugars	.......0.5g
Protein	........30g	Fat	.........14g
Carbohydrate	....2g	Saturates	.......5g

 5 MINS   30 MINS

SERVES 4

I N G R E D I E N T S

1 lb 6 oz–1 lb 10 oz white fish fillets (cod, haddock, etc.)

pinch of Chinese five-spice powder

4 sprigs fresh thyme

large pinch saffron threads

1 cup boiling fish or vegetable stock

2 tbsp sunflower oil

4½ oz small mushrooms, thinly sliced

grated zest of ½ lemon

1 tbsp lemon juice

½ tsp freshly chopped thyme or ¼ tsp dried thyme

½ bunch watercress, chopped

1½ tsp cornstarch

3 tbsp light or heavy cream

salt and pepper

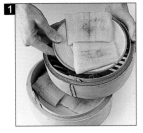  

1 Skin the fish and cut into 4 even-sized portions. Season with salt and pepper and five-spice powder. Arrange the fish on a plate and place in the bottom of a bamboo steamer, laying a sprig of thyme on each piece of fish.

2 Stand a low metal trivet in a wok and add water to come almost to the top of it. Bring to a boil, stand the bamboo steamer on the trivet, and cover with the bamboo lid and then the lid of the wok or a piece of foil. Simmer for 20 minutes until the fish is tender, adding more boiling water to the wok if necessary. Meanwhile, soak the saffron threads in the boiling stock.

3 When the fish is tender, remove and keep warm. Empty the wok and wipe dry. Heat the oil in the wok and stir-fry the mushrooms for about 2 minutes. Add the saffron stock, lemon zest and juice, and chopped thyme and bring to a boil. Add the watercress and simmer for 1–2 minutes.

4 Blend the cornstarch with the cream, add a little of the sauce from the wok, then return to the wok and heat gently until thickened. Serve the fish surrounded by the sauce.

Sesame Salmon with Cream

Salmon fillet holds its shape when tossed in sesame seeds and stir-fried.
It is served in a creamy sauce of diced zucchini.

NUTRITIONAL INFORMATION

Calories 550	Sugars 1g
Protein 35g	Fat 45g
Carbohydrate 2g	Saturates 12g

5 MINS   10 MINS

SERVES 4

INGREDIENTS

1 lb 6 oz–1 lb 10 oz salmon or pink trout fillets

2 tbsp light soy sauce

3 tbsp sesame seeds

3 tbsp sunflower oil

4 green onions, thinly sliced diagonally

2 large zucchini, diced, or 5-inch piece cucumber, diced

grated zest of ½ lemon

1 tbsp lemon juice

½ tsp turmeric

6 tbsp fish stock or water

3 tbsp heavy cream

salt and pepper

curly endive, to garnish

1 Skin the fish and cut into strips about 1 1/2 x 3/4 inch. Pat dry on paper towels. Season lightly, then brush with soy sauce and sprinkle all over with sesame seeds.

2 Heat 2 tablespoons of oil in the wok. Add the pieces of fish and stir-fry for 3-4 minutes until lightly browned all over. Remove with a fish slice, drain on paper towels and keep warm.

3 Heat the remaining oil in the wok and add the green onions and zucchini or cucumber and stir-fry for 1-2 minutes. Add the lemon zest and juice, turmeric, stock, and seasoning and bring to a boil for 1 minute. Stir in the cream.

4 Return the fish pieces to the wok and toss gently in the sauce until they are really hot. Garnish and serve.

COOK'S TIP

Lay the fillet skin-side down. Insert a sharp, flexible knife at one end between the flesh and the skin. Hold the skin tightly at the end and push the knife along, keeping the knife blade as flat as possible against the skin.

Crispy Fish

This is a very hot dish—not for the faint hearted! It may be made without the chili flavorings, if preferred.

NUTRITIONAL INFORMATION

Calories 281   Sugars 3g
Protein . . . . .25g   Fat 12g
Carbohydrate . . .15g   Saturates 2g

30 MINS   40 MINS

SERVES 4

INGREDIENTS

1 lb white fish fillets

BATTER

½ cup all-purpose flour

1 egg, separated

1 tbsp peanut oil

4 tbsp milk

vegetable oil, for deep-frying

SAUCE

1 fresh red chili, chopped

2 garlic cloves, crushed

pinch of chili powder

3 tbsp tomato paste

1 tbsp rice wine vinegar

2 tbsp dark soy sauce

2 tbsp Chinese rice wine

2 tbsp water

pinch of sugar

1 Cut the fish into 1 inch cubes and set aside until required.

2 Sift the all-purpose flour into a mixing bowl and make a well in the center. Add the egg yolk and peanut oil to the mixing bowl and gradually stir in the milk, incorporating the flour to form a smooth batter. Leave to stand for about 20 minutes.

3 Whisk the egg white until it forms peaks and fold into the batter until thoroughly incorporated.

4 Heat the vegetable oil in a preheated wok or large skillet. Dip the fish into the batter and fry, in batches, for 8–10 minutes, until cooked through. Remove the fish from the wok with a slotted spoon, set aside and keep warm until required.

5 Pour off all but 1 tablespoon of oil from the wok and return to the heat. Add the chili, garlic, chili powder, tomato paste, rice wine vinegar, soy sauce, Chinese rice wine, water, and sugar and cook, stirring, for 3–4 minutes.

6 Return the fish to the wok and stir gently to coat it in the sauce. Cook for 2-3 minutes, until hot. Transfer to a serving dish and serve immediately.

Braised Fish Fillets

Any white fish, such as lemon sole or plaice, is ideal for this delicious dish.

NUTRITIONAL INFORMATION

Calories	107	Sugars	.........2g
Protein	........17g	Fat	...........2g
Carbohydrate	....6g	Saturates	.....0.3g

🍲 4 HOURS 🕐 10 MINS

SERVES 4

INGREDIENTS

3-4 small Chinese dried mushrooms

10½-12 oz fish fillets

1 tsp salt

½ egg white, lightly beaten

1 tsp cornstarch paste
(see page 31)

2½ cups vegetable oil

1 tsp finely chopped fresh ginger

2 green onions, finely chopped

1 garlic clove, finely chopped

½ small green bell pepper, seeded
and cut into small cubes

½ small carrot, thinly sliced

½ cup canned sliced bamboo shoots, rinsed
and drained

½ tsp sugar

1 tbsp light soy sauce

1 tsp rice wine or dry sherry

1 tbsp chili bean sauce

2-3 tbsp Chinese Stock (see page 30)
or water

a few drops of sesame oil

1 Soak the dried mushrooms in a bowl of warm water for 30 minutes. Drain thoroughly on paper towels, reserving the soaking water for stock or soup. Squeeze the mushrooms to extract all of the moisture, cut off and discard any hard stems, and slice thinly.

2 Cut the fish into bite-sized pieces, then place in a shallow dish and mix with a pinch of salt, the egg white and cornstarch paste, turning the fish to coat well.

3 Heat the oil in a preheated wok. Add the fish pieces to the wok and deep-fry for about 1 minute. Remove the fish pieces with a slotted spoon and leave to drain on paper towels.

4 Pour off the excess oil, leaving about 1 tablespoon in the wok. Add the ginger, green onions, and garlic to flavor the oil for a few seconds, then add the bell pepper, carrots, and bamboo shoots and stir-fry for about 1 minute.

5 Add the sugar, soy sauce, wine, chili bean sauce, stock or water, and the remaining salt and bring to a boil. Add the fish pieces, stirring to coat with the sauce, and braise for 1 minute. Sprinkle with sesame oil and serve.

Baked Crab with Ginger

In Chinese restaurants, only live crabs are used, but ready-cooked ones can be used at home quite successfully.

NUTRITIONAL INFORMATION

Calories 261   Sugars 0.5g
Protein . . . . .18g   Fat 17g
Carbohydrate . . . .5g   Saturates 2g

3³/₄ HOURS   10 MINS

SERVES 4

INGREDIENTS

1 large or 2 medium crabs, weighing about
    1 lb 10 oz in total

2 tbsp Chinese rice wine or dry sherry

1 egg, lightly beaten

1 tbsp cornstarch

3-4 tbsp vegetable oil

1 tbsp finely chopped fresh ginger

3-4 green onions, cut into sections

2 tbsp light soy sauce

1 tsp sugar

⅓ cup Chinese Stock (see page 30)
    or water

½ tsp sesame oil

cilantro leaves, to garnish

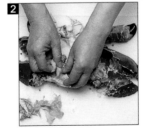
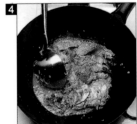

1 Cut the crab in half from the under-belly. Break off the claws and crack them with the back of a cleaver or a large kitchen knife.

2 Discard the legs and crack the shell, breaking it into several pieces. Discard the feathery gills and the stomach sac. Place the crab meat in a bowl.

3 Mix together the wine or sherry, egg and cornstarch. Pour the mixture over the crab and leave to marinate for 10-15 minutes.

4 Heat the vegetable oil in a preheated wok and stir-fry the crab with the chopped ginger and green onions for 2-3 minutes.

5 Add the soy sauce, sugar, and Chinese stock or water, blend well and bring to a boil. Cover and cook for 3-4 minutes, then remove the lid, sprinkle with sesame oil and serve, garnished with a few fresh cilantro leaves.

COOK'S TIP

Crabs are often sold ready-cooked. The crab should feel heavy for its size, and when it is shaken, there should be no sound of water inside. A good medium-sized crab should yield about 1 lb 2 oz meat, enough for 3-4 people.

Stir-fried Shrimp

The bell peppers in this dish can be replaced by either snow peas or broccoli to maintain the attractive pink-green contrast.

NUTRITIONAL INFORMATION

Calories 116   Sugars 1g
Protein ....10g   Fat 6g
Carbohydrate ....4g   Saturates 1g

5 MINS   10 MINS

SERVES 4

I N G R E D I E N T S

6 oz raw shrimp, peeled

1 tsp salt

¼ tsp egg white

2 tsp cornstarch paste (see page 31)

1¼ cups vegetable oil

1 green onion, cut into short sections

1 inch piece fresh ginger, thinly sliced

1 small green bell pepper, cored, seeded, and cubed

½ tsp sugar

1 tbsp light soy sauce

1 tsp rice wine or dry sherry

a few drops sesame oil

VARIATION

1-2 small green or red hot chilies, sliced, can be added with the green bell pepper to create a more spicy dish. Leave the chilies unseeded for a very hot dish.

1 Mix the shrimp with a pinch of the salt, the egg white, and cornstarch paste until well coated.

2 Heat the oil in a preheated wok and stir-fry the shrimp for 30-40 seconds only. Remove and drain on paper towels.

3 Pour off the oil, leaving about 1 tablespoon in the wok. Add the green onion and ginger to flavor the oil for a few seconds, then add the green bell pepper and stir-fry for about 1 minute.

4 Add the remaining salt and the sugar followed by the shrimp. Continue stirring for another minute or so, then add the soy sauce and wine and blend well. Sprinkle with sesame oil and serve immediately.

Steamed Stuffed Snapper

Red mullet may be used instead of the snapper, although they are a little more difficult to stuff because of their size. Use one mullet per person.

NUTRITIONAL INFORMATION

Calories	406	Sugar	.........4g
Protein	........68g	Fat	...........9g
Carbohydrate	....9g	Saturates	.......0g

🥔 20 MINS   🕐 10 MINS

SERVES 4

INGREDIENTS

3 lb whole snapper, cleaned and scaled

16 oz spinach

orange slices and shredded green onion , to garnish

STUFFING

2 cups cooked long-grain rice

1 tsp grated fresh ginger

2 green onions, finely chopped

2 tsp light soy sauce

1 tsp sesame oil

½ tsp ground star anise

1 orange, segmented and chopped

1 Rinse the fish inside and out under cold running water and pat dry with paper towels.

2 Blanch the spinach for 40 seconds, rinse in cold water and drain well, pressing out as much moisture as possible.

3 Arrange the spinach on a heatproof plate and place the fish on top.

4 To make the stuffing, mix together the cooked rice, grated ginger, green onions, soy sauce, sesame oil, star anise, and orange in a bowl.

5 Spoon the stuffing into the body cavity of the fish, pressing it in well with a spoon.

6 Cover the plate and cook in a steamer for 10 minutes, or until the fish is cooked through.

7 Transfer the fish to a warmed serving dish, garnish with orange slices and shredded green onion, and serve.

COOK'S TIP

The name snapper covers a family of tropical and subtropical fish that vary in color. They may be red, orange, pink, grey or blue-green. Some are striped or spotted and they range in size from about 6 inches to 3 ft.

Octopus & Squid with Chili

Try to buy cleaned squid tubes for this dish; if they are not available, see page 278 for instructions on preparing squid.

NUTRITIONAL INFORMATION

Calories	.319	Sugars	.2g
Protein	.40g	Fat	.13g
Carbohydrate	.4g	Saturates	.1g

🍲 8¹/₂ HOURS   🕐 10 MINS

SERVES 6

INGREDIENTS

⅔ cup rice vinegar

¼ cup dry sherry

2 red chilies, chopped

1 tsp sugar

4 tbsp oil

12 baby octopus

12 small squid tubes, cleaned

2 green onions, sliced

1 garlic clove, crushed

1 inch piece fresh ginger, grated

4 tbsp sweet chili sauce

salt

1 Combine the vinegar, dry sherry, red chilies, sugar, 2 tbsp of the oil, and a pinch of salt in a large bowl.

2 Wash each octopus under cold running water and drain. Lay each on its side on a cutting board. Find the "neck" and cut through. The "beak" of the octopus should be left in the head; if it is not, make a cut nearer the tentacles and check again. Discard the head and beak, and put the tentacles, which should all be in one piece, into the vinegar mixture.

3 Put the squid tubes into the vinegar mixture and turn to coat well. Cover and chill for 8 hours or overnight.

4 Heat the remaining oil in a wok and stir-fry the green onions, garlic, and ginger for 1 minute over a very hot grill. Remove from the heat and add the chili sauce. Set aside.

5 Drain the fish from the marinade. Cut the pointed bottom end off each squid tube, so the tubes are of even width. Open out the squid so that it is flat. Score the squid to create a lattice pattern.

6 Cook the octopus and squid over the hottest part of the grill for 4–5 minutes, turning them constantly. The octopus tentacles will curl up, and are cooked when the flesh is no longer translucent. The squid tubes will curl back on themselves, revealing the lattice cuts.

7 When cooked, toss them into the pan with the chili sauce to coat completely and serve immediately.

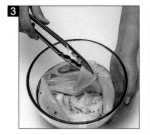

Tuna & Vegetable Stir-Fry

Fresh tuna is a dark, meaty fish and is now widely available at fresh fish counters. It lends itself perfectly to the rich flavors in this recipe.

NUTRITIONAL INFORMATION

Calories ....245 Sugars 11g
Protein ....30g Fat 7g
Carbohydrate ...14g Saturates 1g

10 MINS   10 MINS

SERVES 4

INGREDIENTS

8 oz carrots

1 onion

1¾ cups baby corn-on-the-cobs

2 tbsp corn oil

2½ cups snow peas

1 lb fresh tuna

2 tbsp fish sauce

1 tbsp brown sugar

finely grated zest and juice of 1 orange

2 tbsp sherry

1 tsp cornstarch

rice or noodles, to serve

1 Using a sharp knife, cut the carrots into thin sticks, slice the onion and halve the baby corn-on-the-cobs.

2 Heat the corn oil in a large preheated wok or skillet.

3 Add the onion, carrots, snow peas, and baby corn to the wok or skillet and stir-fry for 5 minutes.

4 Using a sharp knife, thinly slice the fresh tuna.

5 Add the tuna slices to the wok or skillet and then stir-fry for about 2–3 minutes, or until the tuna turns opaque.

6 Mix together the fish sauce, brown sugar, orange zest and juice, sherry and cornstarch.

7 Pour the mixture over the tuna and vegetables and cook for 2 minutes, or until the juices thicken. Serve the stir-fry with rice or noodles.

VARIATION

Try using swordfish steaks instead of the tuna. Swordfish steaks are widely available and similar in texture to tuna.

Snapper with Ginger

Ginger is used widely in Chinese cooking for its strong, pungent flavor. Although fresh ginger is best, ground ginger may be used instead.

NUTRITIONAL INFORMATION

Calories	195	Sugars	.........6g
Protein	........31g	Fat	...........3g
Carbohydrate	....9g	Saturates	.......0g

 10 MINS   15 MINS

SERVES 4

INGREDIENTS

3 lb whole snapper, cleaned and scaled

2 green onions, chopped

1 tsp grated fresh ginger

½ cup garlic wine vinegar

½ cup light soy sauce

3 tsp sugar

dash of chili sauce

½ cup fish stock

1 green bell pepper, seeded and
   thinly sliced

1 large tomato, skinned, seeded, and
   cut into thin strips

salt and pepper

sliced tomato, to garnish

1 Rinse the fish inside and out and pat dry with paper towels.

2 Make 3 diagonal slits in the flesh on each side of the fish. Season the fish with salt and pepper inside and out, according to taste.

3 Place the fish on a heatproof plate and scatter the chopped green onions and grated ginger over the top. Cover and steam for 10 minutes, or until the fish is cooked through.

4 Meanwhile, place the garlic wine vinegar, light soy sauce, sugar, chili sauce, fish stock, bell pepper, and tomato in a saucepan and bring to a boil, stirring occasionally.

5 Cook the sauce over a high heat until the sauce has slightly reduced and thickened.

6 Remove the fish from the steamer and transfer to a warm serving dish. Pour the sauce over the fish, garnish with tomato slices and serve immediately.

VARIATION

Use fillets of fish for this recipe if preferred, and reduce the cooking time to 5–7 minutes.

Squid with Oyster Sauce

Squid is a delicious fish, which if prepared and cooked correctly, is a quick cooking, attractive, and tasty ingredient.

NUTRITIONAL INFORMATION

Calories ....320 Sugars 1g
Protein ....18g Fat 26g
Carbohydrate ....2g Saturates 3g

5 MINS   15 MINS

SERVES 4

INGREDIENTS

1 lb squid

⅔ cup vegetable oil

½ inch piece fresh ginger, grated

2 oz snow peas

5 tbsp hot fish stock

red bell pepper triangles, to garnish

SAUCE

1 tbsp oyster sauce

1 tbsp light soy sauce

pinch of sugar

1 garlic clove, crushed

1 To prepare the squid, cut down the center of the body lengthwise. Flatten the squid out, inside uppermost, and score a lattice design deep into the flesh, using a sharp knife.

2 To make the sauce, combine the oyster sauce, soy sauce, sugar, and garlic in a small bowl. Stir to dissolve the sugar and set aside until required.

3 Heat the oil in a preheated wok until almost smoking. Lower the heat slightly, add the squid and stir-fry until they curl up. Remove with a slotted spoon and drain thoroughly on paper towels.

4 Pour off all but 2 tablespoons of the oil and return the wok to the heat. Add the ginger and snow peas and stir-fry for 1 minute.

5 Return the squid to the wok and pour in the sauce and hot fish stock. Leave to simmer for 3 minutes until thickened. Transfer to a warm serving dish, garnish with bell pepper triangles and serve immediately.

COOK'S TIP

Take care not to overcook the squid, otherwise it will be rubbery and unappetizing.

Shrimp Omelet

This really is a meal in minutes, combining many Chinese ingredients for a truly tasty dish.

NUTRITIONAL INFORMATION

Calories 270   Sugars 1g
Protein . . . . .30g   Fat 15g
Carbohydrate . . . .3g   Saturates 3g

 5 MINS   10 MINS

SERVES 4

INGREDIENTS

2 tbsp sunflower oil

4 green onions

12 oz peeled shrimp

1 cup bean sprouts

1 tsp cornstarch

1 tbsp light soy sauce

6 eggs

3 tbsp cold water

1 Heat the sunflower oil in a large preheated wok or skillet.

2 Using a sharp knife, trim the green onions and cut into slices.

3 Add the shrimp, green onions, and bean sprouts to the wok and stir-fry for 2 minutes.

4 In a small bowl, mix together the cornstarch and soy sauce until well combined.

5 In a separate bowl, beat the eggs with the water, using a metal fork, and then blend with the cornstarch and soy mixture.

6 Add the egg mixture to the wok and cook for 5–6 minutes, or until the mixture sets.

7 Transfer the omelette to a warm serving plate and cut into quarters to serve.

COOK'S TIP

It is important to use fresh bean sprouts for this dish—the canned ones don't have the crunchy texture necessary.

Trout with Pineapple

Pineapple is widely used in Chinese cooking. The tartness of fresh pineapple complements fish particularly well.

NUTRITIONAL INFORMATION

Calories	243	Sugars	........4g
Protein	........30g	Fat	..........11g
Carbohydrate	....6g	Saturates	.......2g

5 MINS   15 MINS

SERVES 4

INGREDIENTS

4 trout fillets, skinned

2 tbsp vegetable oil

2 garlic cloves, cut into slivers

4 slices fresh pineapple, peeled and diced

1 celery stalk, sliced

1 tbsp light soy sauce

¼ cup fresh or unsweetened pineapple juice

⅔ cup fish stock

1 tsp cornstarch

2 tsp water

shredded celery leaves and fresh red chili slices, to garnish

1 Cut the trout fillets into strips. Heat 1 tablespoon of the vegetable oil in a preheated wok until almost smoking. Reduce the heat slightly, add the fish and sauté for 2 minutes. Remove from the wok and set aside.

2 Add the remaining oil to the wok, reduce the heat and add the garlic, diced pineapple, and celery. Stir-fry for 1–2 minutes.

3 Add the soy sauce, pineapple juice, and fish stock to the wok. Bring to a boil and cook, stirring, for 2–3 minutes, or until the sauce has reduced.

4 Blend the cornstarch with the water to form a paste and stir it into the wok. Bring the sauce to a boil and cook, stirring constantly, until the sauce thickens and clears.

5 Return the fish to the wok, and cook, stirring gently, until heated through. Transfer to a warmed serving dish and serve, garnished with shredded celery leaves and red chili slices.

VARIATION

Use canned pineapple instead of fresh pineapple if you wish, choosing slices in unsweetened, natural juice in preference to a syrup.

Szechuan Shrimp

Raw shrimp should be used if possible, otherwise add cooked shrimp at the beginning of step 3.

NUTRITIONAL INFORMATION

Calories 315   Sugars 1g
Protein . . . . .16g   Fat 27g
Carbohydrate . . . .3g   Saturates 3g

 3¹/₂ HOURS   🕐 10 MINS

SERVES 4

INGREDIENTS

9-10½ oz raw jumbo shrimp

pinch of salt

½ egg white, lightly beaten

1 tsp cornstarch paste
  (see page 31)

2½ cups vegetable oil

fresh cilantro leaves,
  to garnish

SAUCE

1 tsp finely chopped fresh ginger

2 green onions, finely chopped

1 garlic clove, finely chopped

3-4 small dried red chilies, seeded and
  chopped

1 tbsp light soy sauce

1 tsp rice wine or dry sherry

1 tbsp tomato paste

1 tbsp oyster sauce

2-3 tbsp Chinese Stock (see page 30) or
  water

a few drops sesame oil

1 Peel the raw shrimp, then mix with the salt, egg white, and cornstarch paste until the shrimp are well coated.

2 Heat the oil in a preheated wok or large skillet until it is smoking, then deep-fry the shrimp in hot oil for about 1 minute. Remove with a slotted spoon and drain on paper towels.

3 Pour off the oil, leaving about 1 tablespoon in the wok. Add all the ingredients for the sauce, in the order listed, bring to a boil and stir until smooth and well blended.

4 Add the shrimp to the sauce and stir until blended well.

5 Serve the shrimp garnished with fresh cilantro leaves.

Spiced Scallops

Scallops are available both fresh and frozen. Make sure they are completely defrosted before cooking.

NUTRITIONAL INFORMATION

Calories 276   Sugar 6g
Protein ....25g   Fat 15g
Carbohydrate ....8g   Saturates 2g

10 MINS   10 MINS

SERVES 4

INGREDIENTS

12 large scallops with roe attached,
   defrosted if frozen, or
   12 oz small scallops without
   roe, defrosted

4 tbsp sunflower oil

4-6 green onions, thinly sliced diagonally

1 garlic clove, crushed

1 inch piece fresh ginger,
   finely chopped

9 oz snow peas

4½ oz small mushrooms, sliced

2 tbsp sherry

2 tbsp soy sauce

1 tbsp honey

¼ tsp ground allspice

salt and pepper

1 tbsp sesame seeds, toasted

1 Wash and dry the scallops, discarding any black pieces and detach the roe, if using.

2 Slice each scallop into 3-4 pieces and if the roes are large, halve them.

3 Heat 2 tablespoons of the sunflower oil in a preheated wok or large, heavy-bottomed skillet, swirling it around until it gets really hot.

4 Add the green onions, garlic, and ginger to the wok or skillet and stir-fry for about 1 minute.

5 Add the snow peas to the wok and continue to cook for 2-3 minutes more, stirring continuously. Remove to a bowl and set aside.

6 Add the remaining sunflower oil to the wok and when really hot add the scallops and roes and stir-fry for a couple of minutes.

7 Add the mushrooms and continue to cook for a minute or so more.

8 Add the sherry, soy sauce, honey, and allspice to the wok, with salt and pepper to taste. Mix thoroughly, then return the snow peas mixture to the wok.

9 Season well with salt and pepper and toss together over a high heat for a minute or so until piping hot. Serve the scallops and vegetables immediately, sprinkled with sesame seeds.

Seafood Medley

Use any combination of fish and seafood in this delicious dish of coated fish served in a wine sauce.

NUTRITIONAL INFORMATION

Calories 168   Sugars 2g
Protein ....29g   Fat 3g
Carbohydrate ....4g   Saturates 1g

🍲 5 MINS   🕐 15 MINS

SERVES 4

I N G R E D I E N T S

2 tbsp dry white wine

1 egg white, lightly beaten

½ tsp Chinese five-spice powder

1 tsp cornstarch

10½ oz raw shrimp,
    peeled and deveined

4½ oz prepared squid,
    cut into rings

4½ oz white fish fillets,
    cut into strips

vegetable oil, for deep-frying

1 green bell pepper, seeded and
    cut into thin strips

1 carrot, cut into thin strips

4 baby corn-on-the-cobs, halved
    lengthwise

1 Mix the wine, egg white, five-spice powder, and cornstarch in a large bowl. Add the shrimp, squid rings, and fish fillets and stir to coat evenly. Remove the fish and seafood with a slotted spoon, reserving any leftover cornstarch mixture.

2 Heat the oil in a preheated wok and deep-fry the shrimp, squid, and fish for 2–3 minutes. Remove the seafood mixture from the wok with a slotted spoon and set aside.

3 Pour off all but 1 tablespoon of oil from the wok and return to the heat. Add the bell pepper, carrot, and corn and stir-fry for 4–5 minutes.

4 Return the seafood to the wok with any remaining cornstarch mixture. Heat through, stirring, and serve.

COOK'S TIP

Open up the squid rings and using a sharp knife, score a lattice pattern on the flesh to make them look attractive.

Salmon with Pineapple

Presentation plays a major part in Chinese cooking and this dish demonstrates this perfectly with the wonderful combination of colors.

NUTRITIONAL INFORMATION

Calories 347	Sugars 12g
Protein 24g	Fat 20g
Carbohydrate . . .16g	Saturates 3g

 10 MINS   15 MINS

SERVES 4

I N G R E D I E N T S

2 tbsp sunflower oil

1 red onion, sliced

1 orange bell pepper, seeded and sliced

1 green bell pepper, seeded and sliced

1 cup baby corn-on-the-cobs

1 lb salmon fillet, skin removed

1 tbsp paprika

8 oz can cubed pineapple, drained

1 cup bean sprouts

2 tbsp tomato ketchup

2 tbsp soy sauce

2 tbsp medium sherry

1 tsp cornstarch

1 Cut each baby corn cob in half. Heat the sunflower oil in a large preheated wok. Add the onion, bell peppers and baby corn to the wok and stir-fry for 5 minutes.

2 Rinse the salmon fillet under cold running water and pat dry with absorbent paper towels.

3 Cut the salmon flesh into thin strips and place in a large bowl. Sprinkle with the paprika and toss well to coat.

4 Add the salmon to the wok together with the pineapple and stir-fry for 2–3 minutes more, or until the fish is tender.

5 Add the bean sprouts to the wok and toss well.

6 Mix together the tomato ketchup, soy sauce, sherry, and cornstarch. Add to the wok and cook until the juices start to thicken. Transfer to warm serving plates and serve immediately.

VARIATION

You can use trout fillets instead of the salmon as an alternative, if you prefer.

Crab in Ginger Sauce

In this recipe, the crabs are served in the shell for ease and visual effect and coated in a glossy ginger sauce.

NUTRITIONAL INFORMATION

Calories	125	Sugars	.........2g
Protein	.........8g	Fat	...........8g
Carbohydrate	....5g	Saturates	.......1g

10 MINS   10 MINS

SERVES 4

INGREDIENTS

2 small cooked crabs

2 tbsp vegetable oil

3 inch piece fresh ginger, grated

2 garlic cloves, thinly sliced

1 green bell pepper, seeded and cut into thin strips

6 green onions, cut into 1 inch lengths

2 tbsp dry sherry

½ tsp sesame oil

⅔ cup fish stock

1 tsp light brown sugar

2 tsp cornstarch

⅔ cup water

VARIATION

If preferred, remove the crab meat from the shells before stir-frying and add to the wok with the bell pepper.

1 Rinse the crabs and gently loosen around the shell at the top. Using a sharp knife, cut away the grey tissue and discard. Rinse the crabs again.

2 Twist off the legs and claws from the crabs. Using a pair of crab claw crackers or a cleaver, gently crack the claws to break through the shell to expose the flesh. Remove and discard any loose pieces of shell.

3 Separate the body and discard the inedible lungs and sac. Cut down the center of each crab to separate the body into two pieces and then cut each of these in half again.

4 Heat the oil in a preheated wok. Add the ginger and garlic and stir-fry for 1 minute. Add the crab pieces and stir-fry for another minute.

5 Stir in the bell pepper, green onions, sherry, sesame oil, stock, and sugar. Bring to a boil, reduce the heat, cover, and simmer for 3–4 minutes.

6 Blend the cornstarch with the water and stir into the wok. Bring to a boil, stirring, until the sauce is thickened and clear. Transfer to a warm serving dish and serve immediately.

Squid with Black Bean Sauce

Squid really is wonderful if quickly cooked as in this recipe, and contrary to popular belief it is not tough and rubbery unless it is overcooked.

NUTRITIONAL INFORMATION

Calories	180	Sugars	.........2g
Protein	........19g	Fat	...........7g
Carbohydrate	...10g	Saturates	.......1g

5 MINS   20 MINS

SERVES 4

INGREDIENTS

1 lb squid rings

2 tbsp all-purpose flour

½ tsp salt

1 green bell pepper

2 tbsp peanut oil

1 red onion, sliced

5¾ oz jar black bean sauce

1 Rinse the squid rings under cold running water and pat dry thoroughly with absorbent paper towels.

2 Place the all-purpose flour and salt in a bowl and mix together. Add the squid rings and toss until they are evenly coated.

3 Using a sharp knife, seed the bell pepper. Slice the bell pepper into thin strips.

4 Heat the peanut oil in a large preheated wok or heavy-bottomed skillet, swirling the oil around the base of the wok until it is really hot.

5 Add the bell pepper slices and red onion to the wok or skillet and stir-fry for about 2 minutes, or until the vegetables are just beginning to soften.

6 Add the squid rings to the wok or skillet and cook for 5 minutes more, or until the squid is cooked through. Be careful not to overcook the squid.

7 Add the black bean sauce to the wok and heat through until the juices are bubbling. Transfer the squid stir-fry to warm serving bowls and serve immediately.

COOK'S TIP

Serve this recipe with fried rice or noodles tossed in soy sauce, if you wish.

Seared Scallops

Scallops have a terrific, subtle flavor which is complemented in this dish by the buttery sauce.

NUTRITIONAL INFORMATION

Calories 272	Sugars 0g	
Protein 28g	Fat 17g	
Carbohydrate 2g	Saturates 8g	

5 MINS 10 MINS

SERVES 4

INGREDIENTS

1 lb fresh scallops, without roe, or the same amount of frozen scallops, defrosted thoroughly

6 green onions

2 tbsp vegetable oil

1 green chili, seeded and sliced

3 tbsp sweet soy sauce

1½ tbsp butter, cubed

1 Rinse the scallops thoroughly under cold running water, drain and pat the scallops dry with absorbent paper towels.

2 Using a sharp knife, slice each scallop in half horizontally.

3 Using a sharp knife, trim and slice the green onions.

4 Heat the vegetable oil in a large preheated wok or heavy-bottomed skillet, swirling the oil around the base of the wok until it is really hot.

5 Add the sliced green chili, green onions, and scallops to the wok and stir-fry over a high heat for 4–5 minutes, or until the scallops are just cooked through. If using frozen scallops, be sure not to overcook them as they will easily disintegrate.

6 Add the soy sauce and butter to the scallop stir-fry and heat through until the butter melts.

7 Transfer to warm serving bowls and serve hot.

COOK'S TIP

If you buy scallops on the shell, slide a knife underneath the membrane to loosen it and cut off the tough muscle that holds the scallop to the shell. Discard the black stomach sac and intestinal vein.

Fish in Szechuan Hot Sauce

This is a classic Szechuan recipe. When served in a restaurant, the fish head and tail are removed before cooking.

NUTRITIONAL INFORMATION

Calories	470	Sugar	.....3g
Protein	....45g	Fat	....29g
Carbohydrate	....7g	Saturates	....4g

3³/₄ HOURS   15 MINS

SERVES 4

INGREDIENTS

1 snapper, sea bass, trout,
    grouper, about 1 lb 10 oz, gutted

1 tbsp light soy sauce

1 tbsp Chinese rice wine or dry sherry

vegetable oil, for deep-frying

flat-leaf parsley or cilantro sprigs, to
    garnish

SAUCE

2 garlic cloves, finely chopped

2-3 green onions, finely chopped

1 tsp finely chopped fresh ginger

2 tbsp chili bean sauce

1 tbsp tomato paste

2 tsp sugar

1 tbsp rice vinegar

½ cup Chinese Stock
    (see page 30) or water

1 tbsp cornstarch paste
    (see page 31)

½ tsp sesame oil

1 Wash the fish and dry well on absorbent paper towels.

2 Score both sides of the fish to the bone with a sharp knife, making diagonal cuts at intervals of 1 inch.

3 Rub the fish with the soy sauce and rice wine or sherry on both sides. Transfer the fish to a plate, cover with plastic wrap and leave to marinate in the refrigerator for 10-15 minutes.

4 Heat the oil in a preheated wok or large skillet until just smoking.

5 Deep-fry the fish in the hot oil for about 3-4 minutes on both sides, or until golden brown.

6 Pour off the oil, leaving about 1 tablespoon in the wok. Push the fish to one side of the wok and add the garlic, white parts of the onions, ginger, chili bean sauce, tomato paste, sugar, vinegar, and Chinese stock or water.

7 Bring the mixture in the wok to a boil and braise the fish in the sauce for 4-5 minutes, turning it over once.

8 Add the green parts of the onions and stir in the cornstarch paste to thicken the sauce.

9 Sprinkle with sesame oil and serve immediately, garnished with fresh parsley or cilantro.

Shrimp with Vegetables

This colorful and delicious dish is cooked with vegetables: vary them according to seasonal availability.

NUTRITIONAL INFORMATION

Calories 298   Sugars 1g
Protein . . . . .13g   Fat 26g
Carbohydrate . . . .3g   Saturates 3g

5 MINS   10 MINS

SERVES 4

I N G R E D I E N T S

2 oz snow peas

½ small carrot

2 oz baby corn-on-the-cob

2 oz straw mushrooms

6-9 oz raw jumbo shrimp, peeled

1 tsp salt

½ egg white, lightly beaten

1 tsp cornstarch paste
    (see page 31)

about 1¼ cups vegetable oil

1 green onion, cut into short sections

4 slices fresh ginger, peeled and finely
    chopped

½ tsp sugar

1 tbsp light soy sauce

1 tsp Chinese rice wine or dry sherry

a few drops sesame oil

lemon slices and chopped fresh chives,
    to garnish

1 Using a sharp knife, top and tail the snow peas; cut the carrot into the same size as the snow peas; halve the baby corn and straw mushrooms.

2 Mix the shrimp with a pinch of the salt, the egg white, and cornstarch paste until the shrimp are evenly coated.

3 Preheat a wok over a high heat for 2-3 minutes, then add the vegetable oil and heat to medium-hot.

4 Add the shrimp to the wok, stirring to separate them. Remove the shrimp with a slotted spoon as soon as the color changes.

5 Pour off the oil, leaving about 1 tablespoon in the wok. Add the snow peas, carrot, corn, mushrooms, and green onions.

6 Add the shrimp together with the ginger, sugar, soy sauce, and wine or sherry, blending well.

7 Sprinkle with the sesame oil and serve hot, garnished with lemon slices and chopped fresh chives.

Fish & Ginger Stir-fry

This delicious and spicy recipe is a really quick fish dish, ideal for midweek family meals or light lunches on weekends.

NUTRITIONAL INFORMATION

Calories 280	Sugars 2g	
Protein 31g	Fat 10g	
Carbohydrate ...17g	Saturates 2g	

5 MINS   15 MINS

SERVES 4

INGREDIENTS

4 tbsp cornstarch

½ tsp ground ginger

1½ lb firm white fish fillets, skinned and cubed

3 tbsp peanut oil

1 inch fresh ginger, grated

1 leek, thinly sliced

1 tbsp white wine vinegar

2 tbsp Chinese rice wine or dry sherry

3 tbsp dark soy sauce

1 tsp sugar

2 tbsp lemon juice

finely shredded leek, to garnish

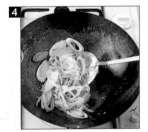

1 Mix the cornstarch and ground ginger in a bowl.

2 Add the cubes of fish, in batches, to the cornstarch mixture, turning to coat the fish thoroughly in the mixture.

3 Heat the peanut oil in a preheated wok or large, heavy-bottomed frying pan, swirling the oil around the base of the wok until it is really hot.

4 Add the grated fresh ginger and sliced leek to the wok or skillet and stir-fry for 1 minute.

5 Add the coated fish to the wok and cook for 5 minutes more, until browned, stirring to prevent the fish from sticking to the base of the wok.

6 Add the remaining ingredients and cook over a low heat for 3–4 minutes, until the fish is cooked through.

7 Transfer the fish and ginger stir-fry to a serving dish and serve immediately.

VARIATION

Use any firm white fish that will hold its shape, such as cod, haddock, or monkfish.

Stir-Fried Cod with Mango

Fish and fruit are a classic combination, and in this recipe a tropical flavor is added which gives a great scented taste to the dish.

NUTRITIONAL INFORMATION

Calories	200	Sugars	........12g
Protein	........21g	Fat	...........7g
Carbohydrate	...14g	Saturates	.......1g

10 MINS   15 MINS

SERVES 4

I N G R E D I E N T S

6 oz carrots

2 tbsp vegetable oil

1 red onion, sliced

1 red bell pepper, seeded
   and sliced

1 green bell pepper, seeded
   and sliced

1 lb skinless cod fillet

1 ripe mango

1 tsp cornstarch

1 tbsp soy sauce

1⅓ cups tropical fruit juice

1 tbsp lime juice

1 tbsp chopped fresh cilantro,
   to garnish

1 Using a sharp knife, slice the carrots into thin sticks.

2 Heat the oil in a preheated wok and stir-fry the onion, carrots, and bell peppers for 5 minutes.

3 Using a sharp knife, cut the cod into small cubes. Peel the mango, then carefully remove the flesh from the center stone. Cut the flesh into thin slices.

4 Add the cod and mango to the wok and stir-fry for another 4–5 minutes, or until the fish is cooked through. Be careful not to break the fish up.

5 Mix together the cornstarch, soy sauce, fruit juice, and lime juice. Pour the mixture into the wok and stir until the mixture bubbles and the juices thicken. Scatter with cilantro and serve immediately.

VARIATION

You can use papaya as an alternativeto the mango, if you prefer.

Fish with Coconut & Basil

Fish curries are sensational and this is no exception. Red curry and coconut are fantastic flavors with the fried fish.

NUTRITIONAL INFORMATION

Calories ....209 Sugars 10g
Protein ....21g Fat 8g
Carbohydrate ...15g Saturates 1g

5 MINS   15 MINS

SERVES 4

INGREDIENTS

2 tbsp vegetable oil

1 lb skinless cod fillet

¼ cup seasoned flour

1 clove garlic, crushed

2 tbsp red curry paste

1 tbsp fish sauce

1¼ cups coconut milk

6 oz cherry tomatoes, halved

20 fresh basil leaves

fragrant rice, to serve

1 Heat the vegetable oil in a large preheated wok.

2 Using a sharp knife, cut the fish into large cubes, removing any bones with a pair of clean tweezers.

3 Place the seasoned flour in a bowl. Add the cubes of fish and mix until well coated.

4 Add the coated fish to the wok and stir-fry over a high heat for 3–4 minutes, or until the fish just begins to brown at the edges.

5 In a small bowl, mix together the garlic, curry paste, fish sauce, and coconut milk. Pour the mixture over the fish and bring to a boil.

6 Add the tomatoes to the mixture in the wok and leave to simmer for 5 minutes.

7 Roughly chop or tear the fresh basil leaves. Add the basil to the wok, stir carefully to combine, taking care not to break up the cubes of fish.

8 Transfer to serving plates and serve hot with fragrant rice.

COOK'S TIP

Take care not to overcook the dish once the tomatoes are added, otherwise they will break down and the skins will come away.

Scallop Pancakes

Scallops, like most shellfish, require very little cooking, and this original dish is a perfect example of how to use shellfish to its full potential.

NUTRITIONAL INFORMATION

Calories ....240 Sugars 1g
Protein ....29g Fat 9g
Carbohydrate ....11g Saturates 1g

 5 MINS   30 MINS

SERVES 4

INGREDIENTS

3½ oz green beans

1 red chili

1 lb scallops, without roe

1 egg

3 green onions, sliced

½ cup rice flour

1 tbsp fish sauce

oil, for frying

salt

sweet chili dip, to serve

1 Using a sharp knife, trim the green beans and slice them very thinly.

2 Using a sharp knife, seed and very finely chop the red chili.

3 Bring a small saucepan of lightly salted water to a boil. Add the green beans to the pan and cook for 3–4 minutes or until just softened.

4 Roughly chop the scallops and place them in a large bowl. Add the cooked beans to the scallops.

5 Mix the egg with the green onions, rice flour, fish sauce, and chili until well combined. Add to the scallops and mix well.

6 Heat about 1 inch of oil in a large preheated wok. Add a ladleful of the mixture to the wok and cook for 5 minutes until golden and set.

7 Remove the pancake from the wok and leave to drain on absorbent paper towels. Keep warm while cooking the remaining pancake mixture. Serve the pancakes hot with a sweet chili dip.

VARIATION

You could use shrimp or shelled clams instead of the scallops, if you prefer.

Shrimp & Corn Patties

Chopped shrimp and corn are combined in a light batter, which is dropped in spoonfuls into hot fat to make these tasty patties.

NUTRITIONAL INFORMATION

Calories	250	Sugars	.........1g
Protein	........17g	Fat	..........9g
Carbohydrate	...26g	Saturates	.......2g

🦐🦐

🍲 35 MINS 🕐 20 MINS

SERVES 4

INGREDIENTS

1 cup all-purpose flour

1½ tsp baking powder

2 eggs

about 1 cup cold water

1 garlic clove, very finely chopped

3 green onions, trimmed and very finely chopped

1 cup peeled small shrimp, chopped

½ cup canned corn kernels, drained

vegetable oil for frying

salt and pepper

TO GARNISH

green onion brushes (see Cook's Tip, right)

lime slices

1 chili flower (see Cook's Tip, page 269)

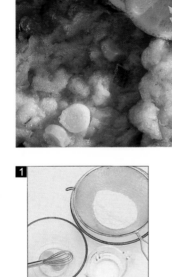

1 Sift the flour, baking powder and ½ tsp salt into a bowl. Add the eggs and half the water and beat to make a smooth batter, adding extra water to give the consistency of heavy cream. Add the garlic and green onions. Cover and leave for 30 minutes.

2 Stir the shrimp and corn into the batter. Season with pepper.

3 Heat 2–3 tablespoons of oil in a wok. Drop tablespoonfuls of the batter into the wok and cook over a medium heat until bubbles rise and the surface just sets. Flip the patties over and cook the other side until golden brown. Drain on paper towels.

4 Cook the remaining batter in the same way, adding more oil to the wok if required. Garnish and serve at once.

COOK'S TIP

Make a green onion brush by trimming off the tips of the leaves and making several fine cuts from the leaf tips to the top of the bulb. Place in iced water to make the leaves curl.

Crispy Fried Squid

Squid tubes are classically used in Chinese cooking and are most attractive when presented as in the following recipe.

NUTRITIONAL INFORMATION

Calories 156   Sugars 0g
Protein ....17g   Fat 6g
Carbohydrate ....7g   Saturates 8g

 10 MINS   10 MINS

SERVES 4

INGREDIENTS

1 lb squid, cleaned

4 tbsp cornstarch

1 tsp salt

1 tsp freshly ground black pepper

1 tsp chili flakes

peanut oil, for frying

dipping sauce, to serve

1 Using a sharp knife, remove the tentacles from the squid and trim. Slice the bodies down one side and open out to give a flat piece.

2 Score the flat pieces with a criss-cross pattern then cut each piece into 4.

3 Mix together the cornstarch, salt, pepper, and chili flakes.

COOK'S TIP

Squid tubes may be purchased frozen if they are not available fresh. They are usually ready-cleaned and are easy to use. Make sure that they are completely defrosted before cooking.

4 Place the salt and pepper mixture in a large plastic bag. Add the squid pieces and shake the bag thoroughly to coat the squid in the flour mixture.

5 Heat about 2 inches of peanut oil in a large preheated wok.

6 Add the squid pieces to the wok and stir-fry, in batches, for about 2 minutes, or until the squid pieces start to curl up. Do not overcook or the squid will become tough.

7 Remove the squid pieces with a slotted spoon, transfer to absorbent paper towels and leave to drain thoroughly.

8 Transfer the fried squid pieces to serving plates and serve immediately with a dipping sauce.

Cantonese Shrimp

This shrimp dish is very simple and is ideal for supper or lunch when time is short.

NUTRITIONAL INFORMATION

Calories	460	Sugar	.........3g
Protein	........53g	Fat	24
Carbohydrate	....6g	Saturates	.......5g

10 MINS   20 MINS

SERVES 4

INGREDIENTS

5 tbsp vegetable oil

4 garlic cloves, crushed

1½lb raw shrimp, shelled and deveined

2 inch piece fresh ginger, chopped

6 oz lean pork, diced

1 leek, sliced

3 eggs, beaten

shredded leek and red bell pepper cut in
   thin sticks, to garnish

rice, to serve

SAUCE

2 tbsp Chinese rice wine or dry sherry

2 tbsp light soy sauce

2 tsp sugar

⅔ cup fish stock

4½ tsp cornstarch

3 tbsp water

change color. Remove the shrimp from the wok or skillet with a slotted spoon, set aside and keep warm.

4 Add the remaining oil to the wok and heat, swirling the oil around the base of the wok until it is really hot.

5 Add the ginger, diced pork, and leek to the wok and stir-fry over a medium heat for 4-5 minutes, or until the pork is lightly colored and sealed.

6 To make the sauce, add the rice wine or sherry, soy sauce, sugar, and fish stock to the wok and stir to blend.

7 In a small bowl, blend the cornstarch with the water to form a smooth paste and stir it into the wok. Cook, stirring, until the sauce thickens and clears.

8 Return the shrimp to the wok and add the beaten eggs. Cook for 5–6 minutes, gently stirring occasionally, until the eggs set.

9 Transfer to a warm serving dish, garnish with shredded leek and bell pepper sticks, and serve immediately with rice.

1 Heat 2 tablespoons of the vegetable oil in a preheated wok.

2 Add the garlic to the wok and stir-fry for 30 seconds.

3 Add the shrimp to the wok and stir-fry for 5 minutes, or until they

Scallops in Ginger Sauce

Scallops are both attractive and delicious. Cooked with ginger and orange, this dish is perfect served with plain rice.

NUTRITIONAL INFORMATION

Calories 216	Sugars 4g
Protein 30g	Fat 8g
Carbohydrate 8g	Saturates 1g

5 MINS   10 MINS

SERVES 4

I N G R E D I E N T S

2 tbsp vegetable oil

1 lb scallops, cleaned and halved

1 inch piece fresh ginger,
    finely chopped

3 garlic cloves, crushed

2 leeks, shredded

¾ cup shelled peas

4½ oz canned bamboo shoots, drained and
    rinsed

2 tbsp light soy sauce

2 tbsp unsweetened orange juice

1 tsp sugar

orange zest, to garnish

1 Heat the vegetable oil in a preheated wok or large skillet. Add the scallops and stir-fry for 1–2 minutes. Remove the scallops from the wok with a slotted spoon, keep warm and set aside until required.

2 Add the ginger and garlic to the wok and stir-fry for 30 seconds. Stir in the leeks and peas and cook, stirring, for 2 minutes more.

3 Add the bamboo shoots and return the scallops to the wok. Stir gently to mix without breaking up the scallops.

4 Stir in the soy sauce, orange juice, and sugar and cook for 1–2 minutes.

5 Transfer the stir-fry to a serving dish, garnish with the orange zest and serve immediately.

COOK'S TIP

The edible parts of a scallop are the round white muscle and the orange and white roe. The frilly skirt surrounding the muscle—the gills and mantle—may be used for making shellfish stock. All other parts should be discarded.

Mussels with Lettuce

Mussels require careful preparation but very little cooking. They are available fresh or in vacuum packs when out of season.

NUTRITIONAL INFORMATION

Calories	205	Sugars	.......0.3g
Protein	........31g	Fat	...........9g
Carbohydrate	....1g	Saturates	.......4g

 15 MINS   5 MINS

SERVES 4

I N G R E D I E N T S

2 lb 4 oz mussels in their shells, scrubbed

2 stalks lemon grass

1 Iceberg lettuce

2 tbsp lemon juice

⅓ cup water

2 tbsp butter

finely grated zest of 1 lemon

2 tbsp oyster sauce

1 Place the scrubbed mussels in a large saucepan.

2 Using a sharp knife, thinly slice the lemon grass and shred the lettuce.

3 Add the lemon grass, lemon juice, and water to the pan of mussels, cover with a tight-fitting lid, and cook for 5 minutes or until the mussels have opened. Discard any mussels that do not open.

4 Carefully remove the cooked mussels from their shells, using a fork and set aside until required.

5 Heat the butter in a large preheated wok or skillet. Add the lettuce and finely grated lemon zest to the wok or fying pan and stir-fry for 2 minutes, or until the lettuce begins to wilt.

6 Add the oyster sauce to the mixture in the wok and heat through, stirring well until the sauce is thoroughly incorporated in the mixture.

7 Transfer the mixture in the wok to a warm serving dish and serve immediately.

COOK'S TIP

When using fresh mussels, be sure to discard any opened mussels before scrubbing and any unopened mussels after cooking.

Gingered Monkfish

This dish is a real treat and is perfect for special occasions. Monkfish has a tender flavor which is ideal with asparagus, chili, and ginger.

NUTRITIONAL INFORMATION

Calories	133	Sugars	.........0g
Protein	........21g	Fat	...........5g
Carbohydrate	....1g	Saturates	.......1g

5 MINS   10 MINS

SERVES 4

INGREDIENTS

1 lb monkfish

1 tbsp freshly grated ginger

2 tbsp sweet chili sauce

1 tbsp corn oil

1 cup thin-stemmed asparagus

3 green onions, sliced

1 tsp sesame oil

1 Using a sharp knife, slice the monkfish into thin flat rounds. Set aside until required.

2 Mix together the freshly grated root ginger and the sweet chili sauce in a small bowl until thoroughly blended. Brush the ginger and chili sauce mixture over the monkfish pieces, using a pastry brush.

3 Heat the corn oil in a large preheated wok or heavy-bottomed skillet.

4 Add the monkfish pieces, asparagus, and chopped green onions to the wok or skillet and cook for about 5 minutes, stirring gently so the fish pieces do not break up.

5 Remove the wok or skillet from the heat, drizzle the sesame oil over the stir-fry and toss well to combine.

6 Transfer the stir-fried gingered monkfish to warm serving plates and serve immediately.

COOK'S TIP

Monkfish is quite expensive, but it is well worth using because it has a wonderful flavor and texture. Alternatively, you could use cubes of chunky cod fillet.

Mussels with Lemon Grass

Give fresh mussels a Far Eastern flavor by using some kaffir lime leaves, garlic, and lemon grass in the stock used for steaming them.

NUTRITIONAL INFORMATION

Calories	194	Sugar	.........0g
Protein	........33g	Fat	...........7g
Carbohydrate	....1g	Saturates	.......1g

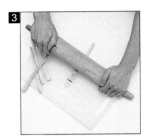

 10 MINS 10 MINS

SERVES 4

INGREDIENTS

1 lb 10 oz live mussels

1 tbsp sesame oil

3 shallots, chopped finely

2 garlic cloves, chopped finely

1 stalk lemon grass

2 kaffir lime leaves

2 tbsp chopped fresh cilantro

finely grated zest of 1 lime

2 tbsp lime juice

1¼ cups hot vegetable stock

crusty bread, to serve

fresh cilantro, to garnish

1 Using a small sharp knife, scrape the beards off the mussels under cold running water. Scrub them well, discarding any that are damaged or remain open when tapped. Keep rinsing until there is no trace of sand.

2 Heat the sesame oil in a large saucepan and fry the shallots and garlic gently until softened, about 2 minutes.

3 Bruise the lemon grass, using a meat mallet or rolling pin, and add to the pan with the kaffir lime leaves, cilantro, lime zest and juice, mussels and stock. Put the lid on the saucepan and cook over a moderate heat for 3–5 minutes. Shake the pan from time to time.

4 Lift the mussels out into 4 warmed soup plates, discarding any that remain shut. Boil the remaining liquid rapidly to reduce slightly. Remove the lemon grass and lime leaves, then pour the liquid over the mussels.

5 Garnish with cilantro and lime wedges, and serve at once.

COOK'S TIP

Mussels are now farmed, so they should be available in fish stores throughout the year.

Seafood Omelet

This delicious omelet is filled with a mixture of fresh vegetables, sliced squid, and shrimp.

NUTRITIONAL INFORMATION

Calories 216	Sugars 2g
Protein 20g	Fat 13g
Carbohydrate 4g	Saturates 4g

5 MINS   10 MINS

SERVES 4

INGREDIENTS

4 eggs

3 tbsp milk

1 tbsp fish sauce or light soy sauce

1 tbsp sesame oil

3 shallots, sliced finely

1 small red bell pepper, cored, seeded, and sliced very finely

1 small leek, trimmed and cut into thin sticks

4½ oz squid rings

⅔ cup cooked peeled shrimp

1 tbsp chopped fresh basil

1 tbsp butter

salt and pepper

sprigs of fresh basil, to garnish

1 Beat the eggs, milk, and fish sauce or soy sauce together.

2 Heat the sesame oil in a wok or large skillet and add the shallots, bell pepper, and leek. Stir-fry briskly for 2–3 minutes.

3 Add the squid rings, shrimp, and chopped basil to the wok or skillet. Stir-fry for 2–3 minutes more, until the squid looks opaque.

4 Season the mixture in the wok with salt and pepper to taste. Transfer to a warmed plate and keep warm until required.

5 Melt the butter in a large omelet pan or skillet and add the beaten egg mixture. Cook over a medium-high heat until just set.

6 Spoon the vegetable and seafood mixture in a line down the middle of the omelet, then fold each side of the omelet over.

7 Transfer the omelet to a warmed serving dish and cut into 4 portions. Garnish with sprigs of fresh basil and serve at once.

VARIATION

Chopped, cooked chicken makes a delicious alternative to the squid.

Use fresh cilantro instead of the basil, if desired.

Shrimp with Ginger

Crispy ginger is a wonderful garnish which offsets the spicy shrimp both visually and in flavor.

NUTRITIONAL INFORMATION

Calories	229	Sugars	.........7g
Protein	........29g	Fat	...........8g
Carbohydrate	...10g	Saturates	.......1g

10 MINS   15 MINS

SERVES 4

INGREDIENTS

2 inch piece fresh ginger

oil, for frying

1 onion, diced

8 oz carrots, diced

½ cup frozen peas

1 cup bean sprouts

1 lb peeled jumbo shrimp

1 tsp Chinese five-spice powder

1 tbsp tomato paste

1 tbsp soy sauce

1 Using a sharp knife, peel the ginger and slice it into very thin sticks.

2 Heat about 1 inch of oil in a large preheated wok. Add the ginger and stir-fry for 1 minute or until the ginger is crispy. Remove the ginger with a slotted spoon and leave to drain on absorbent paper towels.

3 Drain all of the oil from the wok except for about 2 tablespoons. Add the onions and carrots to the wok and stir-fry for 5 minutes. Add the peas and bean sprouts and stir-fry for 2 minutes.

4 Rinse the shrimp under cold running water and pat dry with absorbent paper towels.

5 Combine the five-spice, tomato paste and soy sauce. Brush the mixture over the shrimp.

6 Add the shrimp to the wok and stir-fry for 2 minutes more, or until the shrimp are completely cooked through. Transfer the shrimp mixture to a warm serving bowl and top with the reserved crispy ginger. Serve immediately.

VARIATION

Use slices of white fish instead of the shrimp as an alternative, if you wish.

Mussels in Black Bean Sauce

This dish looks so impressive, the combination of colors making it look almost too good to eat!

NUTRITIONAL INFORMATION

Calories	174	Sugars	.........4g
Protein	........19g	Fat	...........8g
Carbohydrate	....6g	Saturates	.......1g

5 MINS   10 MINS

SERVES 4

INGREDIENTS

12 oz leeks

12 oz cooked green-lipped mussels (shelled)

1 tsp cumin seeds

2 tbsp vegetable oil

2 cloves garlic, crushed

1 red bell pepper, seeded and sliced

¾ cup canned bamboo shoots, drained

6 oz baby spinach

5¾ oz jar black bean sauce

1 Using a sharp knife, trim the leeks and shred them.

2 Place the cooked green-lipped mussels in a large bowl, sprinkle with the cumin seeds and toss well to coat all over. Set aside until required.

COOK'S TIP

If the green-lipped mussels are not available they can be bought shelled in cans and jars from large supermarkets.

3 Heat the vegetable oil in a preheated wok, swirling the oil around the base of the wok until it is really hot.

4 Add the shredded leeks, garlic, and sliced red bell pepper to the wok and stir-fry for 5 minutes, or until the vegetables are tender.

5 Add the bamboo shoots, baby spinach leaves and cooked green-lipped mussels to the wok and stir-fry for about 2 minutes.

6 Pour the black bean sauce over the ingredients in the wok, toss well to coat all the ingredients in the sauce and leave to simmer for a few seconds, stirring occasionally.

7 Transfer the stir-fry to warm serving bowls and serve immediately.

Fish with Ginger Butter

Whole mackerel or trout are stuffed with herbs, wrapped in foil, baked, and then drizzled with a fresh ginger butter.

NUTRITIONAL INFORMATION

Calories 328	Sugar 0g	
Protein 24g	Fat 25g	
Carbohydrate 1g	Saturates 13g	

10 MINS   30 MINS

SERVES 4

I N G R E D I E N T S

4 x 9 oz whole trout or mackerel, gutted

4 tbsp chopped fresh cilantro

5 garlic cloves, crushed

2 tsp grated lemon or lime zest

2 tsp vegetable oil

banana leaves, for wrapping (optional)

6 tbsp butter

1 tbsp grated fresh ginger

1 tbsp light soy sauce

salt and pepper

cilantro sprigs and lemon or lime wedges, to garnish

1 Wash and dry the fish. Mix the cilantro with the garlic, lemon or lime zest, and salt and pepper to taste. Spoon into the fish cavities.

2 Brush the fish with a little oil, season well, and place each fish on a double thickness sheet of baking parchment or foil and wrap up well to enclose. Alternatively, wrap in banana leaves (see right).

3 Place on a cookie sheet and bake in a preheated oven for about 25 minutes or until the flesh will flake easily.

4 Meanwhile, melt the butter in a small pan. Add the ginger and mix well.

5 Stir the light soy sauce into the saucepan.

6 To serve, unwrap the fish parcels, drizzle over the ginger butter, and garnish with cilantro and lemon or lime wedges.

COOK'S TIP

For a really authentic touch, wrap the fish in banana leaves, which can be ordered from oriental supermarkets. They are not edible, but impart a delicate flavor to the fish.

Chili Shrimp

Jumbo shrimp are marinated in a chili mixture then stir-fried with cashews. Serve with a fluffy rice and braised vegetables.

NUTRITIONAL INFORMATION

Calories	435	Sugars	........2g
Protein	........4.2g	Fat	23
Carbohydrate	...10g	Saturates	.......4g

2¼ HOURS   5 MINS

SERVES 4

INGREDIENTS

5 tbsp soy sauce

5 tbsp dry sherry

3 dried red chilies, seeded and chopped

2 garlic cloves, crushed

2 tsp grated fresh ginger

5 tbsp water

1 lb 6 oz shelled jumbo shrimp

1 large bunch green onions, chopped

⅔ cup salted cashews

3 tbsp vegetable oil

2 tsp cornstarch

1 Mix the soy sauce, sherry, chilies, garlic, ginger, and water in a bowl.

2 Add the jumbo shrimp, green onions, and cashews and mix well. Cover tightly and leave to marinate for at least 2 hours, stirring occasionally.

3 Heat the oil in a large wok. Remove the shrimp, green onions, and cashews from the marinade with a slotted spoon and add to the wok, reserving the marinade. Stir-fry over a high heat for 1-2 minutes.

4 Mix the reserved marinade with the cornstarch, add to the wok, and stir-fry for about 30 seconds, until the marinade forms a slightly thickened shiny glaze over the shrimp mixture. Serve immediately.

COOK'S TIP

For an attractive presentation, serve this dish on mixed wild rice and basmati rice. Start cooking the wild rice in boiling water. After 10 minutes, add the basmati rice or other rice and continue boiling until all grains are tender. Drain well and adjust the seasoning.

Shrimp Stir-fry

A very quick and tasty stir-fry using shrimp and cucumber, cooked with lemon grass, chili, and ginger.

NUTRITIONAL INFORMATION

Calories 178	Sugars 1g	
Protein 22g	Fat 7g	
Carbohydrate 3g	Saturates 1g	

5 MINS   5 MINS

SERVES 4

INGREDIENTS

½ cucumber

2 tbsp sunflower oil

6 green onions, halved lengthwise and cut into 1½ inch lengths

1 stalk lemon grass, sliced thinly

1 garlic clove, chopped

1 tsp chopped fresh red chili

4½ oz oyster mushrooms

1 tsp chopped ginger

12 oz cooked peeled shrimp

2 tsp cornstarch

2 tbsp water

1 tbsp dark soy sauce

½ tsp fish sauce

2 tbsp dry sherry or rice wine

boiled rice, to serve

1 Cut the cucumber into strips about ¼ x 1¾ inches.

2 Heat the sunflower oil in a wok or large skillet.

3 Add the green onions, cucumber, lemon grass, garlic, chili, oyster mushrooms, and ginger to the wok or skillet and stir-fry for 2 minutes.

4 Add the shrimp and stir-fry for another minute.

5 Mix together the cornstarch, water, soy sauce, and fish sauce until smooth.

6 Stir the cornstarch mixture and sherry or wine into the wok and heat through, stirring, until the sauce has thickened. Serve with rice.

COOK'S TIP

The white part of the lemon grass stem can be thinly sliced and left in the cooked dish. If using the whole stem, remove it before serving. You can buy lemon grass chopped and dried, or preserved in jars, but neither has the fragrance or delicacy of the fresh variety.

Shrimp with Vegetables

In this recipe, a light Chinese omelet is shredded and tossed back into the dish before serving.

NUTRITIONAL INFORMATION

Calories 258	Sugars 7g
Protein 21g	Fat 15g
Carbohydrate ...10g	Saturates 3g

10 MINS   15 MINS

SERVES 4

INGREDIENTS

8 oz zucchini

3 tbsp vegetable oil

2 eggs

2 tbsp cold water

8 oz carrots, grated

1 onion, sliced

1½ cups bean sprouts

8 oz peeled shrimp

2 tbsp soy sauce

pinch of Chinese five-spice powder

¼ cup peanuts, chopped

2 tbsp fresh chopped cilantro

1 Finely grate the zucchini.

2 Heat 1 tablespoon of the vegetable oil in a large preheated wok.

3 Beat the eggs with the water and pour the mixture into the wok and cook for 2–3 minutes or until the egg sets.

4 Remove the omelet from the wok and transfer to a clean board. Fold the omelet, cut it into thin strips and set aside until required.

5 Add the remaining oil to the wok. Add the carrots, onion, and zucchini and stir-fry for 5 minutes.

6 Add the bean sprouts and shrimp to the wok and cook for another 2 minutes, or until the shrimp are heated through.

7 Add the soy sauce, Chinese five-spice powder, and peanuts to the wok, together with the strips of omelet and heat through. Garnish with chopped fresh cilantro and serve.

COOK'S TIP

The water is mixed with the egg in step 3 for a lighter, less rubbery omelet.

Crab with Chinese Cabbage

The delicate flavor of Chinese cabbage and crab meat are enhanced by the coconut milk in this recipe.

NUTRITIONAL INFORMATION

Calories 109	Sugars 1g
Protein 11g	Fat 6g
Carbohydrate 2g	Saturates 1g

5 MINS   10 MINS

SERVES 4

INGREDIENTS

8 oz shiitake mushrooms

2 tbsp vegetable oil

2 cloves garlic, crushed

6 green onions, sliced

1 head Chinese cabbage, shredded

1 tbsp mild curry paste

6 tbsp coconut milk

7 oz can white crab meat, drained

1 tsp chili flakes

1 Using a sharp knife, cut the mushrooms into slices.

2 Heat the vegetable oil in a large preheated wok or heavy-bottomed skillet.

3 Add the mushrooms and garlic to the wok or skillet and stir-fry for 3 minutes or until the mushrooms have softened.

4 Add the green onions and shredded Chinese cabbage to the wok and stir-fry until the leaves have wilted.

5 Mix together the mild curry paste and coconut milk in a small bowl.

6 Add the curry paste and coconut milk mixture to the wok, together with the crab meat and chili flakes. Mix together until well combined.

7 Heat the mixture in the wok until the juices start to bubble.

8 Transfer the crab and vegetable stir-fry to warm serving bowls and serve immediately.

COOK'S TIP

Shiitake mushrooms are available in the fresh vegetable section of most large supermarkets.

Hot & Sweet Shrimp

Uncooked shrimp are speared on skewers, brushed with a sesame oil, lime juice, and cilantro baste, and then broiled.

NUTRITIONAL INFORMATION

Calories	.239	Sugars	.8g
Protein	.28g	Fat	.11g
Carbohydrate	.8g	Saturates	.2g

 1 HOUR   10 MINS

SERVES 4

INGREDIENTS

wooden skewers soaked in warm water for 20 minutes

1 lb 2 oz uncooked shrimp

3 tbsp sesame oil

2 tbsp lime juice

1 tbsp chopped fresh cilantro

SAUCE

4 tbsp light malt vinegar

2 tbsp fish sauce or light soy sauce

2 tbsp water

2 tbsp light brown sugar

2 garlic cloves, crushed

2 tsp grated fresh ginger

1 red chili, seeded and chopped finely

2 tbsp chopped fresh cilantro

salt

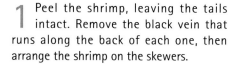

1 Peel the shrimp, leaving the tails intact. Remove the black vein that runs along the back of each one, then arrange the shrimp on the skewers.

2 Mix together the sesame oil, lime juice and chopped cilantro in a shallow bowl. Lay the skewered shrimp in this mixture. Cover and chill in the refrigerator for 30 minutes, turning once, so that the shrimp absorb the marinade.

3 Meanwhile, make the sauce. Heat the vinegar, fish sauce or soy sauce, water, sugar, and salt to taste until boiling. Remove from the heat and leave to cool.

4 Mix together the crushed garlic, grated ginger, red chili and cilantro in a small serving bowl. Add the cooled vinegar mixture and stir until well combined.

5 Place the shrimp on a foil-lined broiler pan under a preheated broiler for about 6 minutes, turning once and basting often with the marinade, until cooked.

6 Transfer to a warmed serving platter and serve with the dipping sauce.

Crab Claws with Chili

Crab claws are frequently used in Chinese cooking, and look sensational. They are perfect with this delicious chili sauce.

NUTRITIONAL INFORMATION

Calories	154	Sugar	.........3g
Protein	........16g	Fat	..........7g
Carbohydrate	....8g	Saturates	.......1g

5 MINS   10 MINS

SERVES 4

INGREDIENTS

1 lb 9 oz crab claws

1 tbsp corn oil

2 cloves garlic, crushed

1 tbsp grated fresh ginger

3 red chilies, seeded and finely chopped

2 tbsp sweet chili sauce

3 tbsp tomato ketchup

1¼ cups cooled fish stock

1 tbsp cornstarch

salt and pepper

1 tbsp fresh chives, snipped

1 Gently crack the crab claws with a nut cracker. This process will allow the flavors of the chili, garlic, and ginger to fully penetrate the crab meat.

2 Heat the corn oil in a large preheated wok.

3 Add the crab claws to the wok and stir-fry for about 5 minutes.

4 Add the garlic, ginger, and chilies to the wok and stir-fry for 1 minute, tossing the crab claws to coat all over.

5 Mix together the sweet chili sauce, tomato ketchup, fish stock, and cornstarch in a small bowl. Add this mixture to the wok and cook, stirring occasionally, until the sauce starts to thicken.

6 Season the mixture in the wok with salt and pepper to taste.

7 Transfer the crab claws and chili sauce to warm serving dishes, garnish with snipped fresh chives and serve.

COOK'S TIP

If crab claws are not easily available, use a whole crab, cut into eight pieces, instead.

Coconut Shrimp

Butterfly shrimp make any meal a special occasion, especially when cooked in such a delicious crispy coating.

NUTRITIONAL INFORMATION

Calories	236	Sugars	.........1g
Protein	........27g	Fat	..........13g
Carbohydrate	....3g	Saturates	.......7g

5 MINS   10 MINS

SERVES 4

I N G R E D I E N T S

½ cup shredded coconut

½ cup fresh white breadcrumbs

1 tsp Chinese five-spice powder

½ tsp salt

finely grated zest of 1 lime

1 egg white

1 lb butterfly shrimp

sunflower or corn oil, for frying

lemon wedges, to garnish

soy or chili sauce, to serve

1 Mix together the shredded coconut, white breadcrumbs, Chinese five-spice powder, salt, and finely grated lime zest in a bowl.

2 Lightly whisk the egg white in a separate bowl.

3 Rinse the shrimp under cold running water, and pat dry with paper towels.

4 Dip the shrimp into the egg white then into the coconut and breadcrumb mixture, so that they are evenly coated.

5 Heat about 2 inches of sunflower or corn oil in a large preheated wok.

6 Add the shrimp to the wok and stir-fry for about 5 minutes or until golden and crispy.

7 Remove the shrimp with a slotted spoon and leave to drain on paper towels.

8 Transfer the coconut shrimp to warm serving dishes and garnish with lemon wedges. Serve immediately with a soy or chili sauce.

COOK'S TIP

Chinese five-spice powder is a mixture of star anise, fennel seeds, cloves, cinnamon bark, and Szechuan pepper. It is very pungent, so should be used sparingly. It will keep indefinitely in an airtight container.

Crab Meat Cakes

Make these tasty crab meat cakes as a snack or first course, or as an accompaniment to a main meal.

NUTRITIONAL INFORMATION

Calories 262	Sugars 4g
Protein 13g	Fat 17g
Carbohydrate . . .14g	Saturates 3g

20 MINS   55 MINS

SERVES 4

INGREDIENTS

generous 1 cup long-grain rice

1 tbsp sesame oil

1 small onion, chopped finely

1 large garlic clove, crushed

2 tbsp chopped fresh cilantro

7 oz can crab meat, drained

1 tbsp fish sauce or light soy sauce

1 cup coconut milk

2 eggs

4 tbsp vegetable oil

salt and pepper

sliced green onions, to garnish

1 Cook the rice in plenty of boiling, lightly salted water until just tender, about 12 minutes. Rinse with cold water and drain well.

2 Heat the sesame oil in a small skillet and fry the onion and garlic gently for about 5 minutes, until softened and golden brown.

3 Combine the rice, onion, garlic, cilantro, crab meat, fish sauce or soy sauce, and coconut milk. Season. Beat the eggs and add to the mixture. Divide the mixture between 8 greased ramekin dishes or teacups and place them in a baking

dish or roasting pan with enough warm water to come halfway up their sides. Place in a preheated oven at 350°F for 25 minutes, until set. Leave to cool.

4 Turn the crab cakes out of the ramekin dishes . Heat the oil in a wok or skillet and fry the crab cakes in the oil until golden brown. Drain on paper towels, garnish, and serve.

COOK'S TIP

If you want, you can prepare these crab cakes up to the point where they have been baked. Cool them, then cover and chill, ready for frying when needed.

Vegetables

The Chinese eat much more vegetables than meat or poultry. This is partly because of widespread poverty, which means that many people cannot afford meat, and also because of religious reasons. Vegetables are used extensively in all meals; even meat and poultry dishes include some kind of vegetable as a supplementary

ingredient in order to give the dish a harmonious balance of color, aroma, flavor, and texture. The Chinese like their vegetables crisp so they are cooked for only a very short time, thus preserving their bright colors as well as valuable nutrients. As with most ingredients in Chinese cooking, it is important to choose the freshest vegetables available to ensure maximum flavor and crispness. As well as side dishes, this chapter also contains deliciously filling main meals.

Green Bean Stir-fry

These beans are simply cooked in a spicy, hot sauce for a tasty and very easy recipe.

NUTRITIONAL INFORMATION

Calories 86	Sugars 4g
Protein 2g	Fat 6g
Carbohydrates 6g	Saturates 1g

 5 MINS   5 MINS

SERVES 4

I N G R E D I E N T S

1 lb green beans

2 fresh red chilies

2 tbsp peanut oil

½ tsp ground star anise

1 garlic clove, crushed

2 tbsp light soy sauce

2 tsp honey

½ tsp sesame oil

1 Using a sharp knife, cut the green beans in half.

2 Slice the fresh chilies, removing the seeds first if you prefer a milder dish.

3 Heat the oil in a preheated wok or large skillet until the oil is almost smoking.

4 Lower the heat slightly, add the halved green beans to the wok, and stir-fry for 1 minute.

5 Add the sliced red chilies, star anise, and garlic to the wok and stir-fry for 30 seconds more.

6 Mix together the soy sauce, honey, and sesame oil in a small bowl.

7 Stir the sauce mixture into the wok. Cook for 2 minutes, tossing the beans to ensure that they are thoroughly coated in the sauce.

8 Transfer the mixture in the wok or pan to a warm serving dish and serve immediately.

VARIATION

This recipe is surprisingly delicious made with brussels sprouts instead of green beans. Trim the sprouts, then shred them finely. Stir-fry the sprouts in hot oil for 2 minutes, then proceed with the recipe from step 4.

Bean Sprouts & Vegetables

This dish is served cold as a salad or appetizer and is very easy to make. It is a form of cold *chop suey*.

NUTRITIONAL INFORMATION

Calories 56   Sugars 5g
Protein ....4g   Fat 1g
Carbohydrate ....9g   Saturates 0.2g

3¼ HOURS   0 MINS

SERVES 4

INGREDIENTS

1 lb bean sprouts

2 fresh red chilies, seeded and finely chopped

1 red bell pepper, seeded and thinly sliced

1 green bell pepper, seeded and thinly sliced

2 oz water chestnuts, quartered

1 celery stalk, sliced

Chinese roasted meats and noodles, to serve

MARINADE

3 tbsp rice wine vinegar

2 tbsp light soy sauce

2 tbsp chopped chives

1 garlic clove, crushed

pinch of Chinese curry powder

1 Place the bean sprouts, chopped red chilies, red and green bell peppers, water chestnuts, and celery in a large bowl and mix well to combine all the ingredients.

2 To make the marinade, mix together the rice wine vinegar, light soy sauce, chopped chives, crushed garlic, and Chinese curry powder in a bowl.

3 Pour the marinade over the prepared vegetables. Toss to mix the vegetables thoroughly in the marinade.

4 Cover the salad with plastic wrap and leave to chill in the refrigerator for at least 3 hours.

5 Drain the vegetables thoroughly, transfer to a serving dish and serve with Chinese roasted meats or noodles.

COOK'S TIP

There are hundreds of varieties of chilies and it is not always possible to tell how hot they are going to be. As a general rule, dark green chilies are hotter than light green and red chilies. Thin, pointed chilies are usually hotter than fatter, blunter chilies.

Honey-fried Chinese Leaves

Chinese cabbage are rather similar to lettuce in that the leaves are delicate with a sweet flavor.

NUTRITIONAL INFORMATION

Calories 121	Sugars 6g
Protein 5g	Fat 7g
Carbohydrate . . .10g	Saturates 1g

 5 MINS   10 MINS

SERVES 4

I N G R E D I E N T S

1 lb Chinese cabbage

1 tbsp peanut oil

½ inch piece fresh ginger, grated

2 garlic cloves, crushed

1 fresh red chili, sliced

1 tbsp Chinese rice wine or dry sherry

4½ tsp light soy sauce

1 tbsp honey

½ cup orange juice

1 tbsp sesame oil

2 tsp sesame seeds

orange zest, to garnish

COOK'S TIP

Single-flower honey has a better, more individual flavor than blended honey. Acacia honey is typically Chinese, but you could also try clover, lemon blossom, lime flower, or orange blossom.

1 Separate the cabbage leaves and shred finely, using a sharp knife.

2 Heat the peanut oil in a preheated wok. Add the ginger, garlic, and chili to the wok and stir-fry the mixture for about 30 seconds.

3 Add the Chinese cabbage, Chinese rice wine or sherry, soy sauce, honey, and orange juice to the wok. Reduce the heat and leave to simmer for 5 minutes.

4 Add the sesame oil to the wok, sprinkle the sesame seeds on top and mix to combine.

5 Transfer to a warm serving dish, garnish with the orange zest and serve immediately.

Vegetable Sesame Stir-fry

Sesame seeds add a delicious flavor to any recipe and are particularly good with vegetables in this soy and rice wine or sherry sauce.

NUTRITIONAL INFORMATION

Calories 118   Sugars 2g
Protein . . . . .3g   Fat 9g
Carbohydrate . . . .5g   Saturates 1g

5 MINS   10 MINS

SERVES 4

INGREDIENTS

2 tbsp vegetable oil

3 garlic cloves, crushed

1 tbsp sesame seeds,
   plus extra to garnish

2 celery stalks, sliced

2 baby corn-on-the-cobs, sliced

2 oz small mushrooms

1 leek, sliced

1 zucchini, sliced

1 small red bell pepper, sliced

1 fresh green chili, sliced

2 oz Chinese cabbage, shredded

rice or noodles, to serve

SAUCE

½ tsp Chinese curry powder

2 tbsp light soy sauce

1 tbsp Chinese rice wine or dry sherry

1 tsp sesame oil

1 tsp cornstarch

4 tbsp water

1 Heat the vegetable oil in a preheated wok or heavy-bottomed skillet, swirling the oil around the base of the wok until it is almost smoking.

2 Lower the heat slightly, add the garlic and sesame seeds and stir-fry for 30 seconds.

3 Add the celery, baby corn, mushrooms, leek, zucchini, bell pepper, chili, and Chinese cabbage, and stir-fry for 4–5 minutes, until the vegetables are beginning to soften.

4 To make the sauce, mix together the Chinese curry powder, light soy sauce, Chinese rice wine or dry sherry, sesame oil, cornstarch, and water.

5 Stir the sauce mixture into the wok until well combined with the other ingredients.

6 Bring to a boil and cook, stirring constantly, until the sauce thickens and clears.

7 Cook for 1 minute, spoon into a warm serving dish and garnish with sesame seeds. Serve the vegetable sesame stir-fry immediately with rice or noodles.

Bok Choy with Cashews

Plum sauce is readily available in jars and has a terrific, sweet flavor which complements the vegetables.

NUTRITIONAL INFORMATION

Calories	241	Sugars	.......7g
Protein	......7g	Fat	......19g
Carbohydrate	....11g	Saturates	.....4g

 5 MINS   15 MINS

SERVES 4

INGREDIENTS

2 red onions

6 oz red cabbage

2 tbsp peanut oil

8 oz bok choy

2 tbsp plum sauce

1⅓ cup roasted cashews

1 Using a sharp knife, cut the red onions into thin wedges and thinly shred the red cabbage.

2 Heat the peanut oil in a large preheated wok or heavy-bottomed skillet until the oil is really hot.

3 Add the onion wedges to the wok or skillet and stir-fry for about

5 minutes or until the onions are just beginning to brown.

4 Add the red cabbage to the wok and stir-fry for 2–3 minutes more.

5 Add the bok choy leaves to the wok or skillet and stir-fry for about 5 minutes, or until the leaves have just wilted.

6 Drizzle the plum sauce over the vegetables, toss together until well combined, and heat until the liquid is bubbling.

7 Scatter with the roasted cashews and transfer to warm serving bowls.

VARIATION

Use unsalted peanuts instead of the cashews, if you prefer.

Bamboo with Cucumber

A simple stir-fried side dish of canned bamboo shoots and sliced cucumber is the perfect accompaniment to a Chinese main meal.

NUTRITIONAL INFORMATION

Calories	101	Sugars	.......0.2g
Protein	.........3g	Fat	...........7g
Carbohydrate	....7g	Saturates	.......1g

20 MINS   10 MINS

SERVES 4

INGREDIENTS

½ cucumber

2 tbsp sesame oil

4 shallots, chopped finely

1 garlic clove, sliced finely

12 oz can of bamboo shoots, drained

1 tbsp dry sherry

1 tbsp soy sauce

2 tsp cornstarch

1 tsp sesame seeds

salt

TO GARNISH

2 red chili flowers (see page 269)

sliced green onions

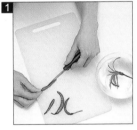  

1 Slice the cucumber thinly and sprinkle with salt. Leave for 10–15 minutes, then rinse with cold water. Prepare the chili and green onion garnish.

2 Heat the sesame oil in a wok or skillet and add the shallots and garlic. Stir-fry for 2 minutes, until golden.

3 Add the bamboo shoots and cucumber to the wok or skillet and stir-fry for 2–3 minutes.

4 Blend together the dry sherry, soy sauce and cornstarch. Add to the bamboo shoots and cucumber, stirring to combine well.

5 Cook for 1–2 minutes to thicken slightly, then add the sesame seeds and stir through.

6 Transfer the vegetables to a warmed serving dish. Garnish with the chili flowers and chopped green onion. Serve immediately.

COOK'S TIP

Salting the cucumber before it is stir-fried draws out some of its moisture so that it stays crisp.

Add some very finely sliced carrot to this dish to add some extra color, if you like.

Shredded Vegetable Omelet

Cook this large omelet and then slice into four portions to serve as a side dish. If you like, double the quantities and serve it as a main course.

NUTRITIONAL INFORMATION

Calories .... .159   Sugars 3g
Protein .... .8g   Fat .... .13g
Carbohydrate ....4g   Saturates 4g

🍲 5 MINS   🕐 10 MINS

SERVES 4

INGREDIENTS

4 eggs

3 tbsp milk

1 tbsp fish sauce or light soy sauce

1 tbsp sesame oil

1 small red onion, very finely sliced

1 small zucchini, trimmed and cut into thin sticks

1 small leek, trimmed and cut into thin sticks

1 small carrot, trimmed and cut into thin sticks

2 inch piece cucumber, cut into thin sticks

1 tbsp chopped fresh cilantro

1 tbsp butter

salt and pepper

TO GARNISH

sprigs of fresh basil

celery leaves

4 chili flowers (see page 269)

1 Beat together the eggs, milk, and fish sauce or soy sauce.

2 Heat the sesame oil in a wok or large skillet, swirling the oil around the base of the wok until it is really hot. Add all the vegetables and stir-fry them briskly for 3–4 minutes, then add the chopped fresh cilantro.

3 Season with salt and pepper to taste. Transfer the stir-fried vegetables to a warmed plate and keep warm.

4 Melt the butter in a large omelet pan or skillet and add the beaten egg mixture.

5 Cook the egg mixture over a medium-high heat until just set.

6 Tip the vegetable mixture along one side of the omelet, then roll up the omelet.

7 Slice into 4 portions and arrange on a warmed serving plate. Garnish with fresh basil, celery leaves, and chili flowers and serve immediately.

Gingered Broccoli

Ginger and broccoli are a perfect combination of flavors and make an exceptionally tasty side dish.

NUTRITIONAL INFORMATION

Calories	118	Sugars	.........3g
Protein	.........8g	Fat	..........7g
Carbohydrate	....6g	Saturates	.......1g

5 MINS   15 MINS

SERVES 4

I N G R E D I E N T S

2 inch piece fresh ginger

2 tbsp peanut oil

1 garlic clove, crushed

1½ lb broccoli flowerets

1 leek, sliced

2¾ oz water chestnuts, halved

½ tsp sugar

½ cup vegetable stock

1 tsp dark soy sauce

1 tsp cornstarch

2 tsp water

1 Using a sharp knife, finely chop the ginger. (Alternatively, cut the ginger into larger strips, to be discarded later, for a slightly milder ginger flavor.)

2 Heat the peanut oil in a preheated wok. Add the garlic and ginger and stir-fry for 30 seconds.

3 Add the broccoli, leek, and water chestnuts and stir-fry for a further 3–4 minutes.

4 Add the sugar, vegetable stock, and dark soy sauce to the wok, reduce the heat and simmer for 4–5 minutes, or until the broccoli is almost cooked.

5 Blend the cornstarch with the water to form a smooth paste and stir it into the wok. Bring to a boil and cook, stirring constantly, for 1 minute or until thickened.

6 If using larger strips of ginger, remove from the wok and discard.

7 Transfer the vegetables to a serving dish and serve immediately.

VARIATION

Use spinach instead of the broccoli, if you prefer. Trim the woody ends and cut the rest into 2 inch lengths, keeping the stalks and leaves separate. Add the stalks with the leek in step 3 and add the leaves 2 minutes later. Reduce the cooking time in step 4 to 3–4 minutes.

Stir-fried Bean Sprouts

Be sure to use fresh bean sprouts, rather than the canned variety, for this crunchy-textured dish.

NUTRITIONAL INFORMATION

Calories 98	Sugars 2g
Protein 2g	Fat 9g
Carbohydrate 3g	Saturates 1g

 5 MINS   5 MINS

SERVES 4

INGREDIENTS

9 oz fresh bean sprouts

2-3 green onions

1 medium red chili pepper (optional)

3 tbsp vegetable oil

½ tsp salt

½ tsp sugar

1 tbsp light soy sauce

a few drops sesame oil (optional)

1 Rinse the bean sprouts in cold water, discarding any husks or small pieces that float to the top.

2 Drain the bean sprouts well on paper towels.

COOK'S TIP

The red chili pepper gives a bite to this dish—leave the seeds in for an even hotter taste. If you prefer a milder, sweeter flavor use red bell pepper instead of the chili pepper. Core, seed, and cut into strips in the same way.

3 Using a sharp knife, cut the green onions into short sections.

4 Thinly shred the red chili pepper, if using, discarding the seeds.

5 Heat the vegetable oil in a preheated wok, swirling the oil around the base of the wok until it is really hot.

6 Add the bean sprouts, green onions, and chili pepper, if using, to the wok and stir-fry the mixture for about 2 minutes.

7 Add the salt, sugar, soy sauce, and sesame oil, if using, to the mixture in the wok. Stir well to blend. Serve the bean sprouts hot or cold.

Braised Chinese Leaves

White cabbage can be used instead of the Chinese cabbage for this dish.

NUTRITIONAL INFORMATION

Calories 138	Sugars 4g	
Protein 6g	Fat 9g	
Carbohydrate ...10g	Saturates 1g	

 5 MINS 5 MINS

SERVES 4

INGREDIENTS

1 lb 2 oz Chinese cabbage
   or white cabbage

3 tbsp vegetable oil

½ tsp Szechuan red peppercorns

5-6 small dried red chilies, seeded and
   chopped

½ tsp salt

1 tbsp sugar

1 tbsp light soy sauce

1 tbsp rice vinegar

a few drops sesame oil (optional)

1 Shred the Chinese cabbage or white cabbage crosswise into thin pieces. (If Chinese cabbage are unavailable, the best alternative to use in this recipe is a firm-packed white cabbage, not the dark green type of cabbage. Cut out the thick core of the cabbage with a sharp knife before shredding.)

2 Heat the vegetable oil in a preheated wok or large skillet, add the Szechuan red peppercorns and dried red chilies, and stir for a few seconds.

3 Add the Chinese cabbage or shredded white cabbage to the peppercorns and chilies and stir-fry for about 1 minute.

4 Add the salt to the mixture in the wok or skillet and continue stirring for another minute.

5 Add the sugar, light soy sauce and rice vinegar, blend well and braise for one more minute.

6 Finally sprinkle on the sesame oil, if using. Serve the braised Chinese cabbage hot or cold.

COOK'S TIP

Szechuan red peppercorns are not true bell peppers, but reddish brown dry berries with a pungent, aromatic odor which distinguishes them from the hotter black peppercorns. Roast them briefly in the oven or dry-fry them. Grind them in a blender and store in a jar until needed.

Bamboo with Spinach

In this recipe, spinach is fried with spices and then braised in a soy-flavored sauce with bamboo shoots for a rich, delicious dish.

NUTRITIONAL INFORMATION

Calories	105	Sugars	.........1g
Protein	.........3g	Fat	...........9g
Carbohydrate	....3g	Saturates	.......2g

5 MINS   10 MINS

SERVES 4

INGREDIENTS

3 tbsp peanut oil

8 oz spinach, chopped

6 oz canned bamboo shoots, drained and rinsed

1 garlic clove, crushed

2 fresh red chilies, sliced

pinch of ground cinnamon

1¼ cups vegetable stock

pinch of sugar

pinch of salt

1 tbsp light soy sauce

COOK'S TIP

Fresh bamboo shoots are rarely available in the West and, in any case, are extremely time-consuming to prepare. Canned bamboo shoots are quite satisfactory, as they are used to provide a crunchy texture, rather than for their flavor, which is fairly insipid.

1 Heat the peanut oil in a preheated wok or large skillet, swirling the oil around the base of the wok until it is really hot.

2 Add the spinach and bamboo shoots to the wok and stir-fry for 1 minute.

3 Add the garlic, chilies, and cinnamon to the mixture in the wok and stir-fry for 30 seconds more.

4 Stir in the stock, sugar, salt, and light soy sauce, cover, and cook over a medium heat for 5 minutes, or until the vegetables are cooked through and the sauce has reduced. If there is too much cooking liquid, blend a little cornstarch with double the quantity of cold water and stir into the sauce.

5 Transfer the bamboo shoots and spinach to a serving dish and serve.

Mushrooms in Coconut Milk

This filling and tasty main course dish, which comprises three varieties of mushroom, can be served over rice or noodles.

NUTRITIONAL INFORMATION

Calories ....189 Sugars 6g
Protein ....6g Fat 15g
Carbohydrate ....7g Saturates 2g

 10 MINS   10 MINS

SERVES 4

INGREDIENTS

2 lemon grass stalks

2 green chilies

1 tbsp light soy sauce

2 garlic cloves, crushed

2 tbsp chopped fresh cilantro

2 tbsp chopped fresh parsley

6 slices Thai ginger, peeled

3 tbsp sunflower oil

1 eggplant, cubed

⅔ cup oyster mushrooms

⅔ cup crimini mushrooms

⅔ cup field mushrooms,
   quartered if large

4½ oz green beans, cut into 2 inch lengths,
   blanched

1¼ cups coconut milk

1 tbsp lemon juice

fresh parsley or cilantro,
   to garnish

rice, to serve

1 Using a sharp knife, thinly slice the lemon grass. Deseed and finely chop the green chilies.

2 Grind together the lemon grass, chilies, light soy sauce, garlic, cilantro, parsley, and Thai ginger in a large pestle and mortar or a food processor. Set aside until required.

3 Heat the sunflower oil in a wok or large, heavy skillet.

4 Add the eggplant to the wok or skillet and stir over a high heat for 3 minutes.

5 Stir in the three varieties of mushrooms and the green beans. Cook for 3 minutes, stirring constantly.

6 Add the ground spice paste to the mixture in the wok or skillet.

7 Add the coconut milk and lemon juice to the pan, bring to a boil and simmer for 2 minutes.

8 Transfer the mushrooms and their sauce to warm serving dishes half-filled with rice, garnish with fresh parsley or cilantro, and serve immediately.

Deep-fried Zucchini

These zucchini fritters are irresistible and could be served as a first course or snack with a chili dip.

NUTRITIONAL INFORMATION

Calories	.117	Sugars	.2g
Protein	.3g	Fat	.6g
Carbohydrate	.14g	Saturates	.1g

 5 MINS   20 MINS

SERVES 4

INGREDIENTS

1 lb zucchini

1 egg white

⅓ cup cornstarch

1 tsp salt

1 tsp Chinese five-spice powder

oil, for deep-frying

chili dip, to serve

1 Using a sharp knife, slice the zucchini into rings or chunky sticks.

2 Place the egg white in a small mixing bowl. Lightly whip the egg white until foamy, using a fork.

3 Mix the cornstarch, salt, and Chinese five-spice powder together and sprinkle onto a large plate.

4 Heat the oil in a large preheated wok or heavy-bottomed skillet.

5 Dip each piece of zucchini into the beaten egg white then coat in the cornstarch and five-spice mixture.

6 Deep-fry the zucchini, in batches, for about 5 minutes or until pale golden and crispy. Repeat with the remaining zucchini.

7 Remove the zucchini with a slotted spoon and leave to drain on absorbent paper towels while deep-frying the remainder.

8 Transfer the zucchini to serving plates and serve immediately with a chili dip.

VARIATION

Alter the seasoning by using chili powder or curry powder instead of the Chinese five-spice powder, if you prefer.

Stuffed Chinese Cabbage

Mushrooms, green onions, celery, and rice are flavored with five-spice powder and wrapped in Chinese cabbage.

NUTRITIONAL INFORMATION

Calories 166	Sugars 3g
Protein 3g	Fat 13g
Carbohydrate ...10g	Saturates 8g

25 MINS   45 MINS

SERVES 4

INGREDIENTS

8 large Chinese cabbage

⅓ cup long-grain rice

½ bouillon cube

¼ cup butter

1 bunch green onions, trimmed and chopped finely

1 celery stalk, chopped finely

1¼ cups small mushrooms, sliced

1 tsp Chinese five-spice powder

1¼ cups passata (strained tomatoes)

salt and pepper

fresh chives, to garnish

1 Blanch the Chinese cabbage in boiling water for 1 minute. Refresh them under cold running water and drain well. Be careful not to tear them.

2 Cook the rice in plenty of boiling water, with the bouillon cube, until just tender. Drain well and set aside until required.

3 Meanwhile, melt the butter in a skillet and fry the green onions and celery gently for 3–4 minutes until softened, but not browned.

4 Add the mushrooms to the wok or skillet and cook for 3–4 minutes more, stirring frequently.

5 Add the cooked rice to the pan with the five-spice powder. Season with salt and pepper and stir well to combine the ingredients.

6 Lay out the Chinese cabbage on a work counter and divide the rice mixture between them. Roll each leaf into a neat pack to enclose the stuffing. Place them, seam-side down, in a greased ovenproof dish. Pour the passata over them and cover with foil. Bake in a preheated oven at 375°F for 25–30 minutes.

7 Serve the stuffed Chinese cabbage immediately, garnished with fresh chives.

Bell Peppers with Chestnuts

This is a crisp and colorful recipe, topped with crisp, shredded leeks for both flavor and color.

NUTRITIONAL INFORMATION

Calories 192   Sugars 5g
Protein ....3g   Fat 14g
Carbohydrate ...13g   Saturates 13g

🥘 5 MINS   🕐 15 MINS

SERVES 4

I N G R E D I E N T S

8 oz leeks

oil, for deep-frying

3 tbsp peanut oil

1 yellow bell pepper, seeded
    and diced

1 green bell pepper, seeded
    and diced

1 red bell pepper, seeded
    and diced

7 oz can water chestnuts,
    drained and sliced

2 cloves garlic, crushed

3 tbsp light soy sauce

1 To make the garnish, finely slice the leeks into thin strips, using a sharp knife.

2 Heat the oil for deep-frying in a wok or large, heavy-bottomed skillet.

3 Add the sliced leeks to the wok or skillet and cook for 2–3 minutes, or until crispy. Set aside until required.

4 Heat the 3 tablespoons of peanut oil in the wok or skillet.

5 Add the yellow, green, and red bell peppers to the wok and stir-fry over a high heat for about 5 minutes, or until they are just beginning to brown at the edges and to soften.

6 Add the sliced water chestnuts, garlic, and light soy sauce to the wok and stir-fry all of the vegetables for 2–3 minutes more.

7 Spoon the bell pepper stir-fry on to warm serving plates, garnish with the crispy leeks, and serve.

COOK'S TIP

Add 1 tbsp of hoisin sauce with the soy sauce in step 6 for extra flavor and spice.

Carrots with Coconut

Sliced carrots and chunks of parsnip are cooked in a creamy coconut sauce with ground almonds and served on a bed of spinach.

NUTRITIONAL INFORMATION

Calories 386   Sugars 14g
Protein ....6g   Fat 32g
Carbohydrate ...20g   Saturates 15g

  10 MINS   35 MINS

SERVES 4

I N G R E D I E N T S

⅓ cup creamed coconut

1¼ cups hot water

2 tbsp slivered almonds

4 tbsp vegetable oil

5 cardamom pods

4 thin slices fresh ginger

2½ cups carrots, sliced

2½ cups parsnips, cut into small chunks

¼ tsp five-spice powder

2 tbsp ground almonds

4 cups young spinach leaves

½ red onion, sliced thinly

1 garlic clove, sliced

salt

1 Crumble the creamed coconut into a bowl or jug, add the hot water, and stir until dissolved.

2 Heat a saucepan and dry-fry the slivered almonds until golden. Remove from the pan and set aside until required.

3 Heat half the oil in the saucepan. Lightly crush the cardamom pods (this helps to release their flavor) and add to the saucepan with the fresh ginger. Fry for 30 seconds to flavor the oil. Add the chopped carrots and parsnips. Stir-fry for 2–3 minutes.

4 Stir in the five-spice powder and ground almonds, and pour in the coconut liquid. Bring to a boil and season with salt to taste. Cover and simmer for 12–15 minutes until the vegetables are tender. Stir occasionally, adding extra water if necessary.

5 Wash and drain the spinach. Remove any stalks. Heat the remaining oil in a wok and stir-fry the onion and garlic for 2 minutes. Add the spinach and stir-fry until it has just wilted. Drain off any excess liquid and season with salt.

6 Remove the cardamom pods and ginger from the carrots and parsnips, and adjust the seasoning. Serve on a bed of the spinach sprinkled with the almonds.

Cantonese Garden Vegetables

This dish tastes as fresh as it looks. Try to obtain baby vegetables as they look and taste so much better in this dish.

NUTRITIONAL INFORMATION

Calories ....130 Sugars 8g
Protein ....6g Fat 8g
Carbohydrate ....8g Saturates 1g

5 MINS   10 MINS

SERVES 4

I N G R E D I E N T S

2 tbsp peanut oil

1 tsp Chinese five-spice powder

2¾ oz baby carrots, halved

2 celery stalks, sliced

2 baby leeks, sliced

1¾ oz snow peas

4 baby zucchini, halved lengthwise

8 baby corn-on-the-cobs

8 oz firm marinated tofu, cubed

4 tbsp fresh orange juice

1 tbsp honey

celery leaves and orange zest,
  to garnish

cooked rice or noodles, to serve

VARIATION

Lemon juice would be just as delicious as the orange juice in this recipe, but use 3 tablespoons instead of 4 tablespoons.

1 Heat the peanut oil in a preheated wok or large skillet until just smoking.

2 Add the Chinese five-spice powder, carrots, celery, leeks, snow peas, zucchini, and corn and stir-fry for 3–4 minutes.

3 Add the tofu to the wok or skillet and cook for 2 minutes more, stirring gently so the tofu does not break up.

4 Stir the fresh orange juice and honey into the wok or skillet, reduce the heat and cook for 1–2 minutes.

5 Transfer the stir-fry to a serving dish, garnish with celery leaves and orange zest, and serve with rice or noodles.

Stir-fried Greens

Eat your greens in this most delicious way—stir-fried so that they retain their color, crunch, and flavor.

NUTRITIONAL INFORMATION

Calories 116	Sugars 3g
Protein 5g	Fat 9g
Carbohydrate 5g	Saturates 1g

5 MINS   10 MINS

SERVES 4

INGREDIENTS

8 green onions

2 celery stalks

4½ oz white radish (daikon)

4½ oz sugar snap peas or snow peas

16 oz Chinese cabbage

6 oz bok choy or spinach

2 tbsp vegetable oil

1 tbsp sesame oil

2 garlic cloves, chopped finely

1 tbsp fish sauce

2 tbsp oyster sauce

1 tsp finely grated fresh ginger

pepper

1 Slice the green onions and celery finely. Cut the white radish (daikon) into thin strips. Trim the sugar snap peas or snow peas. Shred the Chinese cabbage and shred the bok choy or spinach.

2 Heat the vegetable oil and sesame oil together in a wok or large skillet. Add the garlic and fry for 1 minute.

3 Add the green onions, celery, white radish (daikon), and sugar snap peas or snow peas to the wok or skillet and stir-fry for about 2 minutes.

4 Add the Chinese cabbage and bok choy or spinach. Stir-fry for about 1 minute.

5 Stir the fish sauce and oyster sauce into the vegetables with the grated ginger. Cook for 1 minute. Season with pepper to taste, transfer to a warm serving dish and serve immediately.

VARIATION

Any variety—and any amount—of fresh vegetables can be used in this dish. Just make sure that harder vegetables, such as carrots, are cut very finely so that they cook quickly.

Use light soy sauce as an alternative to the fish sauce, if you prefer.

Broccoli in Oyster Sauce

Some Cantonese restaurants use only the stalks of the broccoli for this dish, for the crunchy texture.

NUTRITIONAL INFORMATION

Calories	100	Sugars	. . . . .1g
Protein	. . . . .3g	Fat	. . . . .9g
Carbohydrate	. . . .2g	Saturates	. . . . . . .1g

   3½ HOURS   5 MINS

SERVES 4

I N G R E D I E N T S

9-10½ oz broccoli

3 tbsp vegetable oil

3-4 small slices fresh ginger

½ tsp salt

½ tsp sugar

3-4 tbsp Chinese Stock (see page 30) or water

1 tbsp oyster sauce

COOK'S TIP

The broccoli stalks have to be peeled and cut diagonally to ensure that they will cook evenly. If they are thin stalks, the pieces can be added to the wok at the same time as the flowerets, but otherwise add the stalks first, to ensure that they will be tender.

1 Using a sharp knife, cut the broccoli spears into small flowerets. Trim the stalks, peel off the rough skin, and cut the stalks diagonally into diamond-shaped chunks.

2 Heat the vegetable oil in a preheated wok until really hot.

3 Add the pieces of broccoli stalk and the slices of fresh ginger to the wok and stir-fry for half a minute, then add the flowerets and continue to stir-fry for another 2 minutes.

4 Add the salt, sugar, and Chinese stock or water, and continue stirring for another minute or so.

5 Blend in the oyster sauce. Transfer the broccoli to a serving dish and serve hot or cold.

Eight Jewel Vegetables

This recipe, as the title suggests, is a colorful mixture of eight vegetables, cooked in a black bean and soy sauce.

NUTRITIONAL INFORMATION

Calories 110   Sugars 3g
Protein . . . . .4g   Fat 8g
Carbohydrate . . . .7g   Saturates 1g

 5 MINS   10 MINS

SERVES 4

INGREDIENTS

2 tbsp peanut oil

6 green onions, sliced

3 garlic cloves, crushed

1 green bell pepper, seeded and diced

1 red bell pepper, seeded and diced

1 fresh red chili, sliced

2 tbsp chopped water chestnuts

1 zucchini, chopped

4½ oz oyster mushrooms

3 tbsp black bean sauce

2 tsp Chinese rice wine or dry sherry

4 tbsp dark soy sauce

1 tsp dark brown sugar

2 tbsp water

1 tsp sesame oil

1 Heat the peanut oil in a preheated wok or large skillet until it is smoking.

2 Lower the heat slightly, add the green onions and garlic, and stir-fry for about 30 seconds.

3 Add the red and green bell peppers, fresh red chili, water chestnuts, and zucchini to the wok or skillet and stir-fry for 2–3 minutes, or until the vegetables are just beginning to soften.

4 Add the oyster mushrooms, black bean sauce, Chinese rice wine or dry sherry, dark soy sauce, dark brown sugar, and water to the wok and stir-fry for 4 minutes more.

5 Sprinkle the stir-fry with sesame oil and serve immediately.

COOK'S TIP

Eight jewels or treasures form a traditional part of the Chinese New Year celebrations, which start in the last week of the old year. The Kitchen God, an important figure, is sent to give a report to heaven, returning on New Year's Eve in time for the feasting.

Spicy Mushrooms

A mixture of mushrooms, common in Western cooking, have been used in this recipe for a richly flavored dish.

NUTRITIONAL INFORMATION

Calories 103   Sugars 4g
Protein . . . . .3g   Fat 8g
Carbohydrate . . . .5g   Saturates 2g

5 MINS   10 MINS

SERVES 4

I N G R E D I E N T S

2 tbsp peanut oil

2 garlic cloves, crushed

3 green onions, chopped

10½ oz small mushrooms

2 large open-cap mushrooms, sliced

4½ oz oyster mushrooms

1 tsp chili sauce

1 tbsp dark soy sauce

1 tbsp hoisin sauce

1 tbsp wine vinegar

½ tsp ground Szechuan pepper

1 tbsp dark brown sugar

1 tsp sesame oil

chopped parsley, to garnish

1 Heat the peanut oil in a preheated wok or large skillet until almost smoking.

2 Reduce the heat slightly, add the garlic and green onions to the wok or skillet, and stir-fry for 30 seconds.

3 Add all the mushrooms to the wok, together with the chili sauce, dark soy sauce, hoisin sauce, wine vinegar, ground Szechuan pepper, and dark brown sugar and stir-fry for 4–5 minutes, or until the mushrooms are cooked through. Stir constantly to prevent the mixture sticking to the base of the wok.

4 Sprinkle the sesame oil on top of the mixture in the wok. Transfer to a warm serving dish, garnish with parsley, and serve immediately.

COOK'S TIP

If Chinese dried mushrooms are available, add a small quantity to this dish for texture. Wood ears are widely used and are available dried from Chinese food stores. They should be rinsed, soaked in warm water for 20 minutes, and rinsed again before use.

Golden Needles with Bamboo

Golden needles are the dried flower buds of the tiger lily and have a unique musky flavor. They are available, dried, from Chinese shops.

NUTRITIONAL INFORMATION

Calories 178	Sugars 3g	
Protein 4g	Fat 9g	
Carbohydrate ...22g	Saturates 1g	

35 MINS   25 MINS

SERVES 4

INGREDIENTS

¼ cup dried lily flowers

2 x 8 oz cans bamboo shoots, drained

½ cup cornstarch

vegetable oil, for deep-frying

1 tbsp vegetable oil

scant 2 cups vegetable stock

1 tbsp dark soy sauce

1 tbsp dry sherry

1 tsp sugar

1 large garlic clove, sliced

½ red bell pepper

½ green bell pepper

½ yellow bell pepper

1 Soak the lily flowers in hot water for 30 minutes.

2 Coat the bamboo shoots in cornstarch. Heat enough oil in a large heavy-bottomed saucepan to deep-fry the bamboo shoots in batches until just beginning to color. Remove with a perforated spoon and drain on absorbent paper towels.

3 Drain the lily flowers and trim off the hard ends. Heat 1 tablespoon of oil in a wok or large skillet. Add the lily flowers, bamboo shoots, stock, soy sauce, sherry, sugar, and garlic.

4 Slice the bell peppers thinly and add to the wok or skillet. Bring to a boil, stirring constantly, then reduce the heat and simmer for 5 minutes. Add extra water or stock if necessary.

5 Transfer the mixture in the wok to warm serving dishes and serve.

COOK'S TIP

To coat the bamboo shoots easily with cornstarch, place the cornstarch in a plastic bag, add the bamboo shoots in batches and shake well.

Cauliflower with Greens

This is a delicious way to cook cauliflower—even without the greens.

NUTRITIONAL INFORMATION

Calories	49	Sugars	........2g
Protein	.........2g	Fat	..........3g
Carbohydrate	....3g	Saturates	.....0.5g

5 MINS   5 MINS

SERVES 4

INGREDIENTS

6 oz cauliflower, cut into
    flowerets

1 garlic clove

½ tsp turmeric

1 tbsp cilantro root
    or stem

1 tbsp sunflower oil

2 green onions, cut into 1 inch pieces

4½ oz oriental greens, such as
    bok choy or mustard greens,
    tough stalks removed

1 tsp yellow mustard seeds

1 Blanch the cauliflower, rinse in cold running water, and drain. Set aside until required.

2 Grind together the garlic, turmeric, and cilantro root or stem together in a pestle and mortar or spice grinder.

3 Heat the sunflower oil in a wok or large, heavy-bottomed skillet.

4 Add the green onions to the wok or skillet and cook over a high heat for 2 minutes, stirring constantly.

5 Add the oriental greens and stir-fry for 1 minute. Keep warm and set aside until required.

6 Return the wok or skillet to the heat and add the mustard seeds. Stir until they start to pop, then add the turmeric and cilantro mixture and the cauliflower, and stir until all the cauliflower is coated.

7 Serve the cauliflower with the greens on a warmed serving plate.

COOK'S TIP

Pestle and mortars are available in wood or stone. The stone mortar gives a finer grind than the wooden mortar. A coffee grinder can also be used, but will need a thorough clean afterwards, as some of the spices used in Chinese cooking can be quite pungent!

Sherry & Soy Vegetables

This is a simple, yet tasty side dish which is just as delicious as a snack or main course.

NUTRITIONAL INFORMATION

Calories 374	Sugars 10g	
Protein 14g	Fat 25g	
Carbohydrate ...20g	Saturates 5g	

10 MINS   15 MINS

SERVES 4

I N G R E D I E N T S

2 tbsp sunflower oil

1 red onion, sliced

6 oz carrots, thinly sliced

6 oz zucchini, sliced diagonally

1 red bell pepper, seeded and sliced

1 small head Chinese cabbage, shredded

3 cups bean sprouts

8 oz can bamboo shoots, drained

¼ cup cashews, toasted

S A U C E

3 tbsp medium sherry

3 tbsp light soy sauce

1 tsp ground ginger

1 clove garlic, crushed

1 tsp cornstarch

1 tbsp tomato paste

 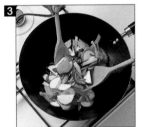 

1 Heat the sunflower oil in a large preheated wok.

2 Add the red onion and stir-fry for 2–3 minutes or until softenened.

3 Add the carrots, zucchini, and bell pepper slices to the wok and stir-fry for 5 minutes more.

4 Add the Chinese cabbage, bean sprouts, and bamboo shoots and heat through for 2–3 minutes, or until the leaves begin to wilt. Stir in the cashews.

5 Combine the sherry, soy sauce, ginger, garlic, cornstarch, and tomato paste. Pour over the vegetables and toss well. Leave to simmer for 2–3 minutes or until the juices start to thicken. Serve immediately.

VARIATION

Use any mixture of fresh vegetables that you have available in this very versatile dish.

Carrots with Pineapple

If you can use fresh pineapple the flavor is even better and the texture crisper.

NUTRITIONAL INFORMATION

Calories 125   Sugars 17g
Protein ....1g   Fat 6g
Carbohydrate ...18g   Saturates 1g

 5 MINS   15 MINS

SERVES 4

INGREDIENTS

1 tbsp sunflower oil

1 tbsp olive oil

1 small onion, finely sliced

1 inch piece fresh ginger, peeled
   and grated

1-2 garlic cloves, crushed

1 lb 2 oz carrots, thinly sliced

1 x 7 oz can pineapple in natural juice,
   chopped, or 9 oz fresh pineapple,
   chopped

2-3 tbsp pineapple juice (from the can or
   fresh)

salt and coarsely ground black pepper

freshly chopped parsley or dill,
   to garnish

COOK'S TIP

If using canned pineapple
make sure it is in natural juice,
not syrup: the sweet taste of
the syrup will ruin the fresh
flavor of this dish. Most fruits
can now be bought canned in
natural juice, which gives a much
fresher, lighter taste.

1 Heat the sunflower and olive oil in a
wok. Add the onion, ginger, and garlic
and stir-fry briskly for 2-3 minutes.

2 Add the carrots and continue to stir-
fry, lowering the heat a little, for
about 5 minutes.

3 Add the pineapple and juice and
plenty of seasoning and continue to
stir-fry for 5-6 minutes, or until the

carrots are tender-crisp and the liquid has
almost evaporated.

4 Adjust the seasoning, adding plenty
of black pepper and turn into a
warmed serving dish. Sprinkle with
chopped parsley or dill and serve as a
vegetable accompaniment. Alternatively,
you can allow the carrots to cool and
serve as a salad, dressed with 2-4
tablespoons French dressing.

Fish Eggplant

Like Fish-flavored Pork (see page 240), there is no fish involved
in this dish, and the meat can be omitted without affecting the flavor.

NUTRITIONAL INFORMATION

Calories	130	Sugars	........3g
Protein	........8g	Fat	..........8g
Carbohydrate	....6g	Saturates	......2g

35 MINS   15 MINS

SERVES 4

INGREDIENTS

1 lb 2 oz eggplant

vegetable oil, for deep-frying

1 garlic clove, finely chopped

½ tsp finely chopped fresh ginger

2 green onions, finely chopped, with the
    white and green parts separated

4½ oz pork, thinly shredded
    (optional)

1 tbsp light soy sauce

2 tsp rice wine or dry sherry

1 tbsp chili bean sauce

½ tsp sugar

1 tbsp rice vinegar

2 tsp cornstarch paste (see page 31)

a few drops sesame oil

salt

2 Heat the vegetable oil in a preheated wok or large skillet until smoking.

3 Add the eggplant chips and deep-fry for about 3-4 minutes, or until soft. Remove and drain on absorbent paper towels.

4 Pour off the hot oil, leaving about 1 tablespoon in the wok. Add the garlic, ginger and the white parts of the green onions, followed by the pork, if using. Stir-fry for about 1 minute or until the color of the meat changes, then add the light soy sauce, rice wine or dry sherry, and chili bean sauce, blending well.

5 Return the eggplant chips to the wok or skillet together with the sugar, ½ teaspoon salt and the rice vinegar.

6 Continue stirring the mixture in the wok for another minute or so, then add the cornstarch paste and stir until the sauce has thickened.

7 Add the green parts of the green onions to the wok and toss to combine. Sprinkle on the sesame oil and serve immediately.

1 Using a sharp knife, cut the eggplant into rounds and then into thin strips about the size of potato chips—the skin can either be peeled or left on. Place the eggplant strips into a colander, sprinkle with salt, and leave to stand for 30 minutes. Rinse thoroughly and pat dry on paper towels. This process removes the bitter juices from the eggplant.

Bamboo with Bell Peppers

This dish has a wonderfully strong ginger flavor which is integral to Chinese cooking. The mixed bell peppers give the dish a burst of color.

NUTRITIONAL INFORMATION

Calories 101   Sugars 5g
Protein . . . . .3g   Fat 6g
Carbohydrate . . . .9g   Saturates 1g

 5 MINS   15 MINS

SERVES 4

I N G R E D I E N T S

2 tbsp peanut oil

8 oz canned bamboo shoots, drained and rinsed

1 inch piece fresh ginger, finely chopped

1 small red bell pepper, seeded and thinly sliced

1 small green bell pepper, seeded and thinly sliced

1 small yellow bell pepper, seeded and thinly sliced

1 leek, sliced

½ cup vegetable stock

1 tbsp light soy sauce

2 tsp light brown sugar

2 tsp Chinese rice wine or dry sherry

1 tsp cornstarch

2 tsp water

1 tsp sesame oil

COOK'S TIP

Add a chopped fresh red chili or a few drops of chili sauce for a spicier dish.

1 Heat the peanut oil in a preheated wok or large skillet, swirling the oil around the base of the wok or pan until it is really hot.

2 Add the bamboo shoots, ginger, bell peppers, and leek to the wok and stir-fry for 2–3 minutes.

3 Stir in the vegetable stock, soy sauce, light brown sugar, and Chinese rice wine or sherry and bring to a boil, stirring.

4 Reduce the heat and simmer for 4–5 minutes, or until the vegetables begin to soften.

5 Blend the cornstarch with the water to form a smooth paste.

6 Stir the cornstarch paste into the wok. Bring to a boil and cook, stirring constantly, until the sauce thickens and clears.

7 Sprinkle the sesame oil over the vegetables and cook for 1 minute. Transfer to a warm serving dish and serve immediately.

Braised Vegetables

This colorful selection of braised vegetables makes a splendid accompaniment to a main dish.

NUTRITIONAL INFORMATION

Calories 170	Sugars 8g	
Protein 7g	Fat 10g	
Carbohydrate ...14g	Saturates 1g	

 10 MINS  10 MINS

SERVES 4

INGREDIENTS

3 tbsp sunflower oil

1 garlic clove, crushed

1 Chinese cabbage, thickly shredded

2 onions, peeled and cut into wedges

9 oz broccoli flowerets

2 large carrots, peeled and cut into thin julienne strips

12 baby corn-on-the-cob, halved if large

2 oz snow peas, halved

3 oz Chinese or oyster mushrooms, sliced

1 tbsp grated fresh ginger

¾ cup vegetable stock

2 tbsp light soy sauce

1 tbsp cornstarch

salt and pepper

½ tsp sugar

1 Heat the oil in a wok. Add the garlic, cabbage, onions, broccoli, carrots, corn, snow peas, mushrooms, and ginger and stir-fry for 2 minutes.

2 Add the stock, cover, and cook for 2–3 minutes more.

3 Blend the soy sauce with the cornstarch and salt and pepper to taste.

4 Remove the braised vegetables from the pan with a slotted spoon and keep warm. Add the soy sauce mixture to the pan juices, mixing well. Bring to a boil, stirring constantly, until the mixture thickens slightly. Stir in the sugar.

5 Return the vegetables to the pan and toss in the slightly thickened sauce. Cook gently to just heat through then serve immediately.

COOK'S TIP

This dish also makes an ideal vegetarian main meal. Double the quantities, to serve 4–6, and serve with noodles or Green Rice (see page 423).

Vegetable & Tofu Pancakes

Chinese pancakes are made with hardly any fat—they are simply flattened white flour dough.

NUTRITIONAL INFORMATION

Calories 312	Sugars 5g
Protein 13g	Fat 19g
Carbohydrate . . .25g	Saturates 7g

5 MINS   15 MINS

SERVES 4

I N G R E D I E N T S

1 tbsp vegetable oil

1 garlic clove, crushed

1 inch piece fresh ginger, grated

1 bunch green onions, trimmed and
   shredded lengthwise

3½ oz snow peas, trimmed and shredded

8 oz tofu, drained and
   cut into ½ inch pieces

2 tbsp dark soy sauce, plus extra
   to serve

2 tbsp hoisin sauce, plus extra
   to serve

2 oz canned bamboo shoots,
   drained

2 oz canned water chestnuts,
   drained and sliced

3½ oz bean sprouts

1 small red chili, seeded and sliced thinly

1 small bunch fresh chives

12 soft Chinese pancakes

TO SERVE

shredded Chinese cabbage

1 cucumber, sliced

strips of red chili

1 Heat the oil in a skillet and stir-fry the garlic and ginger for 1 minute.

2 Add the green onions, snow peas, tofu, soy sauce, and hoisin sauce. Stir-fry for 2 minutes.

3 Add the bamboo shoots, water chestnuts, bean sprouts, and chili to the pan. Stir-fry gently for 2 minutes until the vegetables are just tender but still have bite. Snip the chives into 1 inch lengths and stir into the pan.

4 Meanwhile, heat the pancakes according to the instructions on the pack. Divide the vegetables and tofu among the pancakes. Roll up the pancakes and serve with the Chinese cabbage and extra sauce.

Spicy Eggplants

Try to obtain the smaller Chinese eggplants for this dish, as they have a slightly sweeter taste.

NUTRITIONAL INFORMATION

Calories 120	Sugars 7g	
Protein 2g	Fat 9g	
Carbohydrate 9g	Saturates 1g	

35 MINS   20 MINS

SERVES 4

INGREDIENTS

1 lb eggplant, rinsed

2 tsp salt

3 tbsp vegetable oil

2 garlic cloves, crushed

1 inch piece fresh ginger, chopped

1 onion, halved and sliced

1 fresh red chili, sliced

2 tbsp dark soy sauce

1 tbsp hoisin sauce

½ tsp chili sauce

1 tbsp dark brown sugar

1 tbsp wine vinegar

1 tsp ground Szechuan pepper

1¼ cups vegetable stock

1 Cut the eggplant into cubes if you are using the larger variety, or cut the smaller type in half. Place in a colander and sprinkle with the salt. Let stand for 30 minutes. Rinse under cold running water and pat dry with paper towels.

2 Heat the oil in a preheated wok and add the garlic, ginger, onion, and fresh chili. Stir-fry for 30 seconds and add the eggplant. Continue to cook for 1–2 minutes.

3 Add the soy sauce, hoisin sauce, chili sauce, sugar, wine vinegar, Szechuan pepper, and vegetable stock to the wok, reduce the heat and leave to simmer, uncovered, for 10 minutes, or until the eggplant is cooked.

4 Increase the heat and boil to reduce the sauce until thickened enough to coat the eggplants. Serve immediately.

COOK'S TIP

Sprinkling the eggplant with salt and letting them stand removes the bitter juices, which would otherwise taint the flavor of the dish.

Stir-fried Seasonal Vegetables

When selecting different fresh vegetables for this dish, bear in mind that there should always be a contrast in color as well as texture.

NUTRITIONAL INFORMATION

Calories 108   Sugars 3g
Protein . . . . .3g   Fat 9g
Carbohydrate . . . .4g   Saturates 1g

3¹/₂ HOURS   10 MINS

SERVES 4

I N G R E D I E N T S

1 medium red bell pepper, cored
  and seeded

4½ oz zucchini

4½ oz cauliflower

4½ oz green beans

3 tbsp vegetable oil

a few small slices fresh ginger

½ tsp salt

½ tsp sugar

Chinese Stock (see page 30) or
  water

1 tbsp light soy sauce

a few drops of sesame oil (optional)

1 Using a sharp knife or cleaver, cut the red bell pepper into small squares. Thinly slice the zucchini. Trim the cauliflower and divide into small flowerets, discarding any thick stems. Make sure the vegetables are cut into roughly similar shapes and sizes to ensure even cooking.

2 Top and tail the green beans, then cut them in half.

3 Heat the vegetable oil in a pre-heated wok or large skillet.

4 Add the prepared vegetables to the wok and stir-fry with the ginger for about 2 minutes.

5 Add the salt and sugar to the wok or skillet, and continue to stir-fry for 1-2 minutes, adding a little Chinese stock or water if the vegetables appear to be too dry. Do not add liquid unless necessary.

6 Add the light soy sauce and sesame oil (if using) and stir well to lightly coat the vegetables.

7 Transfer the stir-fried vegetables to a warm serving dish and serve immediately.

VARIATION

Almost any vegetables could be used in this dish but make sure there is a good variety of color, and always include several crisp vegetables such as carrots or snow peas.

Vegetable Chop Suey

Make sure that the vegetables are all cut into pieces of a similar size in this recipe, so that they cook within the same amount of time.

NUTRITIONAL INFORMATION

Calories	155	Sugars	.........6g
Protein	.........4g	Fat	..........12g
Carbohydrate	....9g	Saturates	.......2g

5 MINS   5 MINS

SERVES 4

I N G R E D I E N T S

1 yellow bell pepper, seeded

1 red bell pepper, seeded

1 carrot

1 zucchini

1 fennel bulb

1 onion

2 oz snow peas

2 tbsp peanut oil

3 garlic cloves, crushed

1 tsp grated fresh ginger

4½ oz bean sprouts

2 tsp light brown sugar

2 tbsp light soy sauce

½ cup vegetable stock

  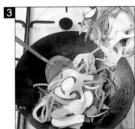

1 Cut the bell peppers, carrot, zucchini, and fennel into thin slices. Cut the onion into quarters and then cut each quarter in half. Slice the snow peas diagonally.

2 Heat the oil in a preheated wok, add the garlic and ginger, and stir-fry for 30 seconds. Add the onion and stir-fry for 30 seconds more.

3 Add the bell peppers, carrot, zucchini, fennel, and snow peas to the wok and stir-fry for 2 minutes.

4 Add the bean sprouts to the wok and stir in the sugar, soy sauce, and stock. Reduce the heat to low and simmer for 1–2 minutes, until the vegetables are tender and coated in the sauce.

5 Transfer the vegetables and sauce to a serving dish and serve immediately.

VARIATION

Use any combination of colorful vegetables that you have available to make this versatile dish.

Caraway Cabbage

This makes a delicious vegetable accompaniment to all types of food: it can also be served as a vegetarian main dish.

NUTRITIONAL INFORMATION

Calories	223	Sugars	........17g
Protein	.........6g	Fat	..........14g
Carbohydrate	...18g	Saturates	.......1g

5 MINS   10 MINS

SERVES 4

INGREDIENTS

1 lb 2 oz white cabbage

1 tbsp sunflower oil

4 green onions, thinly sliced diagonally

6 tbsp raisins

½ cup walnut pieces or pecans, roughly chopped

5 tbsp milk or vegetable stock

1 tbsp caraway seeds

1-2 tbsp freshly chopped mint

salt and pepper

mint sprigs, to garnish

1 Remove any outer leaves from the cabbage and cut out the stem, then shred the leaves very finely, either by hand or using the fine slicing blade on a food processor.

2 Heat the sunflower oil in a wok, swirling it around until it is really hot.

3 Add the green onions to the wok and stir-fry for a minute or so.

4 Add the shredded cabbage and stir-fry for 3-4 minutes, keeping the cabbage moving all the time and stirring from the outside to the center of the wok. Make sure the cabbage does not stick to the wok or go brown.

5 Add the raisins, walnuts or pecans, and milk or vegetable stock and continue to stir-fry for 3-4 minutes until the cabbage begins to soften slightly but is still crisp.

6 Season well with salt and pepper, add the caraway seeds and 1 tablespoon of the chopped mint and continue to stir-fry for a minute or so.

7 Serve sprinkled with the remaining chopped mint and garnish with sprigs of fresh mint.

VARIATION

Red cabbage may be cooked in the same way in the wok, but substitute 2 tablespoons red or white wine vinegar and 3 tablespoons water for the milk and add 1 tablespoon brown sugar. Add a finely chopped apple if you like.

Winter Vegetable Stir-fry

Ordinary winter vegetables are given extraordinary treatment in this lively stir-fry — just the thing for perking up jaded palates.

NUTRITIONAL INFORMATION

Calories	175	Sugars	.........7g
Protein	.........6g	Fat	..........13g
Carbohydrate	....9g	Saturates	.......2g

5 MINS   10 MINS

SERVES 4

I N G R E D I E N T S

3 tbsp sesame oil

¼ cup blanched almonds

1 large carrot, cut into thin strips

1 large turnip, cut into thin strips

1 onion, sliced finely

1 garlic clove, crushed

3 celery stalks, sliced finely

4½ oz brussels sprouts, trimmed and halved

4½ oz cauliflower, broken into flowerets

2 cups white cabbage, shredded

2 tsp sesame seeds

1 tsp grated fresh ginger

½ tsp medium-hot chili powder

1 tbsp chopped fresh cilantro

1 tbsp light soy sauce

salt and pepper

sprigs of fresh cilantro, to garnish

3 Add the cabbage, sesame seeds, ginger, and chili powder and cook, stirring, for 2 minutes. Season to taste.

4 Add the chopped cilantro, soy sauce, and almonds, stirring gently to mix. Serve the vegetables, garnished with cilantro sprigs.

1 Heat the oil in a wok or large skillet. Stir-fry the almonds until lightly browned, then lift them out and drain on paper towels.

2 Add all the vegetables to the wok or skillet, except for the cabbage. Stir-fry the vegetables briskly for 3–4 minutes.

COOK'S TIP

As well as adding protein, vitamins and useful fats to the diet, nuts and seeds add important flavor and texture to vegetarian meals. Sesame seeds are also a good source of vitamin E.

Lemon Chinese Cabbage

These stir-fried Chinese cabbage leaves are served with a tangy sauce made of grated lemon zest, lemon juice, and ginger.

NUTRITIONAL INFORMATION

Calories 120	Sugars 0g	
Protein 5g	Fat 8g	
Carbohydrate 8g	Saturates 1g	

5 MINS   10 MINS

SERVES 4

INGREDIENTS

1 lb 2 oz Chinese cabbage

3 tbsp vegetable oil

½ inch piece fresh ginger, grated

1 tsp salt

1 tsp sugar

½ cup water or vegetable stock

1 tsp grated lemon zest

1 tbsp cornstarch

1 tbsp lemon juice

1 Separate the Chinese cabbage leaves, wash, and drain thoroughly. Pat dry with absorbent paper towels.

2 Cut the Chinese cabbage leaves into 2 inch wide slices.

COOK'S TIP

If Chinese cabbage is unavailable, substitute slices of savoy cabbage. Cook for 1 extra minute to soften the leaves.

3 Heat the oil in a wok and add the grated fresh ginger followed by the Chinese cabbage, stir-fry for 2–3 minutes or until the leaves begin to wilt.

4 Add the salt and sugar, and mix well until the leaves soften. Remove the leaves with a slotted spoon and set aside.

5 Add the water or stock to the wok with the lemon zest. Bring to a boil.

6 Meanwhile, mix the cornstarch to a smooth paste with the lemon juice, then add to the wok. Simmer, stirring constantly, for about 1 minute to make a smooth sauce.

7 Return the cooked Chinese cabbage to the pan and mix thoroughly to coat the leaves in the sauce. Arrange on a serving plate and serve immediately.

Potato Stir-Fry

In this sweet and sour dish, tender vegetables are simply stir-fried with spices and coconut milk, and flavored with lime.

NUTRITIONAL INFORMATION

Calories 138   Sugars 5g
Protein ....2g   Fat 6g
Carbohydrate ...20g   Saturates 1g

10 MINS   20 MINS

SERVES 4

INGREDIENTS

4 waxy potatoes

2 tbsp vegetable oil

1 yellow bell pepper, diced

1 red bell pepper, diced

1 carrot, cut into thin sticks

1 zucchini, cut into thin sticks

2 garlic cloves, crushed

1 red chili, sliced

1 bunch green onions,
  halved lengthwise

8 tbsp coconut milk

1 tsp chopped lemon grass

2 tsp lime juice

finely grated zest of 1 lime

1 tbsp chopped fresh cilantro

1 Using a sharp knife, cut the potatoes into small dice.

2 Bring a large saucepan of water to a boil and cook the diced potatoes for 5 minutes. Drain thoroughly.

3 Heat the vegetable oil in a wok or large skillet, swirling the oil around the base of the wok until it is really hot.

4 Add the potatoes, diced bell peppers, carrot, zucchini, garlic, and chili to the wok and stir-fry the vegetables for 2–3 minutes.

5 Stir in the green onions, coconut milk, chopped lemon grass, and lime juice and stir-fry the mixture for 5 minutes more.

6 Add the lime zest and cilantro and stir-fry for 1 minute. Serve hot.

COOK'S TIP

Check that the potatoes are not overcooked in step 2, otherwise the potato pieces will disintegrate when they are stir-fried in the wok.

Leeks with Yellow Bean Sauce

This is a simple side dish which is ideal with other main meal vegetarian dishes.

NUTRITIONAL INFORMATION

Calories 131	Sugars 3g	
Protein 6g	Fat 9g	
Carbohydrate 7g	Saturates 2g	

 5 MINS   🕐 10 MINS

SERVES 4

I N G R E D I E N T S

1 lb leeks

6 oz baby corn-on-the-cobs

6 green onions

3 tbsp peanut oil

8 oz Chinese cabbage, shredded

4 tbsp yellow bean sauce

1 Using a sharp knife, slice the leeks, halve the baby corn-on-the-cobs and thinly slice the green onions.

2 Heat the peanut oil in a large preheated wok or skillet until smoking.

3 Add the leeks, shredded Chinese cabbage, and corn to the wok or skillet.

4 Stir-fry the vegetables over a high heat for about 5 minutes or until the edges of the vegetables are slightly brown.

5 Add the green onions to the wok or skillet, stirring to combine.

6 Add the yellow bean sauce to the wok or skillet.

7 Stir-fry the mixture in the wok for 2 minutes more, or until heated through and the vegetables are thoroughly coated in the sauce.

8 Transfer the vegetables and sauce to warm serving dishes and serve immediately.

COOK'S TIP

Yellow bean sauce adds an authentic Chinese flavor to stir-fries. It is made from crushed salted soya beans mixed with flour and spices to make a thick paste. It is mild in flavor and is excellent with a range of vegetables.

Vegetables in Coconut Milk

This is a deliciously crunchy way to prepare a mixture of raw vegetables.

NUTRITIONAL INFORMATION

Calories 201   Sugars 10g
Protein . . . . .9g   Fat 13g
Carbohydrate . . .13g   Saturates 3g

 5 MINS   5 MINS

SERVES 4

INGREDIENTS

1 red chili, seeded and chopped

1 tsp coriander seeds

1 tsp cumin seeds

2 garlic cloves, crushed

juice of 1 lime

1 cup coconut milk

2 cups bean sprouts

2 cups white cabbage, shredded

4½ oz snow peas, trimmed

1¼ cups carrots, sliced thinly

1¼ cups cauliflower flowerets

grated or shaved coconut, to serve

3 tbsp peanut butter

1 Grind together the chopped red chili, coriander and cumin seeds, crushed garlic, and lime juice in a pestle and mortar or food processor until a smooth paste is formed.

2 Put the spice paste into a medium-sized saucepan and heat gently for about 1 minute, or until fragrant.

3 Add the coconut milk to the saucepan and stir constantly until just about to boil.

4 Meanwhile, mix together the bean sprouts, shredded white cabbage, trimmed snow peas, sliced carrots, and cauliflower flowerets in a large mixing bowl.

5 Stir the peanut butter into the coconut mixture until well blended and then pour into the pan, stirring to coat the vegetables. Serve garnished with grated or shaved coconut.

COOK'S TIP

If you prefer, the cauliflower, carrots, and snow peas may be blanched first for less bite.

This dish is ideal as a buffet dish as the quantity of dressing is quite sparse, and is only intended to coat.

Sweet & Sour Cauliflower

Although sweet and sour flavorings are mainly associated with pork, they are ideal for flavoring vegetables as in this tasty recipe.

NUTRITIONAL INFORMATION

Calories ....154 Sugars 16g
Protein ....6g Fat 7g
Carbohydrate ...17g Saturates 1g

 5 MINS   20 MINS

SERVES 4

INGREDIENTS

1 lb cauliflower flowerets

2 tbsp sunflower oil

1 onion, sliced

8 oz carrots, sliced

3½ oz snow peas

1 ripe mango, sliced

1 cup bean sprouts

3 tbsp chopped fresh cilantro

3 tbsp fresh lime juice

1 tbsp honey

6 tbsp coconut milk

1 Bring a large saucepan of water to a boil. Add the cauliflower to the pan and cook for 2 minutes. Drain the cauliflower thoroughly.

2 Heat the sunflower oil in a large preheated wok.

3 Add the onion and carrots to the wok and stir-fry for about 5 minutes.

4 Add the drained cauliflower and snow peas to the wok and stir-fry for 2–3 minutes.

5 Add the mango and bean sprouts to the wok and stir-fry for about 2 minutes.

6 Mix together the cilantro, lime juice, honey, and coconut milk in a bowl.

7 Add the cilantro and coconut mixture to the wok and stir-fry for about 2 minutes, or until the juices are bubbling.

8 Transfer the sweet and sour cauliflower stir-fry to serving dishes and serve immediately.

VARIATION

Use broccoli instead of the cauliflower as an alternative, if you prefer.

Ginger & Orange Broccoli

Thinly sliced broccoli flowerets are lightly stir-fried and served in a ginger and orange sauce.

NUTRITIONAL INFORMATION

Calories	133	Sugars	.........6g
Protein	.........9g	Fat	..........7g
Carbohydrate	...10g	Saturates	.......1g

 5 MINS   10 MINS

SERVES 4

I N G R E D I E N T S

1 lb 10 oz broccoli

2 thin slices fresh ginger

2 garlic cloves

1 orange

2 tsp cornstarch

1 tbsp light soy sauce

½ tsp sugar

2 tbsp vegetable oil

1 Divide the broccoli into small flowerets. Peel the stems, using a vegetable peeler, and then cut the stems into thin slices, using a sharp knife.

2 Cut the fresh ginger into thin sticks and slice the garlic.

3 Peel 2 long strips of zest from the orange and cut into thin strips. Place the strips in a bowl, cover with cold water, and set aside.

4 Squeeze the juice from the orange and mix with the cornstarch, light soy sauce, sugar and 4 tablespoons water.

5 Heat the vegetable oil in a wok or large skillet. Add the broccoli stem slices and stir-fry for 2 minutes.

6 Add the fresh ginger slices, garlic, and broccoli flowerets, and stir-fry for 3 minutes more.

7 Stir the orange sauce mixture into the wok and cook, stirring constantly, until the sauce has thickened and coated the broccoli.

8 Drain the reserved orange zest and stir into the wok before serving.

VARIATION

This dish could be made with cauliflower, if you prefer, or a mixture of cauliflower and broccoli.

Carrot & Orange Stir-Fry

Carrots and oranges have long been combined in Oriental cooking, the orange juice bringing out the sweetness of the carrots.

NUTRITIONAL INFORMATION

Calories 341	Sugars 26g
Protein 10g	Fat 21g
Carbohydrate . . .28g	Saturates 4g

10 MINS   10 MINS

SERVES 4

I N G R E D I E N T S

2 tbsp sunflower oil

1 lb carrots, grated

8 oz leeks, shredded

2 oranges, peeled and segmented

2 tbsp tomato ketchup

1 tbsp brown sugar

2 tbsp light soy sauce

½ cup chopped peanuts

VARIATION

You could use pineapple instead of orange, if you prefer. If using canned pineapple, make sure that it is in natural juice not syrup as it will spoil the fresh taste of this dish.

1 Heat the sunflower oil in a large preheated wok.

2 Add the grated carrot and leeks to the wok and stir-fry for 2–3 minutes, or until the vegetables have just softened.

3 Add the orange segments to the wok and heat through gently, ensuring that you do not break up the orange segments as you stir the mixture.

4 Mix the tomato ketchup, brown sugar, and soy sauce together in a small bowl.

5 Add the tomato and sugar mixture to the wok and then stir-fry for 2 minutes more.

6 Transfer the stir-fry to warm serving bowls and scatter with the chopped peanuts. Serve immediately.

Green & Black Bean Stir-fry

A terrific side dish, the variety of greens in this recipe make it as attractive as it is tasty.

NUTRITIONAL INFORMATION

Calories 88   Sugars 2g
Protein . . . . .2g   Fat 7g
Carbohydrate . . . .4g   Saturates 4g

  5 MINS   10 MINS

SERVES 4

I N G R E D I E N T S

8 oz green beans, sliced

4 shallots, sliced

3½ oz shiitake mushrooms, thinly sliced

1 clove garlic, crushed

1 iceberg lettuce, shredded

1 tsp chili oil

2 tbsp butter

4 tbsp black bean sauce

1 Using a sharp knife, slice the fine green beans, shallots, and shiitake mushrooms. Crush the garlic in a pestle and mortar and shred the Iceberg lettuce.

2 Heat the chili oil and butter in a large preheated wok or skillet.

3 Add the green beans, shallots, garlic, and mushrooms to the wok and stir-fry for 2–3 minutes.

4 Add the shredded lettuce to the wok or skillet and stir-fry until the leaves have wilted.

5 Stir the black bean sauce into the mixture in the wok and heat through, tossing gently to mix, until the sauce is bubbling.

6 Transfer the green and black bean stir-fry to a warm serving dish and serve immediately.

COOK'S TIP

If possible, use Chinese green beans which are tender and can be eaten whole. They are available from Chinese grocery stores.

Vegetable Stir-fry with Eggs

Known as Gado Gado in China, this is a true classic which never fades from popularity. A delicious warm salad with a peanut sauce.

NUTRITIONAL INFORMATION

Calories 269   Sugars 12g
Protein . . . . .12g   Fat 19g
Carbohydrate . . .14g   Saturates 3g

10 MINS   15 MINS

SERVES 4

INGREDIENTS

2 eggs

8 oz carrots

12 oz white cabbage

2 tbsp vegetable oil

1 red bell pepper, seeded and thinly sliced

1½ cups bean sprouts

1 tbsp tomato ketchup

2 tbsp soy sauce

⅓ cup salted peanuts, chopped

2 Peel and coarsley grate the carrots.

3 Remove any outer leaves from the white cabbage and cut out the stem, then shred the leaves very finely, either with a sharp knife or by using the fine slicing blade on a food processor.

4 Heat the vegetable oil in a large preheated wok or large skillet.

5 Add the carrots, white cabbage, and bell pepper to the wok and stir-fry for 3 minutes.

6 Add the bean sprouts to the wok and stir-fry for 2 minutes.

7 Combine the tomato ketchup and soy sauce in a small bowl and add to the wok or skillet.

8 Add the chopped peanuts to the wok and stir-fry for 1 minute.

9 Transfer the stir-fry to warm serving plates and garnish with the hard-boiled egg quarters. Serve immediately.

1 Bring a small saucepan of water to a boil. Add the eggs to the pan and cook for about 7 minutes. Remove the eggs from the pan and leave to cool under cold running water for 1 minute. Peel the shell from the eggs and then cut the eggs into quarters.

COOK'S TIP

The eggs are cooled in cold water immediately after cooking in order to prevent the egg yolk blackening around the edges.

Spinach with Mushrooms

For best results, use straw mushrooms, available in cans from oriental shops. If these are unavailable, use small mushrooms instead.

NUTRITIONAL INFORMATION

Calories 201   Sugars 8g
Protein . . . . .7g   Fat 15g
Carbohydrate . . .10g   Saturates 2g

5 MINS   10 MINS

SERVES 4

I N G R E D I E N T S

¼ cup pine nuts

1 lb 2 oz fresh spinach leaves

1 red onion

2 garlic cloves

3 tbsp vegetable oil

15 oz can straw mushrooms, drained

3 tbsp raisins

2 tbsp soy sauce

salt

1 Heat a wok or large, heavy-bottomed skillet.

2 Dry-fry the pine nuts in the wok until lightly browned. Remove with a perforated spoon and set aside until required.

3 Wash the spinach thoroughly, picking the leaves over and removing long stalks. Drain thoroughly and pat dry with absorbent paper towels.

4 Using a sharp knife, slice the red onion and the garlic.

5 Heat the vegetable oil in the wok or skillet. Add the onion and garlic slices and stir-fry for 1 minute until slightly softened.

6 Add the spinach and mushrooms, and continue to stir-fry until the leaves have wilted. Drain off any excess liquid.

7 Stir in the raisins, reserved pine nuts and soy sauce. Stir-fry until thoroughly heated and all the ingredients are well combined.

8 Season to taste with salt, transfer to a warm serving dish, and serve.

COOK'S TIP

Soak the raisins in 2 tablespoons dry sherry before using. This helps to plump them up as well as adding extra flavour to the stir-fry.

Broccoli & Black Bean Sauce

Broccoli works well with the black bean sauce in this recipe, while the almonds add extra crunch and flavor.

NUTRITIONAL INFORMATION

Calories 139   Sugars 3g
Protein ....7g   Fat 10g
Carbohydrate ....5g   Saturates 1g

5 MINS   15 MINS

SERVES 4

INGREDIENTS

1 lb broccoli flowerets

2 tbsp sunflower oil

1 onion, sliced

2 cloves garlic, thinly sliced

¼ cup slivered almonds

1 head Chinese cabbage, shredded

4 tbsp black bean sauce

1 Bring a large saucepan of water to a boil.

2 Add the broccoli flowerets to the pan and cook for 1 minute. Drain the broccoli thoroughly.

3 Meanwhile, heat the sunflower oil in a large preheated wok.

4 Add the onion and garlic slices to the wok and stir-fry until just beginning to brown.

5 Add the drained broccoli flowerets and the slivered almonds to the mixture in the wok and stir-fry for a further 2–3 minutes.

6 Add the shredded Chinese cabbage to the wok and stir-fry for 2 minutes more, stirring the leaves briskly around the wok.

7 Stir the black bean sauce into the vegetables in the wok, tossing to coat the vegetables thoroughly in the sauce and cook until the juices are just beginning to bubble.

8 Transfer the vegetables to warm serving bowls and serve immediately.

VARIATION

Use unsalted cashews instead of the almonds, if preferred.

Vegetable & Nut Stir-fry

A colorful selection of vegetables are stir-fried in a creamy peanut sauce and sprinkled with nuts to serve.

NUTRITIONAL INFORMATION

Calories ....325 Sugars 6g
Protein ....11g Fat 21g
Carbohydrate ...26g Saturates 4g

10 MINS   15 MINS

SERVES 4

INGREDIENTS

3 tbsp crunchy peanut butter

⅔ cup water

1 tbsp soy sauce

1 tsp sugar

1 carrot

½ red onion

4 baby zucchini

1 red bell pepper

9 oz egg thread noodles

¼ cup peanuts, chopped roughly

2 tbsp vegetable oil

1 tsp sesame oil

1 small green chili, seeded and sliced thinly

1 garlic clove, sliced thinly

8 oz can water chestnuts, drained and sliced

3 cups bean sprouts

salt

1 Gradually blend the peanut butter with the water in a small bowl. Stir in the soy sauce and sugar. Set aside.

2 Cut the carrot into thin sticks and slice the red onion. Slice the zucchini on the diagonal and cut the bell pepper into chunks.

3 Bring a large pan of water to a boil and add the egg noodles. Remove from the heat immediately and leave to stand for 4 minutes, stirring occasionally to separate the noodles.

4 Heat a wok or large skillet, add the peanuts, and dry-fry until they are beginning to brown. Remove with a perforated spoon and set aside until required.

5 Add the oils to the pan and heat. Add the carrot, onion, zucchini, bell pepper, chili, and garlic, and stir-fry for 2–3 minutes. Add the water chestnuts, bean sprouts, and peanut sauce. Bring to a boil and heat thoroughly. Season with salt to taste.

6 Drain the noodles and serve with the vegetable and nut stir-fry. Sprinkle with the reserved peanuts.

Tofu & Vegetable Stir-fry

Tofu absorbs all of the flavors in a dish, making it ideal for this recipe.

NUTRITIONAL INFORMATION

Calories 167	Sugars 8g	
Protein 12g	Fat 9g	
Carbohydrate ...10g	Saturates 1g	

 30 MINS   10 MINS

SERVES 4

I N G R E D I E N T S

1 tbsp grated fresh ginger

1 tsp ground ginger

1 tbsp tomato paste

2 tbsp sunflower oil

1 clove garlic, crushed

2 tbsp soy sauce

12 oz soya cubes or tofu cubes

8 oz carrots, sliced

3½ oz green beans, sliced

4 stalks celery, sliced

1 red bell pepper, seeded and
    sliced

boiled rice, to serve

COOK'S TIP

Fresh ginger will keep for
several weeks in a cool, dry
place. Fresh ginger can also be
kept frozen—break off
lumps as needed.

1 Place the grated fresh ginger, ground
   ginger, tomato paste, 1 tablespoon
of the sunflower oil, garlic, soy sauce, and
soya cubes in a large bowl. Mix well
to combine, stirring carefully so that
you don't break up the soya cubes.
Cover and leave to marinate for 20
minutes.

2 Heat the remaining sunflower oil in a
   large preheated wok.

3 Add the marinated mixture
   to the wok and stir-fry for about
2 minutes.

4 Add the carrots, green beans, celery,
   and red bell pepper to the wok and
stir-fry for 5 minutes more.

5 Transfer the stir-fry to warm serving
   dishes and serve immediately with
freshly cooked boiled rice.

Creamy Green Vegetables

This dish is very quick to make. A dash of cream is added to the sauce, but this may be omitted, if preferred.

NUTRITIONAL INFORMATION

Calories 111	Sugars 2g	
Protein 5g	Fat 8g	
Carbohydrate 7g	Saturates 2g	

5 MINS   20 MINS

SERVES 4

I N G R E D I E N T S

1 lb Chinese cabbage, shredded

2 tbsp peanut oil

2 leeks, shredded

4 garlic cloves, crushed

1¼ cups vegetable stock

1 tbsp light soy sauce

2 tsp cornstarch

4 tsp water

2 tbsp light cream or unsweetened plain yogurt

1 tbsp chopped cilantro

1 Blanch the Chinese cabbage in boiling water for 30 seconds. Drain, rinse under cold running water, then drain thoroughly again.

2 Heat the oil in a preheated wok and add the Chinese cabbage, leeks, and garlic. Stir-fry for 2–3 minutes.

3 Add the stock and soy sauce to the wok, reduce the heat to low, cover and simmer for 10 minutes.

4 Remove the vegetables from the wok with a slotted spoon and set aside. Bring the stock to a boil and boil vigorously until reduced by about half.

5 Blend the cornstarch with the water and stir into the wok. Bring to a boil, and cook, stirring constantly, until thickened and clear.

6 Reduce the heat and stir in the vegetables and cream or yogurt. Cook over a low heat for 1 minute.

7 Transfer to a serving dish, sprinkle over the chopped cilantro and serve.

COOK'S TIP

Do not boil the sauce once the cream or yogurt has been added because it will separate.

Crispy Cabbage & Almonds

This dish is better known as crispy seaweed. It does not actually contain seaweed, but consists of collard greens or bok choy.

NUTRITIONAL INFORMATION

Calories 431   Sugars 17g
Protein . . . . .9g   Fat 37g
Carbohydrate . . .17g   Saturates 4g

10 MINS   10 MINS

SERVES 4

INGREDIENTS

2 lb 12 oz bok choy or collard greens

3 cups vegetable oil

¾ cup blanched almonds

1 tsp salt

1 tbsp light brown sugar

pinch of ground cinnamon

1 Separate the leaves from the bok choy or collard greens and rinse them well. Drain thoroughly and pat dry with absorbent paper towels.

2 Shred the collard greens into thin strips, using a sharp knife.

3 Heat the vegetable oil in a preheated wok or large, heavy-bottomed skillet until the oil is almost smoking.

4 Reduce the heat and add the bok choy or collard greens. Cook for 2–3 minutes, or until the greens begin to float in the oil and are crisp.

5 Remove the greens from the oil with a slotted spoon and leave to drain thoroughly on absorbent paper towels.

6 Add the blanched almonds to the oil in the wok and cook for 30 seconds. Remove the almonds from the oil with a slotted spoon and drain thoroughly on absorbent paper towels.

7 Mix together the salt, light brown sugar, and ground cinnamon and sprinkle onto the greens.

8 Toss the almonds into the greens.

9 Transfer the greens and almonds to a warm serving dish and serve immediately.

COOK'S TIP

Make sure that the greens are completely dry before adding them to the oil, otherwise it will spit. The greens will not become crisp if they are wet when placed in the oil.

Chili Eggplant

Strips of eggplant are deep-fried, then served in a fragrant chili sauce with carrot sticks and green onions.

NUTRITIONAL INFORMATION

Calories	119	Sugars	.........2g
Protein	.........1g	Fat	...........11g
Carbohydrate	....3g	Saturates	.......1g

5 MINS   15 MINS

SERVES 4

I N G R E D I E N T S

1 large eggplant

vegetable oil, for deep-frying

2 carrots

4 green onions

2 large garlic cloves

1 tbsp vegetable oil

2 tsp chili sauce

1 tbsp soy sauce

1 tbsp dry sherry

red chili flower, to garnish (see page 269)

1 Slice the eggplant and then cut into strips about the size of french fries.

2 Heat enough oil in a large heavy-bottomed saucepan to deep-fry the eggplant in batches until just browned. Remove the strips with a perforated spoon and drain on paper towels.

3 Using a sharp knife, cut the carrots into thin sticks. Trim and slice the green onions diagonally. Slice the garlic cloves.

4 Heat 1 tablespoon of oil in a wok or large skillet. Add the carrots and stir-fry for 1 minute.

5 Add the chopped green onions and garlic to the wok and stir-fry for another minute.

6 Stir in the chili sauce, soy sauce, and sherry, then stir in the drained eggplant. Mix well so the vegetables are heated through.

7 Transfer to a serving dish, garnish with a red chili flower and serve.

COOK'S TIP

For a milder dish, substitute hoisin sauce for the chili sauce. This can be bought in bottles from supermarkets.

Honey-fried Spinach

This stir-fry is the perfect accompaniment to tofu dishes, and it is so quick and simple to make.

NUTRITIONAL INFORMATION

Calories	146	Sugars	.........9g
Protein	.........4g	Fat	..........9g
Carbohydrate	...10g	Saturates	.......2g

 5 MINS   15 MINS

SERVES 4

INGREDIENTS

4 green onions

3 tbsp peanut oil

12 oz shiitake mushrooms, sliced

2 cloves garlic, crushed

12 oz baby spinach

2 tbsp dry sherry

2 tbsp honey

1 Using a sharp knife, slice the green onions.

2 Heat the peanut oil in a large preheated wok or heavy-bottomed skillet.

3 Add the shiitake mushrooms to the wok and stir-fry for about 5 minutes, or until the mushrooms have softened.

COOK'S TIP

Single-flower honey has a better, more individual flavor than blended honey. Acacia honey is typically Chinese, but you could also try clover, lemon blossom, lime flower, or orange blossom.

4 Stir the crushed garlic into the wok or skillet.

5 Add the baby spinach to the wok or pan and stir-fry for another 2–3 minutes, or until the spinach leaves have just wilted.

6 Mix together the dry sherry and honey in a small bowl until well combined. Drizzle the sherry and honey mixture over the spinach and heat through, stirring to coat the spinach leaves thoroughly in the mixture.

7 Transfer the stir-fry to warm serving dishes, scatter with the chopped green onions, and serve immediately.

Chinese Fried Vegetables

The Chinese are known for their colorful, crisp vegetables, quickly stir-fried. In this recipe, they are tossed in a tasty soy and hoisin sauce.

NUTRITIONAL INFORMATION

Calories 137	Sugars 7g
Protein 8g	Fat 7g
Carbohydrate ...10g	Saturates 11g

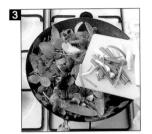

 5 MINS   ⏱ 10 MINS

SERVES 4

INGREDIENTS

2 tbsp peanut oil

12 oz broccoli flowerets

1 tbsp chopped fresh ginger

2 onions, cut into 8

3 celery stalks, sliced

6 oz baby spinach

4½ oz snow peas

6 green onions, quartered

2 garlic cloves, crushed

2 tbsp light soy sauce

2 tsp sugar

2 tbsp dry sherry

1 tbsp hoisin sauce

⅔ cup vegetable stock

1 Heat the peanut oil in a preheated wok until it is almost smoking.

2 Add the broccoli flowerets, chopped ginger, onions, and celery to the wok and stir-fry for 1 minute.

3 Add the spinach, snow peas, green onions, and garlic and stir-fry for 3–4 minutes.

4 Mix together the soy sauce, sugar, sherry, hoisin sauce, and vegetable stock.

5 Pour the stock mixture into the wok, mixing well to coat the vegetables.

6 Cover the wok and cook over a medium heat for 2–3 minutes, or until the vegetables are cooked through, but still crisp.

7 Transfer the Chinese fried vegetables to a warm serving dish and serve immediately.

COOK'S TIP

You could use this mixture to fill Chinese pancakes. They are available from oriental food stores and can be reheated in a steamer in 2–3 minutes.

Chestnut & Vegetable Stir-Fry

In this colorful stir-fry, vegetables are cooked in a wonderfully aromatic sauce which combines peanuts, chili, coconut, cilantro, and turmeric.

NUTRITIONAL INFORMATION

Calories	446	Sugars	........17g
Protein	........14g	Fat	..........25g
Carbohydrate	...42g	Saturates	.......5g

10 MINS   15 MINS

SERVES 4

I N G R E D I E N T S

1 cup unsalted roasted peanuts

2 tsp hot chili sauce

¾ cup coconut milk

2 tbsp soy sauce

1 tbsp ground coriander

pinch of ground turmeric

1 tbsp dark brown sugar

3 tbsp sesame oil

3-4 shallots, finely sliced

1 garlic clove, finely sliced

1-2 red chilies, seeded and finely chopped

1 large carrot, cut into fine strips

1 yellow and 1 red bell pepper, sliced

1 zucchini, cut into fine strips

4½ oz sugar snap peas, trimmed

3 inch piece cucumber, cut into strips

9 oz oyster mushrooms,

9 oz canned chestnuts, drained

2 tsp grated fresh ginger

finely grated zest and juice of 1 lime

1 tbsp chopped fresh cilantro

salt and pepper

slices of lime, to garnish

1 To make the peanut sauce, grind the peanuts in a blender, or chop very finely. Put into a small pan with the hot chili sauce, coconut milk, soy sauce, ground coriander, ground turmeric, and dark brown sugar. Heat gently and simmer for 3–4 minutes. Keep warm and set aside until required.

2 Heat the sesame oil in a wok or large skillet. Add the shallots, garlic, and chilies and stir-fry for 2 minutes.

3 Add the carrot, bell peppers, zucchini, and sugar snap peas to the wok or skillet and stir-fry for 2 more minutes.

4 Add the cucumber, mushrooms, chestnuts, ginger, lime zest and juice, and fresh cilantro to the wok or pan and stir-fry briskly for about 5 minutes, or until the vegetables are crisp, yet crunchy.

5 Season to taste with salt and pepper.

6 Divide the stir-fry between four warmed serving plates, and garnish with slices of lime. Transfer the peanut sauce to a serving dish and serve with the vegetables.

Garlic Spinach

This has to be one of the simplest recipes, yet it is so tasty. Spinach is fried with garlic and lemon grass and tossed in soy sauce and sugar.

NUTRITIONAL INFORMATION

Calories	118	Sugars	6g
Protein	7g	Fat	7g
Carbohydrate	7g	Saturates	1g

 5 MINS   10 MINS

SERVES 4

I N G R E D I E N T S

2 garlic cloves

1 tsp lemon grass

2 lb fresh spinach

2 tbsp peanut oil

salt

1 tbsp dark soy sauce

2 tsp brown sugar

1 Peel the garlic cloves and crush them in a pestle and mortar. Set aside until required.

2 Using a sharp knife, finely chop the lemon grass. Set aside until required.

3 Carefully remove the stems from the spinach. Rinse the spinach leaves and drain them thoroughly, patting them dry with absorbent paper towels.

4 Heat the peanut oil in a preheated wok or large skillet until it is almost smoking.

5 Reduce the heat slightly, add the garlic and lemon grass and stir-fry for 30 seconds.

6 Add the spinach leaves and a pinch of salt to the wok or skillet and stir-fry

for 2–3 minutes, or until the spinach leaves have just wilted.

7 Stir the dark soy sauce and brown sugar into the mixture in the wok or skillet and cook for 3–4 minutes more.

8 Transfer the garlic spinach to a warm serving dish and serve as an accompaniment to a main dish.

COOK'S TIP

Lemon grass is available fresh, dried and canned or bottled. Dried lemon grass must be soaked for 2 hours before using. The stems are hard and are usually used whole and removed from the dish before serving. The roots can be crushed or finely chopped.

Eggplant in Bean Sauce

This dish would go well with rice and another vegetable dish, such as stir-fried baby corn-on-the-cob and green beans.

NUTRITIONAL INFORMATION

Calories 115	Sugars 2g	
Protein 3g	Fat 9g	
Carbohydrate 6g	Saturates 1g	

12¾ HOURS   1¼ HOURS

SERVES 4

INGREDIENTS

generous ⅓ cup dried black beans

scant 2 cups vegetable stock

1 tbsp malt vinegar

1 tbsp dry sherry

1 tbsp soy sauce

1 tbsp sugar

1½ tsp cornstarch

1 red chili, seeded and chopped

½ inch piece fresh ginger, chopped

2 eggplant

2 tsp salt

3 tbsp vegetable oil

2 garlic cloves, sliced

4 green onions, cut diagonally

shredded radishes, to garnish

1 Soak the beans overnight in plenty of cold water. Drain and place in a saucepan. Cover with cold water, bring to a boil, and boil rapidly, uncovered, for 10 minutes. Drain. Return the beans to the saucepan with the vegetable stock and bring to a boil.

2 Blend together the vinegar, sherry, soy sauce, sugar, cornstarch, chili, and ginger in a small bowl. Add to the saucepan, cover and simmer for 40 minutes, or until the beans are tender and the sauce has thickened. Stir occasionally.

3 Cut the eggplant into chunks and place in a colander. Sprinkle over the salt and leave to drain for 30 minutes. Rinse well to remove the salt and dry on paper towels. This process removes the bitter juices which would otherwise spoil the flavor of the dish.

4 Heat the vegetable oil in a wok or large skillet. Add the eggplant chunks and garlic. Stir-fry for 3–4 minutes until the eggplant has started to brown.

5 Add the sauce to the eggplant with the green onions. Heat thoroughly, stirring to coat the eggplant, garnish with radish shreds, and serve.

Vegetable with Hoisin

This vegetable stir-fry has rice added to it and it can be served as a meal in itself.

NUTRITIONAL INFORMATION

Calories 120	Sugars 6g	
Protein 4g	Fat 6g	
Carbohydrate ...12g	Saturates 1g	

20 MINS   10 MINS

SERVES 4

INGREDIENTS

1 red onion

3½ oz carrots

1 yellow bell pepper

2 tbsp sunflower oil

1 cup cooked brown rice

6 oz snow peas

1½ cups bean sprouts

4 tbsp hoisin sauce

1 tbsp snipped fresh chives

1 Using a sharp knife, thinly slice the red onion.

2 Thinly slice the carrots.

3 Seed and dice the yellow bell pepper.

4 Heat the sunflower oil in a large preheated wok or heavy-bottomed skillet.

5 Add the red onion slices, carrots, and yellow bell pepper to the wok and stir-fry for about 3 minutes.

6 Add the cooked brown rice, snow peas, and bean sprouts to the mixture in the wok and stir-fry for 2 minutes

more. Stir briskly to ensure that the ingredients are well mixed and the rice grains are separated.

7 Stir the hoisin sauce into the vegetables and mix until well combined and completely heated through.

8 Transfer the vegetable stir-fry to warm serving dishes and scatter with the snipped fresh chives. Serve immediately.

COOK'S TIP
Hoisin sauce is a dark brown, reddish sauce made from soy beans, garlic, chili, and various other spices, and is commonly used in Chinese cookery. It may also be used as a dipping sauce.

Sweet & Sour Vegetables

Select vegetables from the suggested list, including green onions and garlic. For a hotter, spicier sauce, add chili sauce.

NUTRITIONAL INFORMATION

Calories 160   Sugars 16g
Protein . . . . .6g   Fat 7g
Carbohydrate . . .18g   Saturates 1g

5 MINS   10 MINS

SERVES 4

I N G R E D I E N T S

5-6 vegetables from the following:

1 bell pepper, red, green, or yellow, cored, seeded, and sliced

4½ oz green beans, cut into 2-3 pieces

4½ oz snow peas, cut into 2-3 pieces

9 oz broccoli or cauliflower, divided into tiny flowerets

9 oz zucchini, cut into thin 2 inch lengths

6 oz carrots, cut into julienne strips

4½ oz baby corn-on-the-cob, sliced thinly

2 leeks, sliced thinly and cut into thin strips

4½ oz small mushrooms, thinly sliced

1 x 7 oz can water chestnuts or bamboo shoots, drained and sliced

1 x 15 oz can bean sprouts

4 green onions trimmed and thinly sliced

1 garlic clove, crushed

2 tbsp sunflower oil

S W E E T   &   S O U R   S A U C E

2 tbsp wine vinegar

2 tbsp honey

1 tbsp tomato paste

2 tbsp soy sauce

2 tbsp sherry

1-2 tsp sweet chili sauce (optional)

2 tsp cornstarch

1 Cut the selected vegetables into uniform lengths. Mix the sauce ingredients in a bowl. Heat the oil in the wok, add the green onions and garlic, and stir-fry for 1 minute.

2 Add the prepared vegetables—the harder and firmer ones first—and stir-fry for 2 minutes. Then add the softer ones such as mushrooms and snow peas and stir-fry for 2 minutes.

3 Add the sweet and sour mixture to the wok and bring to a boil quickly, tossing all the vegetables until they are thoroughly coated and the sauce has thickened. Serve hot.

Butternut Squash Stir-fry

Butternut squash is as its name suggests, deliciously buttery and nutty in flavor. If the squash is not in season, use sweet potatoes instead.

NUTRITIONAL INFORMATION

Calories	.301	Sugars	.4g
Protein	.9g	Fat	.22g
Carbohydrate	.19g	Saturates	.4g

 5 MINS   25 MINS

SERVES 4

INGREDIENTS

2 lb 4 oz butternut squash, peeled

3 tbsp peanut oil

1 onion, sliced

2 cloves garlic, crushed

1 tsp coriander seeds

1 tsp cumin seeds

2 tbsp chopped cilantro

⅔ cup coconut milk

½ cup water

⅓ cup salted cashews

TO GARNISH

freshly grated lime zest

fresh cilantro

lime wedges

1 Using a sharp knife, slice the butternut squash into small, bite-sized cubes.

2 Heat the peanut oil in a large preheated wok.

3 Add the butternut squash, onion, and garlic to the wok and stir-fry for 5 minutes.

4 Stir in the coriander seeds, cumin seeds, and fresh cilantro and stir-fry for 1 minute.

5 Add the coconut milk and water to the wok and bring to a boil. Cover the wok and leave to simmer for 10–15 minutes, or until the squash is tender.

6 Add the cashews and stir to combine.

7 Transfer to warm serving dishes and garnish with freshly grated lime zest, fresh cilantro and lime wedges. Serve hot.

COOK'S TIP

If you do not have coconut milk, grate some creamed coconut into the dish with the water in step 5.

Green Stir-fry

The basis of this recipe is bok choy, also known as Chinese greens. If unavailable, use chard or savoy cabbage instead.

NUTRITIONAL INFORMATION

Calories 107   Sugars 6g
Protein ....4g   Fat 8g
Carbohydrate ....6g   Saturates 1g

5 MINS   10 MINS

SERVES 4

INGREDIENTS

2 tbsp peanut oil

2 garlic cloves, crushed

½ tsp ground star anise

1 tsp salt

12 oz bok choy, shredded

8 oz baby spinach

1 oz snow peas

1 celery stalk, sliced

1 green bell pepper, seeded and sliced

¼ cup vegetable stock

1 tsp sesame oil

1 Heat the peanut oil in a preheated wok or large skillet, swirling the oil around the base of the wok until it is really hot.

2 Add the crushed garlic to the wok or skillet and stir-fry for about 30 seconds.

3 Stir in the ground star anise, salt, shredded bok choy, spinach, snow peas, celery, and green bell pepper and stir-fry for 3–4 minutes.

4 Add the vegetable stock, cover the wok, and cook for 3–4 minutes.

5 Remove the lid from the wok and stir in the sesame oil. Mix thoroughly to combine all the ingredients.

6 Transfer the green vegetable stir-fry to a warm serving dish and serve.

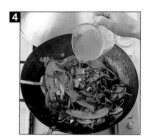

COOK'S TIP

Star anise is an important ingredient in Chinese cuisine. The attractive star-shaped pods are often used whole to add a decorative garnish to dishes. The flavor is similar to liquorice, but with spicy undertones and is quite strong.

Vegetable Stir-Fry

A range of delicious flavors are captured in this simple recipe which is ideal if you are in a hurry.

NUTRITIONAL INFORMATION

Calories 138	Sugars 5g
Protein 3g	Fat 12g
Carbohydrate 5g	Saturates 2g

5 MINS   25 MINS

SERVES 4

I N G R E D I E N T S

3 tbsp vegetable oil

8 baby onions, halved

1 eggplant, cubed

8 oz zucchini, sliced

8 oz open-cap mushrooms, halved

2 cloves garlic, crushed

14 oz can chopped tomatoes

2 tbsp sundried tomato paste

2 tbsp soy sauce

1 tsp sesame oil

1 tbsp Chinese rice wine or dry sherry

freshly ground black pepper

fresh basil leaves, to garnish

1 Heat the vegetable oil in a large preheated wok or skillet until it is almost smoking.

2 Add the baby onions and eggplant to the wok or skillet and stir-fry for 5 minutes, or until the vegetables are golden and just beginning to soften.

3 Add the sliced zucchini, mushrooms, garlic, chopped tomatoes, and tomato paste to the wok and stir-fry for about 5 minutes. Reduce the heat and leave to simmer for 10 minutes, or until the vegetables are tender.

4 Add the soy sauce, sesame oil, and rice wine or sherry to the wok, bring back to a boil and cook for 1 minute.

5 Season the vegetable stir-fry with freshly ground black pepper and scatter with fresh basil leaves. Serve immediately.

COOK'S TIP

Basil has a very strong flavor which is perfect with vegetables and Chinese flavorings. Instead of using basil simply as a garnish in this dish, try adding a handful of fresh basil leaves to the stir-fry in step 4.

Stir-fried Spinach

This is an easy recipe to make as a quick accompaniment to a main course. The water chestnuts give a delicious crunch to the greens.

NUTRITIONAL INFORMATION

Calories	.85	Sugars	.2g
Protein	.4g	Fat	.4g
Carbohydrate	.9g	Saturates	.1g

5 MINS   10 MINS

SERVES 4

INGREDIENTS

1 tbsp sunflower oil

1 garlic clove, halved

2 green onions, sliced finely

8 oz can water chestnuts, drained and sliced finely (optional)

1 lb 2 oz spinach, any tough stalks removed

1 tsp sherry vinegar

1 tsp light soy sauce

pepper

1 Heat the sunflower oil in a wok or large, heavy skillet over a high heat, swirling the oil around the base of the wok until it is really hot.

2 Add the halved garlic clove and cook, stirring, for 1 minute. If the garlic should brown, remove it immediately.

3 Add the finely sliced green onions and water chestnuts, if using, and stir for 2–3 minutes.

4 Add the spinach leaves and stir into the wok.

5 Add the sherry vinegar, soy sauce, and a sprinkling of pepper. Cook, stirring, until the spinach is tender. Remove the garlic.

6 Using a slotted spoon, drain off the excess liquid from the wok and serve the stir-fried greens immediately.

COOK'S TIP

Several types of oriental greens (for example, choy sam and bok choy) are widely available and any of these can be successfully substituted for the spinach.

Stir-fried Mixed Vegetables

The Chinese carefully select vegetables to achieve a harmonious balance of contrasting colors and textures.

NUTRITIONAL INFORMATION

Calories	534	Sugars	.........8g
Protein	........14g	Fat	.........45g
Carbohydrate	...19g	Saturates	.......5g

5 MINS   5 MINS

SERVES 4

INGREDIENTS

2 oz snow peas

1 small carrot

4½ oz Chinese cabbage

2 oz black or white mushrooms

2 oz canned bamboo shoots, rinsed and drained

3-4 tbsp vegetable oil

4½ oz fresh bean sprouts

1 tsp salt

1 tsp sugar

1 tbsp oyster sauce or light soy sauce

a few drops sesame oil (optional)

dip sauce, to serve (optional)

1 Prepare the vegetables: top and tail the snow peas, and cut the carrot, Chinese cabbage, mushrooms, and bamboo shoots into roughly the same shape and size as the snow peas.

2 Heat the vegetable oil in a preheated wok or large skillet and add the carrot. Stir-fry for a few seconds, then add the snow peas and Chinese cabbage and stir-fry for about 1 minute.

3 Add the bean sprouts, mushrooms and bamboo shoots to the wok or skillet and continue to stir-fry for another minute.

  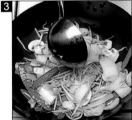

4 Add the salt and sugar, continue stirring for another minute, then add the oyster sauce or light soy sauce, blending well.

5 Sprinkle the vegetables with sesame oil (if using) and serve hot or cold, with a dip sauce, if liked.

COOK'S TIP

Oyster sauce is used in many Cantonese dishes. It is worth buying an expensive brand as it will be noticeably better. Good oyster sauce has a rich, almost beefy flavor. Once opened, a bottle of oyster sauce can be kept for months in the refrigerator.

Deep-fried Vegetables

Choose a selection of your favorite seasonal vegetables, coat them in a light batter, and deep-fry them until crispy to make this delightful dish.

NUTRITIONAL INFORMATION

Calories 333	Sugars 9g	
Protein 7g	Fat 16g	
Carbohydrate ...38g	Saturates 2g	

40 MINS   15 MINS

SERVES 4

INGREDIENTS

1 lb 2 oz selection of fresh vegetables, such as red and green bell peppers, zucchini, carrots, green onions, cauliflower, broccoli, and mushrooms

oil, for deep-frying

BATTER

1 cup all-purpose flour

½ tsp salt

1 tsp sugar

1 tsp baking powder

3 tbsp vegetable oil

scant 1 cup tepid water

SAUCE

1 tbsp light brown sugar

2 tbsp soy sauce

4 tbsp cider vinegar

4 tbsp medium sherry

1 tbsp cornstarch

1 tsp finely grated fresh ginger

TO GARNISH

green onion brushes
  (see page 305)

chopped green onions

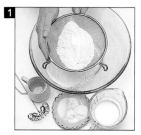

1 To make the batter, sift the flour, salt, sugar, and baking powder into a large bowl. Add the oil and most of the water. Whisk together to make a smooth batter, adding extra water to give it the consistency of light cream. Chill for 20–30 minutes.

2 To make the sauce, put all the ingredients into a small saucepan. Heat, stirring, until thickened and smooth.

3 Cut all the vegetables into even, bite-sized pieces. Heat the oil in a wok or deep fat fryer. Dip the vegetables into the batter and fry them in the hot oil, a few at a time, until golden brown and crispy, about 2 minutes. Drain on paper towels.

4 Garnish and serve the vegetables on a warmed platter accompanied by the dipping sauce.

Spiced Eggplant

This is a spicy and sweet dish, flavored with mango chutney and heated up with chilies for a really wonderful combination of flavors.

NUTRITIONAL INFORMATION

Calories	208	Sugars	........17g
Protein	.........1g	Fat	..........15g
Carbohydrate	...17g	Saturates	.......2g

 5 MINS   25 MINS

SERVES 4

INGREDIENTS

3 tbsp peanut oil

2 onions, sliced

2 cloves garlic, chopped

2 eggplants, diced

2 red chilies, seeded and very finely chopped

2 tbsp brown sugar

6 green onions, sliced

3 tbsp mango chutney

oil, for deep-frying

2 cloves garlic, sliced, to garnish

1 Heat the peanut oil in a large preheated wok or heavy-bottomed skillet, swirling the oil around the base of the wok until it is really hot.

2 Add the onions and chopped garlic to the wok, stirring well.

3 Add the diced eggplant and chilies to the wok and stir-fry for 5 minutes.

4 Add the brown sugar, green onions, and mango chutney to the wok, stirring well.

5 Reduce the heat, cover and leave to simmer, stirring from time to time, for 15 minutes or until the eggplant is tender.

6 Transfer the stir-fry to serving bowls and keep warm.

7 Heat the oil for deep-frying in the wok and quickly stir-fry the slices of garlic, until they brown slightly. Garnish the stir-fry with the deep-fried garlic and serve immediately.

COOK'S TIP

The "hotness" of chilies varies enormously so always use with caution, but as a general guide the smaller they are the hotter they will be. The seeds are the hottest part and so are usually discarded.

Tofu

A popular ingredient in Chinese cooking, tofu, also known as bean curd, is made from puréed and pressed yellow soya beans. Although it has a bland flavor, it blends well with other ingredients and absorbs the flavors of spices and sauces. Tofu is extremely versatile—it can be stir-fried, deep-fried, or added to soups. It is also a healthy

substitute for meat and fish, being high in protein and low in fat. Tofu is sold in cakes and in dried form, and it is also available marinated or smoked. The recipes in this chapter combine tofu with a variety of flavors and ingredients to create a selection of tasty snacks together with more filling main dishes. Try, for example, Fried Tofu with Peanut Sauce, Braised Tofu Homestyle, and Chinese Vegetable Casserole.

Fried Tofu with Peanut Sauce

This is a very sociable dish if put in the center of the table where people can help themselves with cocktail sticks.

NUTRITIONAL INFORMATION

Calories ....338 Sugars 9g
Protein ....16g Fat 22g
Carbohydrate ...21g Saturates 4g

5 MINS   20 MINS

SERVES 4

INGREDIENTS

1 lb 2 oz marinated or plain tofu

2 tbsp rice vinegar

2 tbsp sugar

1 tsp salt

3 tbsp smooth peanut butter

½ tsp chili flakes

3 tbsp barbecue sauce

4 cups sunflower oil

2 tbsp sesame oil

BATTER

4 tbsp all-purpose flour

2 eggs, beaten

4 tbsp milk

½ tsp baking powder

½ tsp chili powder

1 Cut the tofu into 1 inch triangles. Set aside until required.

2 Combine the rice vinegar, sugar, and salt in a saucepan. Bring to a boil and then simmer for 2 minutes.

3 Remove the sauce from the heat and add the smooth peanut butter, chili flakes, and barbecue sauce, stirring well until thoroughly blended.

4 To make the batter, sift the all-purpose flour into a bowl, make a well in the center and add the eggs. Draw in the flour, adding the milk slowly. Stir in the baking powder and chili powder.

5 Heat both the sunflower oil and sesame oil in a deep-fryer or large saucepan until a light haze appears on top.

6 Dip the tofu triangles into the batter and deep-fry until golden brown. You may need to do this in batches. Drain on absorbent paper towels.

7 Transfer the tofu triangles to a serving dish and serve with the peanut sauce.

COOK'S TIP

Tofu is made from puréed soya beans. It is white, with a soft cheese-like texture, and is sold in blocks, either fresh or vacuum-packed. Although it has a bland flavor, it blends well with other ingredients, and absorbs the flavors of spices and sauces.

Tofu Sandwiches

Slices of tofu are sandwiched together with a cucumber and cream cheese filling and coated in batter.

NUTRITIONAL INFORMATION

Calories 398   Sugars 8g
Protein . . . . .13g   Fat 24g
Carbohydrate . . .35g   Saturates 7g

🍲 40 MINS   🕐 15 MINS

MAKES 28

INGREDIENTS

4 Chinese dried mushrooms (if unavailable, use thinly sliced open-cap mushrooms)

9½ oz tofu

½ cucumber, grated

½ inch piece fresh ginger, grated

¼ cup cream cheese

salt and pepper

BATTER

1 cup all-purpose flour

1 egg, beaten

½ cup water

½ tsp salt

2 tbsp sesame seeds

vegetable oil for deep-frying

SAUCE

⅔ cup unsweetened plain yogurt

2 tsp honey

2 tbsp chopped fresh mint

1 Place the dried mushrooms in a small bowl and cover with warm water. Leave to soak for 20–25 minutes.

2 Drain the mushrooms, squeezing out the excess water. Remove the tough centers and chop the mushrooms.

3 Drain the tofu and slice thinly. Then cut each slice to make 1 inch squares.

4 Squeeze the excess liquid from the cucumber and mix the cucumber with the mushrooms, grated ginger, and cream cheese. Season well with salt and pepper. Use as a filling to sandwich slices of tofu together to make about 28 sandwiches.

5 To make the batter, sift the flour into a bowl. Beat in the egg, water and salt to make a thick batter. Stir in the sesame seeds. Heat the oil in a wok. Coat the sandwiches in the batter and deep-fry in batches until golden. Remove and drain on paper towels.

6 To make the dipping sauce, combine the yogurt, honey and mint. Serve with the tofu sandwiches.

Tofu with Hot & Sweet Sauce

Golden pieces of tofu are served in a hot and creamy peanut and chili sauce for a classic vegetarian first course.

NUTRITIONAL INFORMATION

Calories 367	Sugars 5g
Protein 18g	Fat 30g
Carbohydrate 8g	Saturates 5g

5 MINS   15 MINS

SERVES 4

INGREDIENTS

1 lb tofu, cubed

oil, for frying

SAUCE

6 tbsp crunchy peanut butter

1 tbsp sweet chili sauce

⅔ cup coconut milk

1 tbsp tomato paste

¼ cup chopped salted peanuts

1 Pat away any moisture from the tofu using absorbent paper towels.

2 Heat the oil in a large wok or skillet until very hot.

3 Add the tofu to the wok and cook, in batches, for about 5 minutes, or until golden and crispy.

4 Remove the tofu with a slotted spoon, transfer to absorbent paper towels, and leave to drain.

5 To make the peanut and chili sauce, mix together the crunchy peanut butter, sweet chili sauce, coconut milk, tomato paste and chopped salted peanuts in a bowl. Add a little boiling water if necessary to achieve a smooth consistency. Stir well until the ingredients are thoroughly blended.

6 Transfer the tofu to serving plates and pour the sauce over the top. Alternatively, pour the sauce into a serving dish and serve separately.

COOK'S TIP

Make sure that all of the moisture has been absorbed from the tofu before frying, otherwise it will not become crisp.

Cook the peanut and chili sauce in a saucepan over a gentle heat before serving, if you prefer.

Ma-po Tofu

Ma-Po was the wife of a Szechuan chef who created this popular dish in the middle of the 19th century.

NUTRITIONAL INFORMATION

Calories 235   Sugars 1g
Protein . . . . .16g   Fat 18g
Carbohydrate . . . .3g   Saturates 4g

 3½ HOURS   15 MINS

SERVES 4

I N G R E D I E N T S

3 cakes tofu

3 tbsp vegetable oil

4½ oz coarse ground beef

½ tsp finely chopped garlic

1 leek, cut into short sections

½ tsp salt

1 tbsp black bean sauce

1 tbsp light soy sauce

1 tsp chili bean sauce

3-4 tbsp Chinese Stock (see page 30) or
    water

2 tsp cornstarch paste (see page 31)

a few drops sesame oil

black pepper

finely chopped green onions,
    to garnish

1 Cut the tofu into ½ inch cubes, handling it carefully.

2 Bring some water to a boil in a small pan or a wok, add the tofu and blanch for 2-3 minutes to harden. Remove and drain well.

3 Heat the oil in a preheated wok. Add the ground beef and garlic and stir-fry for about 1 minute, or until the color of the beef changes. Add the leek, salt, and sauces and blend well.

4 Add the stock or water followed by the tofu. Bring to a boil and braise gently for 2-3 minutes.

5 Add the cornstarch paste, and stir until the sauce has thickened. Sprinkle with sesame oil and black pepper, garnish, and serve hot.

COOK'S TIP

Tofu has been an important element in Chinese cooking for more than 1000 years. It is made of yellow soya beans, which are soaked, ground and mixed with water. Tofu is highly nutritious, being rich in protein and low in fat.

Braised Vegetables with Tofu

Also known as Buddha's Delight, the original recipe calls for 18 different vegetables to represent the 18 Buddhas—but 6-8 are quite acceptable!

NUTRITIONAL INFORMATION

Calories	300	Sugars	.........2g
Protein	.........8g	Fat	..........28g
Carbohydrate	....6g	Saturates	.......3g

3³/₄ HOURS   10 MINS

SERVES 4

I N G R E D I E N T S

¼ oz dried wood ear mushrooms

1 cake tofu

2 oz snow peas

4½ oz Chinese cabbage

1 small carrot

3 oz canned baby corn-on-the-cob, drained

3 oz canned straw mushrooms, drained

2 oz canned water chestnuts, drained

1¼ cups vegetable oil

1 tsp salt

½ tsp sugar

1 tbsp light soy sauce or oyster sauce

2-3 tbsp Chinese Stock (see page 30) or water

a few drops sesame oil

1 Soak the wood ears in warm water for 15-20 minutes, then rinse and drain, discarding any hard bits, and dry on paper towels.

2 Cut the cake of tofu into about 18 small pieces.

3 Top and tail the snow peas. Cut the Chinese cabbage and the carrot into slices roughly the same size and shape as the snow peas. Cut the corn, the straw mushrooms, and the water chestnuts in half.

4 Heat the oil in a preheated wok. Add the tofu, and deep-fry for about 2 minutes until it turns slightly golden. Remove and drain.

5 Pour off most of the oil, leaving about 2 tablespoons in the wok. Add the carrot, Chinese cabbage and snow peas to the wok and stir-fry for about 1 minute.

6 Add the corn, mushrooms, and water chestnuts. Stir gently for 2 more minutes, then add the salt, sugar, soy sauce or oyster sauce, and Chinese stock or water. Bring to a boil and stir-fry for 1 more minute. Sprinkle with sesame oil and serve hot or cold.

Braised Tofu Home-style

The pork used in the recipe can be replaced by chicken or shrimp, or it can be omitted altogether.

NUTRITIONAL INFORMATION

Calories 218	Sugars 1g
Protein 17g	Fat 16g
Carbohydrate 2g	Saturates 2g

10 MINS   10 MINS

SERVES 4

I N G R E D I E N T S

3 cakes tofu

4½ oz boneless pork (or any other type of meat)

1 leek

a few small dried whole chilies, soaked

vegetable oil, for deep-frying

1-2 green onions, cut into short sections

2 tbsp crushed yellow bean sauce

1 tbsp light soy sauce

2 tsp rice wine or dry sherry

a few drops sesame oil

1 Split each cake of tofu into 3 slices crosswise, then cut each slice diagonally into 2 triangles.

2 Cut the pork into small thin slices or shreds; cut the leek into thin strips.

3 Drain the chilies, remove the seeds using the tip of a knife, then cut into small shreds.

4 Heat the oil in a preheated wok until smoking, then deep-fry the tofu triangles for 2-3 minutes, or until golden brown all over. Remove with a slotted spoon and drain on paper towels.

5 Pour off the hot oil, leaving about 1 tablespoon in the wok. Add the pork strips, green onions, and chilies and stir-fry for about 1 minute or until the pork changes color.

6 Add the leek, tofu, yellow bean sauce, soy sauce, and wine or sherry and braise for 2-3 minutes, stirring gently to blend well. Finally sprinkle on the sesame oil and serve.

COOK'S TIP

Tofu is sold in 2 forms: as firm cakes, or as a thickish junket, known as silken tofu. It is the solid kind that is used for braising and stir-frying. Silken tofu is usually added to soups or sauces.

Tofu with Mushrooms

Chunks of cucumber and smoked tofu stir-fried with straw mushrooms, snow peas, and corn in a yellow bean sauce.

NUTRITIONAL INFORMATION

Calories 130	Sugars 2g	
Protein 9g	Fat 9g	
Carbohydrate 3g	Saturates 1g	

 15 MINS   10 MINS

SERVES 4

INGREDIENTS

1 large cucumber

1 tsp salt

8 oz smoked tofu

2 tbsp vegetable oil

2 oz snow peas

8 baby corn-on-the-cob

1 celery stalk, sliced diagonally

15 oz can straw mushrooms, drained

2 green onions, cut into strips

½ inch piece fresh ginger, chopped

1 tbsp yellow bean sauce

1 tbsp light soy sauce

1 tbsp dry sherry

1 Halve the cucumber lengthwise and remove the seeds, using a teaspoon or melon baller.

2 Cut the cucumber into cubes, place in a colander, and sprinkle over the salt. Leave to drain for 10 minutes. Rinse thoroughly in cold water to remove the salt and drain thoroughly on absorbent paper towels.

3 Cut the tofu into cubes.

4 Heat the vegetable oil in a wok or large skillet until smoking.

5 Add the tofu, snow peas, corn, and celery to the wok. Stir until the tofu is lightly browned.

6 Add the straw mushrooms, green onions, and ginger, and stir-fry for another minute.

7 Stir in the cucumber, yellow bean sauce, light soy sauce, dry sherry, and 2 tablespoons of water. Stir-fry for 1 minute and ensure that all the vegetables are coated in the sauces before serving.

COOK'S TIP

Straw mushrooms are available in cans from oriental suppliers and some supermarkets. If unavailable, substitute 9 oz baby button mushrooms.

Chinese Vegetable Casserole

This mixed vegetable casserole is very versatile and is delicious with any combination of vegetables.

NUTRITIONAL INFORMATION

Calories 218   Sugars 4g
Protein . . . . .7g   Fat 14g
Carbohydrate . . .12g   Saturates 2g

5 MINS   30 MINS

SERVES 4

INGREDIENTS

4 tbsp vegetable oil

2 medium carrots, sliced

1 zucchini, sliced

4 baby corn-on-the-cobs, halved lengthwise

4½ oz cauliflower flowerets

1 leek, sliced

4½ oz water chestnuts, halved

8 oz tofu, diced

1¼ cups vegetable stock

1 tsp salt

2 tsp dark brown sugar

2 tsp dark soy sauce

2 tbsp dry sherry

1 tbsp cornstarch

2 tbsp water

1 tbsp chopped cilantro, to garnish

1 Heat the oil in a preheated wok until it is almost smoking. Lower the heat slightly, add the carrots, zucchini, corn cobs, cauliflower, and leek to the wok and stir-fry for 2–3 minutes.

2 Stir in the water chestnuts, tofu, stock, salt, sugar, soy sauce, and sherry and bring to a boil. Reduce the heat, cover and simmer for 20 minutes.

3 Blend the cornstarch with the water to form a smooth paste.

4 Stir the cornstarch mixture into the wok. Bring the sauce to a boil and cook, stirring constantly until it thickens and clears.

5 Transfer the casserole to a warm serving dish, sprinkle with chopped cilantro and serve immediately.

COOK'S TIP

If there is too much liquid remaining, boil vigorously for 1 minute before adding the cornstarch to reduce it slightly.

Oysters with Tofu

Oysters are often eaten raw, but are delicious when quickly cooked as in this recipe, and mixed with salt and citrus flavors.

NUTRITIONAL INFORMATION

Calories	175	Sugars	.........2g
Protein	........18g	Fat	..........10g
Carbohydrate	....3g	Saturates	.......1g

5 MINS   10 MINS

SERVES 4

INGREDIENTS

8 oz leeks

12 oz tofu

2 tbsp sunflower oil

12 oz shelled oysters

2 tbsp fresh lemon juice

1 tsp cornstarch

2 tbsp light soy sauce

⅓ cup fish stock

2 tbsp chopped fresh cilantro

1 tsp finely grated lemon zest

1 Using a sharp knife, trim and slice the leeks.

2 Cut the tofu into bite-sized pieces.

3 Heat the sunflower oil in a large preheated wok or skillet. Add the leeks to the wok and stir-fry for 2 minutes.

4 Add the tofu and oysters to the wok or skillet and stir-fry for 1–2 minutes.

5 Mix together the lemon juice, cornstarch, light soy sauce, and fish stock in a small bowl, stirring until well blended.

6 Pour the cornstarch mixture into the wok and cook, stirring occasionally, until the juices start to thicken.

7 Transfer to serving bowls and scatter the cilantro and lemon zest on top. Serve immediately.

VARIATION

Shelled clams or mussels could be used instead of the oysters, if you prefer.

Tofu & Vegetable Stir-Fry

This is a quick dish to prepare, making it ideal as a mid-week supper dish, after a busy day at work!

NUTRITIONAL INFORMATION

Calories 124   Sugars 2g
Protein ....6g   Fat 6g
Carbohydrate ....11g   Saturates 1g

 5 MINS   25 MINS

SERVES 4

I N G R E D I E N T S

1¼ cups potatoes, cubed

1 tbsp vegetable oil

1 red onion, sliced

8 oz firm tofu, diced

2 zucchini, diced

8 canned artichoke hearts, halved

⅔ cup passata (strained tomatoes)

1 tbsp sweet chili sauce

1 tbsp soy sauce

1 tsp sugar

2 tbsp chopped basil

salt and pepper

1 Cook the potatoes in a saucepan of boiling water for 10 minutes. Drain thoroughly and set aside until required.

2 Heat the vegetable oil in a wok or large skillet and sauté the red onion for 2 minutes until the onion has softened, stirring.

3 Stir in the diced tofu and zucchini and cook for 3–4 minutes until they begin to brown slightly.

4 Add the cooked potatoes to the wok or skillet, stirring to mix.

5 Stir in the artichoke hearts, passata (strained tomatoes), sweet chili sauce, soy sauce, sugar, and basil.

6 Season to taste with salt and pepper and cook for a further 5 minutes, stirring well.

7 Transfer the tofu and vegetable stir-fry to serving dishes and serve immediately.

COOK'S TIP

Canned artichoke hearts should be drained thoroughly and rinsed before use because they often have salt added.

Black Bean Casserole

This colorful Chinese-style casserole is made with tofu, vegetables, and black bean sauce.

NUTRITIONAL INFORMATION

Calories 513   Sugars 5g
Protein . . . . .19g   Fat 25g
Carbohydrate . . .56g   Saturates 4g

30 MINS   30 MINS

SERVES 4

I N G R E D I E N T S

6 Chinese dried mushrooms

9½ oz tofu

3 tbsp vegetable oil

1 carrot, cut into thin strips

4½ oz snow peas

8 baby corn-on-the-cob, halved lengthwise

8 oz can sliced bamboo shoots, drained

1 red bell pepper, cut into chunks

4½ oz Chinese cabbage, shredded

1 tbsp soy sauce

1 tbsp black bean sauce

1 tsp sugar

1 tsp cornstarch

vegetable oil for deep-frying

9 oz Chinese rice noodles

salt

1 Soak the dried mushrooms in a bowl of warm water for 20–25 minutes. Drain and squeeze out the excess water, reserving the liquid. Remove the tough centers and slice the mushrooms thinly.

2 Cut the tofu into cubes. Boil in a pan of lightly salted water for 2–3 minutes to firm up and then drain.

3 Heat half the oil in a saucepan. Add the tofu and fry until lightly browned. Remove and drain on paper towels.

4 Add the remaining oil and stir-fry the mushrooms, carrot, snow peas, corn, bamboo shoots, and bell pepper for 2–3 minutes. Add the Chinese cabbage and tofu, and stir-fry for another 2 minutes.

5 Stir in the sauces and sugar, and season with salt. Add 6 tbsp of the reserved mushroom liquid mixed with the cornstarch. Bring to a boil, reduce the heat, cover, and braise for 2–3 minutes until the sauce thickens slightly.

6 Heat the oil for deep-frying in a large pan. Deep-fry the noodles, in batches, until puffed up and lightly golden. Drain and serve with the casserole.

Spicy Fried Tofu Triangles

Marinated tofu is ideal in this recipe for added flavor, although the spicy coating is very tasty with plain tofu.

NUTRITIONAL INFORMATION

Calories 224   Sugars 17g
Protein ....10g   Fat 13g
Carbohydrate ...18g   Saturates 2g

1¼ HOURS   10 MINS

SERVES 4

INGREDIENTS

1 tbsp sea salt

4½ tsp Chinese five-spice powder

3 tbsp light brown sugar

2 garlic cloves, crushed

1 tsp grated fresh ginger

2 x 8 oz cakes tofu

vegetable oil, for deep-frying

2 leeks, shredded and halved

shredded leek, to garnish

1 Mix together the salt, Chinese five-spice powder, sugar, garlic, and ginger in a bowl and transfer to a plate.

2 Cut the tofu cakes in half diagonally to form two triangles. Cut each triangle in half and then in half again to form 16 triangles.

3 Roll the tofu triangles in the spice mixture, turning to coat thoroughly. Set aside for 1 hour.

4 Heat the vegetable oil for deep-frying in a wok until it is almost smoking.

5 Reduce the heat slightly, add the tofu triangles and fry for 5 minutes, until golden brown. Remove the tofu from the wok with a slotted spoon, set aside and keep warm until required.

6 Add the leeks to the wok and stir-fry for 1 minute. Remove from the wok and drain on paper towels.

7 Arrange the leeks on a warm serving plate and place the fried tofu on top. Garnish with the fresh shredded leek and serve immediately.

COOK'S TIP

Fry the tofu in batches and keep each batch warm until all of the tofu has been fried and is ready to serve.

Microwave Tofu Casserole

In this quick recipe, all the cooking is done in a microwave—there is not a wok in sight!

NUTRITIONAL INFORMATION

Calories ....222 Sugars 3g
Protein ....11g Fat 13g
Carbohydrate ...16g Saturates 2g

1¼ HOURS   15 MINS

SERVES 4

I N G R E D I E N T S

9½ oz smoked tofu, cubed

2 tbsp soy sauce

1 tbsp dry sherry

1 tsp sesame oil

4 dried Chinese mushrooms

9 oz egg noodles

1 carrot, cut into thin sticks

1 celery stalk, cut into thin sticks

4½ oz (16–18) baby corn-on-the-cobs,
   halved lengthwise

2 tbsp oil

1 zucchini, sliced

4 green onions, chopped

1⅓ cups snow peas, each cut into 3 pieces

2 tbsp black bean sauce

1 tsp cornstarch

salt and pepper

1 tbsp toasted sesame seeds, to garnish

1 Marinate the tofu in the soy sauce, sherry and sesame oil for 30 minutes.

2 Place the mushrooms in a small bowl and pour over boiling water to cover. Leave to soak for 20 minutes.

3 Place the egg noodles in a large bowl. Pour over enough boiling water to cover by 1 inch. Add ½ teaspoon salt, cover, and cook on HIGH power for 4 minutes.

4 Place the carrot, celery, corn, and oil in a large bowl. Cover and cook on HIGH power for 1 minute.

5 Drain the mushrooms, reserving 1 tablespoon of the liquid. Squeeze out excess water from the mushrooms and discard the hard cores. Thinly slice the mushrooms.

6 Add the mushrooms to the bowl of vegetables with the zucchini, green onions, and snow peas. Mix well. Cover and cook on HIGH power for 4 minutes, stirring every minute. Add the black bean sauce to the vegetables, stirring to coat the vegetables in the sauce.

7 Mix the cornstarch with the reserved mushroom water and stir into the vegetables with the tofu and marinade. Cover and cook on HIGH power for 2–3 minutes until heated through and the sauce has thickened slightly. Season with salt and pepper to taste. Drain the noodles. Garnish the vegetables with sesame seeds and serve with the noodles.

Tofu with Bell Peppers

Tofu is perfect for marinating as it readily absorbs flavors for a great tasting main dish.

NUTRITIONAL INFORMATION

Calories	267	Sugars	.........2g
Protein	.........9g	Fat	..........23g
Carbohydrate	....5g	Saturates	.......3g

25 MINS   15 MINS

SERVES 4

INGREDIENTS

12 oz tofu

2 cloves garlic, crushed

4 tbsp soy sauce

1 tbsp sweet chili sauce

6 tbsp sunflower oil

1 onion, sliced

1 green bell pepper, seeded
and diced

1 tbsp sesame oil

1 Using a sharp knife, cut the tofu into bite-sized pieces. Place the tofu in a shallow non-metallic dish.

2 Mix together the garlic, soy sauce, and sweet chili sauce and drizzle over the tofu. Toss well to coat and leave to marinate for about 20 minutes.

3 Meanwhile, heat the sunflower oil in a large preheated wok.

4 Add the onion to the wok and stir-fry over a high heat until brown and crispy. Remove the onion with a slotted spoon and leave to drain on absorbent paper towels.

5 Add the tofu to the hot oil and stir-fry for about 5 minutes.

6 Remove all but 1 tablespoon of the sunflower oil from the wok. Add the bell pepper to the wok and stir-fry for 2–3 minutes, or until softened.

7 Return the tofu and onions to the wok and heat through, stirring occasionally.

8 Drizzle with sesame oil. Transfer to serving plates and serve immediately.

COOK'S TIP

If you are in a real hurry, buy ready-marinated tofu from your supermarket.

Sweet & Sour Tofu

Sweet-and-sour sauce was one of the first Chinese sauces introduced to Western diets, and remains one of the most popular.

NUTRITIONAL INFORMATION

Calories 205	Sugars 12g
Protein 11g	Fat 11g
Carbohydrate . . .17g	Saturates 1g

🥣 5 MINS   🕐 10 MINS

SERVES 4

I N G R E D I E N T S

2 celery stalks

1 carrot

1 green bell pepper, seeded

2¾ oz snow peas

2 tbsp vegetable oil

2 garlic cloves, crushed

8 baby corn-on-the-cobs

4½ oz bean sprouts

1 lb tofu, cubed

rice or noodles, to serve

S A U C E

2 tbsp light brown sugar

2 tbsp wine vinegar

1 cup vegetable stock

1 tsp tomato paste

1 tbsp cornstarch

1 Using a sharp knife, thinly slice the celery, cut the carrot into thin strips, dice the bell pepper, and cut the snow peas in half diagonally.

2 Heat the vegetable oil in a preheated wok until it is almost smoking. Reduce the heat slightly, add the crushed garlic, celery, carrot, bell pepper, snow peas, and corn and stir-fry for 3–4 minutes.

3 Add the bean sprouts and tofu to the wok and cook for 2 minutes, stirring well.

4 To make the sauce, combine the sugar, wine vinegar, stock, tomato paste, and cornstarch, stirring well to mix. Stir into the wok, bring to a boil, and cook, stirring, until the sauce thickens and clears. Continue to cook for 1 minute. Serve with rice or noodles.

COOK'S TIP

Be careful not to break up the tofu when stirring.

Fried Tofu & Vegetables

Tofu is available in different forms from both Chinese and Western supermarkets. The cake form of tofu is used in this recipe.

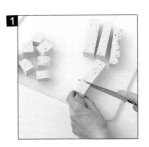

NUTRITIONAL INFORMATION

Calories 367	Sugars 5g	
Protein 13g	Fat 30g	
Carbohydrate 11g	Saturates 4g	

5 MINS　　15 MINS

SERVES 4

INGREDIENTS

1 lb tofu

⅔ cup vegetable oil

1 leek, sliced

4 baby corn-on-the-cobs, halved lengthwise

2 oz snow peas

1 red bell pepper, seeded and diced

2 oz canned bamboo shoots, drained and rinsed

rice or noodles, to serve

SAUCE

1 tbsp Chinese rice wine or dry sherry

4 tbsp oyster sauce

3 tsp light soy sauce

2 tsp sugar

pinch of salt

¼ cup vegetable stock

1 tsp cornstarch

2 tsp water

1 Rinse the tofu in cold water and pat dry with paper towels. Cut the tofu into 1 inch cubes.

2 Heat the oil in a preheated wok until almost smoking. Reduce the heat, add the tofu, and stir-fry until golden brown. Remove from the wok with a slotted spoon and drain on paper towels.

3 Pour all but 2 tablespoons of the oil from the wok and return to the heat. Add the leek, corn, snow peas, bell pepper, and bamboo shoots and stir-fry for 2–3 minutes.

4 Add the Chinese rice wine or sherry, oyster sauce, soy sauce, sugar, salt, and stock to the wok and bring to a boil. Blend the cornstarch with the water to form a smooth paste and stir it into the sauce. Bring the sauce to a boil and cook, stirring constantly, until thickened and clear.

5 Stir the tofu into the mixture in the wok and cook for about 1 minute until hot. Serve with rice or noodles.

Tofu Casserole

Tofu is ideal for absorbing all the other flavors in this dish. If marinated tofu is used, it will add a flavor of its own.

NUTRITIONAL INFORMATION

Calories 228   Sugars 3g
Protein . . . . .16g   Fat 15g
Carbohydrate . . . .7g   Saturates 2g

5 MINS   15 MINS

SERVES 4

INGREDIENTS

1 lb tofu

2 tbsp peanut oil

8 green onions, cut into sticks

2 celery stalks, sliced

4½ oz broccoli flowerets

4½ oz zucchini, sliced

2 garlic cloves, thinly sliced

1 lb baby spinach

rice, to serve

SAUCE

2 cups vegetable stock

2 tbsp light soy sauce

3 tbsp hoisin sauce

½ tsp chili powder

1 tbsp sesame oil

1 Cut the tofu into 1 inch cubes and set aside until required.

2 Heat the peanut oil in a preheated wok or large skillet.

3 Add the green onions, celery, broccoli, zucchini, garlic, spinach, and tofu to the wok or skillet and stir-fry for 3–4 minutes.

4 To make the sauce, mix together the vegetable stock, soy sauce, hoisin sauce, chili powder, and sesame oil in a saucepan and bring to a boil.

5 Add the stir-fried vegetables and tofu to the saucepan, reduce the heat, cover and simmer for 10 minutes.

6 Transfer the tofu and vegetables to a warm serving dish and serve with rice.

VARIATION

This recipe has a green vegetable theme, but alter the color and flavor by adding your favourite vegetables.
Add 2¾ oz fresh or canned and drained straw mushrooms with the vegetables in step 2.

Tofu with Mushrooms & Peas

Chinese mushrooms are available from Chinese supermarkets and health food shops and add a unique flavor to Oriental dishes.

NUTRITIONAL INFORMATION

Calories	.218	Sugars	.1g
Protein	.12g	Fat	.14g
Carbohydrate	.13g	Saturates	.2g

 15 MINS   15 MINS

SERVES 4

INGREDIENTS

1 oz dried Chinese mushrooms

1 lb tofu

4 tbsp cornstarch

oil, for deep-frying

2 cloves garlic, finely chopped

1 inch piece fresh ginger, grated

¾ cup frozen or fresh peas

1 Place the Chinese mushrooms in a large bowl. Pour in enough boiling water to cover and leave to stand for about 10 minutes.

2 Meanwhile, cut the tofu into bite-sized cubes, using a sharp knife.

3 Place the cornstarch in a large bowl.

4 Add the tofu to the bowl and toss in the cornstarch until evenly coated.

5 Heat the oil for deep-frying in a large preheated wok.

6 Add the cubes of tofu to the wok and deep-fry, in batches, for 2–3 minutes or until golden and crispy. Remove the tofu with a slotted spoon and leave to drain on absorbent paper towels.

7 Drain off all but 2 tablespoons of oil from the wok. Add the garlic, ginger, and Chinese mushrooms to the wok and stir-fry for 2–3 minutes.

8 Return the cooked tofu to the wok and add the peas. Heat through for 1 minute then serve hot.

COOK'S TIP

Chinese dried mushrooms add flavor and a distinctive aroma. Sold dried in packs, they can be expensive but only a few are needed per dish and they store indefinitely. If they are unavailable, use open-cap mushrooms instead.

Rice

Together with noodles, rice forms the central part of a Chinese meal, particularly in southern China. In the north, the staple foods tend to be more wheat-based. For an everyday meal, plain rice is served with one or two dishes and a soup. Rice can be boiled and then steamed or it can be fried with other ingredients, such as eggs, shrimp, meat,

and vegetables, and then flavored with soy sauce. The most common type of rice used in Chinese cooking is short-grain or glutinous rice, which become slightly sticky when cooked and is therefore ideal for eating with chopsticks. This chapter includes some delicious rice dishes which can be eaten on their own or as an accompaniment. Fried rice is a particular favorite in Western restaurants, so several variations are included here.

Egg Fried Rice

In this classic Chinese dish, boiled rice is fried with peas, green onions, and egg and flavored with soy sauce.

NUTRITIONAL INFORMATION

Calories	203	Sugars	.........1g
Protein	.........9g	Fat	...........11g
Carbohydrate	...19g	Saturates	.......2g

 20 MINS   10 MINS

SERVES 4

INGREDIENTS

⅔ cup long-grain rice

3 eggs, beaten

2 tbsp vegetable oil

2 garlic cloves, crushed

4 green onions, chopped

1 cup cooked peas

1 tbsp light soy sauce

pinch of salt

shredded green onion,
   to garnish

1 Cook the rice in a pan of boiling water for 10-12 minutes, until almost cooked, but not soft. Drain well, rinse under cold water and drain again.

2 Place the beaten eggs in a saucepan and cook over a gentle heat, stirring until softly scrambled.

3 Heat the vegetable oil in a preheated wok or large skillet, swirling the oil around the base of the wok until it is really hot.

4 Add the crushed garlic, green onions, and peas and sauté, stirring occasionally, for 1-2 minutes. Stir the rice into the wok, mixing to combine.

5 Add the eggs, light soy sauce and a pinch of salt to the wok or skillet and stir to mix the egg in thoroughly.

6 Transfer the egg fried rice to serving dishes and serve garnished with the shredded green onion.

COOK'S TIP

The rice is rinsed under cold water to wash out the starch and prevent it from sticking together.

Fried Rice with Pork

This dish is a meal in itself, containing pieces of pork, fried with rice, peas, tomatoes, and mushrooms.

NUTRITIONAL INFORMATION

Calories 285   Sugars 2g
Protein . . . . .18g   Fat 16g
Carbohydrate . . .19g   Saturates 4g

10 MINS   30 MINS

SERVES 4

I N G R E D I E N T S

⅔ cup long-grain rice

3 tbsp peanut oil

1 large onion, cut into 8

8 oz pork tenderloin, thinly sliced

2 open-cap mushrooms, sliced

2 garlic cloves, crushed

1 tbsp light soy sauce

1 tsp light brown sugar

2 tomatoes, skinned, seeded, and chopped

½ cup cooked peas

2 eggs, beaten

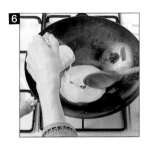

1 Cook the rice in a saucepan of boiling water for about 15 minutes, until tender, but not soft. Drain well, rinse under cold running water, and drain again thoroughly.

2 Heat the peanut oil in a preheated wok. Add the sliced onion and pork and stir-fry for 3-4 minutes, until just beginning to color.

3 Add the mushrooms and garlic to the wok and stir-fry for 1 minute.

4 Add the soy sauce and sugar to the mixture in the wok and stir-fry for 2 minutes more.

5 Stir in the rice, tomatoes, and peas, mixing well. Transfer the mixture to a warmed dish.

6 Stir the eggs into the wok and cook, stirring with a wooden spoon, for 2-3 minutes, until beginning to set.

7 Return the rice mixture to the wok and mix well. Transfer to serving dishes and serve immediately.

COOK'S TIP

You can cook the rice in advance and chill or freeze it until required.

Chili Fried Rice

Not so much a side dish as a meal in itself, this delicious fried rice can be served on its own or as an accompaniment to many Chinese dishes.

NUTRITIONAL INFORMATION

Calories	290	Sugars	.........2g
Protein	........11g	Fat	..........14g
Carbohydrate	...26g	Saturates	.......2g

 20 MINS 15 MINS

SERVES 4

INGREDIENTS

generous 1 cup long-grain rice

4 tbsp vegetable oil

2 garlic cloves, chopped finely

1 small red chili, seeded and chopped finely

8 green onions, trimmed and sliced finely

1 tbsp red curry paste or 2 tsp chili sauce

1 red bell pepper, cored, seeded, and chopped

¾ cup dwarf green beans, chopped

1½ cups cooked peeled shrimp or chopped cooked chicken

2 tbsp fish sauce

TO GARNISH

cucumber slices

shredded green onion

1 Cook the rice in plenty of boiling, lightly salted water until tender, about 12 minutes. Drain, rinse with cold water, and drain thoroughly.

2 Heat the vegetable oil in a wok or large skillet until the oil is really hot.

3 Add the garlic to the wok and fry gently for 2 minutes until golden.

4 Add the chili and green onions and cook, stirring, for 3–4 minutes.

5 Add the red curry paste or chili sauce to the wok or skillet and fry for 1 minute, then add the red bell pepper and green beans. Stir-fry briskly for 2 minutes.

6 Tip the cooked rice into the wok or skillet and add the shrimp or chicken and the fish sauce. Stir-fry over a medium-high heat for about 4–5 minutes, until the rice is hot.

7 Transfer the chili fried rice to warm serving dishes, garnish with cucumber slices and shredded green onion and serve.

COOK'S TIP

Cook the rice the day before if you can remember—it will give an even better result. Alternatively, use rice left over from another dish to make this recipe.

Rice with Seven Spice Beef

Beef fillet is used in this recipe as it is very suitable for quick cooking and has a wonderful flavor.

NUTRITIONAL INFORMATION

Calories	171	Sugars	........8g
Protein	........28g	Fat	..........15g
Carbohydrate	...60g	Saturates	.......6g

5 MINS   30 MINS

SERVES 4

INGREDIENTS

1 cup long-grain white rice

2½ cups water

12 oz beef fillet

2 tbsp soy sauce

2 tbsp tomato ketchup

1 tbsp seven spice seasoning

2 tbsp peanut oil

1 onion, diced

8 oz carrots, diced

¾ cup frozen peas

2 eggs, beaten

2 tbsp cold water

1 Rinse the rice under cold running water, then drain thoroughly. Place the rice in a saucepan with 2½ cups of water, bring to a boil, cover, and leave to simmer for 12 minutes. Turn the cooked rice out onto a tray and leave to cool.

2 Using a sharp knife, thinly slice the beef fillet.

3 Mix together the soy sauce, tomato ketchup, and seven spice seasoning. Spoon over the beef and toss well to coat.

4 Heat the oil in a preheated wok. Add the beef and stir-fry for 3–4 minutes.

5 Add the onion, carrots, and peas to the wok and stir-fry for another 2–3 minutes. Add the cooked rice to the wok and stir to combine.

6 Beat the eggs with 2 tablespoons of cold water. Drizzle the egg mixture over the rice and stir-fry for 3–4 minutes, or until the rice is heated through and the egg has set. Transfer to a warm serving bowl and serve immediately.

VARIATION

You can use pork fillet or chicken instead of the beef, if you prefer.

Chinese Fried Rice

It is essential to use cold, dry rice with separate grains to make this recipe properly.

NUTRITIONAL INFORMATION

Calories ....475 Sugars 3g
Protein ....16g Fat 16g
Carbohydrate ...72g Saturates 3g

5 MINS   30 MINS

SERVES 4

INGREDIENTS

3 cups water

½ tsp salt

1½ cups long-grain rice

2 eggs

4 tsp cold water

3 tbsp sunflower oil

4 green onions, sliced diagonally

1 red, green, or yellow bell pepper, cored,
    seeded, and thinly sliced

3-4 lean bacon slices, cut into strips

7 oz fresh bean sprouts

4½ oz frozen peas, defrosted

2 tbsp soy sauce (optional)

salt and pepper

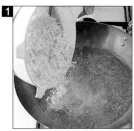

1 Pour the water into the wok with the salt and bring to the boil. Rinse the rice in a strainer under cold water until the water runs clear, drain well and add to the boiling water. Stir well, then cover the wok tightly with the lid or a lid made of foil, and simmer gently for 12-13 minutes. (Don't remove the lid during cooking or the steam will escape and the rice will not be cooked.)

2 Remove the lid, give the rice a good stir, and spread out on a large plate or cookie sheet to cool and dry.

3 Beat each egg separately with salt and pepper and 2 teaspoons of cold water. Heat 1 tablespoon of oil in the wok, pour in the first egg, swirl it around and leave to cook undisturbed until set. Remove to a board and cook the second egg. Cut the omelets into thin slices.

4 Add the remaining oil to the wok and when really hot add the green onions and bell pepper and stir-fry for 1-2 minutes. Add the bacon and continue to

stir-fry for a further 1-2 minutes. Add the bean sprouts and peas and toss together thoroughly; stir in the soy sauce, if using.

5 Add the rice and seasoning and stir-fry for 1 minute or so, then add the strips of omelet and continue to stir for about 2 minutes or until the rice is piping hot. Serve at once.

Chinese Risotto

Risotto is a creamy Italian dish made with arborio or risotto rice. This Chinese version is simply delicious!

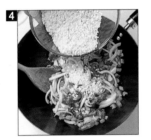

NUTRITIONAL INFORMATION

Calories	436	Sugars	.........7g
Protein	........13g	Fat	..........14g
Carbohydrate	...70g	Saturates	.......4g

 5 MINS   25 MINS

SERVES 4

INGREDIENTS

2 tbsp peanut oil

1 onion, sliced

2 cloves garlic, crushed

1 tsp Chinese five-spice powder

8 oz Chinese sausage, sliced

8 oz carrots, diced

1 green bell pepper, seeded and diced

1⅓ cups risotto rice

1¾ cups vegetable or chicken stock

1 tbsp fresh chives

1 Heat the peanut oil in a large preheated wok or a heavy-bottomed skillet.

2 Add the onion slices, crushed garlic, and Chinese five-spice powder to the wok or skillet and stir-fry for 1 minute.

3 Add the Chinese sausage, carrots, and green bell pepper to the wok and stir to combine.

4 Stir in the risotto rice and cook for 1 minute.

5 Gradually add the vegetable or chicken stock, a little at a time, stirring constantly until the liquid has been completely absorbed and the rice grains are tender.

6 Snip the chives with a pair of clean kitchen shears and stir into the wok with the last of the stock.

7 Transfer the Chinese risotto to warm serving bowls and serve immediately.

COOK'S TIP

Chinese sausage is highly flavored and is made from chopped pork fat, pork meat and spices. Use a spicy Portuguese sausage if Chinese sausage is unavailable.

Fragrant Coconut Rice

This fragrant, sweet rice is delicious served with meat, vegetable or fish dishes as part of a Chinese menu.

NUTRITIONAL INFORMATION

Calories	306	Sugars	........2g
Protein	.........5g	Fat	..........6g
Carbohydrate	...61g	Saturates	.......4g

🍲 5 MINS   🕐 15 MINS

SERVES 4

INGREDIENTS

9½ oz long-grain white rice

2½ cups water

½ tsp salt

⅓ cup coconut milk

¼ cup shredded coconut

1 Rinse the rice thoroughly under cold running water until the water runs completely clear.

2 Drain the rice thoroughly in a sieve set over a large bowl. This is to remove some of the starch and to prevent the grains from sticking together.

3 Place the rice in a wok with 2½ cups of water.

4 Add the salt and coconut milk to the wok and bring to a boil.

5 Cover the wok with a lid or a lid made of foil, curved into a domed shape and resting on the sides of the wok. Reduce the heat and leave to simmer for 10 minutes.

6 Remove the lid from the wok and fluff up the rice with a fork – all of the liquid should be absorbed and the rice grains should be tender. If not, add more water and continue to simmer for a few more minutes until all the liquid has been absorbed.

7 Spoon the rice into a warm serving bowl and scatter with the shredded coconut. Serve immediately.

COOK'S TIP

Coconut milk is not the liquid found inside coconuts— that is called coconut water. Coconut milk is made from the white coconut flesh soaked in water and milk and then squeezed to extract all of the flavor. You can make your own or buy it in cans.

Stir-Fried Rice with Sausage

This is a very quick rice dish as it uses pre-cooked rice. It is therefore ideal when time is short or for a quick lunch-time dish.

NUTRITIONAL INFORMATION

Calories ....383 Sugars 9g
Protein ....19g Fat 17g
Carbohydrate ...42g Saturates 4g

5 MINS   20 MINS

SERVES 4

INGREDIENTS

12 oz Chinese sausage

2 tbsp sunflower oil

2 tbsp soy sauce

1 onion, sliced

6 oz carrots, cut into thin sticks

1¼ cups peas

¾ cup canned pineapple cubes, drained

4¾ cups cooked long-grain rice

1 egg, beaten

1 tbsp chopped fresh parsley

1 Using a sharp knife, thinly slice the Chinese sausage.

2 Heat the sunflower oil in a large preheated wok. Add the sausage to the wok and stir-fry for 5 minutes.

3 Stir in the soy sauce and allow to bubble for about 2–3 minutes, or until syrupy.

4 Add the onion, carrots, peas, and pineapple to the wok and stir-fry for a further 3 minutes.

5 Add the cooked rice to the wok and stir-fry the mixture for about 2–3 minutes, or until the rice is completely heated through.

6 Drizzle the beaten egg over the top of the rice and cook, tossing the ingredients in the wok, until the egg sets.

7 Transfer the stir-fried rice to a large, warm serving bowl and scatter with plenty of chopped fresh parsley. Serve immediately.

COOK'S TIP

Cook extra rice and freeze it in preparation for some of the other rice dishes included in this book, as it saves time and enables a meal to be prepared in minutes. Be sure to cool any leftover cooked rice quickly before freezing to avoid food poisoning.

Egg Fu-Yung with Rice

In this dish, cooked rice is mixed with scrambled eggs and Chinese vegetables. It is a great way of using up leftover cooked rice.

NUTRITIONAL INFORMATION

Calories 258	Sugars 1g
Protein 8g	Fat 16g
Carbohydrate ...21g	Saturates 3g

30 MINS   25 MINS

SERVES 4

INGREDIENTS

generous ¾ cup long-grain rice

2 Chinese dried mushrooms
   (if unavailable, use thinly sliced
   open-cap mushrooms)

3 eggs, beaten

3 tbsp vegetable oil

4 green onions, sliced

½ green bell pepper, chopped

⅓ cup canned bamboo shoots

⅓ cup canned water
   chestnuts, sliced

2 cups bean sprouts

2 tbsp light soy sauce

2 tbsp dry sherry

2 tsp sesame oil

salt and pepper

1 Cook the rice in lightly salted boiling water according to the pack instructions.

2 Place the Chinese dried mushrooms in a small bowl, cover with warm water, and leave to soak for about 20–25 minutes.

3 Mix the beaten eggs with a little salt. Heat 1 tablespoon of the oil in a preheated wok or large skillet. Add the eggs and stir until just set. Remove and set aside.

4 Drain the mushrooms and squeeze out the excess water. Remove the tough centers and chop the mushrooms.

5 Heat the remaining oil in a clean wok or skillet. Add the mushrooms, green onions, and green bell pepper, and stir-fry for 2 minutes. Add the bamboo shoots, water chestnuts, and bean sprouts. Stir-fry for 1 minute.

6 Drain the rice thoroughly and add to the pan with the remaining ingredients. Mix well, heating the rice thoroughly. Season to taste with salt and pepper. Stir in the reserved eggs and serve.

COOK'S TIP

To wash bean sprouts, place them in a bowl of cold water and swirl with your hand. Remove any long tail ends then rinse and drain thoroughly.

Rice with Crab & Mussels

Shellfish makes an ideal partner for rice. Mussels and crab add flavor and texture to this spicy dish.

NUTRITIONAL INFORMATION

Calories	336	Sugars	.........4g
Protein	........32g	Fat	..........10g
Carbohydrate	...33g	Saturates	.......1g

20 MINS   10 MINS

SERVES 4

INGREDIENTS

1½ cups long-grain rice

6 oz white crab meat, fresh, canned or
    frozen (defrosted if frozen), or 8 imitation
    crab/pollock sticks, defrosted if frozen

2 tbsp sesame or sunflower oil

1 inch piece fresh ginger, grated

4 green onions, thinly sliced diagonally

4½ oz snow peas, cut into 2-3 pieces

½ tsp turmeric

1 tsp ground cumin

2 x 7 oz jars mussels, well drained, or 12 oz
    frozen mussels, defrosted

1 x 15 oz can bean sprouts, well drained

salt and pepper

1 Cook the rice in boiling salted water, following the instructions given in Chinese Fried Rice (see page 416).

2 Extract the crab meat, if using fresh crab (see Cook's Tip). Flake the crab meat or cut the crab sticks into 3 or 4 pieces.

3 Heat the oil in a preheated wok and stir-fry the ginger and green onions for a minute or so. Add the snow peas and continue to cook for another minute.

Sprinkle the turmeric, cumin, and seasoning over the vegetables and mix well to combine.

4 Add the crab meat and mussels and stir-fry for 1 minute. Stir in the cooked rice and bean sprouts and stir-fry for 2 minutes or until hot and well mixed.

5 Adjust the seasoning to taste and serve immediately.

COOK'S TIP

To prepare fresh crab, twist off the claws and legs, crack with a heavy knife and pick out the meat with a skewer. Discard the gills and pull out the under shell; discard the stomach sac. Pull the soft meat from the shell. Cut open the body section and pry out the meat with a skewer.

Rice with Five-Spice Chicken

This dish has a wonderful color obtained from the turmeric, and a great spicy flavor, making it very appealing all-round.

NUTRITIONAL INFORMATION

Calories	.412	Sugars	.1g
Protein	.23g	Fat	.13g
Carbohydrate	.53g	Saturates	.2g

5 MINS   20 MINS

SERVES 4

INGREDIENTS

1 tbsp Chinese five-spice powder

2 tbsp cornstarch

12 oz boneless, skinless chicken breasts, cubed

3 tbsp peanut oil

1 onion, diced

1 cup long-grain white rice

½ tsp turmeric

2½ cups chicken stock

2 tbsp snipped fresh chives

1 Place the Chinese five-spice powder and cornstarch in a large bowl. Add the chicken pieces and toss to coat all over.

2 Heat 2 tablespoons of the peanut oil in a large preheated wok. Add the chicken pieces to the wok and stir-fry for 5 minutes. Using a slotted spoon, remove the chicken and set aside.

3 Add the remaining peanut oil to the wok.

4 Add the onion to the wok and stir-fry for 1 minute.

5 Add the rice, turmeric and chicken stock to the wok and gently bring to a boil.

6 Return the chicken pieces to the wok, reduce the heat and leave to simmer for 10 minutes, or until the liquid has been absorbed and the rice is tender.

7 Add the snipped fresh chives, stir to mix, and serve hot.

COOK'S TIP

Be careful when using turmeric as it can stain the hands and clothes a distinctive shade of yellow.

Green Rice

Spinach is used in this recipe to give the rice a wonderful green coloring. Tossed with the carrot strips, it is a really appealing dish.

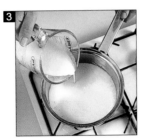

NUTRITIONAL INFORMATION

Calories	582	Sugars	........11g
Protein	........15g	Fat	..........12g
Carbohydrate	...110g	Saturates	.......4g

1¼ HOURS   20 MINS

SERVES 4

I N G R E D I E N T S

2 tbsp olive oil

2¼ cups basmati rice, soaked for 1 hour, washed and drained

3 cups coconut milk

1 tsp salt

1 bay leaf

2 tbsp chopped fresh cilantro

2 tbsp chopped fresh mint

2 green chilies, seeded and chopped finely

1 Heat the olive oil in a saucepan.

2 Add the basmati rice to the saucepan and stir with a wooden spatula until the rice becomes translucent.

3 Add the coconut milk, salt, and bay leaf. Bring to a boil and cook until all the liquid is absorbed.

4 Lower the heat as much as possible, cover the saucepan tightly and cook for 10 minutes.

5 Remove the bay leaf and stir in the cilantro, mint, and chopped green chilies. Fork through the rice gently and serve.

COOK'S TIP

Two segments of fresh lime would make an attractive garnish for this dish and would complement the cilantro perfectly.

Hot & Spicy Chicken Rice

Chicken is cooked with rice and vegetables and flavored with red curry paste, ginger, cilantro, and lime for a deliciously spicy dish.

NUTRITIONAL INFORMATION

Calories 350	Sugars 2g
Protein 26g	Fat 16g
Carbohydrate ...27g	Saturates 3g

 10 MINS   30 MINS

SERVES 4

INGREDIENTS

generous 1 cup white long-grain rice

4 tbsp vegetable oil

2 garlic cloves, chopped finely

6 shallots, sliced finely

1 red bell pepper, seeded and diced

4½ oz green beans, cut into 1 inch lengths

1 tbsp red curry paste

12 oz cooked skinless, boneless chicken, chopped

½ tsp ground coriander seeds

1 tsp finely grated fresh ginger

2 tbsp fish sauce

finely grated zest of 1 lime

3 tbsp lime juice

1 tbsp chopped fresh cilantro

salt and pepper

TO GARNISH

lime wedges

sprigs of fresh cilantro

1 Cook the rice in plenty of boiling, lightly salted water for 12–15 minutes until tender. Drain, rinse in cold water, and drain thoroughly.

2 Heat the vegetable oil in a large preheated wok or skillet.

3 Add the garlic and shallots to the wok or skillet and fry gently for 2–3 minutes until golden.

4 Add the bell pepper and green beans and stir-fry for 2 minutes. Add the red curry paste and stir-fry for 1 minute.

5 Add the cooked rice to the wok or skillet, then add the cooked chicken, ground coriander seeds, ginger, fish sauce, lime zest, and juice, and fresh cilantro.

6 Stir-fry the mixture in the wok over a medium-high heat for about 4–5 minutes, until the rice and chicken are thoroughly reheated. Season to taste.

7 Transfer the chicken and rice mixture to a warm serving dish, garnish with lime wedges and fresh cilantro, and serve immediately.

Chinese Vegetable Rice

This rice can either be served as a meal in itself or as an accompaniment to other vegetable recipes.

NUTRITIONAL INFORMATION

Calories	228	Sugars	........5g
Protein	.........5g	Fat	..........7g
Carbohydrate	...37g	Saturates	.......1g

5 MINS   25 MINS

SERVES 4

I N G R E D I E N T S

1¾ cups long-grain white rice

1 tsp turmeric

2 tbsp sunflower oil

8 oz zucchini, sliced

1 red bell pepper, seeded and sliced

1 green bell pepper, seeded and sliced

1 green chili, seeded and finely chopped

1 medium carrot, coarsley grated

1½ cups bean sprouts

6 green onions, sliced, plus extra to garnish (optional)

2 tbsp soy sauce

salt

1 Place the rice and turmeric in a pan of lightly salted water and bring to a boil. Reduce the heat and leave to simmer until the rice is just tender. Drain the rice thoroughly and press out any excess water with a sheet of paper towels. Set aside until required.

2 Heat the sunflower oil in a large preheated wok.

3 Add the zucchini to the wok and stir-fry for about 2 minutes.

4 Add the bell peppers and chili to the wok and stir-fry for 2–3 minutes.

5 Add the cooked rice to the mixture in the wok, a little at a time, tossing well after each addition.

6 Add the carrots, bean sprouts, and green onions to the wok and stir-fry for a further 2 minutes.

7 Drizzle with soy sauce and serve at once, garnished with extra green onions, if desired.

COOK'S TIP

For real luxury, add a few saffron strands infused in boiling water instead of the turmeric.

Green-fried Rice

Spinach is used in this recipe to give the rice a wonderful green coloring. Tossed with the carrot strips, it is a really appealing dish.

NUTRITIONAL INFORMATION

Calories 139	Sugars 2g	
Protein 3g	Fat 7g	
Carbohydrate ...18g	Saturates 1g	

🍲 5 MINS   🕐 20 MINS

SERVES 4

INGREDIENTS

⅔ cup long-grain rice

2 tbsp vegetable oil

2 garlic cloves, crushed

1 tsp grated fresh ginger

1 carrot, cut into thin sticks

1 zucchini, diced

8 oz baby spinach

2 tsp light soy sauce

2 tsp light brown sugar

1 Cook the rice in a saucepan of boiling water for about 15 minutes. Drain the rice well, rinse under cold running water and then rinse the rice thoroughly again. Set aside until required.

2 Heat the vegetable oil in a preheated wok or large, heavy-bottomed skillet.

3 Add the crushed garlic and grated fresh ginger to the wok or skillet and stir-fry for about 30 seconds.

4 Add the carrot sticks and diced zucchini to the mixture in the wok and stir-fry for about 2 minutes, so the vegetables still retain their crunch.

5 Add the baby spinach and stir-fry for 1 minute, until wilted.

6 Add the rice, soy sauce ,and sugar to the wok and mix together well.

7 Transfer the green-fried rice to serving dishes and serve immediately.

COOK'S TIP

Light soy sauce has more flavor than the sweeter, dark soy sauce, which gives the food a rich, reddish color.

Fruity Coconut Rice

A pale yellow rice flavored with coconut and spices to serve as an accompaniment—or as a main dish with added diced chicken or pork.

NUTRITIONAL INFORMATION

Calories	578	Sugars	........17g
Protein	.........8g	Fat	..........31g
Carbohydrate	....71g	Saturates	......15g

 5 MINS   35 MINS

SERVES 4

INGREDIENTS

3 oz creamed coconut

3 cups boiling water

1 tbsp sunflower oil (or olive oil for a stronger flavor)

1 onion, thinly sliced or chopped

generous 1 cup long-grain rice

¼ tsp turmeric

6 whole cloves

1 cinnamon stick

½ tsp salt

½ cup raisins or golden raisins

½ cup walnut or pecan halves, roughly chopped

2 tbsp pumpkin seeds (optional)

1 Blend the creamed coconut with half the boiling water until smooth, then stir in the rest until well blended.

2 Heat the oil in a preheated wok, add the onion and stir-fry gently for 3-4 minutes until the onion begins to soften.

3 Rinse the rice thoroughly under cold running water, drain well, and add to the wok with the turmeric. Cook for 1-2 minutes, stirring all the time.

4 Add the coconut milk, cloves, cinnamon stick, and salt and bring to a boil. Cover and simmer very gently for 10 minutes.

5 Add the raisins, nuts, and pumpkin seeds, if using, and mix well. Cover the wok again and continue to cook for a further 5-8 minutes or until all the liquid has been absorbed and the rice is tender. Remove from the heat and leave to stand, still tightly covered, for 5 minutes. Remove the cinnamon stick and serve.

COOK'S TIP

Add 1 cup cooked chicken or pork cut into dice or thin slivers with the raisins to turn this into a main dish. The addition of coconut milk makes the cooked rice slightly sticky.

Chinese Chicken Rice

This is a really colorful main meal or side dish which tastes just as good as it looks.

NUTRITIONAL INFORMATION

Calories 324   Sugars 4g
Protein ....24g   Fat 10g
Carbohydrate ...37g   Saturates 2g

5 MINS   25 MINS

SERVES 4

INGREDIENTS

1¾ cups long-grain white rice

1 tsp turmeric

2 tbsp sunflower oil

12 oz skinless, boneless chicken breasts or thighs, sliced

1 red bell pepper, seeded and sliced

1 green bell pepper, seeded and sliced

1 green chili, seeded and finely chopped

1 medium carrot, coarsely grated

1½ cups bean sprouts

6 green onions, sliced, plus extra to garnish

2 tbsp soy sauce

salt

1 Place the rice and turmeric in a large saucepan of lightly salted water and cook until the grains of rice are just tender, about 10 minutes. Drain the rice thoroughly and press out any excess water with paper towels.

2 Heat the sunflower oil in a large preheated wok or skillet.

3 Add the strips of chicken to the wok or skillet and stir-fry over a high heat until the chicken is just beginning to turn a golden color.

4 Add the sliced bell peppers and green chili to the wok and stir-fry for 2–3 minutes.

5 Add the cooked rice to the wok, a little at a time, tossing well after each addition until well combined and the grains of rice are separated.

6 Add the carrot, bean sprouts, and green onions to the wok and stir-fry for another 2 minutes.

7 Drizzle with the soy sauce and toss to combine.

8 Transfer the Chinese chicken rice to a warm serving dish, garnish with extra green onions, if wished and serve at once.

Fried Rice in Pineapple

This looks very impressive on a party buffet. Mix the remaining pineapple flesh with papaya and mango for an exotic fruit salad.

NUTRITIONAL INFORMATION

Calories 197   Sugars 8g
Protein ....5g   Fat 8g
Carbohydrate ...29g   Saturates 1g

 20 MINS   10 MINS

SERVES 4

I N G R E D I E N T S

1 large pineapple

1 tbsp sunflower oil

1 garlic clove, crushed

1 small onion, diced

½ celery stalk, sliced

1 tsp coriander seeds, ground

1 tsp cumin seeds, ground

1½ cups small mushrooms, sliced

1⅓ cups cooked rice

2 tbsp light soy sauce

½ tsp sugar

½ tsp salt

¼ cup cashews

TO GARNISH

1 green onion, sliced finely

fresh cilantro leaves

mint sprig

1 Using a sharp knife, halve the pineapple lengthwise and cut out the flesh to make 2 boat-shaped shells.

2 Cut the flesh into cubes and reserve 1 cup to use in this recipe. (Any remaining pineapple cubes can be served separately.)

3 Heat the sunflower oil in a wok or large, heavy-bottomed skillet.

4 Cook the garlic, onion, and celery over a high heat, stirring constantly, for 2 minutes. Stir in the coriander and cumin seeds, and the mushrooms.

5 Add the reserved pineapple cubes and cooked rice to the wok or skillet and stir well.

6 Stir in the soy sauce, sugar, salt, and cashews.

7 Using 2 spoons, lift and stir the rice for about 4 minutes until it is thoroughly heated.

8 Spoon the rice mixture into the pineapple boats. Garnish with sliced green onion, cilantro leaves, and a mint sprig.

Chatuchak Fried Rice

An excellent way to use up leftover rice. Put it in the freezer as soon as it is cool, and it will be ready to reheat at any time.

NUTRITIONAL INFORMATION

Calories 241   Sugars 5g
Protein . . . . .7g   Fat 5g
Carbohydrate . . .46g   Saturates 1g

 25 MINS   15 MINS

SERVES 4

I N G R E D I E N T S

1 tbsp sunflower oil

3 shallots, chopped finely

2 garlic cloves, crushed

1 red chili, seeded and chopped finely

1 inch piece fresh ginger,
   shredded finely

½ green bell pepper, seeded and
   sliced finely

2-3 baby eggplants, quartered

3 oz sugar snap peas or snow peas,
   trimmed and blanched

6 baby corn-on-the-cob, halved lengthwise
   and blanched

1 tomato, cut into 8 pieces

1½ cups bean sprouts

3 cups cooked jasmine rice

2 tbsp tomato ketchup

2 tbsp light soy sauce

TO GARNISH

fresh cilantro leaves

lime wedges

1 Heat the sunflower oil in a wok or large, heavy-bottomed skillet over a high heat.

2 Add the shallots, garlic, chili, and ginger to the wok or skillet. Stir until the shallots have softened.

3 Add the green bell pepper and baby eggplants and stir well.

4 Add the sugar snap peas or snow peas, corn, tomato, and bean sprouts. Stir-fry for 3 minutes.

5 Add the cooked jasmine rice to the wok, and lift and stir with two spoons for 4–5 minutes, until no more steam is released.

6 Stir the tomato ketchup and soy sauce into the mixture in the wok.

7 Serve the Chatuchak fried rice immediately, garnished with cilantro leaves and lime wedges to squeeze over.

Curried Rice with Tofu

Cooked rice is combined with marinated tofu, vegetables, and peanuts to make this deliciously rich curry.

NUTRITIONAL INFORMATION

Calories 598	Sugars 2g
Protein 16g	Fat 25
Carbohydrate . . .81g	Saturates 4g

 15 MINS   15 MINS

SERVES 4

I N G R E D I E N T S

1 tsp coriander seeds

1 tsp cumin seeds

1 tsp ground cinnamon

1 tsp cloves

1 whole star anise

1 tsp cardamom pods

1 tsp white peppercorns

1 tbsp oil

6 shallots, chopped very roughly

6 garlic cloves, chopped very roughly

2 inch piece lemon grass, sliced

4 fresh red chilies, seeded and chopped

grated zest of 1 lime

1 tsp salt

3 tbsp sunflower oil

1 cup marinated tofu, cut into 1 inch cubes

4½ oz green beans, cut into 1 inch lengths

6 cups cooked rice (1½ cups raw weight)

3 shallots, diced finely and deep-fried

1 green onion, chopped finely

2 tbsp chopped roast peanuts

1 tbsp lime juice

1 To make the curry paste, grind together the seeds and spices in a pestle and mortar or spice grinder.

2 Heat the sunflower oil in a preheated wok until it is really hot. Add the shallots, garlic, and lemon grass and cook over a low heat until soft, about 5 minutes. Add the chilies and grind together with the dry spices. Stir in the lime zest and salt.

3 To make the curry, heat the oil in a wok or large, heavy-bottomed skillet. Cook the tofu over a high heat for 2 minutes to seal. Stir in the curry paste and beans. Add the rice and stir over a high heat for about 3 minutes.

4 Transfer to a warmed serving dish. Sprinkle with the deep-fried shallots, green onion, and peanuts. Squeeze over the lime juice.

Crab Congee

This is a typical Chinese breakfast dish although it is probably best served as a lunch or supper dish at a Western table!

NUTRITIONAL INFORMATION

Calories	327	Sugars	.......0.1g
Protein	........18g	Fat	...........7g
Carbohydrate	...50g	Saturates	.......2g

 5 MINS   1¼ HOURS

SERVES 4

I N G R E D I E N T S

1 cup short-grain rice

6¼ cups fish stock

½ tsp salt

3½ oz Chinese sausage,
    thinly sliced

8 oz white crab meat

6 green onions, sliced

2 tbsp chopped fresh cilantro

freshly ground black pepper,
    to serve

1 Place the short-grain rice in a large preheated wok or skillet.

2 Add the fish stock to the wok or skillet and bring to a boil.

3 Reduce the heat, then simmer gently for 1 hour, stirring the mixture from time to time.

4 Add the salt, sliced Chinese sausage, white crab meat, sliced green onions, and chopped fresh cilantro to the wok and heat through for about 5 minutes.

5 Add a little more water to the wok if the congee "porridge" is too thick, stirring well.

6 Transfer the crab congee to warm serving bowls, sprinkle with freshly ground black pepper and serve immediately.

COOK'S TIP

Always buy the freshest possible crab meat; fresh is best, although frozen or canned will work for this recipe. In the West, crabs are often sold ready-cooked. The crab should feel heavy for its size, and when it is shaken, there should be no sound of water inside.

Curried Rice with Pork

This rice dish is flavored with vegetables and pork, soy sauce, and curry spices with strips of omelet added as a topping.

NUTRITIONAL INFORMATION

Calories	436	Sugars	.........2g
Protein	........30g	Fat	..........20g
Carbohydrate	...37g	Saturates	.......5g

10 MINS   35 MINS

SERVES 4

INGREDIENTS

1½ cups long-grain rice

12 oz–1 lb 2 oz pork fillet or lean pork slices

3 tomatoes, peeled, quartered, and seeded

2 eggs

4 tsp water

3 tbsp sunflower oil

1 onion, thinly sliced

1–2 garlic cloves, crushed

1 tsp medium or mild curry powder

½ tsp ground coriander

¼ tsp medium-hot chili powder or 1 tsp bottled sweet chili sauce

2 tbsp soy sauce

4½ oz frozen peas, defrosted

salt and pepper

1 Cook the rice in boiling salted water, following the instructions given in Chinese Fried Rice (see page 416) and keep warm until required.

2 Meanwhile, cut the pork into narrow strips across the grain, discarding any fat. Slice the tomatoes.

3 Beat each egg separately with 2 teaspoons cold water and salt and pepper. Heat 2 teaspoons of oil in the wok until really hot. Pour in the first egg, swirl it around and cook undisturbed until set. Remove to a plate or board and repeat with the second egg. Cut the omelets into strips about ½ inch wide.

4 Heat the remaining oil in the wok and when really hot add the onion and garlic and stir-fry for 1–2 minutes. Add the pork and continue to stir-fry for about 3 minutes or until almost cooked.

5 Add the curry powder, coriander, chili powder or chili sauce, and soy sauce to the wok and cook for another minute, stirring constantly.

6 Stir in the rice, tomatoes, and peas and stir-fry for about 2 minutes until piping hot. Adjust the seasoning to taste and turn into a heated serving dish. Arrange the strips of omelet on top and serve at once.

Steamed Rice in Lotus Leaves

The fragrance of the leaves penetrates the rice, giving it a unique taste. Lotus leaves can be bought from Chinese food stores.

NUTRITIONAL INFORMATION

Calories ....163 Sugars 0.1g
Protein ....5g Fat 6g
Carbohydrate ...2.1g Saturates 1g

🍚 1 HOUR 🕐 40 MINS

SERVES 4

INGREDIENTS

2 lotus leaves

4 Chinese dried mushrooms (if unavailable, use thinly sliced open-cap mushrooms)

generous ¾ cup long-grain rice

1 cinnamon stick

6 cardamom pods

4 cloves

1 tsp salt

2 eggs

1 tbsp vegetable oil

2 green onions, chopped

1 tbsp soy sauce

2 tbsp sherry

1 tsp sugar

1 tsp sesame oil

1 Unfold the lotus leaves carefully and cut along the fold to divide each leaf in half. Lay on a large cookie sheet and pour over enough hot water to cover. Soak for about 30 minutes until softened.

2 Place the dried mushrooms in a small bowl and cover with warm water. Leave to soak for 20–25 minutes.

3 Cook the rice in a saucepan of boiling water with the cinnamon stick, cardamom pods, cloves, and salt for about

10 minutes—the rice should be partially cooked. Drain thoroughly and remove the cinnamon stick. Place the rice in a bowl.

4 Beat the eggs lightly. Heat the oil in a wok and cook the eggs quickly, stirring until set. Remove and set aside.

5 Drain the mushrooms, squeezing out the excess water. Remove the tough centers and chop the mushrooms. Stir into

the rice with the cooked egg, green onions, soy sauce, sherry, sugar, and sesame oil.

6 Drain the lotus leaves and divide the rice into four portions. Place a portion in the center of each leaf and fold up to form a pack. Place in a steamer, cover, and steam over simmering water for 20 minutes. To serve, cut the tops of the lotus leaves open to expose the rice inside.

Vegetable Fried Rice

This dish can be served as part of a substantial meal for a number of people or as a vegetarian meal in itself for four.

NUTRITIONAL INFORMATION

Calories 175   Sugars 3g
Protein ....3g   Fat 10g
Carbohydrate ...20g   Saturates 2g

 10 MINS   20 MINS

SERVES 4

INGREDIENTS

⅔ cup long-grain white rice

3 tbsp peanut oil

2 garlic cloves, crushed

½ tsp Chinese five-spice powder

⅓ cup green beans

1 green bell pepper, seeded and chopped

4 baby corn-on-the-cobs, sliced

1 oz bamboo shoots, chopped

3 tomatoes, skinned, seeded and chopped

½ cup cooked peas

1 tsp sesame oil

1 Bring a large saucepan of water to a boil.

2 Add the long-grain white rice to the saucepan and cook for about 15 minutes. Drain the rice well, rinse under cold running water and drain thoroughly again.

3 Heat the peanut oil in a preheated wok or large skillet. Add the garlic and Chinese five-spice and stir-fry for 30 seconds.

4 Add the green beans, chopped green bell pepper and sliced corn and stir-fry the ingredients in the wok for 2 minutes.

5 Stir the bamboo shoots, tomatoes, peas, and rice into the mixture in the wok and stir-fry for 1 further minute.

6 Sprinkle with sesame oil and transfer to serving dishes. Serve immediately.

VARIATION

Use a selection of vegetables of your choice in this recipe, cutting them to a similar size to make sure that they cook in the same amount of time.

Coconut Rice with Lentils

Rice and green lentils are cooked with coconut, lemon grass, and curry leaves. It will serve 2 people as a main course or 4 as a side dish.

NUTRITIONAL INFORMATION

Calories 511   Sugars 3g
Protein . . . . .12g   Fat 24g
Carbohydrate . . .67g   Saturates 15g

  5 MINS   50 MINS

SERVES 4

I N G R E D I E N T S

⅓ cup green lentils

generous 1 cup long-grain rice

2 tbsp vegetable oil

1 onion, sliced

2 garlic cloves, crushed

3 curry leaves

1 stalk lemon grass, chopped (if unavailable, use grated zest of ½ lemon)

1 green chili, seeded and chopped

½ tsp cumin seeds

1½ tsp salt

⅓ cup creamed coconut

2½ cups hot water

2 tbsp chopped fresh cilantro

TO GARNISH

shredded radishes

shredded cucumber

1 Wash the lentils and place in a saucepan. Cover with cold water, bring to a boil and boil rapidly for 10 minutes.

2 Wash the rice thoroughly and drain well. Set aside until required.

3 Heat the vegetable oil in a large saucepan which has a tight-fitting lid

and fry the onion for 3–4 minutes. Add the garlic, curry leaves, lemon grass, chili, cumin seeds, and salt, and stir well.

4 Drain the lentils and rinse. Add to the onion and spices with the rice and mix well.

5 Add the creamed coconut to the hot water and stir until dissolved. Stir the coconut liquid into the rice mixture and bring to a boil. Turn down the heat to low,

put the lid on tightly and leave to cook undisturbed for 15 minutes.

6 Without removing the lid, remove the pan from the heat and leave to rest for 10 minutes to allow the rice and lentils to finish cooking in their own steam.

7 Stir in the cilantro and remove the curry leaves. Serve garnished with the radishes and cucumber.

Fried Rice with Shrimp

Use either large or jumbo peeled shrimp for this rice dish.

NUTRITIONAL INFORMATION

Calories 599	Sugars 0g	
Protein 26g	Fat 16g	
Carbohydrate ...94g	Saturates 3g	

🐡 🐡 🐡

🍲 5 MINS   🕐 35 MINS

SERVES 4

I N G R E D I E N T S

1½ cups long-grain rice

2 eggs

4 tsp cold water

salt and pepper

3 tbsp sunflower oil

4 green onions, thinly sliced diagonally

1 garlic clove, crushed

4½ oz small mushrooms, thinly sliced

2 tbsp oyster or anchovy sauce

1 x 7 oz can water chestnuts, drained and sliced

9 oz peeled shrimp, defrosted if frozen

½ bunch watercress, roughly chopped

watercress sprigs, to garnish (optional)

1 Cook the rice in boiling salted water, following the instructions given in Chinese Fried Rice (see page 416) and keep warm.

2 Beat each egg separately with 2 teaspoons of cold water and salt and pepper.

3 Heat 2 teaspoons of sunflower oil in a wok or large skillet, swirling it around until really hot. Pour in the first egg, swirl it around and leave to cook undisturbed until set. Remove to a plate or board and repeat with the second egg. Cut the omelets into 1 inch squares.

4 Heat the remaining oil in the wok and when really hot add the green onions and garlic and stir-fry for 1 minute. Add the mushrooms and continue to cook for another 2 minutes.

5 Stir in the oyster or anchovy sauce and seasoning and add the water chestnuts, and shrimp; stir-fry for 2 minutes.

6 Stir in the cooked rice and stir-fry for 1 minute, then add the watercress and omelet squares and stir-fry for another 1-2 minutes until piping hot. Serve at once garnished with sprigs of watercress, if liked.

Chicken & Rice Casserole

This is a quick-cooking, spicy casserole of rice, chicken, vegetables, and chili in a soy and ginger flavored liquor.

NUTRITIONAL INFORMATION

Calories	502	Sugars	........2g
Protein	........55g	Fat	..........9g
Carbohydrate	...52g	Saturates	.......3g

35 MINS   50 MINS

SERVES 4

I N G R E D I E N T S

⅔ cup long-grain rice

1 tbsp dry sherry

2 tbsp light soy sauce

2 tbsp dark soy sauce

2 tsp dark brown sugar

1 tsp salt

1 tsp sesame oil

2 lb skinless, boneless chicken meat, diced

3¾ cups chicken stock

2 open-cap mushrooms, sliced

2 oz water chestnuts, halved

2¾ oz broccoli flowerets

1 yellow bell pepper, sliced

4 tsp grated fresh ginger

whole chives, to garnish

VARIATION

This dish would work equally well with beef or pork. Chinese dried mushrooms may be used instead of the open-cap mushrooms, if rehydrated before adding to the dish.

1 Cook the rice in a saucepan of boiling water for about 15 minutes. Drain well, rinse under cold water, and drain again thoroughly.

2 Mix together the sherry, soy sauces, sugar, salt, and sesame oil.

3 Stir the chicken into the soy mixture, turning to coat the chicken well. Leave to marinate for about 30 minutes.

4 Bring the stock to a boil in a saucepan or preheated wok. Add the chicken with the marinade, mushrooms, water chestnuts, broccoli, bell pepper, and ginger.

5 Stir in the rice, reduce the heat, cover, and cook for 25-30 minutes, until the chicken and vegetables are cooked through. Transfer to serving plates, garnish with chives, and serve.

Special Fried Rice

This dish is a popular choice in Chinese restaurants. Ham and shrimp are mixed with vegetables in a soy-flavored rice.

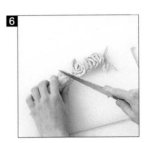

NUTRITIONAL INFORMATION

Calories 301	Sugars 1g
Protein 26g	Fat 13g
Carbohydrate ...21g	Saturates 3g

 5 MINS   30 MINS

SERVES 4

INGREDIENTS

⅔ cup long-grain rice

2 tbsp vegetable oil

2 eggs, beaten

2 garlic cloves, crushed

1 tsp grated fresh ginger

3 green onions, sliced

¾ cup cooked peas

⅔ cup bean sprouts

1⅓ cups shredded ham

15½ oz peeled, cooked shrimp

2 tbsp light soy sauce

1 Cook the rice in a saucepan of boiling water for about 15 minutes. Drain well, rinse under cold water, and drain thoroughly again.

2 Heat 1 tablespoon of the vegetable oil in a preheated wok.

3 Add the beaten eggs and another 1 teaspoon of oil. Tilt the wok so that the egg covers the base to make a thin pancake.

4 Cook until lightly browned on the underside, then flip the pancake over and cook on the other side for 1 minute. Remove from the wok and leave to cool.

5 Heat the remaining oil in the wok and stir-fry the garlic and ginger for 30 seconds. Add the green onions, peas, bean sprouts, ham, and shrimp. Stir-fry for 2 minutes.

6 Stir in the soy sauce and rice and cook for a further 2 minutes. Transfer the rice to serving dishes. Roll up the pancake, slice it very thinly and use to garnish the rice. Serve immediately.

COOK'S TIP

As this recipe contains meat and fish, it is ideal served with simpler vegetable dishes.

Sweet Chili Pork Fried Rice

This is a variation of egg fried rice which may be served as an accompaniment to a main meal dish.

NUTRITIONAL INFORMATION

Calories	366	Sugars	.........5g
Protein	........29g	Fat	..........16g
Carbohydrate	...28g	Saturates	.......4g

🍲 25 MINS 🕑 20 MINS

SERVES 4

I N G R E D I E N T S

1 lb pork tenderloin

2 tbsp sunflower oil

2 tbsp sweet chili sauce, plus extra
   to serve

1 onion, sliced

6 oz carrots, cut into thin sticks

6 oz zucchini, cut into thin sticks

1 cup canned bamboo shoots, drained

4¾ cups cooked long-grain rice

1 egg, beaten

1 tbsp chopped fresh parsley

1 Using a sharp knife, cut the pork tenderloin into thin slices.

2 Heat the sunflower oil in a large preheated wok or skillet.

3 Add the pork to the wok and stir-fry for 5 minutes.

4 Add the chili sauce to the wok and allow to bubble, stirring, for 2–3 minutes or until syrupy.

5 Add the onion, carrots, zucchini, and bamboo shoots to the wok and stir-fry for another 3 minutes.

6 Add the cooked rice and stir-fry for 2–3 minutes, or until the rice is heated through.

7 Drizzle the beaten egg over the top of the fried rice and cook, tossing the ingredients in the wok with two spoons, until the egg sets.

8 Scatter with chopped fresh parsley and serve immediately, with extra sweet chili sauce, if desired.

COOK'S TIP

For a really quick dish,
add frozen mixed vegetables
to the rice instead of the freshly
prepared vegetables.

Crab Fried Rice

Canned crab meat is used in this recipe for convenience, but fresh white crab meat could be used – quite deliciously – instead.

NUTRITIONAL INFORMATION

Calories	225	Sugars	.........1g
Protein	........12g	Fat	...........11g
Carbohydrate	...20g	Saturates	.......2g

 5 MINS   25 MINS

SERVES 4

I N G R E D I E N T S

⅔ cup long-grain rice

2 tbsp peanut oil

4½ oz canned white crab meat, drained

1 leek, sliced

⅔ cup bean sprouts

2 eggs, beaten

1 tbsp light soy sauce

2 tsp lime juice

1 tsp sesame oil

salt

sliced lime, to garnish

1 Cook the rice in a saucepan of boiling salted water for 15 minutes. Drain well, rinse under cold running water and drain again thoroughly.

2 Heat the peanut oil in a preheated wok until it is really hot.

3 Add the crab meat, leek, and bean sprouts to the wok and stir-fry for 2-3 minutes. Remove the mixture from the wok with a slotted spoon and set aside until required.

4 Add the eggs to the wok and cook, stirring occasionally, for 2-3 minutes, until they begin to set.

5 Stir the rice and the crab meat, leek, and bean sprout mixture into the eggs in the wok.

6 Add the soy sauce and lime juice to the mixture in the wok. Cook for 1 minute, stirring to combine, and sprinkle with the sesame oil.

7 Transfer the crab fried rice to a serving dish, garnish with the sliced lime, and serve immediately.

VARIATION

Cooked lobster may be used instead of the crab for a really special dish.

Noodles

Noodles are a symbol of longevity in China and are always served at birthday and New Year celebrations. It is considered bad luck to cut noodles into shorter lengths because the Chinese believe the longer they are, the longer and happier your life will be. Noodles are available in several varieties, both fresh and dried, made from wheat,

buckwheat, or rice flours, or you can even make your own if you have time! They come in fine threads, strings, or flat ribbons and can be bought from large supermarkets or oriental food stores. Like rice, noodles are very versatile and can be boiled, fried, added to soups, or served plain. Noodles are precooked as part of the manufacturing process, so most only need soaking in hot water to rehydrate them.

Beef Chow Mein

Chow mein must be the best-known and most popular noodle dish on any Chinese menu. You can use any meat or vegetables instead of beef.

NUTRITIONAL INFORMATION

Calories 341   Sugars 3g
Protein . . . . .27g   Fat 17g
Carbohydrate . . .20g   Saturates 4g

10 MINS   20 MINS

SERVES 4

I N G R E D I E N T S

1 lb egg noodles

4 tbsp peanut oil

1 lb lean beef steak, cut into thin strips

2 garlic cloves, crushed

1 tsp grated fresh ginger

1 green bell pepper, thinly sliced

1 carrot, thinly sliced

2 celery stalks, sliced

8 green onions

1 tsp dark brown sugar

1 tbsp dry sherry

2 tbsp dark soy sauce

few drops of chili sauce

1 Cook the noodles in a saucepan of boiling salted water for 4-5 minutes. Drain well, rinse under cold running water and drain again thoroughly.

2 Toss the noodles in 1 tablespoon of the peanut oil.

3 Heat the remaining oil in a preheated wok. Add the beef and stir-fry for 3-4 minutes, stirring constantly.

4 Add the crushed garlic and grated fresh ginger to the wok and stir-fry for 30 seconds.

5 Add the bell pepper, carrot, celery, and green onions and stir-fry for about 2 minutes.

6 Add the dark brown sugar, dry sherry, dark soy sauce, and chili sauce to the mixture in the wok and cook, stirring, for 1 minute.

7 Stir in the noodles, mixing well, and cook until completely warmed through.

8 Transfer the noodles to warm serving bowls and serve immediately.

VARIATION

A variety of different vegetables may be used in this recipe for color and flavor—try broccoli, red bell peppers, green beans, or baby corn-on-the-cobs.

Cellophane Noodles & Shrimp

Jumbo shrimp are cooked with orange juice, bell peppers, soy sauce, and vinegar and served on a bed of cellophane noodles.

NUTRITIONAL INFORMATION

Calories	118	Sugar	.........4g
Protein	.........7g	Fat	..........4g
Carbohydrate	...15g	Saturates	.......1g

  10 MINS 25 MINS

SERVES 4

I N G R E D I E N T S

6 oz cellophane noodles

1 tbsp vegetable oil

1 garlic clove, crushed

2 tsp grated fresh ginger

24 raw jumbo shrimp, peeled and deveined

1 red bell pepper, seeded and thinly sliced

1 green bell pepper, seeded and thinly sliced

1 onion, chopped

2 tbsp light soy sauce

juice of 1 orange

2 tsp wine vinegar

pinch of brown sugar

⅔ cup fish stock

1 tbsp cornstarch

2 tsp water

orange slices, to garnish

1 Cook the noodles in a pan of boiling water for 1 minute. Drain well, rinse under cold water, and then drain again.

2 Heat the oil in a wok and stir-fry the garlic and ginger for 30 seconds.

3 Add the shrimp and stir-fry for 2 minutes. Remove with a slotted spoon and keep warm.

4 Add the bell peppers and onion to the wok and stir-fry for 2 minutes. Stir in the soy sauce, orange juice, vinegar, sugar, and stock. Return the shrimp to the wok and cook for 8-10 minutes, until cooked through.

5 Blend the cornstarch with the water and stir into the wok. Bring to a boil, add the noodles and cook for 1-2 minutes. Garnish and serve.

VARIATION

Lime or lemon juice and slices may be used instead of the orange. Use 3-5½ tsp of these juices.

Cantonese Fried Noodles

This dish is usually served as a snack or light meal. It may also be served as an accompaniment to plain meat and fish dishes.

NUTRITIONAL INFORMATION

Calories ....385 Sugars 6g
Protein ....38g Fat 17g
Carbohydrate ...21g Saturates 4g

5 MINS   15 MINS

SERVES 4

INGREDIENTS

12 oz egg noodles

3 tbsp vegetable oil

1½ lb lean steak, cut into thin strips

4½ oz green cabbage, shredded

2¾ oz bamboo shoots

6 green onions, sliced

1 oz green beans, halved

1 tbsp dark soy sauce

2 tbsp beef stock

1 tbsp dry sherry

1 tbsp light brown sugar

2 tbsp chopped parsley, to garnish

1 Cook the noodles in a saucepan of boiling water for 2-3 minutes. Drain well, rinse under cold running water, and drain thoroughly again.

2 Heat 1 tablespoon of the oil in a preheated wok or skillet, swirling it around until it is really hot

3 Add the noodles and stir-fry for 1-2 minutes. Drain the noodles and set aside until required.

4 Heat the remaining oil in the wok. Add the beef and stir-fry for 2-3 minutes. Add the cabbage, bamboo shoots, green onions, and beans to the wok and stir-fry for 1-2 minutes.

5 Add the soy sauce, beef stock, dry sherry, and light brown sugar to the wok, stirring to mix well.

6 Stir the noodles into the mixture in the wok, tossing to mix well. Transfer to serving bowls, garnish with chopped parsley, and serve immediately.

VARIATION

You can vary the vegetables in this dish depending on seasonal availability or whatever you have on hand—try broccoli, green bell pepper, or spinach.

Sweet & Sour Noodles

This delicious dish combines sweet and sour flavors with the addition of egg, rice noodles, shrimp, and vegetables for a real treat.

NUTRITIONAL INFORMATION

Calories	352	Sugars	........14g
Protein	........23g	Fat	..........17g
Carbohydrate	...29g	Saturates	.......3g

10 MINS   10 MINS

SERVES 4

INGREDIENTS

3 tbsp fish sauce

2 tbsp distilled white vinegar

2 tbsp sugar

2 tbsp tomato paste

2 tbsp sunflower oil

3 cloves garlic, crushed

12 oz rice noodles, soaked in boiling water for 5 minutes

8 green onions, sliced

6 oz carrot, grated

1¼ cups bean sprouts

2 eggs, beaten

8 oz peeled large shrimp

½ cup chopped peanuts

1 tsp chili flakes, to garnish

1 Mix together the fish sauce, vinegar, sugar, and tomato paste.

2 Heat the sunflower oil in a large preheated wok.

3 Add the garlic to the wok and stir-fry for 30 seconds.

4 Drain the noodles thoroughly and add them to the wok together with the fish sauce and tomato paste mixture. Mix well to combine.

5 Add the green onions, carrot, and bean sprouts to the wok and stir-fry for 2–3 minutes.

6 Move the contents of the wok to one side, add the beaten eggs to the empty part of the wok, and cook until the egg sets. Add the noodles, shrimp, and peanuts to the wok and mix well. Transfer to warm serving dishes and garnish with chili flakes. Serve hot.

COOK'S TIP

Chili flakes may be found in the spice section of large supermarkets.

Noodles with Chili & Shrimp

This is a simple dish to prepare and is packed with flavor, making it an ideal choice for special occasions.

NUTRITIONAL INFORMATION

Calories 259	Sugars 9g
Protein 28g	Fat 8g
Carbohydrate . . .20g	Saturates 1g

  10 MINS   5 MINS

SERVES 4

I N G R E D I E N T S

9 oz thin glass noodles

2 tbsp sunflower oil

1 onion, sliced

2 red chilies, seeded and very finely chopped

4 lime leaves, thinly shredded

1 tbsp fresh cilantro

2 tbsp sugar

2 tbsp fish sauce

1 lb raw jumbo shrimp, peeled

1 Place the noodles in a large bowl. Pour over enough boiling water to cover the noodles and leave to stand for 5 minutes. Drain thoroughly and set aside until required.

COOK'S TIP

If you cannot buy raw jumbo shrimp, use cooked shrimp instead and cook them with the noodles for 1 minute only, just to heat through.

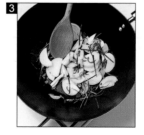 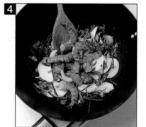 

2 Heat the sunflower oil in a large preheated wok or skillet until it is really hot.

3 Add the onion, red chilies, and lime leaves to the wok and stir-fry for 1 minute.

4 Add the cilantro, sugar, fish sauce, and shrimp and then stir-fry for 2 minutes or until the shrimp turn pink.

5 Add the drained noodles to the wok, toss to mix well, and stir-fry for 1–2 minutes or until heated through.

6 Transfer the noodles and shrimp to warm serving bowls and serve immediately.

Chicken & Noodle One-Pot

Flavorsome chicken and vegetables cooked with Chinese egg noodles in a coconut sauce. Serve in deep soup bowls.

NUTRITIONAL INFORMATION

Calories	256	Sugars 7g
Protein	........30g	Fat 8g
Carbohydrate	...18g	Saturates 2g

 5 MINS   20 MINS

SERVES 4

INGREDIENTS

1 tbsp sunflower oil

1 onion, sliced

1 garlic clove, crushed

1 inch ginger, peeled and grated

1 bunch green onions, sliced diagonally

1 lb 2 oz chicken breast fillet, skinned and cut into bite-sized pieces

2 tbsp mild curry paste

2 cups coconut milk

1¼ cups chicken stock

9 oz Chinese egg noodles

2 tsp lime juice

salt and pepper

basil sprigs, to garnish

1 Heat the sunflower oil in a wok or large, heavy-bottomed skillet.

2 Add the onion, garlic, ginger, and green onions to the wok and stir-fry for 2 minutes until softened.

3 Add the chicken and curry paste and stir-fry for 4 minutes, or until the vegetables and chicken are golden brown. Stir in the coconut milk, stock, and salt and pepper to taste, and mix well.

4 Bring to a boil, break the noodles into large pieces, if necessary, add to the pan, cover, and simmer for about 6-8 minutes until the noodles are just tender, stirring occasionally.

5 Add the lime juice and adjust the seasoning, if necessary.

6 Serve the chicken and noodle one-pot at once in deep soup bowls, garnished with basil sprigs.

COOK'S TIP

If you enjoy hot flavors, substitute the mild curry paste in the above recipe with hot curry paste (found in Asian markets) but reduce the quantity to 1 tablespoon.

Quick Chicken Chow Mein

A quick stir-fry of chicken and vegetables which are mixed with Chinese egg noodles and a dash of sesame oil.

NUTRITIONAL INFORMATION

Calories 300   Sugars 5g
Protein . . . . .23g   Fat 15g
Carbohydrate . . .18g   Saturates 2g

20 MINS   15 MINS

SERVES 4

INGREDIENTS

2 tbsp sesame seeds

9 oz thread egg noodles

6 oz broccoli flowerets

3 tbsp sunflower oil

1 garlic clove, sliced

1 inch piece fresh ginger,
    peeled and chopped

9 oz chicken fillet, sliced thinly

1 onion, sliced

4½ oz shiitake mushrooms,
    sliced

1 red bell pepper, seeded and
    cut into thin strips

1 tsp cornstarch

2 tbsp water

15 oz can baby corn-on-the-cob,
    drained and halved

2 tbsp dry sherry

2 tbsp soy sauce

1 tsp sesame oil

1 Put the sesame seeds in a heavy-bottomed skillet and cook for 2–3 minutes until they turn brown and begin to pop. Cover the pan so the seeds do not jump out and shake them constantly to prevent them burning. Remove from the pan and set aside until required.

2 Put the noodles in a bowl, cover with boiling water, and leave to stand for 4 minutes. Drain thoroughly.

3 Meanwhile, blanch the broccoli in boiling salted water for 2 minutes, then drain.

4 Heat the sunflower oil in a wok or large skillet, add the garlic, ginger, chicken, and onion and stir-fry for 2 minutes until the chicken is golden and the onion softened.

5 Add the broccoli, mushrooms, and red bell pepper and stir-fry for another 2 minutes.

6 Mix the cornstarch with the water then stir into the pan with the corn, sherry, soy sauce, drained noodles, and sesame oil and cook, stirring, until the sauce is thickened and the noodles warmed through. Sprinkle with the sesame seeds and serve.

COOK'S TIP

As well as adding protein, vitamins and useful fats to the diet, nuts and seeds add important flavor and texture.

Lamb with Noodles

Lamb is quick fried, coated in a soy sauce, and served on a bed of transparent noodles for a richly flavored dish.

NUTRITIONAL INFORMATION

Calories	285	Sugars	.........1g
Protein	........27g	Fat	..........16g
Carbohydrate	...10g	Saturates	.......6g

5 MINS   15 MINS

SERVES 4

INGREDIENTS

5½ oz cellophane noodles

2 tbsp peanut oil

1 lb lean lamb, thinly sliced

2 garlic cloves, crushed

2 leeks, sliced

3 tbsp dark soy sauce

1 cup lamb stock

dash of chili sauce

red chili strips, to garnish

1 Bring a large saucepan of water to a boil. Add the cellophane noodles and cook for 1 minute. Drain the noodles well, place in a strainer, rinse under cold running water, and drain thoroughly again. Set aside until required.

2 Heat the peanut oil in a preheated wok or skillet, swirling the oil around until it is really hot.

3 Add the lamb to the wok or skillet and stir-fry for about 2 minutes.

4 Add the crushed garlic and sliced leeks to the wok and stir-fry for 2 minutes more.

5 Stir in the dark soy sauce, lamb stock, and chili sauce and cook for

3-4 minutes, stirring frequently, until the meat is cooked through.

6 Add the drained cellophane noodles to the wok or skillet and cook for about 1 minute, stirring, until heated through.

7 Transfer the lamb and cellophane noodles to serving plates, garnish with red chili strips, and serve.

COOK'S TIP

Transparent noodles are available in Chinese supermarkets. Use egg noodles instead if transparent noodles are unavailable, and cook them according to the instructions on the pack.

Fried Vegetable Noodles

In this recipe, noodles are first boiled and then deep-fried for a crisply textured dish, and tossed with fried vegetables.

NUTRITIONAL INFORMATION

Calories . . . . . . .229 Sugars 4g
Protein . . . . .5g Fat 15g
Carbohydrate . . .20g Saturates 2g

  5 MINS 🕐 25 MINS

SERVES 4

I N G R E D I E N T S

3 cups dried egg noodles

2 tbsp peanut oil

2 garlic cloves, crushed

½ tsp ground star anise

1 carrot, cut into thin sticks

1 green bell pepper, cut into thin sticks

1 onion, quartered and sliced

4½ oz broccoli flowerets

2¾ oz bamboo shoots

1 celery stalk, sliced

1 tbsp light soy sauce

⅔ cup vegetable stock

oil, for deep-frying

1 tsp cornstarch

2 tsp water

1 Cook the noodles in a saucepan of boiling water for 1-2 minutes. Drain well and rinse under cold running water. Leave the noodles to drain thoroughly in a colander until required.

2 Heat the peanut oil in a preheated wok until smoking. Reduce the heat, add the crushed garlic and ground star anise, and stir-fry for 30 seconds. Add the remaining vegetables and stir-fry for 1-2 minutes.

3 Add the soy sauce and vegetable stock to the wok and cook over a low heat for 5 minutes.

4 Heat the oil for deep-frying in a separate wok to 350°F, or until a cube of bread browns in 30 seconds.

5 Using a fork, twist the drained noodles and form them into rounds. Deep-fry them in batches until crisp, turning once. Leave to drain thoroughly on paper towels.

6 Blend the cornstarch with the water to form a paste and stir into the vegetables. Bring to a boil, stirring until the sauce is thickened and clear.

7 Arrange the noodles on a warm serving plate, spoon the vegetables on top, and serve immediately.

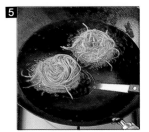

Pork Chow Mein

This is a basic recipe—the meat and/or vegetables can be varied as much as you like.

NUTRITIONAL INFORMATION

Calories	239	Sugars 1g
Protein	........17g	Fat 14g
Carbohydrate	...12g	Saturates 2g

15 MINS   15 MINS

SERVES 4

INGREDIENTS

9 oz egg noodles

4-5 tbsp vegetable oil

9 oz pork fillet, cooked

4½ oz green beans

2 tbsp light soy sauce

1 tsp salt

½ tsp sugar

1 tbsp Chinese rice wine or dry sherry

2 green onions, finely shredded

a few drops sesame oil

chili sauce, to serve (optional)

1 Cook the noodles in boiling water according to the instructions on the pack, then drain and rinse under cold water. Drain again then toss with 1 tablespoon of the oil.

2 Slice the pork into thin shreds and trim the beans.

3 Heat 3 tablespoons of oil in a preheated wok until hot. Add the noodles and stir-fry for 2-3 minutes with 1 tablespoon soy sauce, then remove to a serving dish. Keep warm.

4 Heat the remaining oil and stir-fry the beans and meat for 2 minutes. Add the salt, sugar, wine or sherry, the remaining soy sauce and about half the green onions to the wok.

5 Stir the mixture in the wok, adding a little stock if necessary, then pour on top of the noodles, and sprinkle with sesame oil and the remaining green onions.

6 Serve the chow mein hot or cold with chili sauce, if desired.

COOK'S TIP

Chow mein literally means "stir-fried noodles" and is highly popular in the West as well as in China. Almost any ingredient can be added, such as fish, meat, poultry, or vegetables. It is very popular for lunch and makes a tasty salad served cold.

Fried Noodles (Chow Mein)

This is a basic recipe for chow mein. Additional ingredients such as chicken or pork can be added if you like.

NUTRITIONAL INFORMATION

Calories	716	Sugars	.....2g
Protein	.....4g	Fat	.....12g
Carbohydrate	...14g	Saturates	.....1g

 5 MINS   15 MINS

SERVES 4

INGREDIENTS

9½ oz egg noodles

3-4 tbsp vegetable oil

1 small onion, finely shredded

4½ oz fresh bean sprouts

1 green onion, finely shredded

2 tbsp light soy sauce

a few drops of sesame oil

salt

1 Bring a wok or saucepan of salted water to a boil.

2 Add the egg noodles to the saucepan or wok and cook according to the instructions on the pack (usually no more than 4-5 minutes).

COOK'S TIP

Noodles, a symbol of longevity, are made from wheat or rice flour, water, and egg. Handmade noodles are made by an elaborate process of kneading, pulling, and twisting the dough, and it takes years to learn the art.

3 Drain the noodles well and rinse in cold water; drain thoroughly again, then transfer to a large mixing bowl and toss with a little vegetable oil.

4 Heat the remaining vegetable oil in a preheated wok or large skillet until really hot.

5 Add the shredded onion to the wok and stir-fry for about 30-40 seconds.

6 Add the bean sprouts and drained noodles to the wok, stir, and toss for 1 more minute.

7 Add the shredded green onion and light soy sauce and blend well.

8 Transfer the noodles to a warm serving dish, sprinkle with the sesame oil, and serve immediately.

Noodles with Shrimp

This is a simple dish using egg noodles and large shrimp, which give the dish a wonderful flavor, texture, and color.

NUTRITIONAL INFORMATION

Calories 142	Sugars 0.4g	
Protein 11g	Fat 7g	
Carbohydrate 11g	Saturates 1g	

5 MINS   10 MINS

SERVES 4

INGREDIENTS

8 oz thin egg noodles

2 tbsp peanut oil

1 garlic clove, crushed

½ tsp ground star anise

1 bunch green onions, cut into 2 inch pieces

24 raw jumbo shrimp, peeled with tails intact

2 tbsp light soy sauce

2 tsp lime juice

lime wedges, to garnish

1 Blanch the noodles in a saucepan of boiling water for about 2 minutes.

2 Drain the noodles well, rinse under cold water, and drain thoroughly again. Keep warm and set aside until required.

3 Heat the peanut oil in a preheated wok or large skillet until almost smoking.

4 Add the crushed garlic and ground star anise to the wok and stir-fry for 30 seconds.

5 Add the green onions and jumbo shrimp to the wok and stir-fry for 2-3 minutes.

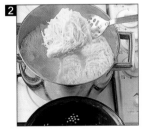

6 Stir in the light soy sauce, lime juice, and noodles and mix well.

7 Cook the mixture in the wok for about 1 minute until thoroughly heated through and all the ingredients are thoroughly incorporated.

8 Spoon the noodle and shrimp mixture into a warm serving dish. Transfer to serving bowls, garnish with lime wedges, and serve immediately.

COOK'S TIP

If fresh egg noodles are available, these require very little cooking: simply place in boiling water for about 3 minutes, then drain and toss in oil. Noodles can be boiled and eaten plain, or stir-fried with meat and vegetables for a light meal or snack.

Homemade Noodles

These noodles are simple to make; you do not need a pasta-making machine because they are rolled out by hand.

NUTRITIONAL INFORMATION

Calories	294	Sugars	........3g
Protein	.........7g	Fat	.........15g
Carbohydrate	...35g	Saturates	.......2g

  20 MINS · 15 MINS

SERVES 2–4

INGREDIENTS

NOODLES

1 cup all-purpose flour

2 tbsp cornstarch

½ tsp salt

½ cup boiling water

5 tbsp vegetable oil

STIR-FRY

1 zucchini, cut into thin sticks

1 celery stalk, cut into thin sticks

1 carrot, cut into thin sticks

4½ oz open-cap mushrooms, sliced

14½ oz broccoli flowerets and stalks, peeled and thinly sliced

1 leek, sliced

2 cups bean sprouts

1 tbsp soy sauce

2 tsp rice wine vinegar

½ tsp sugar

  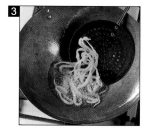

1 To prepare the noodles, sift the flour, cornstarch, and salt into a bowl. Make a well in the center and pour in the boiling water and 1 teaspoon of oil. Mix quickly to make a soft dough. Cover and leave for 5–6 minutes.

2 Make the noodles by breaking off small pieces of dough and rolling into balls. Roll each ball across a very lightly oiled work counter with the palm of your hand to form thin noodles. Do not worry if some of the noodles break into shorter lengths. Set the noodles aside.

3 Heat 3 tablespoons of oil in a wok. Add the noodles in batches and fry over a high heat for 1 minute. Reduce the heat and cook for another 2 minutes. Remove and drain on paper towels. Set aside.

4 Heat the remaining oil in the pan. Add the zucchini, celery, and carrot, and stir-fry for 1 minute. Add the mushrooms, broccoli, and leek, and stir-fry for another minute. Stir in the remaining ingredients and mix well until thoroughly heated through.

5 Add the noodles and cook over a high heat, tossing to mix the ingredients. Serve immediately.

Special Noodles

This dish combines meat, vegetables, shrimp, and noodles in a curried coconut sauce. Serve as a main meal or as an accompaniment.

NUTRITIONAL INFORMATION

Calories	409	Sugars	........12g
Protein	........24g	Fat	..........23g
Carbohydrate	...28g	Saturates	.......8g

5 MINS   25 MINS

SERVES 4

INGREDIENTS

9 oz thin rice noodles

4 tbsp peanut oil

2 cloves garlic, crushed

2 red chilies, seeded and very
  finely chopped

1 tsp grated fresh ginger

2 tbsp Madras curry paste

2 tbsp rice wine vinegar

1 tbsp sugar

8 oz cooked ham, finely shredded

1¼ cups canned water chestnuts, sliced

3½ oz mushrooms, sliced

¾ cup peas

1 red bell pepper, seeded and
  thinly sliced

3½ oz peeled shrimp

2 large eggs

4 tbsp coconut milk

¼ cup shredded coconut

2 tbsp chopped fresh cilantro

1 Place the rice noodles in a large bowl, cover with boiling water, and leave to soak for about 10 minutes. Drain the noodles thoroughly, then toss with 2 tablespoons of peanut oil.

2 Heat the remaining peanut oil in a large preheated wok until the oil is really hot.

3 Add the garlic, chilies, ginger, curry paste, rice wine vinegar, and sugar to the wok and stir-fry for 1 minute.

4 Add the ham, water chestnuts, mushrooms, peas, and red bell pepper to the wok and stir-fry for 5 minutes.

5 Add the noodles and shrimp to the wok and stir-fry for 2 minutes.

6 In a small bowl, beat together the eggs and coconut milk. Drizzle over the mixture in the wok and stir-fry until the egg sets.

7 Add the shredded coconut and chopped fresh cilantro to the wok and toss to combine. Transfer the noodles to warm serving dishes and serve immediately.

Seafood Chow Mein

Use whatever seafood is available for this delicious noodle dish—mussels or crab would also be suitable.

NUTRITIONAL INFORMATION

Calories	.281	Sugars	.1g
Protein	.15g	Fat	.18g
Carbohydrate	.16g	Saturates	.2g

15 MINS ⏱ 15 MINS

SERVES 4

INGREDIENTS

3 oz squid, cleaned

3-4 fresh scallops

3 oz raw shrimp, shelled

½ egg white, lightly beaten

1 tbsp cornstarch paste
(see page 31)

9½ oz egg noodles

5-6 tbsp vegetable oil

2 tbsp light soy sauce

2 oz snow peas

½ tsp salt

½ tsp sugar

1 tsp Chinese rice wine

2 green onions, finely shredded

a few drops of sesame oil

1 Open up the squid and score the inside in a criss-cross pattern, then cut into pieces about the size of a postage stamp. Soak the squid in a bowl of boiling water until all the pieces curl up. Rinse in cold water and drain.

2 Cut each scallop into 3-4 slices. Cut the shrimp in half lengthwise if large. Mix the scallops and shrimp with the egg white and cornstarch paste.

3 Cook the noodles in boiling water according to the pack instructions, then drain and rinse under cold water. Drain well, then toss with about 1 tablespoon of oil.

4 Heat 3 tablespoons of oil in a preheated wok. Add the noodles and 1 tablespoon of the soy sauce and stir-fry for 2-3 minutes. Remove to a large serving dish.

5 Heat the remaining oil in the wok and add the snow peas and seafood. Stir-fry for about 2 minutes, then add the salt, sugar, wine, remaining soy sauce, and about half the green onions. Blend well and add a little stock or water if necessary. Pour the seafood mixture on top of the noodles and sprinkle with sesame oil. Garnish with the remaining green onions and serve.

COOK'S TIP

Chinese rice wine, made from glutinous rice, is also known as "yellow wine" because of its golden amber color. If it is unavailable, a good dry or medium sherry is an acceptable substitute.

Sesame Hot Noodles

Plain egg noodles are tossed in a dressing made with sesame oil, soy sauce, peanut butter, cilantro, lime, chili, and sesame seeds.

NUTRITIONAL INFORMATION

Calories ....300 Sugars 1g
Protein ....7g Fat 21g
Carbohydrate ...21g Saturates 3g

5 MINS   10 MINS

SERVES 4

INGREDIENTS

2 x 9 oz packs medium egg noodles

3 tbsp sunflower oil

2 tbsp sesame oil

1 garlic clove, crushed

1 tbsp smooth peanut butter

1 small green chili, seeded and very finely chopped

3 tbsp toasted sesame seeds

4 tbsp light soy sauce

½ tbsp lime juice

salt and pepper

4 tbsp chopped fresh cilantro

1 Place the noodles in a large pan of boiling water, then immediately remove from the heat. Cover and leave to stand for 6 minutes, stirring once halfway through the time. At the end of 6 minutes the noodles will be perfectly cooked. Alternatively, cook the noodles following the pack instructions.

2 Meanwhile, make the dressing. Mix together the sunflower oil, sesame oil, crushed garlic, and peanut butter in a mixing bowl until smooth.

3 Add the chopped green chili, sesame seeds, and light soy sauce to the

other dressing ingredients. Add the lime juice, according to taste, and mix well. Season with salt and pepper.

4 Drain the noodles thoroughly, then place in a heated serving bowl.

5 Add the dressing and chopped fresh cilantro to the noodles and toss well to mix. Serve hot as a main meal accompaniment.

COOK'S TIP

If you are cooking the noodles ahead of time, toss the cooked, drained noodles in 2 teaspoons of sesame oil, then turn into a bowl. Cover and keep warm until required.

Mushroom & Pork Noodles

This dish benefits from the use of colored oyster mushrooms. If these are unavailable, ordinary mushrooms will suffice.

NUTRITIONAL INFORMATION

Calories	286	Sugars	.........3g
Protein	........23g	Fat	..........13g
Carbohydrate	...21g	Saturates	.......3g

  10 MINS   20 MINS

SERVES 4

INGREDIENTS

1 lb thin egg noodles

2 tbsp peanut oil

12 oz pork tenderloin, sliced

2 garlic cloves, crushed

1 onion, cut into 8 pieces

8 oz oyster mushrooms

4 tomatoes, skinned, seeded, and thinly sliced

2 tbsp light soy sauce

¼ cup pork stock

1 tbsp chopped fresh cilantro

1 Cook the noodles in a saucepan of boiling water for 2-3 minutes. Drain well, rinse under cold running water, and drain thoroughly again.

2 Heat 1 tablespoon of the oil in a preheated wok or skillet.

3 Add the noodles to the wok or skillet and stir-fry for about 2 minutes.

4 Using a slotted spoon, remove the noodles from the wok, drain well, and set aside until required.

5 Heat the remaining peanut oil in the wok. Add the pork slices and stir-fry for 4-5 minutes.

6 Stir in the crushed garlic and chopped onion and stir-fry for another 2-3 minutes.

7 Add the oyster mushrooms, tomatoes, light soy sauce, pork stock, and drained noodles. Stir well and cook for 1-2 minutes.

8 Sprinkle with chopped cilantro and serve immediately.

COOK'S TIP

For crisper noodles, add 2 tablespoons of oil to the wok and fry the noodles for 5-6 minutes, spreading them thinly in the wok and turning halfway through cooking.

Beef with Crispy Noodles

Crispy noodles are terrific and may also be served on their own as a side dish, sprinkled with sugar and salt.

NUTRITIONAL INFORMATION

Calories ....244 Sugars 9g
Protein ....20g Fat 10g
Carbohydrate ...19g Saturates 2g

 5 MINS   30 MINS

SERVES 4

INGREDIENTS

8 oz medium egg noodles

12 oz beef fillet

2 tbsp sunflower oil

1 tsp ground ginger

1 clove garlic, crushed

1 red chili, seeded and very finely chopped

3½ oz carrots, cut into thin sticks

6 green onions, sliced

2 tbsp lime marmalade

2 tbsp soy sauce

oil, for frying

1 Place the noodles in a large dish or bowl. Pour over enough boiling water to cover the noodles and leave to stand for about 10 minutes while you stir-fry the rest of the ingredients.

2 Using a sharp knife, thinly slice the beef fillet.

3 Heat the sunflower oil in a large preheated wok or skillet.

4 Add the beef and ground ginger to the wok or skillet and stir-fry for about 5 minutes.

5 Add the crushed garlic, chopped red chili, carrots, and green onions to the wok and stir-fry for another 2–3 minutes.

6 Add the lime marmalade and soy sauce to the wok and allow to bubble for 2 minutes. Remove the chili beef and ginger mixture, set aside and keep warm until required.

7 Heat the oil for frying in the wok or skillet.

8 Drain the noodles thoroughly and pat dry with absorbent paper towels. Carefully lower the noodles into the hot oil and cook for 2–3 minutes or until crispy. Drain the noodles on absorbent paper towels.

9 Divide the noodles between 4 warm serving plates and top with the chili beef and ginger mixture. Serve immediately. Alternatively, serve the noodles separately.

Egg Noodles with Beef

Quick and easy, this mouth-watering Chinese-style noodle dish can be cooked in minutes.

NUTRITIONAL INFORMATION

Calories	329	Sugars	.........3g
Protein	........23g	Fat	..........16g
Carbohydrate	...20g	Saturates	.......4g

 10 MINS 15 MINS

SERVES 4

I N G R E D I E N T S

10 oz egg noodles

3 tbsp walnut oil

1 inch piece fresh ginger,
  cut into thin strips

5 green onions, finely shredded

2 garlic cloves, finely chopped

1 red bell pepper, cored, seeded, and
  thinly sliced

3½ oz small mushrooms, thinly sliced

12 oz fillet steak, cut into thin strips

1 tbsp cornstarch

5 tbsp dry sherry

3 tbsp soy sauce

1 tsp soft brown sugar

1 cup bean sprouts

1 tbsp sesame oil

salt and pepper

green onion strips,
  to garnish

1 Bring a large saucepan of water to a boil. Add the egg noodles and cook according to the instructions on the pack. Drain the noodles, rinse under cold running water, drain thoroughly again, and set aside.

2 Heat the walnut oil in a preheated wok until it is really hot.

3 Add the grated fresh ginger, shredded green onions, and chopped garlic and stir-fry for 45 seconds.

4 Add the red bell pepper, mushrooms, and steak and stir-fry for 4 minutes. Season to taste with salt and pepper.

5 Mix together the cornstarch, dry sherry, and soy sauce in a small jug to form a paste, and pour into the wok. Sprinkle over the brown sugar and stir-fry all of the ingredients for another 2 minutes.

6 Add the bean sprouts, drained noodles, and sesame oil to the wok, stir and toss together for 1 minute.

7 Transfer the stir-fry to warm serving dishes, garnish with strips of green onion, and serve.

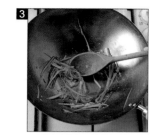

Chili Shrimp Noodles

Cellophane or "glass" noodles are made from mung beans. They are sold dried, so they need soaking before use.

NUTRITIONAL INFORMATION

Calories	152	Sugars	........2g
Protein	........11g	Fat	..........8g
Carbohydrate	...10g	Saturates	.......1g

 25 MINS   10 MINS

SERVES 4

I N G R E D I E N T S

2 tbsp light soy sauce

1 tbsp lime or lemon juice

1 tbsp fish sauce

4½ oz firm tofu, cut into chunks

4½ oz cellophane noodles

2 tbsp sesame oil

4 shallots, sliced finely

2 garlic cloves, crushed

1 small red chili, seeded and chopped finely

2 celery stalks, sliced finely

2 carrots, sliced finely

⅔ cup cooked, peeled small shrimp

1 cup bean sprouts

T O   G A R N I S H

celery leaves

fresh chilies

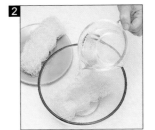

1 Mix together the light soy sauce, lime or lemon juice, and fish sauce in a small bowl. Add the tofu cubes and toss them until coated in the mixture. Cover and set aside for 15 minutes.

2 Put the noodles into a large bowl and cover with warm water. Leave them to soak for about 5 minutes, and then drain them well.

3 Heat the sesame oil in a wok or large skillet. Add the shallots, garlic, and red chili, and stir-fry for 1 minute.

4 Add the sliced celery and carrots to the wok or pan and stir-fry for 2–3 minutes more.

5 Tip the drained noodles into the wok or skillet and cook, stirring, for 2 minutes, then add the small shrimp, bean sprouts, and tofu, with the soy sauce mixture. Cook over a medium high heat for 2–3 minutes until heated through.

6 Transfer the mixture in the wok to a serving dish and garnish with celery leaves and chilies.

Noodles with Cod & Mango

Fish and fruit are tossed with a trio of bell peppers in this spicy dish served with noodles for a quick, healthy meal.

NUTRITIONAL INFORMATION

Calories	274	Sugars	........11g
Protein	........25g	Fat	...........8g
Carbohydrate	...26g	Saturates	.......1g

 10 MINS   25 MINS

SERVES 4

I N G R E D I E N T S

9 oz pack egg noodles

1 lb skinless cod fillet

1 tbsp paprika

2 tbsp sunflower oil

1 red onion, sliced

1 orange bell pepper, seeded and sliced

1 green bell pepper, seeded and sliced

3½ oz baby corn-on-the-cobs, halved

1 mango, sliced

1 cup bean sprouts

2 tbsp tomato ketchup

2 tbsp soy sauce

2 tbsp medium sherry

1 tsp cornstarch

  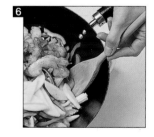

1 Place the egg noodles in a large bowl and cover with boiling water. Leave to stand for about 10 minutes.

2 Rinse the cod fillet and pat dry with absorbent paper towels. Cut the cod flesh into thin strips.

3 Place the cod strips in a large bowl. Add the paprika and toss well to coat the fish.

4 Heat the sunflower oil in a large preheated wok.

5 Add the onion, bell peppers, and baby corn to the wok and stir-fry for about 5 minutes.

6 Add the cod to the wok together with the sliced mango and stir-fry for another 2–3 minutes or until the fish is tender.

7 Add the bean sprouts to the wok and toss well to combine.

8 Mix together the tomato ketchup, soy sauce , sherry and cornstarch. Add the mixture to the wok and cook, stirring occasionally, until the juices thicken.

9 Drain the noodles thoroughly and transfer to warm serving bowls. Transfer the cod and mango stir-fry to separate serving bowls and serve immediately.

Chicken Noodles

Rice noodles are used in this recipe. They are available in large supermarkets or Chinese markets.

NUTRITIONAL INFORMATION

Calories	169	Sugars	.........2g
Protein	........14g	Fat	...........7g
Carbohydrate	...12g	Saturates	.......2g

5 MINS   15 MINS

SERVES 4

I N G R E D I E N T S

8 oz rice noodles

2 tbsp peanut oil

8 oz skinless, boneless chicken breast, sliced

2 garlic cloves, crushed

1 tsp grated fresh ginger

1 tsp Chinese curry powder

1 red bell pepper, seeded and thinly sliced

2¾ oz snow peas, shredded

1 tbsp light soy sauce

2 tsp Chinese rice wine

2 tbsp chicken stock

1 tsp sesame oil

1 tbsp chopped fresh cilantro

1 Soak the rice noodles for 4 minutes in warm water. Drain thoroughly and set aside until required.

2 Heat the peanut oil in a preheated wok or large heavy-bottomed skillet and stir-fry the chicken slices for 2-3 minutes.

3 Add the garlic, ginger, and Chinese curry powder and stir-fry for another 30 seconds. Add the red bell pepper and snow peas to the mixture in the wok and stir-fry for 2-3 minutes.

4 Add the noodles, soy sauce, Chinese rice wine, and chicken stock to the wok and mix well, stirring occasionally, for 1 minute.

5 Sprinkle the sesame oil and chopped cilantro over the noodles. Transfer to serving plates and serve.

VARIATION

You can use pork or duck in this recipe instead of the chicken, if you prefer.

Noodles in Soup

Noodles in soup are far more popular than fried noodles in China. You can use different ingredients for the dressing according to taste.

NUTRITIONAL INFORMATION

Calories 231   Sugars 1g
Protein . . . . .18g   Fat 11g
Carbohydrate . . .16g   Saturates 2g

4 HOURS   15 MINS

SERVES 4

INGREDIENTS

9 oz chicken, pork, or any other ready-cooked meat

3-4 Chinese dried mushrooms, soaked

4½ oz canned sliced bamboo shoots, rinsed and drained

4½ oz spinach leaves, lettuce hearts, or Chinese cabbage, shredded

2 green onions, finely shredded

9 oz egg noodles

about 2½ cups Chinese Stock (see page 30)

2 tbsp light soy sauce

2 tbsp vegetable oil

1 tsp salt

½ tsp sugar

2 tsp Chinese rice wine or dry sherry

a few drops sesame oil

1 tsp red chili oil (optional)

1 Using a sharp knife or meat cleaver, cut the meat into thin shreds.

2 Squeeze dry the soaked Chinese mushrooms and discard the hard stalk.

3 Thinly shred the mushrooms, bamboo shoots, spinach leaves, and green onions.

4 Cook the noodles in boiling water according to the instructions on the pack, then drain and rinse under cold water. Place the noodles in a bowl.

5 Bring the Chinese stock to a boil, add about 1 tablespoon soy sauce and pour over the noodles. Keep warm.

6 Heat the vegetable oil in a preheated wok, add about half of the green onions, the meat and the vegetables (mushrooms, bamboo shoots, and greens). Stir-fry for about 2-3 minutes. Add all the seasonings and stir until well combined.

7 Pour the mixture in the wok over the noodles, garnish with the remaining onions, and serve immediately.

COOK'S TIP

Noodle soup is wonderfully satisfying and is ideal to serve on cold winter days.

Speedy Peanut Pan-fry

Thread egg noodles are the ideal accompaniment to this quick dish because they can be cooked quickly and easily while the stir-fry sizzles.

NUTRITIONAL INFORMATION

Calories	563	Sugars	.........7g
Protein	........45g	Fat	..........33g
Carbohydrate	...22g	Saturates	.......7g

🍲 5 MINS   🕐 15 MINS

SERVES 4

INGREDIENTS

2 cups zucchini

1⅓ cups baby corn-on-the-cob

9 oz thread egg noodles

2 tbsp corn oil

1 tbsp sesame oil

8 boneless chicken thighs or 4 breasts, sliced thinly

3¾ cups small mushrooms

1½ cups bean sprouts

4 tbsp smooth peanut butter

2 tbsp soy sauce

2 tbsp lime or lemon juice

½ cup roasted peanuts

salt and pepper

cilantro, to garnish

1 Using a sharp knife, trim and thinly slice the zucchini and baby corn-on-the-cob. Set the vegetables aside until required.

2 Cook the noodles in lightly salted boiling water for 3–4 minutes.

3 Meanwhile, heat the corn oil and sesame oil in a large wok or skillet and fry the chicken over a fairly high heat for 1 minute.

4 Add the zucchini, corn, and mushrooms and stir-fry for 5 minutes.

5 Add the bean sprouts, peanut butter, soy sauce, lime or lemon juice, and pepper, then cook for 2 minutes more.

6 Drain the noodles thoroughly. Scatter with the roasted peanuts and serve with the zucchini and mushroom mixture. Garnish with fresh cilantro.

COOK'S TIP

Try serving this stir-fry with rice sticks. These are broad, pale, translucent ribbon noodles made from ground rice.

Chicken Chow Mein

This classic dish requires no introduction as it is already a favorite among most Chinese food-eaters.

NUTRITIONAL INFORMATION

Calories 230	Sugars 2g	
Protein 19g	Fat 11g	
Carbohydrate ...14g	Saturates 2g	

🕭 🕭

🍲 5 MINS   🕙 20 MINS

SERVES 4

I N G R E D I E N T S

9 oz pack medium egg noodles

2 tbsp sunflower oil

9½ oz cooked chicken breasts, shredded

1 clove garlic, finely chopped

1 red bell pepper, seeded and thinly sliced

3½ oz shiitake mushrooms, sliced

6 green onions, sliced

1 cup bean sprouts

3 tbsp soy sauce

1 tbsp sesame oil

VARIATION

You can make the chow mein with a selection of vegetables for a vegetarian dish, if you prefer.

1 Place the egg noodles in a large bowl or dish and break them up slightly. Pour over enough boiling water to cover the noodles and leave to stand.

2 Heat the sunflower oil in a large preheated wok. Add the shredded chicken, finely chopped garlic, bell pepper slices, mushrooms, green onions, and bean sprouts to the wok and stir-fry for about 5 minutes.

3 Drain the noodles thoroughly. Add the noodles to the wok, toss well and stir-fry for another 5 minutes.

4 Drizzle the soy sauce and sesame oil over the chow mein and toss until well combined.

5 Transfer the chicken chow mein to warm serving bowls and serve immediately.

Garlic Pork & Noodles

This is a wonderful one-pot dish of stir-fried pork fillet with small shrimps and noodles that is made in minutes.

NUTRITIONAL INFORMATION

Calories 424	Sugars 1g
Protein 33g	Fat 27g
Carbohydrate ...13g	Saturates 5g

 5 MINS 15 MINS

SERVES 4

INGREDIENTS

9 oz pack medium egg noodles

3 tbsp vegetable oil

2 garlic cloves, crushed

12 oz pork tenderloin, cut into strips

⅓ cup dried small shrimp, or
   4½ oz peeled shrimp

1 bunch green onions, finely chopped

¾ cup chopped roasted and shelled
   unsalted peanuts

3 tbsp fish sauce

1½ tsp brown sugar

1-2 small red chilies, seeded and finely
   chopped (to taste)

3 tbsp lime juice

3 tbsp chopped fresh cilantro

1 Place the noodles in a large pan of boiling water, then immediately remove from the heat. Cover and leave to stand for 6 minutes, stirring once halfway through the time. After 6 minutes the noodles will be perfectly cooked. Alternatively, follow the instructions on the pack. Drain and keep warm.

2 Heat the oil in a wok, add the garlic and pork, and stir-fry until the pork strips are browned, about 2-3 minutes.

3 Add the dried small shrimp or shelled shrimp, green onions, peanuts, fish sauce, brown sugar, chilies to taste, and lime juice. Stir-fry for another 1 minute.

4 Add the cooked noodles and chopped fresh cilantro and stir-fry until heated through, about 1 minute. Serve the stir-fry immediately.

COOK'S TIP

Fish sauce is made from pressed, salted fish and is available in gourmet supermarkets and oriental stores. It is very salty, so no extra salt should be added.

Yellow Bean Noodles

Cellophane or thread noodles are excellent re-heated, unlike other noodles which must be served as soon as they are ready.

NUTRITIONAL INFORMATION

Calories 212	Sugars 0.5g
Protein 28g	Fat 7g
Carbohydrate . . .10g	Saturates 2g

 5 MINS   30 MINS

SERVES 4

I N G R E D I E N T S

6 oz cellophane noodles

1 tbsp peanut oil

1 leek, sliced

2 garlic cloves, crushed

1 lb ground chicken

1 cup chicken stock

1 tsp chili sauce

2 tbsp yellow bean sauce

4 tbsp light soy sauce

1 tsp sesame oil

chopped chives, to garnish

1 Place the cellophane noodles in a bowl, pour over boiling water, and soak for 15 minutes.

2 Drain the noodles thoroughly and cut into short lengths with a pair of kitchen shears.

3 Heat the oil in a wok or skillet and stir-fry the leek and garlic for 30 seconds.

4 Add the chicken to the wok and stir-fry for 4-5 minutes, until the chicken is completely cooked through.

5 Add the chicken stock, chili sauce, yellow bean sauce, and soy sauce to the wok and cook for 3-4 minutes.

6 Add the drained noodles and sesame oil to the wok and cook, tossing to mix well, for 4-5 minutes.

7 Spoon the mixture into warm serving bowls, sprinkle with chopped chives, and serve immediately.

COOK'S TIP

Cellophane noodles are available from gourmet supermarkets and all Chinese food stores.

Crispy Noodles & Tofu

This dish requires a certain amount of care and attention to get the crispy noodles properly cooked, but it is worth the extra effort.

NUTRITIONAL INFORMATION

Calories 242	Sugars 2g
Protein 13g	Fat 17g
Carbohydrate ...10g	Saturates 3g

 35 MINS   25 MINS

SERVES 4

INGREDIENTS

6 oz thread egg noodles

2½ cups sunflower oil, for deep-frying

2 tsp grated lemon zest

1 tbsp light soy sauce

1 tbsp rice vinegar

1 tbsp lemon juice

1½ tbsp sugar

1 cup marinated tofu, diced

2 garlic cloves, crushed

1 red chili, sliced finely

1 red bell pepper, diced

4 eggs, beaten

red chili flower, to garnish (see Cook's Tip page 269)

temperature with a few strands of noodles. They should swell to many times their size, but if they do not, wait until the oil is hot enough; otherwise they will be tough and stringy, not puffy and light.

4 Cook the noodles in batches. As soon as they turn a pale gold color, scoop them out and drain on plenty of absorbent paper towels. Leave to cool.

5 Reserve 2 tablespoons of the oil and drain off the rest. Heat the reserved oil in the wok or pan.

6 Add the marinated tofu to the wok or skillet and cook quickly over a high heat to seal.

7 Add the crushed garlic cloves, sliced red chili, and diced red bell pepper to the wok. Stir-fry for 1–2 minutes.

8 Add the reserved vinegar mixture to the wok, stir to mix well, and add the beaten eggs, stirring until they are set.

9 Serve the tofu mixture with the crispy fried noodles, garnished with a red chili flower.

1 Blanch the egg noodles briefly in hot water, to which a little of the oil has been added. Drain the noodles and spread out to dry for at least 30 minutes. Cut into threads about 3 inches long.

2 Combine the lemon zest, light soy sauce, rice vinegar, lemon juice, and sugar in a small bowl. Set the mixture aside until required.

3 Heat the sunflower oil in a wok or large, heavy skillet, and test the

Twice-cooked Lamb

Here lamb is first boiled and then fried with soy sauce, oyster sauce, and spinach and finally tossed with noodles for a richly flavored dish.

NUTRITIONAL INFORMATION

Calories 315   Sugars 5g
Protein . . . . .27g   Fat 16g
Carbohydrate . . .16g   Saturates 6g

 5 MINS   30 MINS

SERVES 4

I N G R E D I E N T S

9 oz egg noodles

1 lb lamb loin fillet, thinly sliced

2 tbsp soy sauce

2 tbsp sunflower oil

2 cloves garlic, crushed

1 tbsp sugar

2 tbsp oyster sauce

6 oz baby spinach

1 Place the egg noodles in a large bowl and cover with boiling water. Leave to soak for about 10 minutes.

2 Bring a large saucepan of water to a boil. Add the lamb and cook for 5 minutes. Drain thoroughly.

3 Place the slices of lamb in a bowl and mix with the soy sauce and 1 tablespoon of the sunflower oil.

4 Heat the remaining sunflower oil in a large preheated wok, swirling the oil around until it is really hot.

5 Add the marinated lamb and crushed garlic to the wok and stir-fry for about 5 minutes or until the meat is just beginning to brown.

6 Add the sugar and oyster sauce to the wok and stir well to combine.

7 Drain the noodles thoroughly. Add the noodles to the wok and stir-fry for another 5 minutes.

8 Add the spinach to the wok and cook for 1 minute or until the leaves just wilt. Transfer the lamb and noodles to serving bowls and serve hot.

COOK'S TIP

If using dried noodles, follow the instructions on the pack as they require less soaking.

Quick Chicken Noodles

Chicken and fresh vegetables are flavored with ginger and Chinese five-spice powder in this speedy stir-fry.

NUTRITIONAL INFORMATION

Calories 266	Sugars 4g	
Protein 25g	Fat 13g	
Carbohydrate ...12g	Saturates 2g	

10 MINS   15 MINS

SERVES 4

I N G R E D I E N T S

6 oz Chinese thread egg noodles

2 tbsp sesame or vegetable oil

¼ cup peanuts

1 bunch green onions, sliced

1 green bell pepper, seeded and cut into thin strips

1 large carrot, cut into thin sticks

4½ oz cauliflower, broken into small flowerets

12 oz skinless, boneless chicken, cut into strips

9 oz mushrooms, sliced

1 tsp finely grated fresh ginger

1 tsp Chinese five-spice powder

1 tbsp chopped fresh cilantro

1 tbsp light soy sauce

salt and pepper

fresh chives, to garnish

pan. Stir-fry the mixture over a high heat for 4–5 minutes.

1 Put the noodles in a large bowl and cover with boiling water. Leave to soak for 6 minutes.

2 Heat the oil in a wok and stir-fry the peanuts for 1 minute until browned. Remove from the wok and leave to drain.

3 Add the green onions, bell pepper, carrot, cauliflower, and chicken to the

4 Drain the noodles thoroughly and add to the wok. Add the mushrooms and stir-fry for 2 minutes. Add the ginger, five-spice, and cilantro; stir-fry for 1 minute.

5 Season with soy sauce and salt and pepper. Sprinkle with the peanuts, garnish, and serve.

VARIATION

Instead of fresh ginger, ½ teaspoon ground ginger can be used.

Vary the vegetables according to what is in season. Make the most of bargains bought from your local vegetable market.

Oyster Sauce Noodles

Chicken and noodles are cooked and then tossed in an oyster sauce and egg mixture in this delicious recipe.

NUTRITIONAL INFORMATION

Calories 278	Sugars 2g
Protein 30g	Fat 12g
Carbohydrate ...13g	Saturates 3g

 5 MINS   25 MINS

SERVES 4

I N G R E D I E N T S

9 oz egg noodles

1 lb chicken thighs

2 tbsp peanut oil

3½ oz carrots, sliced

3 tbsp oyster sauce

2 eggs

3 tbsp cold water

1 Place the egg noodles in a large bowl or dish. Pour enough boiling water over the noodles to cover and leave to stand for 10 minutes.

2 Meanwhile, remove the skin from the chicken thighs. Cut the chicken flesh into small pieces, using a sharp knife.

VARIATION

Flavor the eggs with soy sauce or hoisin sauce as an alternative to the oyster sauce, if you prefer.

3 Heat the peanut oil in a large preheated wok or skillet, swirling the oil around the base of the wok until it is really hot.

4 Add the pieces of chicken and the carrot slices to the wok and stir-fry for about 5 minutes.

5 Drain the noodles thoroughly. Add the noodles to the wok and stir-fry for

2–3 minutes more, or until the noodles are heated through.

6 Beat together the oyster sauce, eggs, and 3 tablespoons of cold water. Drizzle the mixture over the noodles and stir-fry for another 2–3 minutes or until the eggs set.

7 Transfer the mixture in the wok to warm serving bowls and serve hot.

Satay Noodles

Rice noodles and vegetables are tossed in a crunchy peanut and chili sauce for a quick satay-flavored recipe.

NUTRITIONAL INFORMATION

Calories 281   Sugars 7g
Protein . . . . .9g   Fat 20g
Carbohydrate . . .18g   Saturates 4g

5 MINS   20 MINS

SERVES 4

INGREDIENTS

9½ oz rice sticks (wide, flat rice-flour noodles)

3 tbsp peanut oil

2 cloves garlic, crushed

2 shallots, sliced

8 oz green beans, sliced

3¾ oz cherry tomatoes, halved

1 tsp chili flakes

4 tbsp crunchy peanut butter

⅔ cup coconut milk

1 tbsp tomato paste

sliced green onions, to garnish

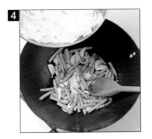

1 Place the rice sticks (wide, flat rice-flour noodles) in a large bowl and pour over enough boiling water to cover. Leave to stand for 10 minutes.

2 Heat the oil in a large preheated wok or heavy-bottomed skillet.

3 Add the crushed garlic and sliced shallots to the wok or skillet and stir-fry for 1 minute.

4 Drain the rice sticks thoroughly. Add the green beans and drained noodles to the wok or skillet and stir-fry for about 5 minutes.

5 Add the cherry tomatoes to the wok and mix well.

6 Mix together the chili flakes, peanut butter, coconut milk, and tomato paste until well combined.

7 Pour the chili mixture over the noodles, toss well until all the ingredients are thoroughly combined, and heat through.

8 Transfer the satay noodles to warm serving dishes and garnish with green onion slices and serve immediately.

Curried Rice Noodles

Rice noodles or vermicelli are also known as rice sticks. The ideal meat to use in this dish is Barbecue Pork (see page 115).

(see page 115)

NUTRITIONAL INFORMATION

Calories	223	Sugars	.........2g
Protein	........15g	Fat	..........13g
Carbohydrate	....11g	Saturates	.......2g

15 MINS   15 MINS

SERVES 4

INGREDIENTS

7 oz rice vermicelli

4½ oz cooked chicken or pork

2 oz peeled shrimp, defrosted if frozen

4 tbsp vegetable oil

1 medium onion, thinly shredded

4¼ oz fresh bean sprouts

1 tsp salt

1 tbsp mild curry powder

2 tbsp light soy sauce

2 green onions, thinly shredded

1-2 small fresh green or red chili peppers, seeded and thinly shredded

1 Soak the rice vermicelli in boiling water for about 8-10 minutes, then rinse in cold water and drain well. Set aside until required.

2 Using a sharp knife or meat cleaver, thinly slice the cooked meat.

3 Dry the shrimp on absorbent paper towels.

4 Heat the vegetable oil in a preheated wok or large skillet.

5 Add the shredded onion to the wok or pan and stir-fry until opaque. Add the bean sprouts and stir-fry for 1 minute.

6 Add the drained noodles with the meat and shrimp, and continue stirring for another minute.

7 Mix together the salt, curry powder, and soy sauce in a little bowl.

8 Blend the sauce mixture into the wok, followed by the green onions and chili peppers. Stir-fry for one more minute, then serve immediately.

COOK'S TIP

Rice noodles are made from rice flour. They become soft and pliable after being soaked for 15 minutes. If you wish to store them after they have been soaked, toss them in a few drops of sesame oil, then place them in a sealed container in the refrigerator.

Hot & Crispy Noodles

These crispy noodles will add a delicious crunch to your Chinese meal. They can be served as a side dish or as an appetizer for people to share.

NUTRITIONAL INFORMATION

Calories	104	Sugars	0.3g
Protein	2g	Fat	6g
Carbohydrate	11g	Saturates	1g

5 MINS   15 MINS

SERVES 4

INGREDIENTS

9 oz rice noodles

oil, for deep-frying

2 garlic cloves, chopped finely

8 green onions, trimmed and chopped finely

1 small red or green chili, seeded and chopped finely

2 tbsp fish sauce

2 tbsp light soy sauce

2 tbsp lime or lemon juice

2 tbsp sugar

TO GARNISH

green onions, shredded

cucumber, sliced thinly

fresh chilies

1 Break the noodles into smaller pieces with your hands. Heat the oil for deep-frying in a wok or large skillet and fry small batches of the noodles until pale golden brown and puffed up. Lift the noodles out with a perforated spoon and leave to drain on paper towels.

2 When all the noodles are cooked, carefully pour off the oil, leaving 3 tablespoons in the wok. Add the garlic, green onions, and chili, and stir-fry for about 2 minutes.

3 Mix together the fish sauce, soy sauce, lime or lemon juice, and sugar. Add to the wok or skillet and cook for 2 minutes, until the sugar has dissolved. Tip all the noodles back into the wok and toss lightly to coat with the sauce mixture.

4 Serve the noodles garnished with shredded green onions, thinly sliced cucumber, and chilies.

VARIATION

Stir-fry some uncooked peeled shrimp or chopped raw chicken with the green onions and garlic in step 2. Cook for an extra 3–4 minutes to make sure they are thoroughly cooked.

Chicken on Crispy Noodles

Blanched noodles are fried in the wok until crisp and brown, and then topped with a shredded chicken sauce for a delightfully tasty dish.

NUTRITIONAL INFORMATION

Calories 376   Sugars 2g
Protein . . . . .15g   Fat 27g
Carbohydrate . . .17g   Saturates 4g

 35 MINS   25 MINS

SERVES 4

INGREDIENTS

8 oz skinless, boneless chicken breasts, shredded

1 egg white

5 tsp cornstarch

8 oz thin egg noodles

1⅔ cups vegetable oil

2½ cups chicken stock

2 tbsp dry sherry

2 tbsp oyster sauce

1 tbsp light soy sauce

1 tbsp hoisin sauce

1 red bell pepper, seeded and very thinly sliced

2 tbsp water

3 green onions, chopped

1 Mix together the chicken, egg white, and 2 teaspoons of the cornstarch in a bowl. Leave to stand for at least 30 minutes.

2 Blanch the noodles in boiling water for 2 minutes, then drain thoroughly.

3 Heat the vegetable oil in a preheated wok. Add the noodles, spreading them to cover the base of the wok. Cook over a low heat for about 5 minutes, until the noodles are browned on the underside.

Flip the noodles over and brown on the other side. Remove from the wok when crisp and browned, place on a serving plate, and keep warm. Drain the oil from the wok.

4 Add 1¼ cups of the chicken stock to the wok. Remove from the heat and add the chicken, stirring well so that it does not stick. Return to the heat and cook for 2 minutes. Drain, discarding the stock.

5 Wipe the wok with paper towels and return to the heat. Add the sherry, sauces, bell pepper, and the remaining stock and bring to a boil. Blend the remaining cornstarch with the water and stir it into the mixture.

6 Return the chicken to the wok and cook over a low heat for 2 minutes. Place the chicken on top of the noodles and sprinkle with green onions.

Chili Pork Noodles

This is quite a spicy dish, with a delicious peanut flavor. Increase or reduce the amount of chili to your liking.

NUTRITIONAL INFORMATION

Calories	421	Sugars	.........3g
Protein	........27g	Fat	.........26g
Carbohydrate	...20g	Saturates	.......6g

  35 MINS   10 MINS

SERVES 4

INGREDIENTS

12 oz ground pork

1 tbsp light soy sauce

1 tbsp dry sherry

12 oz egg noodles

2 tsp sesame oil

2 tbsp vegetable oil

2 garlic cloves, crushed

2 tsp grated fresh ginger

2 fresh red chilies, sliced

1 red bell pepper, seeded and finely sliced

¼ cup unsalted peanuts

3 tbsp peanut butter

3 tbsp dark soy sauce

dash of chili oil

1¼ cups pork stock

1 Mix together the pork, light soy sauce and dry sherry in a large bowl. Cover and leave to marinate for 30 minutes.

2 Meanwhile, cook the noodles in a saucepan of boiling water for 4 minutes. Drain well, rinse in cold water, and drain again. Toss the noodles in the sesame oil.

3 Heat the vegetable oil in a preheated wok and stir-fry the garlic, ginger, chilies, and bell pepper for 30 seconds.

4 Add the pork to the mixture in the wok, together with the marinade. Continue cooking for about 1 minute, until the pork is sealed.

5 Add the peanuts, peanut butter, soy sauce, chili oil, and stock and cook for 2-3 minutes.

6 Toss the noodles in the mixture and serve immediately.

VARIATION

Ground chicken or lamb would also be excellent in this recipe instead of the pork.

Curried Shrimp Noodles

Athough these noodles are almost a meal in themselves, if served as an accompaniment, they are ideal with plain vegetable or fish dishes.

NUTRITIONAL INFORMATION

Calories	246	Sugars	.........1g
Protein	........17g	Fat	..........14g
Carbohydrate	...14g	Saturates	.......2g

  5 MINS   15 MINS

SERVES 4

I N G R E D I E N T S

8 oz rice noodles

4 tbsp vegetable oil

1 onion, sliced

2 ham slices, shredded

2 tbsp Chinese curry powder

⅔ cups fish stock

8 oz peeled, raw shrimp

2 garlic cloves, crushed

6 green onions, chopped

1 tbsp light soy sauce

2 tbsp hoisin sauce

1 tbsp dry sherry

2 tsp lime juice

fresh snipped chives, to garnish

COOK'S TIP

Hoisin sauce is made from soy beans, sugar, flour, vinegar, salt, garlic, chili, and sesame seed oil. Sold in cans or jars, it will keep in the refrigerator for several months.

1 Cook the noodles in a pan of boiling water for 3-4 minutes. Drain well, rinse under cold water, and drain again.

2 Heat 2 tablespoons of the oil in a wok. Add the onion and ham and stir-fry for 1 minute. Add the curry powder and stir-fry for another 30 seconds.

3 Stir the noodles and fish stock into the wok and cook for 2-3 minutes.

Remove the noodles from the wok and keep warm.

4 Heat the remaining oil in the wok. Add the shrimp, garlic, and green onions and stir-fry for about 1 minute.

5 Stir in the remaining ingredients. Pour the mixture over the noodles, toss to mix, and garnish with fresh chives.

Chilled Noodles & Peppers

This is a convenient dish to serve when you are arriving home just before family or friends. Quick to prepare and assemble, it is ready in minutes.

NUTRITIONAL INFORMATION

Calories	260	Sugars	.........4g
Protein	.........4g	Fat	..........21g
Carbohydrate	...15g	Saturates	.......4g

5 MINS   15 MINS

SERVES 4–6

INGREDIENTS

9 oz ribbon noodles, or Chinese egg noodles

1 tbsp sesame oil

1 red bell pepper

1 yellow bell pepper

1 green bell pepper

6 green onions, cut into thin strips

salt

DRESSING

5 tbsp sesame oil

2 tbsp light soy sauce

1 tbsp tahini (sesame seed paste)

4-5 drops hot pepper sauce

1 Preheat the broiler to medium. Cook the noodles in a large pan of boiling, salted water until they are almost tender. Drain them in a colander, run cold water through them, and drain thoroughly. Tip the noodles into a bowl, stir in the sesame oil, cover, and chill.

2 Cook the bell peppers under the broiler, turning them frequently, until they are blackened on all sides. Plunge into cold water, then skin them. Cut in half, remove the core and seeds, and cut the flesh into thick strips. Set aside in a covered container.

3 To make the dressing, mix together the sesame oil, light soy sauce, tahini (sesame seed paste), and hot pepper sauce until well combined.

4 Pour the dressing on the noodles, reserving 1 tablespoon, and toss well. Turn the noodles into a serving dish, arrange the broiled bell peppers over the noodles, and spoon on the reserved dressing. Scatter on the green onion strips.

COOK'S TIP

If you have time, another way of peeling bell peppers is to first broil them, then place in a plastic bag, seal, and leave for about 20 minutes. The skin will then peel off easily.

Desserts

Desserts are rarely eaten in ordinary Chinese households except on special occasions. Sweet dishes are usually served as snacks between main meals, but fresh fruit is considered to be very refreshing at the end of a meal. The recipes in this chapter are adaptations of Imperial recipes or use Chinese cooking methods and ingredients to produce

mouthwatering desserts that round off any meal perfectly. There are delicious dinner party desserts, which look as good as they taste, pastries, which can be eaten on a coffee break, and a selection of refreshing fruit salads. Among the recipes to choose from are Sweet Fruit Wontons, in which a sweet date filling is sealed in wonton wrappers and laced with honey, or Battered Bananas, in which pieces of banana are deep-fried and then sprinkled with brown sugar.

Sweet Fruit Wontons

These sweet wontons are very adaptable and may be filled with whole, small fruits or a spicy chopped mixture as here.

NUTRITIONAL INFORMATION

Calories	244	Sugars	.......25g
Protein	.........2g	Fat	..........12g
Carbohydrate	...35g	Saturates	.......3g

10 MINS   15 MINS

SERVES 4

INGREDIENTS

12 wonton skins

2 tsp cornstarch

6 tsp cold water

oil, for deep-frying

2 tbsp honey

selection of fresh fruit (such as kiwi, limes, oranges, mango, and apples), sliced, to serve

FILLING

1 cup chopped dried, pitted dates

2 tsp dark brown sugar

½ tsp ground cinnamon

1 To make the filling, mix together the dates, sugar, and cinnamon in a bowl.

2 Spread out the wonton skins on a cutting board and spoon a little of the filling into the center of each skin.

COOK'S TIP

Wonton skins may be found in Chinese supermarkets. Alternatively, make 1 quantity of the dough used for Shrimp Dumpling Soup (see page 51).

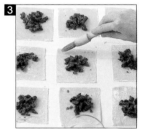

3 Blend the cornstarch and water and brush this mixture around the edges of the wonton skins.

4 Fold the wonton skins over the filling, bringing the edges together, then bring the two corners together, sealing with the cornstarch mixture.

5 Heat the oil for deep-frying in a wok to 350°F, or until a cube of bread browns in 30 seconds. Fry the wontons, in batches, for 2-3 minutes, until golden. Remove the wontons from the oil with a slotted spoon and leave to drain on absorbent paper towels.

6 Place the honey in a bowl and stand it in warm water, to soften it slightly. Drizzle the honey over the sweet fruit wontons and serve with a selection of fresh fruit.

Mango Mousse

This is a light, softly set and tangy mousse, which is perfect for clearing the palate after a Chinese meal of mixed flavors.

NUTRITIONAL INFORMATION

Calories ....346 Sugars 27g
Protein ....7g Fat 24g
Carbohydrate ...27g Saturates 15g

40 MINS   0 MINS

SERVES 4

I N G R E D I E N T S

14 oz can mangoes in syrup

2 pieces candied ginger,
  chopped

1 cup heavy cream

4 tsp powdered gelatin

2 tbsp hot water

2 egg whites

1½ tbsp light brown sugar

candied ginger and lime rind,
  to decorate

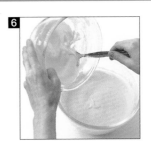

1 Drain the mangoes, reserving the syrup. Blend the mango pieces and ginger in a food processor or blender for 30 seconds, or until smooth.

2 Measure the purée and make up to 1¼ cups with the reserved mango syrup.

3 In a separate bowl, whip the cream until it forms soft peaks. Fold the mango mixture into the cream until well combined.

4 Dissolve the gelatin in the hot water and leave to cool slightly.

5 Pour the gelatin into the mango mixture in a steady stream, stirring.

Leave to cool in the refrigerator for 30 minutes, until almost set.

6 Beat the egg whites in a clean bowl until they form soft peaks, then beat in the sugar. Gently fold the egg whites into the mango mixture with a metal spoon.

7 Spoon the mousse into individual serving dishes, decorate with preserved ginger and lime rind, and serve.

COOK'S TIP

The gelatin must be stirred into the mango mixture in a gentle, steady stream to prevent it from setting in lumps when it comes into contact with the cold mixture.

Litchis with Orange Sorbet

This dish is truly delicious! The fresh flavor of the sorbet perfectly complements the spicy litchis.

NUTRITIONAL INFORMATION

Calories 313	Sugars 82g
Protein 1g	Fat 0g
Carbohydrate . . .82g	Saturates 0g

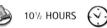

🥧 10½ HOURS   🕐 5 MINS

SERVES 4

I N G R E D I E N T S

S O R B E T

¼ cups sugar

2 cups cold water

12 oz can mandarin oranges, in natural juice

2 tbsp lemon juice

S T U F F E D   L I T C H I S

15 oz can litchis, drained

2 oz preserved ginger, drained and finely chopped

lime rind, cut into diamond shapes, to decorate

1 To make the sorbet, place the sugar and water in a saucepan, and stir over a low heat until the sugar has dissolved. Bring the mixture to a boil, and boil vigorously for 2-3 minutes.

2 Blend the mandarins in a food processor until smooth. Press the purée through a strainer then stir into the syrup, together with the lemon juice. Set aside to cool. Once cooled, pour the mixture into a rigid, plastic container and freeze until set, stirring occasionally.

3 Meanwhile, drain the litchis on absorbent paper towels. Spoon the chopped ginger into the centre of the litchis.

4 Arrange the litchis on serving plates, and serve with scoops of orange sorbet. Decorate with lime rind.

COOK'S TIP

It is best to leave the sorbet in the refrigerator for 10 minutes, so that it softens slightly, allowing you to scoop it to serve.

Exotic Fruit Crêpes

These pancakes are filled with an exotic array of tropical fruits. Decorate lavishly with tropical flowers or mint sprigs.

NUTRITIONAL INFORMATION

Calories 382   Sugars 24g
Protein ....7g   Fat 17g
Carbohydrate ...53g   Saturates 3g

40 MINS   35 MINS

SERVES 4

INGREDIENTS

BATTER

1 cup all-purpose flour

pinch of salt

1 egg

1 egg yolk

1¼ cups coconut milk

4 tsp vegetable oil, plus oil for frying

FILLING

1 banana

1 papaya

juice of 1 lime

2 passion-fruit

1 mango, peeled, pitted, and sliced

4 litchis, pitted and halved

1-2 tbsp honey

flowers or mint sprigs, to decorate

1 Sift the flour and salt into a bowl. Make a well in the center and add the egg, egg yolk, and a little of the coconut milk. Gradually draw the flour into the egg mixture, beating well and slowly adding the remaining coconut milk to make a smooth batter. Stir in the oil. Cover and chill for 30 minutes.

2 Peel and slice the banana and place in a bowl. Peel and slice the papaya, discarding the seeds. Add to the banana with the lime juice and mix well. Cut the passion-fruit in half and scoop out the flesh and seeds into the fruit bowl. Stir in the mango, litchis, and honey.

3 Heat a little oil in a 6 inch skillet. Pour in just enough of the batter to cover the base of the pan and tilt so that it spreads thinly and evenly. Cook until the pancake is just set and the underside is lightly browned, turn, and briefly cook the other side. Remove from the pan and keep warm. Repeat with the remaining batter to make a total of 8 crêpes.

4 To serve, place a little of the prepared fruit filling along the center of each crêpe and then roll it into a cone shape. Lay seam-side down on warmed serving plates, decorate with flowers or mint sprigs, and serve.

Mango & Passion-fruit Salad

The rich mascarpone cream which accompanies the exotic fruit salad gives this Chinese dessert an Italian twist.

NUTRITIONAL INFORMATION

Calories 211   Sugars 18g
Protein . . . . .6g   Fat 10g
Carbohydrate . . .18g   Saturates 6g

    1¼ HOURS   🕐 0 MINS

SERVES 4

INGREDIENTS

1 large mango

2 oranges

4 passion-fruit

2 tbsp orange-flavored liqueur such as Grand Marnier

mint or geranium leaves, to decorate

MASCARPONE CREAM

½ cup mascarpone cheese

1 tbsp honey

4 tbsp plain yogurt

few drops vanilla extract

1 Using a sharp knife, cut the mango in half lengthwise as close to the pit as possible. Remove the pit, using a sharp knife.

2 Peel off the mango skin, cut the flesh into slices, and place into a large bowl.

3 Peel the oranges, removing all the white membrane, and cut into segments. Add to the bowl with any juices.

4 Halve the passion-fruit, scoop out the flesh, and add to the bowl with the orange-flavored liqueur. Mix together all the ingredients in the bowl.

5 Cover the bowl with plastic wrap and chill in the refrigerator for 1 hour. Turn into glass serving dishes.

6 To make the mascarpone cream, blend the mascarpone cheese and honey together. Stir in the plain yogurt and vanilla extract until thoroughly blended.

7 Serve the fruit salad with the mascarpone cream, decorated with mint or geranium leaves.

COOK'S TIP

Passion-fruit are ready to eat when their skins are well dimpled. They are mostly available in the summer. Substitute guava or pineapple for the passion-fruit, if you prefer.

Baked Coconut Rice Pudding

A wonderful baked rice pudding cooked with delicious coconut milk and a little lime rind. Serve hot or chilled with fresh or stewed fruit.

NUTRITIONAL INFORMATION

Calories	211	Sugars	....27g
Protein	....5g	Fat	....2g
Carbohydrate	...46g	Saturates	....1g

 5 MINS   2½ HOURS

SERVES 4–6

I N G R E D I E N T S

⅓ cup short-grain rice

2½ cups coconut milk

1¼ cups milk

1 large strip lime rind

¼ cup sugar

butter

pinch of ground star anise (optional)

fresh or stewed fruit, to serve

1 Lightly grease a 2½ pint shallow flameproof dish.

2 Mix the short-grain rice with the coconut milk, milk, lime rind, and sugar until all the ingredients are well blended.

3 Pour the rice mixture into the greased ovenproof dish and dot the surface with a little butter. Bake in the oven for about 30 minutes.

4 Remove the dish from the oven. Remove and discard the strip of lime from the rice pudding.

5 Stir the pudding well, add the pinch of ground star anise, if using, return to the oven and cook for another 1-2

hours or until almost all the milk has been absorbed and a golden brown skin has baked on the top of the pudding.

6 Cover the top of the pudding with foil if it starts to brown too much towards the end of the cooking time.

7 Serve the baked coconut rice pudding warm, or chilled if you prefer, with fresh or stewed fruit.

COOK'S TIP

As the mixture cools, it thickens. If you plan to serve the rice chilled, then fold in about 3 tablespoons cream or extra coconut milk before serving to give a thinner consistency.

Passion-fruit Rice

This creamy rice pudding, adapted for the microwave, is spiced with cardamom, cinnamon, and bay leaf and served with passion-fruit.

NUTRITIONAL INFORMATION

Calories	534	Sugars	........42g
Protein	.........9g	Fat	..........22g
Carbohydrate	...80g	Saturates	......13g

1¼ HOURS   30 MINS

SERVES 4

INGREDIENTS

1 cup jasmine fragrant rice

2½ cups milk

1½ cup sugar

6 cardamom pods, split open

1 dried bay leaf

1 cinnamon stick

⅔ cup heavy cream, whipped

4 passion-fruit

berries, to decorate

COOK'S TIP

If you are unable to obtain passion-fruit, you can use a purée of another fruit of your choice, such as kiwi fruit, raspberry, or strawberry.

1 Place the jasmine fragrant rice in a large bowl with the milk, sugar, cardamom pods, bay leaf, and cinnamon stick. Cover and cook on medium power for 25–30 minutes, stirring occasionally. The rice should be just tender and have

absorbed most of the milk. Add a little extra milk, if necessary.

2 Leave the rice to cool, still covered. Remove the bay leaf, cardamom husks, and cinnamon stick.

3 Gently fold the cream into the cooled rice mixture.

4 Halve the passion-fruits and scoop out the centers into a bowl.

5 Layer the rice with the passion-fruit in 4 tall glasses, finishing with a layer of passion-fruit. Leave to chill in the refrigerator for 30 minutes.

6 Decorate the passion-fruit rice with berries and serve immediately.

Chinese Fruit Salad

The syrup for this colorful dish is filled with Chinese flavors for a refreshing dessert.

NUTRITIONAL INFORMATION

Calories	405	Sugars	.......81g
Protein	.........3g	Fat	..........6g
Carbohydrate	...83g	Saturates	.......1g

 1¾ HOURS   ⏱ 10 MINS

SERVES 4

I N G R E D I E N T S

3 fl oz Chinese rice wine or dry sherry

rind and juice of 1 lemon

3 cups water

8 oz sugar

2 cloves

1 inch piece cinnamon stick, bruised

1 vanilla bean

pinch of apple pie spice

1 star anise pod

1 inch piece fresh ginger, sliced

1¾ oz unsalted cashews

2 kiwis

1 star fruit

4 oz strawberries

14 oz can litchis in syrup,
    drained

1 piece candied ginger, drained and sliced

chopped mint, to decorate

1 Put the Chinese rice wine or sherry, lemon rind and juice, and water in a saucepan.

2 Add the sugar, cloves, cinnamon stick, vanilla bean, apple pie spice, star anise, and fresh ginger to the saucepan.

3 Heat the mixture in the pan gently, stirring constantly, until the sugar has dissolved and then bring to a boil. Reduce the heat and simmer for 5 minutes. Set aside to cool completely.

4 Strain the syrup, discarding the flavorings. Stir in the cashews, cover with plastic wrap, and chill in the refrigerator.

5 Meanwhile, prepare the fruits: halve and slice the kiwi, slice the star fruit, and hull and slice the strawberries.

6 Spoon the prepared fruit into a dish with the litchis and ginger. Stir through gently to mix.

7 Pour the syrup over the fruit, decorate with chopped mint, and serve.

Banana Pastries

These pastries require a little time to prepare, but are worth the effort. A sweet banana filling is wrapped in dough and baked.

NUTRITIONAL INFORMATION

Calories	745	Sugars	.......24g
Protein	........13g	Fat	.........30g
Carbohydrate	...112g	Saturates	......15g

  45 MINS   25 MINS

SERVES 4

I N G R E D I E N T S

D O U G H

4 cups all-purpose flour

4 tbsp shortening

4 tbsp unsalted butter

½ cup water

F I L L I N G

2 large bananas

⅓ cup finely chopped dried apricots

pinch of nutmeg

dash of orange juice

1 egg yolk, beaten

icing sugar, for dusting

cream or ice cream, to serve

1 To make the dough, sift the flour into a large mixing bowl. Add the shortening and butter and cut into the flour with the fingertips until the mixture resembles breadcrumbs. Gradually blend in the water to make a soft dough. Wrap in plastic wrap and chill in the refrigerator for 30 minutes.

2 Mash the bananas in a bowl with a fork and stir in the apricots, nutmeg, and orange juice, mixing well.

3 Roll the dough out on a lightly floured surface and cut out 4 inch rounds.

4 Spoon a little of the banana filling onto one half of each round and fold the dough over the filling to make semi-circles. Pinch the edges together and seal by pressing with the prongs of a fork.

5 Arrange the pastries on a non-stick cookie sheet and brush them with the beaten egg yolk. Cut a small slit in each pastry and cook in a preheated oven at 350°F for about 25 minutes, or until golden brown.

6 Dust the banana pastries with icing sugar and serve with cream or ice cream.

VARIATION

Use a fruit filling of your choice, such as apple or plum, as an alternative.

Fruit Salad with Ginger Syrup

This is a very special fruit salad made from the most exotic and colorful fruits that are soaked in a syrup made with fresh ginger and ginger wine.

NUTRITIONAL INFORMATION

Calories	225	Sugars	........45g
Protein	.........2g	Fat	...........4g
Carbohydrate	...45g	Saturates	.......3g

  4¹/₂ HOURS   5 MINS

SERVES 4

INGREDIENTS

1 inch fresh ginger, peeled and chopped

¼ cup sugar

⅔ cup water

grated rind and juice of 1 lime

⅓ cup ginger wine

1 fresh pineapple, peeled, cored, and cut into bite-sized pieces

2 ripe mangoes, peeled, pitted, and diced

4 kiwi, peeled and sliced

1 papaya, peeled, seeded, and diced

2 passion-fruit, halved and flesh removed

12 oz litchis, peeled and pitted

¼ fresh coconut, grated

2 oz cape gooseberries, to decorate (optional)

coconut ice-cream, to serve (optional)

 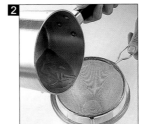 

1 Place the ginger, sugar, water, and lime juice in a pan and bring slowly to a boil. Simmer for 1 minute, remove from the heat and allow to cool slightly.

2 Strain the syrup, add the ginger wine, and mix well. Cool completely.

3 Place the fruit in a serving bowl. Add the cold syrup and mix well. Cover and chill in the refrigerator for 2-4 hours.

4 Just before serving, add half of the grated coconut to the salad and mix well. Sprinkle the remainder on top.

5 If using cape gooseberries to decorate the salad, peel back each calyx to form a flower. Wipe the berries clean, then arrange them around the side of the fruit salad before serving.

COOK'S TIP

Despite their name, cape gooseberries (physalis) are golden in color and more similar in appearance to ground cherries. They make a delightful decoration to many fruit-based desserts.

Honeyed Rice Puddings

These small rice puddings are quite sweet, but have a wonderful flavor because of the combination of ginger, honey, and cinnamon.

NUTRITIONAL INFORMATION

Calories	199	Sugars	........15g
Protein	.........3g	Fat	...........1g
Carbohydrate	...46g	Saturates	.......0g

🍰 10 MINS   🕐 50 MINS

SERVES 4

INGREDIENTS

1½ cups short-grain rice

2 tbsp honey, plus extra
   for drizzling

large pinch of ground cinnamon

15 dried apricots, chopped

3 pieces candied ginger, drained and
   chopped

8 whole dried apricots, to decorate

1 Put the rice in a saucepan and just cover with cold water. Bring to a boil, reduce the heat, cover, and cook for about 15 minutes, or until the water has been absorbed. Stir the honey and cinnamon into the rice.

2 Grease 4 x ⅔ cup ramekin dishes.

3 Blend the chopped dried apricots and ginger in a food processor to make a smooth paste.

4 Divide the paste into 4 equal portions and shape each into a flat round to fit into the base of the ramekin dishes.

5 Divide half of the rice between the ramekin dishes and place the apricot paste on top.

6 Cover the apricot paste with the remaining rice. Cover the ramekins with wax paper and foil and steam for 30 minutes, or until set.

7 Remove the ramekins from the steamer and let stand for 5 minutes.

8 Unmold the puddings onto warm serving plates and drizzle with honey. Decorate with dried apricots and serve.

COOK'S TIP

The puddings may be left to chill in their ramekin dishes in the refrigerator, then unmolded and served with ice cream or cream.

Green Fruit Salad

This delightfully refreshing fruit salad is the perfect finale for a Chinese meal. It has a lovely light syrup made with fresh mint and honey.

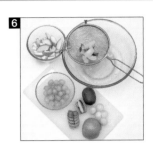

NUTRITIONAL INFORMATION

Calories 157	Sugars 34g	
Protein 1g	Fat 0.2g	
Carbohydrate ...34g	Saturates 0g	

30 MINS   15 MINS

SERVES 4

INGREDIENTS

1 small honeydew melon

2 green apples

2 kiwi

1 cup seedless green grapes

fresh mint sprigs, to decorate

SYRUP

1 lemon

1⅓ cup white wine

⅔ cup water

4 tbsp honey

few sprigs of fresh mint

1 To make the syrup, pare the rind from the lemon using a potato peeler.

2 Put the lemon rind in a saucepan with the white wine, water, and honey. Bring to a boil, then simmer gently for 10 minutes.

3 Remove the syrup from the heat. Add the sprigs of mint and leave to cool.

4 To prepare the fruit, first slice the melon in half and scoop out the seeds. Use a melon baller or a teaspoon to make melon balls.

5 Core and chop the apples. Peel and slice the kiwi.

6 Strain the cooled syrup into a serving bowl, removing and reserving the lemon rind and discarding the mint sprigs.

7 Add the apple, grapes, kiwi fruit and melon. Stir through gently to mix.

8 Serve, decorated with sprigs of fresh mint and some of the reserved lemon rind.

COOK'S TIP

Single-flower honey has a better, more individual flavor than blended honey. Acacia honey is typically Chinese, but you could also try clove, lemon blossom, lime flower, or orange blossom.

Chinese Custard Tarts

These small tarts are irresistible—a custard is baked in a rich, sweet pastry. The tarts may be served warm or cold.

NUTRITIONAL INFORMATION

Calories	474	Sugars	........30g
Protein	.........9g	Fat	..........22g
Carbohydrate	...64g	Saturates	......12g

20 MINS 30 MINS

SERVES 4

INGREDIENTS

DOUGH

1½ cups all-purpose flour

3 tbsp sugar

4 tbsp unsalted butter

2 tbsp shortening

2 tbsp water

CUSTARD

2 small eggs

¼ cup sugar

¾ cup milk

½ tsp ground nutmeg, plus extra for sprinkling

cream, to serve

1 To make the dough, sift the all-purpose flour into a bowl. Add the sugar and cut in the butter and shortening until the mixture resembles breadcrumbs. Add the water and mix to form a firm dough.

2 Transfer the dough to a lightly floured surface and knead for 5 minutes, until smooth. Cover with plastic wrap and leave to chill in the refrigerator while you prepare the filling.

3 To make the custard, beat the eggs and sugar together. Gradually add the milk and ground nutmeg and beat until well combined.

4 Separate the dough into 15 even-sized pieces. Flatten the dough pieces into rounds and press into shallow patty pans.

5 Spoon the custard into the tart shells and cook in a preheated oven at 300°F, for 25-30 minutes.

6 Transfer the Chinese custard tarts to a wire rack, leave to cool slightly, then sprinkle with nutmeg. Serve hot or cold with cream.

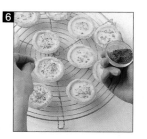

COOK'S TIP

For extra convenience, make the dough in advance, cover, and leave to chill in the refrigerator until required.

Coconut Bananas

This elaborate dessert is the perfect finale for a Chinese banquet. Bananas are fried in a citrus-flavored butter and served with coconut.

NUTRITIONAL INFORMATION

Calories	.514	Sugars	.70g
Protein	.4g	Fat	.21g
Carbohydrate	.75g	Saturates	.14g

  10 MINS   10 MINS

SERVES 4

INGREDIENTS

3 tbsp shredded fresh coconut

¼ cup unsalted butter

1 tbsp grated fresh ginger

grated rind of 1 orange

¼ cup sugar

4 tbsp fresh lime juice

6 bananas

6 tbsp orange-flavored liqueur (Cointreau or Grand Marnier, for example)

3 tsp toasted sesame seeds

lime slices, to decorate

ice-cream, to serve (optional)

1 Heat a small non-stick skillet until hot. Add the coconut and cook, stirring constantly, for 1 minute until lightly colored. Remove from the pan and allow to cool.

2 Melt the butter in a large skillet and add the ginger, orange rind, sugar, and lime juice. Mix well.

3 Peel and slice the bananas lengthwise (and halve if they are very large). Place the bananas cut-side down in the butter mixture and cook for 1-2 minutes or until the sauce mixture starts to become sticky. Turn the bananas to coat in the sauce.

4 Remove the bananas and place on heated serving plates. Keep warm.

5 Return the pan to the heat and add the orange liqueur, blending well. Ignite, allow the flames to die down, then pour over the bananas.

6 Sprinkle with the reserved coconut and sesame seeds and serve immediately, decorated with slices of lime.

COOK'S TIP

For a very special treat try serving this with a flavored ice-cream such as coconut, ginger, or praline.

Exotic Fruit Salad

This is a sophisticated fruit salad that makes use of some of the exotic fruits that are now available in gourmet supermarkets.

NUTRITIONAL INFORMATION

Calories	149	Sugars	........39g
Protein	.........1g	Fat	..........0.1g
Carbohydrate	...39g	Saturates	.......0g

  10 MINS   15 MINS

SERVES 6

INGREDIENTS

3 passion-fruit

½ cup sugar

⅔ cup water

1 mango

10 litchis, canned or fresh

1 carambola

1 Halve the passion-fruit and press the flesh through a strainer into a saucepan.

2 Add the sugar and water to the saucepan and bring to a gentle boil, stirring frequently.

3 Put the mango on a cutting board and cut a thick slice from either side, cutting as near to the pit as possible. Cut away as much flesh as possible in large chunks from the pit.

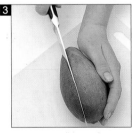 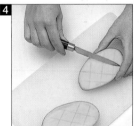 

4 Take the 2 side slices and make 3 cuts through the flesh but not the skin, and 3 more at right angles to make a lattice pattern.

5 Push inside out so that the cubed flesh is exposed and you can easily cut it off.

6 Peel and pit the litchis and cut the carambola into 12 slices.

7 Add all the mango flesh, the litchis, and carambola to the passion-fruit syrup and poach gently for 5 minutes. Remove the fruit with a perforated spoon.

8 Bring the syrup to a boil and cook for 5 minutes until it thickens slightly.

9 To serve, transfer all the fruit to individual serving glasses, pour over the sugar syrup, and serve warm.

COOK'S TIP

A delicious accompaniment to any exotic fruit dish is cardamom cream. Crush the seeds from 8 cardamom pods, add 1¼ cups whipping cream and whip until soft peaks form.

Sweet Rice

This dessert is served at banquets and celebratory meals in China because it looks wonderful when sliced.

NUTRITIONAL INFORMATION

Calories 213   Sugars 15g
Protein . . . . .2g   Fat 7g
Carbohydrate . . .37g   Saturates 4g

20 MINS   1¹⁄₄ HOURS

SERVES 4

I N G R E D I E N T S

¾ cup rice

2 tbsp unsalted butter

1 tbsp sugar

8 dried dates, pitted and chopped

1 tbsp raisins

5 candied cherries, halved

5 pieces angelica, chopped

5 walnut halves

½ cup canned chestnut paste

S Y R U P

⅔ cup water

2 tbsp orange juice

4½ tsp light brown sugar

1½ tsp cornstarch

1 tbsp cold water

1 Put the rice in a saucepan, cover with cold water, and bring to the boil. Reduce the heat, cover and simmer for about 15 minutes, or until the water has been absorbed. Stir in the butter and superfine sugar.

2 Grease a 1 pint heatproof pudding bowl. Cover the base and sides of the bowl with a thin layer of the rice, pressing with the back of a spoon.

3 Mix the fruit and walnuts together and press them into the rice.

4 Spread a thicker layer of rice on top, and then fill the centre with the chestnut paste. Cover with the remaining rice, pressing the top down to seal in the paste completely.

5 Cover the bow) with pleated wax paper and foil and secure with string. Place in a steamer, or stand the bow) in a pan and fill with hot water until it reaches halfway up the sides of the bowl. Cover and steam for 45 minutes. Leave to stand for 10 minutes.

6 Before serving, gently heat the water and orange juice in a small saucepan. Add the light brown sugar and stir to dissolve. Bring the syrup to a boil.

7 Mix the cornstarch with the cold water to form a smooth paste, then stir into the boiling syrup. Cook for 1 minute until thickened and clear.

8 Turn the pudding out on to a serving plate. Pour the syrup over the top, cut into slices and serve.

Mango Dumplings

Fresh mango and canned litchis fill these small steamed dumplings, making a really colorful and tasty treat.

NUTRITIONAL INFORMATION

Calories 434	Sugars 16g
Protein 12g	Fat 4g
Carbohydrate . . .93g	Saturates 1g

1³/₄ HOURS   25 MINS

SERVES 4

INGREDIENTS

DOUGH

2 tsp baking powder

1 tbsp sugar

²⁄₃ cup water

²⁄₃ cup milk

3½ cups all-purpose flour

FILLING AND SAUCE

1 small mango

3½ oz can litchis, drained

1 tbsp ground almonds

4 tbsp orange juice

ground cinnamon, for dusting

1 To make the dough, place the baking powder and caster superfine sugar in a large mixing bowl.

2 Mix the water and milk together, and then stir this mixture into the baking powder and sugar mixture until well combined. Gradually stir in the all-purpose flour to make a soft dough. Set the dough aside in a warm place for about 1 hour.

3 To make the filling, peel the mango and cut the flesh from the pit. Roughly chop the mango flesh; reserve half and set aside for the sauce.

4 Chop the litchis, and add to half of the chopped mango, together with the ground almonds. Leave to stand for 20 minutes.

5 Meanwhile, make the sauce. Blend the reserved mango and the orange juice in a food processor until smooth. Using the back of a spoon, press the mixture through a sieve to make a smooth sauce.

6 Divide the dough into 16 equal pieces. Roll each piece out on a lightly floured surface into 3-inch rounds.

7 Spoon a little of the mango and litchi filling on to the centre of each round, and fold the dough over the filling to make semi-circles. Pinch the edges together to seal firmly.

8 Place the dumplings on a heatproof plate in a steamer, cover and steam for about 20-25 minutes, or until cooked through.

9 Remove the mango dumplings from the steamer, dust with a little ground cinnamon and serve with the mango sauce.

Battered Bananas

These bananas are quite irresistible, therefore it may be best to make double quantities for weak-willed guests!

NUTRITIONAL INFORMATION

Calories	562	Sugars	........79g
Protein	.........6g	Fat	..........10g
Carbohydrate	...118g	Saturates	.......1g

10 MINS   20 MINS

SERVES 4

I N G R E D I E N T S

8 medium bananas

2 tsp lemon juice

⅔ cup self-rising flour

⅔ cup rice flour

1 tbsp cornstarch

½ tsp ground cinnamon

1 cup water

oil, for deep-frying

4 tbsp light brown sugar

cream or ice cream, to serve

1 Cut the bananas into even-sized chunks and place them in a large mixing bowl.

2 Sprinkle the lemon juice over the bananas to prevent discoloration.

3 Sift the self-raising flour, rice flour, cornstarch, and cinnamon into a mixing bowl. Gradually stir in the water to make a thin batter.

4 Heat the oil in a preheated wok until smoking, then reduce the heat slightly.

5 Place a piece of banana on the end of a fork and carefully dip it into the batter, draining off any excess. Repeat with the remaining banana pieces.

6 Sprinkle the light brown sugar on to a large plate.

7 Carefully place the banana pieces in the oil and cook for 2-3 minutes, until golden. Remove the banana pieces from the oil with a slotted spoon and roll them in the sugar.

8 Transfer the battered bananas to serving bowls and serve immediately with cream or ice cream.

COOK'S TIP

Rice flour can be bought from health food stores or from Chinese supermarkets.

Melon & Kiwi Salad

A refreshing fruit salad, ideal to serve after a rich meal. Cantaloupe melons are also good.

NUTRITIONAL INFORMATION

Calories	88	Sugars	........17g
Protein	.........1g	Fat	..........0.2g
Carbohydrate	...17g	Saturates	.......0g

🍓 1¹/₄ HOURS   🕐 0 MINS

SERVES 4

INGREDIENTS

½ small honeydew melon

2 kiwi

1 cup green seedless grapes

1 papaya, halved

3 tbsp orange-flavored liqueur such as Cointreau

1 tbsp chopped lemon verbena, lemon balm, or mint

sprigs of lemon verbena, to decorate

1 Remove the seeds from the melon, cut into 4 slices, and cut away the skin. Cut the flesh into cubes and put into a bowl.

2 Peel the kiwi and cut across into slices. Add to the melon with the grapes.

3 Remove the seeds from the papaya and cut off the skin. Slice the flesh thickly and cut into diagonal pieces. Add to the fruit bowl and mix well.

4 Mix together the liqueur and lemon verbena, pour over the fruit and leave for 1 hour, stirring occasionally.

5 Spoon the fruit salad into glasses, pour over the juices, and decorate with lemon verbena sprigs or cape gooseberries.

COOK'S TIP

Lemon balm or sweet balm is a fragrant lemon-scented plant with slightly hairy serrated leaves and a pronounced lemon flavor. Lemon verbena can also be used—this has an even stronger lemon flavor and smooth elongated leaves.

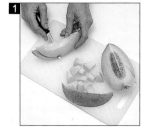

Poached Allspice Pears

These pears are moist and delicious after poaching in a sugar and allspice mixture. They are wonderful served hot or cold.

NUTRITIONAL INFORMATION

Calories	157	Sugars	........17g
Protein	.........5g	Fat	..........19g
Carbohydrate	...17g	Saturates	......12g

5 MINS   15 MINS

SERVES 4

I N G R E D I E N T S

4 large, ripe pears

1¼ cups orange juice

2 tsp ground allspice

⅓ cup raisins

2 tbsp light brown sugar

grated orange rind, to decorate

1 Using an apple corer, core the pears.

2 Using a sharp knife, peel the pears and cut them in half.

3 Place the pear halves in a large saucepan.

4 Add the orange juice, ground allspice, raisins, and light brown sugar to the saucepan and heat gently, stirring, until the sugar has dissolved.

5 Bring the mixture in the saucepan to a boil and continue to boil for 1 minute.

6 Reduce the heat to low and leave to simmer for about 10 minutes, or until the pears are cooked, but still fairly firm. Test whether the pears are cooked or not by inserting the tip of a sharp knife.

7 Remove the pears from the pan with a slotted spoon and transfer to serving plates.

8 Decorate the poached allspice pears with grated orange rind and serve hot with the syrup.

COOK'S TIP

The Chinese do not usually have desserts to finish off a meal, except at banquets and special occasions. Sweet dishes are usually served in between main meals as snacks, but fruit is refreshing at the end of a big meal.

Mangoes with Sticky Rice

These delightful rice puddings make a lovely dessert or afternoon snack. You can have fun experimenting with different-shaped rice molds.

NUTRITIONAL INFORMATION

Calories ....202 Sugars 31g
Protein ....2g Fat 2g
Carbohydrate ...47g Saturates 0.3g

   12³/₄ HOURS   50 MINS

SERVES 4

I N G R E D I E N T S

½ cup glutinous or sticky rice

1 cup coconut milk

⅓ cup light brown sugar

½ tsp salt

1 tsp sesame seeds, toasted

4 ripe mangoes, peeled, halved, pitted, and sliced

2 Line a bamboo basket or steamer with cheesecloth or finely woven cotton cloth. Add the rice and steam over a pan of gently simmering water until the rice is tender, about 40 minutes.

3 Remove the rice from the heat and transfer to a large mixing bowl.

4 Reserve 4 tablespoons of the coconut milk and put the remainder into a small saucepan with the light brown sugar and salt. Heat and simmer gently for about 8 minutes until reduced by about one third.

5 Pour the coconut milk mixture over the rice, fluffing up the rice with a fork so that the mixture is absorbed. Set aside for 10–15 minutes.

6 Pack the rice into individual molds and then invert them onto serving plates.

7 Pour a little reserved coconut milk over each rice mound and sprinkle with the sesame seeds.

8 Arrange the sliced mango on the plates and serve, decorated with pieces of mango cut into different shapes with tiny cutters.

1 Put the glutinous rice into a colander and rinse well with plenty of cold water until the water runs clear. Transfer the rice to a large bowl, cover with cold water, and leave to soak overnight, or for at least 12 hours. Drain the rice thoroughly.

COOK'S TIP

Glutinous or sticky rice is available from stores that sell Thai ingredients, although you can try making this recipe with short-grain pudding rice instead.

Lime Mousse with Mango

Lime-flavored cream molds, served with a fresh mango and lime sauce, make a stunning dessert.

NUTRITIONAL INFORMATION

Calories 254	Sugars 17g
Protein 5g	Fat 19g
Carbohydrate ...17g	Saturates 12g

🏠 🏠

🍲 10 MINS   🕐 0 MINS

SERVES 4

I N G R E D I E N T S

1 cup fresh cheese

grated rind of 1 lime

1 tbsp sugar

½ cup heavy cream

M A N G O   S A U C E

1 mango

juice of 1 lime

4 tsp sugar

T O   D E C O R A T E

4 cape gooseberries

strips of lime rind

1 Put the fromage frais, lime rind, and sugar in a bowl and mix together.

2 Whisk the heavy cream in a separate bowl and fold into the fromage frais.

3 Line 4 decorative molds or ramekin dishes with cheesecloth or plastic wrap and divide the mixture evenly between them. Fold the cheesecloth over the top and press down firmly.

4 To make the sauce, slice through the mango on each side of the large flat stone, then cut the flesh from the pit. Remove the skin.

5 Cut off 12 thin slices and set aside. Chop the remaining mango, put into a food processor with the lime juice and sugar. Blend until smooth. Alternatively, push the mango through a strainer then mix with the lime juice and sugar.

6 Unmold the molds onto serving plates. Arrange 3 slices of mango on each plate, pour some sauce around, decorate, and serve.

COOK'S TIP

Cape gooseberries have a tart and mildly scented flavor and make an excellent decoration for many desserts. Peel back the papery husks to expose the bright orange fruits.

Index

Index compiled by Hilary Bird.